Secondary Classroom Management

Secondary Classroom Management

Lessons from Research and Practice

Second Edition

Carol Simon Weinstein

Rutgers, the State University of New Jersey

Boston   Burr Ridge, IL   Dubuque, IA   Madison, WI   New York
San Francisco   St. Louis   Bangkok   Bogotá   Caracas   Kuala Lumpur
Lisbon   London   Madrid   Mexico City   Milan   Montreal   New Delhi
Santiago   Seoul   Singapore   Sydney   Taipei   Toronto

McGraw-Hill Higher Education

A Division of The **McGraw-Hill** *Companies*

SECONDARY CLASSROOM MANAGEMENT
LESSONS FROM RESEARCH AND PRACTICE
Published by McGraw-Hill, a business unit of The McGraw-Hill Companies, Inc. 1221 Avenue of the Americas, New York, NY, 10020. Copyright © 2003, 1996, by The McGraw-Hill Companies, Inc. All rights reserved. No part of this publication may be reproduced or distributed in any form or by any means, or stored in a database or retrieval system, without the prior written consent of The McGraw-Hill Companies, Inc., including but not limited to, in any network or other electronic storage or transmission, or broadcast for distance learning.

Some ancillaries, including electronic and print components, may not be available to customers outside the United States.

This book is printed on acid-free paper.

2 3 4 5 6 7 8 9 0 FGR/FGR 0 9 8 7 6 5 4 3 2

ISBN 0-07-232270-5

Editorial director: *Jane Karpacz*
Sponsoring editor: *Beth Kaufman*
Developmental editor: *Cara Harvey*
Marketing manager: *Dan Loch*
Project manager: *Diane M. Folliard*
Production supervisor: *Heather D. Burbridge*
Coordinator freelance design: *Pam Verros*
Cover design: *Asylum Studios*
Photo research coordinator: *David A. Tietz*
Photographer: *Suzanne Karp Krebs*
Compositor: *Carlisle Communications, Ltd.*
Typeface: *10/12 Times Roman*
Printer: *Quebecor World Fairfield Inc.*

Library of Congress Cataloging-in-Publication Data

Weinstein, Carol Simon.
    Secondary classroom management : lessons from research and practice / Carol Simon Weinstein.—2nd ed.
        p. cm.
    Includes bibliographical references and index.
    ISBN 0-07-232270-5 (alk. paper)
    1. Classroom management.   2. Education, Secondary.   3. Classroom environment.   I. Title.
LB3013.W46 2003
373.1102′4—dc21

2001054380

www.mhhe.com

About the Author

Carol Simon Weinstein is professor of education in the Department of Learning and Teaching at Rutgers Graduate School of Education. She received her bachelor's degree in psychology from Clark University in Worcester, Massachusetts, and her master's and doctoral degrees from Harvard Graduate School of Education.

It was at Harvard that Dr. Weinstein first became interested in the impact of classroom design on students' behavior and attitudes. She pursued this topic for many years, writing about the ways that classroom environments can be designed to facilitate teachers' goals and to foster children's learning and development. Dr. Weinstein's interest in organizing classroom space eventually expanded to include classroom organization and management in general. She is the author (with Andrew J. Mignano, Jr.) of *Elementary Classroom Management* (McGraw-Hill, 2003), as well as numerous chapters and articles on classroom management and teacher education students' beliefs about caring and control. In 1998, she took part in writing and producing the CD-ROM, *Effective Classroom Management: An Interactive Multimedia Professional Development Tool for Educators.* Dr. Weinstein currently works with teachers on conflict resolution and peacemaking and is a trainer for *Second Step,* a violence prevention program.

In 2000, Dr. Weinstein was recognized for her efforts with the "Contributing Researcher Award" from the American Federation of Teachers for "Bridging the Gap between Theory and Practice in Effective Classroom Management."

Dedication

For our Superbunny,
Bernice Weinstein,
with love

Brief Contents

Contents

Preface

In the years since the first edition of *Secondary Classroom Management,* the challenges of classroom management have grown dramatically. Classes are more heterogeneous than ever, with students from a wide range of cultural and linguistic backgrounds. Youngsters with disabilities are educated in classes with their nondisabled peers. Increasing numbers of youngsters come to school with emotional and psychological problems. Block scheduling is growing in popularity, requiring more complex, varied instruction. The horror of Columbine and other incidents of school violence have heightened anxiety. At the same time, there has been more attention to the need to make schools safer, more caring places; more attention to problems of bullying and peer harassment; and greater effort to reach out to alienated, isolated youth.

Given these challenges, teacher education students and beginning teachers need clear, practical, research-based suggestions for organizing and managing classrooms. *Secondary Classroom Management* responds to that need. My goal has been to write a book that uses research on teaching in a reasonable, responsible way, yet is accessible, even enjoyable to read. Chapters address the ongoing management tasks that teachers face, such as organizing physical space, creating community, teaching and enforcing norms for behavior, motivating students, and responding to misbehavior. Each of these topics is like a piece of a jigsaw puzzle; no one piece is sufficient by itself, but when they are all put into place the result is a classroom environment that is respectful, orderly, and productive.

A Case Study Approach

The full title of this book is *Secondary Classroom Management: Lessons from Research and Practice.* As the subtitle indicates, the book combines what research has to say about effective classroom management with knowledge culled from practice. This is done by weaving together discussions of research-based management principles with both the thinking and the actual management practices of four real secondary teachers. Fred Cerequas (social studies), Donnie Collins (mathematics), and Sandra Krupinski (chemistry) teach different subjects in very different school districts, but they are all experienced teachers who are able to create productive, respectful classrooms. Christina Lugo Vreeland is a second-year English teacher who is new to this edition. She is still "learning the ropes," but like her three more experienced colleagues, she demonstrates the ability to be reflective and articulate. She has also shown a great deal of courage in allowing me to observe in her classroom!

Readers will come to know these four teachers—to hear their thinking on various aspects of classroom management and to see the ways they interact with students. Their stories provide real-life illustrations of the concepts and principles derived from research. In addition, excerpts from the journal entries of my own student teachers reveal the frustrations and uncertainties they experience, the situations they encounter, and the new understandings they develop. I hope these journal entries resonate with readers who are also beginning the process of learning to teach.

The Second Edition: New Coverage

Like the first edition, this edition of *Secondary Classroom Management* is more comprehensive than many management texts, with chapters on working with families; using time effectively; and working with troubled students. The book also addresses the managerial challenges involved in a variety of instructional formats, such as recitations, discussions, and groupwork, topics more commonly found in general methods books. This material has been updated to reflect recent scholarship and current concerns. In addition, this edition contains three new chapters.

- *Beyond Rules and Routines: Creating Safer, More Caring Classrooms* (Chapter 5) addresses the need to build caring, supportive relationships with and among students, a theme that is echoed throughout the book. This new emphasis is intended to convey the message that classroom management is not simply about rules, rewards, and consequences, but also about building connections with students and creating safer, more caring classrooms.
- *Enhancing Students' Motivation* (Chapter 8) is an expanded version of the discussion of motivation that appeared in the first edition as part of a chapter on gaining students' cooperation. The chapter begins by reflecting on what is realistic and appropriate with respect to motivating secondary students. It then examines the factors that give rise to motivation and considers a variety of motivational strategies drawn from research, theory, and the practice of the four teachers.
- *Preventing and Responding to Violence* (Chapter 14) is a sad necessity in this post-Columbine era. The chapter discusses the ways that individual teachers can build a climate of tolerance, teach conflict resolution, recognize the early warning signs of potential violence, de-escalate potentially explosive situations, be alert for gang activity, and deal effectively with aggression and fighting.

Other new content includes:

- Block scheduling.
- "Thorny" problems such as cheating, not turning in homework, and defiance.
- Additional attention to the inclusion of students with disabilities and working with culturally diverse learners.
- Bullying and peer harassment, including student-to-student sexual harassment and sexual-orientation harassment.

Writing Style and Features

Although the subject matter is serious, I have written *Secondary Classroom Management* in a somewhat informal, conversational style. Readers of the previous edition have told me that the book is unlike any textbook they have read; I take that as a compliment. In addition, chapters contain photographs and cartoons; checklists of key points; models of letters, forms, assessments, and contracts; summaries of major ideas; activities to extend understanding; and suggestions for further reading. All of these features are intended to engage the reader, promote comprehension, and facilitate application of the material.

Acknowledgements

I wish to express my gratitude to all the people who helped to make this edition a reality. A fervent thank you goes to Fred, Donnie, Sandy, and Christina for allowing me to observe in their classrooms and ask them endless questions. They have been gracious and welcoming, and they have generously shared the lessons they have learned in their combined 90 years of teaching. Thank you, also, to the superintendents, assistant superintendents, and principals who gave me permission to carry out this project in their schools and districts: Ronald Larkin and Penelope Lattimer of New Brunswick; Marylu Simon of Highland Park; Willa Spicer of South Brunswick; and LeRoy Seitz and Michael Cilento of Woodbridge Township. I am also grateful to the counselors and psychologists who took the time to speak with me during the preparation of this edition and the previous one: Nancy Carringer, Carol Lowinger, Lindy Mandy, Tonia Moore, Gail Reynolds, Andree Robinson, Shirley Sexton, and Dr. Marilyn Weichman. Many thanks to the student teachers who shared their experiences and their journal entries with me. Special thanks go to Geoffrey Alpaugh, Cynthia Braslow, Patti Hearn, Dave Pellicare, Michelle Poremski, Kerri Quinn, Sandra Roth, Jennifer Saniscalchi, Laurie Savitt, Dixie Shafer, and Amy Wojdyla. It should be noted that in several cases, details have been changed to avoid embarrassment to anyone, and at times, composite journal entries have been created.

I want to express my appreciation to Suzanne Karp Krebs, photographer and friend. Her ability to take such graceful photographs amid the hyperkinetic activity of a group of teenagers is truly impressive. I thank Claire Swedberg and Samantha Johnson for conscientiously performing so many of the tedious tasks that are involved in producing a manuscript. I am also grateful to the individuals who provided thoughtful, comprehensive, helpful reviews:

Melva M. Burke, East Carolina University
Kay Alderman, The University of Akron
Leslie Huling, Southwest Texas State University
Charles W. Anderson, Michigan State University
Rita Silverman, Pace University
Maura L. Roberts, Arizona State University
Michael Hawke, Tarleton State University
Linda T. Jones, Mississippi State University

Thanks also to Lois Weiner from New Jersey City University, who reminded me about Molnar and Lindquist's work on changing problem behavior, and to Mary Morcos, one of Lois's students, who allowed me to use her case study on reframing.

I also wish to acknowledge the support and understanding of Beth Kaufman and Cara Harvey at McGraw-Hill. They have been extremely patient during difficult times, and I appreciate their faith in me. Finally, a special thank you to Neil, for putting up with all my whining, and for everything else too.

Carol Simon Weinstein

Secondary Classroom Management

PART I

Introduction

Chapter One

The Secondary Classroom Environment

Guiding Assumptions

Plan of the Book

Summary

For many prospective and beginning teachers, entering a secondary classroom is like returning home after a brief absence. So little has changed: desks with oversized arms are still arranged in straggly rows; the musty odor of chalk still permeates the air; bells still signal the end of classes; and bulletin boards still display faded copies of bell schedules and fire drill instructions. The familiarity of these sights, sounds, and smells makes us feel comfortable and at ease; in fact, it may lead us to conclude that the transition from student to teacher will be relatively easy. Yet, ironically, this very familiarity can be a trap; it can make it difficult to appreciate what a curious and demanding place the secondary classroom really is. Looking at the classroom as if we have never seen one before may help us recognize some of its strange characteristics and contradictions.

Viewed from a fresh perspective, the secondary classroom turns out to be an extremely crowded place. It is more like a subway or a bus than a place designed for learning, and it is hard to think of another setting (except prison, perhaps) where such large groups of individuals are packed so closely together for so many hours. Nonetheless, amid this crowdedness, students are often not permitted to interact. As Philip Jackson (1968) has noted, "students must try to behave as if they were in solitude, when in point of fact they are not. . . . These young people, if they are to become successful students, must learn how to be alone in a crowd" (p. 16).

There are other contradictions in this curious place. High school students are expected to work together in harmony, yet they may be strangers—even rivals—and may come from very different cultural backgrounds. Students are urged to help one another,

"I expect you all to be independent, innovative, critical thinkers who will do exactly as I say."

FIGURE 1-1. Students are urged to be independent and responsible, yet they are also expected to show complete obedience to the teacher. (Reprinted by permission of Warren.)

but they are also told to keep their eyes on their own papers. They are encouraged to co-operate, but they are often in competition, especially if they are concerned about class rank and college admission. They are lectured about being independent and responsible, yet they are also expected to show complete, unquestioning obedience to the teacher's dictates. (This peculiar situation is captured in the cartoon that appears in Figure 1-1.) They are urged to work slowly and carefully, but they are often reminded that 42- (or even 84-) minute periods require adherence to a rigid time schedule.

In addition to these contradictions, Walter Doyle (1986) has pointed out some features of the classroom setting that make it even more complex. First, classrooms are characterized by *multidimensionality.* Unlike a post office or a restaurant, places devoted to a single activity, the classroom is the setting for a broad range of events. Within its boundaries, students read, write, and discuss. They work on projects, view videotapes, and listen to lectures. They also form friendships, argue, and evaluate last Saturday's basketball game. Teachers lead whole-class discussions, coordinate small-group activities, and administer tests. They also take attendance, settle disputes, and counsel students with problems. Somehow, the classroom environment must be able to accommodate all these activities.

A second characteristic of classrooms is the rapid pace at which things happen. Classroom events occur with an *immediacy* that makes it impossible to think through every action ahead of time. An argument erupts over a perceived insult; a student complains that a neighbor is copying; a normally silent student makes a serious, but irrelevant, comment during a group discussion. Each of these incidents requires a quick response, an on-the-spot decision about how to proceed. Furthermore, classroom incidents like these cannot always be anticipated, despite the most careful planning. This *unpredictability* is a third characteristic of classrooms. It ensures that being a teacher is rarely boring, but unpredictability can also be exhausting.

A fourth characteristic of classrooms is the *lack of privacy*. Classrooms are remarkably public places. Within their four walls, each person's behavior can be observed by many others. Teachers talk of feeling as though they are always "on stage" or living in a "fishbowl" (Lortie, 1975). Their feelings are understandable. With 20 or 30 pairs of eyes watching, it is difficult to find a moment for a private chuckle or an unobserved groan. But the scrutiny goes two ways: Teachers constantly monitor students' behavior as well. And in response to this sometimes unwelcome surveillance, students develop an "active underlife" (Hatch, 1986) in which to pursue their own personal agendas. With skills that increase as they progress from grade to grade, students learn to pass notes, comb their hair, and do homework for another course, all—they hope—without the teacher's ever noticing. Yet, even if they avoid the teacher's eyes, there are always peers watching. It is difficult for students to have a private interaction with the teacher, to conceal a grade on a test, or to make a mistake without someone noticing.

Finally, over the course of the academic year, classes construct a joint *history*. This fifth characteristic means that classes, like families, remember past events—both positive and negative. They remember who got yelled at, who got away with being late to class, and what the teacher said about homework assignments. They remember who was going to have only "one more chance" before getting detention, and if the teacher didn't follow through, they remember that too. The class memory means that what happens today affects what happens tomorrow. It also means that teachers must work to shape a history of shared experiences that will support, rather than frustrate, future activities.

Crowded, competitive, contradictory, multidimensional, fast-paced, unpredictable, public—this portrait of the classroom highlights characteristics that we often overlook. I have begun the book with this portrait because I believe that *effective organization and management require an understanding of the unique features of the classroom*. Many of the management problems encountered by beginning teachers can be traced back to their failure to understand the complex setting in which they work.

Past experiences with children and adolescents may also mislead beginning teachers. For example, you may have tutored an individual student who was having academic difficulties, or perhaps you have been a camp counselor or a swim-club instructor. Although these are valuable experiences, they are very different from teaching in classrooms. Teachers do not work one-on-one with students in a private room; they seldom lead recreational activities that participants have themselves selected. Teachers do not even work with people who have chosen to be present. (See Figure 1-2 for Calvin's perspective on compulsory attendance.) Instead, *teachers work with captive groups of students, on academic agendas that students have not helped to set, in a crowded, public setting*. Within this setting, you must gain the cooperation of students

Calvin and Hobbes   by Bill Watterson

FIGURE 1-2. Teachers work with captive groups of students.
(CALVIN AND HOBBES © Watterson. Reprinted with permission of UNIVERSAL PRESS SYNDICATE. All rights reserved.)

and get them involved in educational activities. This is not a simple task. As Tracy Kidder (1989) has noted:

> *The problem is fundamental. Put twenty or more children of roughly the same age in a little room, confine them to desks, make them wait in lines, make them behave. It is as if a secret committee, now lost to history, had made a study of children and, having figured out what the greatest number were least disposed to do, declared that all of them should do it. (p. 115)*

Secondary Classroom Management is designed to help prospective and beginning teachers understand the special characteristics of the classroom setting and their implications for organization and management. I hope to provide concepts and principles that you can use to think about the managerial tasks you will encounter as a teacher. For example, once you recognize that students are a captive audience, you are better able to see why it's necessary to stimulate interest in lessons. Comprehending the norms of the traditional classroom leads you to appreciate the difficulty that students have in cooperative learning situations. Being aware of the crowded, public nature of classrooms helps you to understand the importance of dealing with behavior problems in an unobtrusive way.

Guiding Assumptions

Sometimes, we become so preoccupied with basic management issues (like getting everyone to sit down), we forget that classroom management is not about achieving order for order's sake; it's about achieving order so that productive learning can occur. In other words, *the ultimate goal of classroom management is to promote learning*. Keeping this in mind, let us consider six underlying assumptions that have guided the content and organization of this book.

The first assumption is that *successful classroom management fosters self-discipline and personal responsibility.* Let's be honest: Every teacher's worst fear is the prospect of losing control—of being helpless and ineffectual in the face of unruly, anarchic classes. Given this nightmare, it's tempting to create a coercive, top-down management system that relies heavily on the use of rewards and penalties to gain obedience. Yet, such an approach does little to teach students to make good choices about how to act (Covaleski, 1993). Furthermore, as Mary McCaslin and Tom Good (1998) point out, "the success of a compliance model depends upon constant monitoring (if the teacher turns her or his back, students misbehave . . .)" (p. 170). An emphasis on external control is also inconsistent with current thinking about curriculum and instruction (McCaslin & Good, 1992, 1998). It doesn't make sense to design learning activities that encourage independence, problem solving, and critical thinking, and then use managerial strategies that encourage dependence on points, popcorn parties, and punishment. This is not to discount the importance of teachers' authority; clearly, in order to be effective, you must be willing to set limits and guide students' behavior. Nonetheless, what you are aiming toward is an environment in which students behave appropriately, not out of fear of punishment or desire for reward, but out of a sense of personal responsibility.

The second assumption is that *most problems of disorder in classrooms can be avoided if teachers use good preventive management strategies.* Thus, I emphasize the prevention of misbehavior, rather than strategies for coping with misbehavior. This emphasis is consistent with pivotal research conducted in the '70s and '80s—research that dramatically changed the way we think about students' behavior. In a now classic study, Jacob Kounin (1970) set out to explain the differences between orderly and disorderly classes by examining how teachers responded to misconduct. To his surprise, he found that the reactions of effective and ineffective managers were quite similar. What accounted then for the differences in order? Kounin eventually determined that the orderly classes were more the result of a teacher's ability to *manage the activities of the group* than of particular ways of handling student misconduct. As a result of Kounin's study, we now distinguish between *discipline*—responding to inappropriate behavior—and *classroom management*—ways of creating a caring, respectful environment that promotes involvement in academic activities and minimizes off-task or disruptive behavior.

A third assumption of this book is that *the way teachers think about management strongly influences what they do.* Research has provided some fascinating examples of the links between teachers' beliefs about management and their behavior. Consider Sarah, for example, a first-year teacher who was having difficulty managing her class (Ulerick & Tobin, 1989). Sarah's behavior in the classroom seemed to reflect her belief that effective teachers should use charm and humor to engage students in learning and gain their cooperation. In short, her thinking about management reflected a metaphor of "teacher as comedian." Eventually, Sarah reconceptualized the role of teacher, discarding the comedian metaphor and adopting a metaphor of teacher as "social director." As "social director," the teacher's job was to "invite students to appropriate, interesting, and meaningful learning activities" (p. 12) and to assist students in directing their own learning activities. This change in Sarah's thinking about classroom management led to changes in her behavior and to dramatic improvements in the atmosphere of her classes.

In a similar study, Carter (1985) reviewed narrative descriptions of life in the classrooms of an effective and an ineffective classroom manager. Carter's analysis led her to conclude that the two teachers thought about classroom management in very different ways. The effective manager saw her managerial role as "a driver navigating a complex and often treacherous route" (p. 89). From this perspective, her responsibility was to guide classroom events smoothly and efficiently; she emphasized the academic tasks that students needed to accomplish and did not allow minor misbehaviors and interruptions to get her off course. In contrast, the ineffective manager seemed to see her role as "defender of a territory." Constantly vigilant for threats to order, she was careful to catch all misbehaviors whenever they occurred and used reprimands and appeals to authority in order to control inappropriate behavior.

Taken together, these studies suggest that teachers who view classroom management as a process of guiding and structuring classroom events tend to be more effective than teachers who stress their disciplinary role or who see classroom management as a product of personal charm (Brophy, 1988). This perspective on classroom management is also consistent with an emphasis on prevention.

Fourth, *the need for order must not supersede the need for meaningful instruction.* It is commonly acknowledged that management and instruction are complementary, with good classroom management a prerequisite for good instruction. Certainly, instruction cannot take place in an environment that is chaotic and disorderly. On the other hand, an excessive focus on management can sometimes *hinder* instruction (Doyle, 1986). For example, a teacher may wish to divide the class into small groups for a cooperative learning activity. Yet her anxiety about the noise level and her fear that students may not work well together could make her abandon the small-group project and substitute an individual worksheet assignment. Academic work that is more intellectually and socially challenging may also be more challenging from a managerial perspective. Yet, it is crucial that teachers not sacrifice the curriculum in order to achieve an orderly classroom. As Doyle (1985) comments, "A well-run lesson that teaches nothing is just as useless as a chaotic lesson in which no academic work is possible" (p. 33).

The fifth assumption is that *the tasks of classroom management vary across different classroom situations.* Ecological psychologists remind us that the classroom is not a "homogenized glob" (Kounin & Sherman, 1979, p. 150). Rather, it is composed of distinct "subsettings"—teacher presentations, whole-class discussions, transition times, small-group activities, laboratory investigations—and what constitutes order may be different in each of these subsettings. For example, "calling out" may be a problem during a teacher-directed question and answer session (often referred to as "recitation"), but it may be perfectly acceptable in a more student-centered discussion. Similarly, students may be prohibited from helping one another during an independent writing assignment, but they may be encouraged to work together during a cooperative learning activity.

Students have the right to know what is expected of them in these different classroom situations. This means that teachers must think about the unique management needs of each classroom subsetting and make a point of teaching students the appropriate ways of behaving in each one. In order to assist in this task, *Secondary Classroom Management* discusses the specific management "hazards" associated with independent work, groupwork, recitations, and discussions (Carter, 1985) and suggests ways of preventing these hazards from occurring.

The final assumption is that *becoming an effective classroom manager requires knowledge, reflection, hard work, and time.* Despite numerous books that provide "101 guaranteed ways of creating order," classroom management cannot be reduced to a set of recipes or gimmicks. As we have seen, the classroom environment is crowded, multidimensional, fast-paced, unpredictable, and public. In this complex setting, pat answers just won't work. Similarly, well-managed classrooms are not achieved by following "gut instinct" or doing "what feels right." Classroom management is a *learned craft.* That means that you must become familiar with the knowledge base that undergirds effective management. You must also be ready and willing to anticipate problems, analyze situations, generate solutions, make thoughtful decisions—and learn from your mistakes.

Plan of the Book

Secondary Classroom Management focuses first on ways of creating a classroom environment that supports learning and self-regulation, such as designing an appropriate physical setting, developing standards for behavior, building an atmosphere of caring and respect, and using time wisely. It then moves to the managerial tasks directly related to instruction—for example, motivating students to learn, organizing groupwork, and managing student-centered discussions. Finally, the book examines the inevitable challenges associated with classroom management, such as responding to inappropriate behavior, helping students with special needs, and preventing and coping with violence.

Throughout the book, concepts and principles derived from research are woven together with the wisdom and experiences of four real secondary teachers. You learn about the classes they teach and about the physical constraints of their rooms; you hear them reflect on their rules and routines and watch as they teach them to students. You listen as they talk about motivating students and fostering cooperation, and as they discuss appropriate ways to deal with misbehavior. In sum, *this book focuses on real decisions made by real teachers as they manage the complex environment of the secondary classroom.* By sharing their stories, I do not mean to suggest that their ways of managing classrooms are the only effective ways. Rather, my goal is to illustrate how four reflective, caring, and very different individuals approach the tasks involved in classroom management.

Now, let's meet the teachers.

🧩 Summary

This chapter examined some of the contradictions and special characteristics of classrooms. It argued that effective management requires an understanding of the unique features of the classroom environment and stressed the fact that teachers work with captive groups of students on academic agendas that students have not helped to set. It then discussed six assumptions that guided the content and organization of the book.

Contradictions of the classroom environment

- Classrooms are crowded, yet students are often not allowed to interact.
- Students are expected to work together harmoniously, yet they may not know or like each other.
- Students are urged to cooperate, yet they often work in individual or competitive situations.
- Students are encouraged to be independent, yet they are also expected to conform to the teacher's dictates.
- Students are instructed to work slowly and carefully, but they have to be aware of the "press of time" in a 42- (or an 84-) minute period.

Characteristics of the classroom environment

- Multidimensionality
- Immediacy
- Unpredictability
- Lack of privacy
- History

Guiding assumptions of the book

- Successful classroom management promotes self-regulation.
- Most problems of disorder can be avoided if teachers use good preventive management strategies.
- The way teachers think about management influences the way they behave.
- The need for order must not supersede the need for meaningful instruction.
- Behavioral expectations vary across different subsettings of the classroom.
- Becoming an effective classroom manager requires knowledge, reflection, hard work, and time.

In an effort to illustrate various ways of managing classrooms effectively, the book focuses on real decisions made by real teachers as they manage the complex environment of the secondary classroom.

✿ References

Brophy, J. (1988). Educating teachers about managing classrooms and students. *Teaching and Teacher Education, 4*(1), 1–18.

Carter, K. (March–April 1985). Teacher comprehension of classroom processes: An emerging direction in classroom management research. Paper presented at the annual meeting of the American Educational Research Association, Chicago.

Covaleskie, J. F. (1993). Discipline and morality: Beyond rules and consequences. In J. W. Noll (Ed.), *Taking sides: Clashing views on controversial educational issues.* Guilford, CT: The Dushkin Publishing Group, pp. 319–326. Reprinted from *The Educational Forum,* Winter 1992, *56*[2].

Doyle, W. (1985). Recent research on classroom management: Implications for teacher preparation. *Journal of Teacher Education, 36*(3), 31–35.

Doyle, W. (1986). Classroom organization and management. In M. C. Wittrock (Ed.), *Handbook of research on teaching.* New York: Macmillan, pp. 392–431.

Hatch, J. A. (March 1986). Alone in a crowd: Analysis of covert interactions in a kindergarten. Presented at the annual meeting of the American Educational Research Association, San Francisco. ERIC Document Reproduction Service No. ED 272 278.

Jackson, P. (1968). *Life in classrooms.* New York: Holt, Rinehart & Winston.

Kidder, T. (1989). *Among schoolchildren.* Boston: Houghton Mifflin.

Kounin, J. S. (1970). *Discipline and group management in classrooms.* New York: Holt, Rinehart & Winston.

Kounin, J. S., & Sherman, L. (1979). School environments as behavior settings. *Theory into practice, 14,* 145–151.

Lortie, D. (1975). *Schoolteacher.* Chicago: University of Chicago Press.

McCaslin, M., & Good, T. L. (1992). Compliant cognition: The misalliance of management and instructional goals in current school reform. *Educational Researcher, 21*(3), 4–17.

McCaslin, M., & Good, T. L. (1998). Moving beyond management as sheer compliance: Helping students to develop goal coordination strategies. *Educational Horizons,* Summer, 169–176.

Ulerick, S. L., & Tobin, K. (March 1989). The influence of a teacher's beliefs on classroom management. Paper presented at the annual meeting of the American Educational Research Association, San Francisco.

Chapter Two

Meeting the Teachers (and Their Students)

Donnie Collins

Sandra Krupinski

Fred Cerequas

Christina Lugo Vreeland

What Do the Students Say?

Concluding Comments

Summary

All four of our teachers work in central New Jersey, a densely populated area characterized by ethnic, racial, and socioeconomic diversity. *Donnie Collins* is a mathematics teacher in New Brunswick, a mid-sized urban district. Across the Raritan River from New Brunswick is Highland Park, where *Sandra Krupinski* is a high school chemistry teacher. *Fred Cerequas* ("Ser-a-kwas") teaches social studies in nearby South Brunswick. Finally, *Christina Lugo Vreeland* teaches English at John F. Kennedy Memorial High School in Woodbridge Township, a geographically sprawling district about 20 miles north. This chapter introduces all four teachers and briefly describes the districts in which they work. Then the chapter considers what their *students* have to say about the characteristics of successful classroom managers.

Donnie Collins

Of the 6,500 students who attend this district's 10 schools, 54 percent are Latino and 41 percent are African American. Many of the children come from poor or low-income families, evidenced by the fact that 80 percent of the students qualify for the federal free or reduced-price lunch program. The socioeconomic conditions breed other problems—drugs, transiency, homelessness, teenage pregnancy, physical abuse.

About 20 years ago, after receiving some of the lowest scores in New Jersey on a statewide standardized test, New Brunswick instituted a highly structured curriculum. Objectives were developed for every subject at every grade level, along with time lines for teaching each objective. Teachers must submit plan books and grade books to building principals or department chairpersons, who closely monitor when each objective is taught and evaluated and how students are progressing.

Critics argued that the new curriculum restricted creativity and burdened teachers with unnecessary paperwork, but academic achievement has steadily increased in the last two decades. This improvement is evident in the scores on the High School Proficiency Test (HSPT) that New Jersey requires for graduation. In 1998, 87.2 percent of 11th-graders passed the reading portion of the test; 86.2 percent passed the math portion; 88.3 percent passed the writing portion; and 74.5 percent passed all three portions. These results compare favorably with other urban school districts in the state, and teachers and administrators are convinced that New Brunswick has been moving in the right direction. Financial support from local corporations (in particular, Johnson & Johnson, whose world headquarters is located in the city) and collaborative projects with Rutgers, the state university, have also aided the district's quest for improvement.

New Brunswick High School is a few miles from the heart of downtown, a low brick building set back from the street on a wide expanse of lawn. Built in the 1960s, the school currently accommodates 788 students in grades 9 through 12. A large sign just inside the main entrance proclaims "Care and Excellence—Our #1 Goal," and fancifully painted murals honor the school's mascot, the zebra. The long hallways are lined with metal lockers in banks of red, green, blue, orange, and yellow. On the walls are posters advertising school clubs and activities; one announces a meeting of WWF—Working With Fathers—an organization for adolescent fathers.

On the second floor, in a corner classroom opposite the math department office, we find Donnie Collins, a 9th- through 12th-grade mathematics teacher. A 56-year-old mother of one, Donnie began teaching math in 1964 in Birmingham, Alabama. She moved to New Brunswick in 1969 and has been teaching in the district ever since, first on the junior high level and then at the high school. This year, since New Brunswick High School is now on block scheduling (a topic we will discuss in Chapter 7), Donnie teaches two 80-minute classes at the high school—Algebra I and "SRA," a special review course for students who have failed the mathematics portion of the HSPT. She then drives to a nearby elementary school, where she teaches mathematics to eighth-graders in the gifted and talented program.

Donnie Collins

Being a teacher was Donnie's childhood dream. "As a child I always wanted to play school," she recalls, "and I always wanted to be the teacher, never one of the pupils." Reflecting on this early dream, Donnie acknowledges the influence of her grandmother, who had been an elementary teacher before she opened a beauty school and shop. Although Donnie's parents were farmers, they recognized that farming was not for her. As Donnie puts it, "My calling was to be a teacher."

Donnie was influenced not only by her grandmother but also by two of her own teachers. Her fifth-grade teacher, Mrs. Poole, was intimidating at first, but Donnie soon realized that she needn't be frightened. Mrs. Poole wasn't mean; she was just concerned about students' achievement and well-being. "From Mrs. Poole, I learned about the importance of maintaining discipline, about the need to be firm and fair, and the value of keeping in touch with parents." Later, in high school, Donnie encountered Miss Anchrum, a young math teacher fresh out of college, with lots of new ideas about how to make math exciting: "Miss Anchrum made math real, and she would accept nothing less than our best." From her, Donnie learned the importance of motivating students and holding high expectations.

Donnie eventually earned both a bachelor's degree and a master's degree in mathematics, along with certification to teach. But the impact of Mrs. Poole and Miss Anchrum has stayed with her, and her teaching reflects the lessons she learned from them. When asked about her goals, she answers without hesitation:

> *I want the same things my teachers wanted. I want my students to become creative, independent thinkers; I want them to be able to function effectively in our everyday world; I want them to make a positive contribution to society. I continually stress that there is always more than one way to solve a problem and I encourage them to find alternative solutions. I believe strongly in the importance of groupwork and peer tutoring so that students can learn to work together and to take constructive criticism. When students say, "Oh, Ms. Collins, I don't need to know this; all I need to know is how to count my money," I tell them: "But first you have to make the money, and once you've made your money, you have to keep it." And you have to know math to do that.*

Donnie's goals are not achieved easily. She is frustrated by those students "who can't see beyond today," who cause disruption, and who create problems for those who do want to learn. She is also concerned about a lack of parental involvement (a topic we will discuss in Chapter 6), and the problems that her students face. As she puts it, "Education is just not a priority for many of my students. *Survival* is the priority." Sometimes she has to forgo a math lesson in order to discuss the more immediate problems of her students: conflicts with families, pregnancy, parenting (New Brunswick High School has a day care center for the children of its students), running away from home, violence in the community, drugs. With a certain amount of resignation, Donnie comments:

> *If you try to go ahead with a math lesson when they're all riled up about something that has happened at home or in the neighborhood, you're doomed. There's just no point to it. It's better to put away the quadratic equations and talk.*

In a continuing effort to meet the needs of her students, Donnie has served as a trainer in New Brunswick High School's Peer Leadership Program. During a week-long retreat, 15 to 20 high school seniors are taught interpersonal, communication, and problem-solving skills so that they can then help freshmen make the adjustment from junior to senior high. Donnie is also committed to her own professional development—she frequently attends workshops and courses on a variety of topics, such as classroom management, dealing with diverse students, sensitivity training, even teaching the Holocaust. But it is the daily help provided by her colleagues for which she is most grateful: "It's important to know that you're not alone in dealing with a student. I am lucky to have colleagues I can go to for advice and support."

Despite the difficulties of teaching in an urban district, Donnie is still enthusiastic and optimistic about her chosen career. One of the major satisfactions is the fact that each day brings something new. Another is "seeing the light come on," and knowing that a student suddenly understands what the lesson is all about. Particularly satisfying is sharing the successes of former students—and knowing that she played a part:

> *I was recently given a surprise birthday party, and one of my former students was invited. He's currently working for the General Electric Corporation, and there he was at my party, talking about having had me in eighth grade and the impact I had on his life. That's the real reward of teaching.*

Listening to Donnie Collins speak about the goals she has for her students and the satisfactions she derives from teaching, it is obvious that the legacy of Mrs. Poole and Miss Anchrum lives on in this New Brunswick High School mathematics teacher.

Sandra Krupinski

The tree-lined borough of Highland Park lies on the other side of the Raritan River from New Brunswick. The population of this small community is extremely diverse. The district's three schools serve children who live in homes valued at $500,000 as well as those from low-income apartment complexes. The student population of 1,650 is 53 percent European American, 17 percent African American, 14 percent Latino, and 16 percent Asian American. About 26 percent of the children qualify for the federal free or reduced-price lunch program. HSPT results from fall 1998 indicate that 96.3 percent of 11th-graders passed the reading portion of the test; 100 percent passed the math portion; 100 percent passed the writing portion; and 96.3 percent passed all three portions. These results reinforce Highland Park's reputation as a district that works hard to promote academic excellence, no mean accomplishment in the face of budget problems and changing demographics.

Highland Park High School currently houses 650 students in grades 7 through 12. Built in 1925, the building was recently renovated and expanded, thanks to the passage of a $15-million-dollar bond referendum that allowed the district to make long-overdue capital improvements.

In the science wing on the second floor is the chemistry classroom where Sandra Krupinski, a 50-year-old mother of two, teaches three classes of chemistry—two college prep and one advanced placement. This year, Sandy's classes are larger and more diverse than in previous years. In her sixth-period class, for example, there are 25 students, including five African Americans, one Latino, one Asian American, and one whose family has come from India. The class also includes a student classified as emotionally disturbed.

Sandy's love of science was awakened when she herself was a student at Highland Park High School, and teaching seemed like the obvious, logical career. "At that time," Sandy remembers, "women just weren't encouraged to consider other options. It was either teaching or nursing." Her father, a construction worker, and her mother, an office manager for an insurance company, applauded the decision to be a teacher, proud that Sandy would be the first in her family to attend college.

Sandy Krupinski

Although Sandy recognizes that becoming a teacher was not the result of thoughtful deliberation, she is confident that she pursued the right course. After 22 years of teaching, she still doesn't regard it as a "just a job." Even in the summer, after only a few weeks of vacation, she finds herself gravitating back to school so she can begin to prepare for classes.

Sandy is very clear about what she is trying to achieve with her students. She sees chemistry as a vehicle for helping students develop problem-solving skills, self-discipline ("a new experience for some"), and self-confidence:

> *Chemistry is seen as a difficult subject, and some students begin the year thinking they'll never be able to master it. They'll come up to me with a blank paper and say, "I couldn't do this, Mrs. K." I can't stand that. My hope is that by the end of the year these students will have the confidence to attack problems and the ability to develop appropriate strategies. That's much more important to me than getting the right answers.*

In order to achieve this goal, Sandy tries hard to create an accepting, nonthreatening atmosphere in her class. On the first day of school, for example, she gives her students an index card and asks them to answer four questions: (1) How do you learn best? (2) What do you expect to be excited about in chemistry? (3) What do you expect to be nervous about? and (4) What can I do to help? Their responses are revealing, particularly to the third and fourth questions. One student shares his fear of talking in front of the class and asks her not to call on him. Several confide that they are anxious about the difficulty of the course, particularly the mathematics and the need to memorize "lots of itsy, bitsy facts"; they ask her to be patient and to take extra time. One girl with limited proficiency in English writes about the fact that her "language is not good," and asks Sandy to speak slowly and to "sometimes explain something for me."

When students return on the second day of class, Sandy addresses each concern that has been raised (telling students that these are the fears expressed by "two or more students"). She thanks them for sharing information that will help her to help them and reassures them that she will be patient, that they will proceed slowly, and that she will always be available for extra help outside of class. Afterwards, thinking about why she takes the time to do this, Sandy comments:

As I talk about each fear they've expressed, I can actually see their shoulders drop, and I can feel the anxiety level in the class go down. Doing this also gives me information that I can use to help them. For example, take the boy who's afraid of speaking in front of the class. Today, students were putting problems on the board that they had done for homework. Normally, I don't particularly want people with the right answers to put the problems up on the board, because I want them to see that what's important is developing a strategy, not just getting the correct answer. In this case, however, it was important for him to feel confident about going up to the board. So, as I walked around the room, I glanced at his paper and saw that he had a particular problem correct. I told him he had done a good job with it and asked him to put it on the board. Instead of getting anxious, he smiled at me! This couldn't have happened if I hadn't asked students to share their concerns with me.

Sandy may be sensitive to students' anxieties about chemistry, but she still communicates high expectations and a no-nonsense attitude. This year, during an unexpectedly long "vacation" brought about by a fierce blizzard, Sandy called all of her Advanced Placement students to give them an assignment "so they wouldn't fall behind." Her students weren't surprised; one of them told her, "Oh, Mrs. K., we just *knew* you'd call!"

Sandy's no-nonsense attitude is also apparent in an incident that occurred during very different weather many months earlier. Last year, on a hot spring day when temperatures in the chemistry lab hovered around 100° Fahrenheit, Sandy glanced out the window and saw one of her students lying on the lawn. The girl was blatantly cutting class. Sandy called the vice-principal and asked her to bring the student to the classroom. "Are you sure you don't want me to take her to the detention room?" asked the vice-principal. "Of course not," Sandy told her. "I want her in here, where I can teach her something!"

Sandy is troubled by incidents like this; it is hard for her to accept the fact that she doesn't succeed with every student, and she continually takes courses and workshops to find ways to reach even the least motivated youngster. Yet, it is incidents like this that have helped to build Sandy Krupinski's reputation as a teacher who is passionate about chemistry and fiercely committed to students' learning—a teacher who manages to be both demanding and caring.

Fred Cerequas

Not far from New Brunswick is the community of South Brunswick. The school district has a reputation for innovation. Four of its 11 schools have been designated "Blue Ribbon Schools" by national review panels assembled by the United States Department of Education, and three have received New Jersey "Star School" status. In recent years, the district has worked closely with the Educational Testing Service to pilot procedures for the National Board for Professional Teaching Standards. South Brunswick has also devoted considerable effort to developing alternative ways to measure student understanding, such as portfolio and performance assessments.

This well-regarded school district currently has about 7,500 students and is gaining more than 400 a year. The student population is also becoming increasingly diverse; it is now 64 percent European American, 20 percent Asian American, 10 percent African American, and 6 percent Latino. More than 50 different first languages are spoken—in particular, Spanish, Gujarati, Hindi, Cantonese, and Arabic—and like Highland Park, the socioeconomic range is striking. Although people think of South Brunswick as a middle- to upper-middle-class community, a sizable number of its children live in low-cost mobile home parks. About 12 percent are eligible for the federal free or reduced-price lunch program. The HSPT results from 1998 show that 95.5 percent of the 11th-graders passed the reading portion of the test; 96.6 percent passed the math; 98.6 percent passed the writing; and 93.2 percent passed all three portions.

Fred Cerequas, a 58-year-old father of three, is a member of the 10-person social studies department at South Brunswick High School. The building is only three years old—a sleek, modern facility with state-of-the-art laboratories, an auditorium with 1,000 seats, and wide, spacious hallways. It currently houses 1,800 students (up from 1,200 only five years ago), but an addition is already needed because of the continuing population growth.

Fred's route to teaching was circuitous. As the son of factory workers who had to leave school for economic reasons, Fred went into the United States Army after high school. He worked as an information specialist in Alaska, where he had a radio and television show, narrated troop information films, and wrote for several army newspapers. When he was discharged in 1962, he began to work his way through college by driving a school bus for high school students. It was then that he discovered he was able to "connect with kids" and decided to earn a teaching certificate "just in case." A successful and

Fred Cerequas

gratifying student teaching experience led him to decide that this was the career he wanted to pursue. His first teaching position was in South Brunswick, and he's been there ever since—a total of 34 years. Far from being burned out, Fred still believes he learns as much from his students as they do from him. In fact, he proclaims that last year was the most interesting and exciting of his career—and that this one looks even better.

Fred currently teaches five classes: two sections of U.S. History I (honors); one section of the Institute for Political and Legal Education (IPLE), a practicum in law, government, and politics for a heterogeneous group of seniors; and two sections of Contemporary World Issues, a non-Western history course for seniors (one honors and one "regular"). It is the Contemporary World Issues course that excites Fred the most; here, students study non-Western cultures and examine the impact—positive and negative—of Western influence.

Fred articulates his goals for his students by telling the story of Tanida, a senior he had in class last year. After learning about the problems of women and children in the third world, Tanida organized her classmates to sponsor a little girl in Africa through *Save the Children*—all without prompting from the teacher. To Fred, Tanida's efforts represent a combination of knowledge and compassion, and it is this combination that he strives for in his classes. He tells us:

> *I believe real teachers are cultivators. They nurture the seeds of wisdom in their students by helping them become independent, eager learners who combine experience and knowledge with the genuine concern for others that gives life its meaning.*

Fred admits that his goals are not easily achieved in today's typical high school, where an "Industrial Revolution mentality" dominates:

> *Buildings like factories; seats in rows; rigid schedules; production quotas; quality controls. . . . The whole system seems geared to efficiency rather than humanity. At times, it seems to me that schools as they are designed actually inhibit education.*

Despite the obstacles to learning that he sees in our current system of schooling, Fred is energetic and optimistic, and he continually seeks better and more interesting ways to teach. Several years ago, he participated in a summer institute at the National Humanities Center in North Carolina, along with 20 other outstanding teachers from around the country. He was also named a Dodge Foundation Fellow and received a grant from the National Endowment for the Humanities to study ways of integrating literature more effectively into a history curriculum. He regularly works with student teachers from Rutgers and Princeton.

Professional activities like these fuel his determination to connect with kids and to "nurture wisdom." Early in the fall, for example, Fred led a discussion in Contemporary World Issues on the social institutions common to all cultures. Although students were generally cooperative, about one-half of the class wasn't fully engaged—a fact that did not escape his notice. Fred stopped the lesson and addressed the students' apathy in his characteristically direct, down-to-earth manner:

> *Listen, we don't study junk in here. What we're doing in here is trying to understand processes of change. This affects us; this stuff can make a difference in your life. And if you can be more than just bored seniors, we can do some really important stuff in here.*

After class, Fred sat in the teachers' room reflecting on the students' resistance. He reviewed the class roster, noting which youngsters had participated and which had remained silent. He spoke of the skepticism and detachment frequently displayed by students, particularly seniors; he acknowledged the difficulty of convincing them that what they were studying held meaning for their lives. Nonetheless, he vowed to "convert" them, and looked ahead to the day when he would actually have to chase them out after class. Given Fred's commitment and passion for teaching, there was little doubt that he would succeed. After all, according to Fred, "*Teacher* is not a word that describes what I do for a living; rather, it defines who I am."

Christina Lugo Vreeland

With 24 schools and 12,900 students, Woodbridge Township is the largest of our four districts. John F. Kennedy Memorial High School, one of the district's three high schools, was built in 1963. A two-story, yellow brick building, it is tucked away—almost hidden—behind a residential development of small one-story houses. A mural on the front of the building announces that JFK is the "Home of the Mustangs," and famous quotations from the school's namesake are painted on walls throughout the school.

JFK draws almost 900 students from the 10 different towns that comprise Woodbridge Township. In addition, the high school houses the district's English-as-a-Second-Language (ESL) program, providing instruction for 80 students who have recently arrived from non-English-speaking countries. The student body is predominantly European American (61 percent), but the racial and ethnic diversity is steadily increasing (African American, 8 percent; Latino, 10 percent; Asian American, 20 percent; Native American, 1 percent), and 13 percent of the students qualify for the federal free or reduced-price lunch program. HSPT results for 1998 indicate that 93.3 percent of all 11th-graders passed the reading section; 96 percent passed the mathematics section; 97.3 percent passed the writing section; and 89.9 percent passed all sections.

In the English wing on the second floor, we find Christina Lugo Vreeland—24 years old, newly married, and in her second year of teaching English and journalism. Christina grew up in Woodbridge Township, the daughter of a truck driver whose family emigrated from Puerto Rico when he was three, and an office worker raised in a nearby community. She attended Rutgers, the state university of New Jersey, where she majored in English and minored in Spanish. After receiving her bachelor's degree in 1997, Christina continued on for a master's degree and certification in English Education. Her academic achievements at Rutgers were impressive: In addition to being elected to Phi Beta Kappa, Christina received a James Dickson Carr Scholarship and a Martin Luther King, Jr. Scholarship, highly prestigious awards for outstanding minority students.

Like Donnie and Sandy, Christina never really considered a career other than teaching (except for a time in eighth grade when she wanted to be a fashion designer). Even as a little girl, Christina "always had to be the teacher and tell everyone else what to do." But it wasn't until her junior year in high school that Christina began to think seriously about the kind of teacher she wanted to be:

I had an excellent teacher, Helaine Rasmussen. She was very strict, and we were afraid of her before we actually had her, but then we got to like her. She really enjoyed what she was doing. I have one vision of her teaching The Great Gatsby. *She was sitting on the window sill, and she was describing a scene in the novel where there are two girls sitting in flowing dresses. She was acting it out, showing how their flowing dresses would look. It was so exciting. I had read the novel, but I hadn't pictured it. She made it real for me. . . .*

We also had to do a big term paper that year. . . . We knew from 10th grade that we were going to have to do this. It seemed insurmountable— 20 pages! But Mrs. Rasmussen had former students come in and talk about how they had done the project, and she took us through it step by step, so that . . . everything just seemed to fall into place. We were able to compose this paper we had never thought we would be able to do.

Then in my senior year, I had Angela Korodan for honors English. She started off by meeting with us at the end of junior year to give us the summer reading assignment. She gave us her address and opened the lines of communication. We had to mail her one of our assignments over the summer. She started teaching before she had to. And then the first two or three days of school, we sat in a circle, and talked about ourselves. These were people I had known for a long time, but I still learned things. She did the same; she told us about how she became a teacher, and how she had been a nun.

From Mrs. Rasmussen, Christina learned the importance of making literature vivid for students and being rigorous, yet systematic, when teaching research skills. From Mrs. Korodan, she learned about the value of building communication and a sense of community. These are lessons that Christina tries hard to remember now that she is on the other side of the desk.

Like New Brunswick High School, JFK is on block scheduling, so Christina meets three 84-minute classes a day, with one professional or "prep" period. Given the double periods, "year-long" classes last for half a year; this means that Christina gets new students and new courses every January. Her current schedule calls for two 10th-grade English classes, one with 29 students and one with 25 students, and one basic skills class for 11 students who have failed the HSPT.

One of Christina's major goals is to help her students "make a place for reading and writing in their everyday lives." She explains:

I think that lots of times English teachers are so passionate about literature and analysis of literature that we forget that our students are not preparing to be English teachers. . . . The way I read and the way my students read is different, and that's okay. What I need to do is foster the kind of reading and writing that will be useful for them and to create the desire to read and write.

To promote students' fluency in writing, Christina begins every class period with journal writing. As soon as the bell rings, students glance at the journal topic on the chalkboard, take out their journals, and begin writing. Sometimes journal entries serve as a lead-in to the day's lesson; for example, when students were about to discuss Antigone's decision to bury her brother, they wrote on a journal topic related to civil disobedience: "If you believed that what you were doing was right, would you break a law knowing that the penalty would be five years in jail?" Sometimes, journal entries are intended to stimulate thinking about the character traits we value in people ("Whom do you admire and why?" "What is patience, and who is the most patient person you know?); sometimes, they're responses to music ("Describe the music you're listening to").

In addition to teaching, Christina is a coadvisor for the school's newspaper, *The Torch*. Only five students were consistently involved when Christina and Karen Black, a colleague in the English Department, took on the challenge of advising; now there are about 50, and the increased participation is a source of great satisfaction. Christina also likes the fact that she's "involved in something extracurricular that shows the fruits of what I teach—writing, editing skills, thinking skills." Christina is also active in the school's "Learn and Serve" program, which integrates community service with the life and curriculum of the school. JFK has been recognized at both state and national levels as a "Learn and Serve Leader School." This means that Christina and her students are involved in a variety of service learning projects, such as the construction of a neighborhood playground for toddlers and an interdisciplinary project to create, dramatize, and donate children's books to a local elementary school.

One day in midwinter, Christina reminisced about her first year and a half of teaching. She was still recovering from a bout of flu, and she was feeling upset about having missed several school days right at the beginning of the new term. She talked about

Christina Lugo Vreeland

feeling overwhelmed by the stacks of ungraded essays, the service learning project, and the classes that were larger than usual. With an embarrassed smile, Christina expressed some of the doubts she had recently been feeling:

> *For the last few days, I've been questioning, "Why do I want to be here? Why do I say I enjoy this?" And then today, we had a great discussion about* Ethan Frome. *The kids really understood things. They really got into it; they got excited about it. I had kids making important points—I didn't have to ask the leading questions each time. And they had the desire to discuss with each other and to read more. . . . At the end of the class [in the English Department office], the other teachers looked at me and saw me smiling. They knew I'd been feeling overwhelmed. And one of them asked, "Why are you so happy?" And I told them, "I just had an experience that renewed my faith in my ability to do this for the rest of my life."*

What Do the Students Say?

While working with these four teachers, I became curious about the perceptions of students in their classrooms. In particular, I was interested in why they thought secondary students were cooperative and well behaved in some classes and uncooperative and ill behaved in others, as well as their views of the particular classes I was observing. In each class, the teacher left the room so that the students and I could talk more comfortably. I explained that I wanted the "student perspective" on classroom management and asked them to explain in writing "why kids behave in some classes," "why kids misbehave in some classes," and "how kids generally behave in this class and why." After students had a chance to write down their thoughts, they shared their responses.

Across classes, students demonstrated extraordinary consistency. Whether students were 9th-graders or 12th-graders, basic skills or honors students, their responses reflected three main themes. First, students stressed the importance of teachers' *relating to students with caring and respect.* They talked about teachers who "can relate to our teenage lifestyle," who "try to get to know us and understand us," who "create trust," who "help you and explain what they want," and "who work with you not against you." One student in Fred's class put it this way: "When a teacher takes some time to get to know students and shows some humor or shares a bit of their personal life, students may relate to them better." In Sandy's class, students also echoed the importance of relationships: "The teacher must relate to the students. Understand when there is a problem and try to solve it. When the students see a teacher doing his/her best to make them feel comfortable with what they're learning, they behave well." And one of Christina's students wrote this:

> *I want to cooperate in this class because she is not all serious, she can laugh, have fun, and still get all the work done. Students can tell when a*

teacher wants to help you and teach you, and when they just do it because they have to.

Clearly, not all teachers relate to students in this way. Students wrote about teachers "who put students down" and treat them like "little kids," about teachers who "don't care," and about teachers who are "beyond strict and just don't want to hear what we have to say." As one student wrote:

Sometimes, if a teacher really demands the respect from day one, instead of earning it, a disliking developes [sic]. If a teacher doesn't think about what the students are feeling, they won't like him/her. Students can always detect those sort of things. Dislike = misbehave.

Many students used the word *respect* in both their written and oral comments, and I pressed them to tell me what "respecting students" looks like. They didn't have difficulty: Teachers respect students when they give them their grades privately, when they come prepared for class, when they don't tell students a question is dumb, when they "scold a child quietly instead of in class in front of others," when they take time to help kids who are confused, when they allow students to give their own opinions, when they make sure that students treat each other well (e.g., they don't allow kids to talk when another kid is talking), and when they show students that they *care*.

A second theme to emerge from students' comments was the importance of *teaching in a way that is motivating and interesting.* One of Donnie's students captured this widely shared perspective:

Teachers have to make the class fun, but organized. Have a lot of interaction between students and challenge them. . . . Sometimes teachers are boring. The class drags on and the students lose attention span towards the teacher and the class. If the teacher teaches in an old-fashion [sic] style, the kids become frustrated.

These ideas were expressed in a number of ways: Teachers need to be knowledgeable and to *love* what they do ("kids can tell"); teachers need to teach in creative ways—not just out of the book; they need to get the whole class involved; they need to relate the material to students' lives. Although a lot of people used the word *fun,* one of Fred's students wrote, "Not everything can be fun; it doesn't have to be fun, but there are ways teachers can make it more interesting and more challenging." For Christina's students, the "cool things Mrs. Vreeland picks for us to do" were especially important, since their classes are 84 minutes long. They clearly appreciated the fact that class sessions are "not just lectures and question and answer" and that Christina "uses different ways to teach us as opposed to 'open your book, read questions 1 to 5 and answer them.' "

The final theme that students discussed was the need for teachers to "*set the rules and follow them.*" This was expressed in a number of different ways: "Teachers need to be a strong authority figure"; "teachers need to tell kids what they expect and give no second tries"; "teachers need to show strength"; "teachers need to be strict (but not mean)"; "teachers need to come off as someone who has control." What is clearly conveyed by these responses is students' lack of respect for teachers who are too permissive, who are "too cowardly to take charge," and who "let kids run all over them." One student wrote: "Kids misbehave when the teacher lets them pretty much do whatever they want. If they're disrupting class the teacher will try to go on with her class by maybe trying to speak above the person disrupting the class or ignoring it." This view was reiterated in another student's response: "Usually misbehavior happens in classes when teachers are too lenient. Every class needs to have some time to relax and fool around, but the teacher should know the limit." Still another summed it up this way:

> *Some teachers seem very insecure about misbehaving students. They tend to say "stop or I'll send you to the office" too much. When a teacher first meets his/her class they need to set down guidelines and go over them confidently and be sure of what he/she is doing.*

These themes—respect, motivation, and limits—characterize the behavior of the four teachers featured in this book. As I watched them teach, I was repeatedly struck by the caring and sensitivity they showed to students, by their efforts to stimulate students' interest and engagement in lessons, and by their authoritative, "no-nonsense" attitudes. We will address these themes in the three sections of the book that follow.

Concluding Comments

Donnie, Sandy, Fred, and Christina teach different subjects in different settings. Grade levels range from 9th to 12th. Sandy, Fred, and Christina teach classes that are predominantly white, while Donnie's classes are predominantly African American and Latino. Fred and Christina work in districts where about 12 percent of the children are eligible for free or reduced-price lunch, compared with the 26 percent figure in Sandy's district, and the 80 percent figure in Donnie's district. Sandy teaches an advanced placement class, while Donnie and Christina teach basic skills classes for students who have failed portions of the High School Proficiency Test. Donnie and Christina teach in schools that have adopted block scheduling and where teachers must follow a carefully prescribed curriculum; in contrast, Fred and Sandy's classes are 45 minutes and teachers in their schools are given a great deal of autonomy. In order to be effective, our four teachers must be sensitive and responsive to these differences in age, race, culture, socioeconomic conditions, achievement levels, and district policy.

Despite these differences, Donnie, Sandy, Fred, and Christina are alike in many ways. Obvious similarities emerge when they talk about the tasks of classroom management. Chapter 1 discussed the assumption that the way teachers think about management strongly influences how they behave. I cited research suggesting that teachers who view classroom management as a process of guiding and structuring classroom events tend to be more effective than teachers who stress their disciplinary role. Interestingly, when Donnie, Sandy, Fred, and Christina speak about classroom management, they rarely use the words *discipline* or *punishment, confrontation* or *penalty.* Instead, they emphasize mutual respect; they talk about the importance of being organized and well prepared; they stress the need to develop a "caring community," in which all individuals are contributing, valued members (Battistich, Watson, Solomon, Lewis, & Schaps, 1999); they speak about involving students and helping them to achieve.

It's important to remember that Donnie, Sandy, Fred, and Christina are real human beings working in the complex, uncertain environment of the secondary classroom. Although they are intelligent, skillful teachers who are extremely effective at preventing misbehavior, their classrooms are not free of problems. (In fact, Chapter 12 focuses specifically on the ways they deal with misbehavior.) Like all of us, they make mistakes; they become frustrated and impatient; they sometimes fail to live up to their own images of the ideal teacher. By their own testimony, they are all "still learning how to run more effective classrooms."

It is also important to remember that these four teachers do not follow recipes or prescriptions for classroom management, so their ways of interacting with students often look very different. Nonetheless, underlying the differences in behavior, it is often possible to detect the same guiding principles. The chapters that follow will try to convey the ways these four excellent teachers tailor the principles to fit their own particular contexts.

Finally, it is necessary to point out that these teachers do not work in schools where conditions are so bad that classes have to be held in stairwells or storage closets, where windows remain broken for years, and where 40 students in a class have to share a handful of books. Nor do they teach in schools that have installed metal detectors, where students regularly carry weapons, and where gang activity is common. In recent years, New Brunswick, Highland Park, South Brunswick, and Woodbridge Township have all experienced an increase in serious problems, but violence is certainly not an everyday occurrence. Whether the strategies discussed here are generalizable to severely troubled schools is not clear. Nevertheless, I hope that *Secondary Classroom Management* will prove to be a useful starting point for teachers everywhere.

✵ Summary

This chapter introduced the four teachers whose thinking and experiences will be described throughout the rest of the book. They work in four school districts in central New Jersey.

- **New Brunswick:** an urban district of 6,500 students (54 percent Latino and 41 percent African American); 80 percent of the students qualify for the federal free or reduced-price lunch program.
  Donnie Collins: a mathematics teacher at New Brunswick High School.
- **Highland Park:** a small district of 1,650 students (53 percent European American, 17 percent African American, 14 percent Latino, and 16 percent

Asian American); about 26 percent of the students qualify for the federal free or reduced-price lunch program.

Sandra Krupinski: a chemistry teacher at Highland Park High School.

- **South Brunswick:** a district of about 7,500 students and growing fast; student population is 64 percent European American, 20 percent Asian American, 10 percent African American, and 6 percent Latino; about 12 percent of the students are eligible for the federal free or reduced-price lunch program.

Fred Cerequas: a social studies teacher at South Brunswick High School.

- **Woodbridge Township:** a district of 12,900 students in 24 schools (61 percent European American, 20 percent Asian American, 10 percent Latino, 8 percent African American); about 13 percent of the students qualify for the federal free or reduced-price lunch program.

Christina Vreeland: an English teacher at JFK Memorial High School.

Although these four teachers teach different subjects in very different settings, they are alike in many ways. In particular, they speak about classroom management in very similar terms: They emphasize the prevention of behavior problems, mutual respect, involving students in learning activities, and the importance of being organized and well prepared.

The four teachers' views of effective classroom management mirror their students' conceptions. When asked why they behave well in certain classes and not in others, students consistently voiced three themes: relating to students with caring and respect; teaching in a way that is motivating and interesting; and setting limits and enforcing them. We will return to these three themes in subsequent chapters.

References

Battistich, V., Watson, M., Solomon, D., Lewis, C., & Schaps, E. (1999). Beyond the three R's: A broader agenda for school reform. *The Elementary School Journal, 99*(5), 415–432.

PART II

Establishing an Environment for Learning

Designing the Physical Environment

Discussions of organization and management often neglect the physical characteristics of the classroom. Unless it becomes too hot, too cold, too crowded, or too noisy, we tend to think of the classroom setting as an unimportant backdrop for interaction. This general tendency to ignore the physical environment is especially prevalent in secondary schools, where many teachers are like nomads, moving from room to room throughout the day. In this unfortunate situation, it is difficult to create a classroom setting that is more than simply adequate. Nonetheless, it is important to recognize that the *physical environment can influence the way teachers and students feel, think, and behave.* Careful planning of this environment—within the constraints of your daily schedule—is an integral part of good classroom management. Moreover, *creating a comfortable, functional classroom is one way of showing your students that you care about them.*

Environmental psychologists point out that the effects of the classroom setting can be both *direct* and *indirect* (Proshansky & Wolfe, 1974). For example, if students seated in straight rows are unable to carry on a class discussion because they can't hear one another, the *environment is directly hindering their participation.* Students might also be affected *indirectly* if they infer from the seating arrangement that the teacher does not really want them to interact. In this case, the arrangement of the desks is sending a message to the students about how they are supposed to behave. Their reading of this message would be accurate if the teacher had deliberately arranged the seats to inhibit discussion. More likely, however, the teacher genuinely desires class participation, but has never thought about the link between the classroom environment and student behavior.

This chapter is intended to help you develop *"environmental competence"* (Steele, 1973): awareness of the physical environment and its impact and the ability to use that environment to meet your goals. Even when they share space or move from room to room, environmentally competent teachers are sensitive to the messages communicated by the physical setting. They plan spatial arrangements that support their instructional plans. They know how to evaluate the effectiveness of a classroom environment. They are alert to the possibility that physical factors might contribute to behavioral problems, and they modify at least some aspects of the classroom environment when the need arises.

As you read this chapter, remember that classroom management is not simply a matter of dealing with misbehavior. As I stressed in the first two chapters, successful managers *promote students' involvement in educational activities, foster self-regulation, prevent disruption, and relate to students with care and respect.* My discussion of the classroom environment reflects this perspective: I am concerned not only with reducing distraction and minimizing congestion through good environmental design, but also with ways the environment can promote students' security, increase their comfort, and stimulate their interest in learning tasks.

Throughout this chapter, I will illustrate major points with examples from the classrooms of the four teachers you have just met. Interestingly, Donnie, Sandy, and Fred happen to teach their classes in one room this year, although they share their room with other teachers. For Donnie and Fred, teaching in one room is a substantial improvement from past years, when they had to move from room to room. Last year was particularly difficult for Fred: He taught his five classes in four different rooms! This year, it is Christina who has to move; another English teacher uses her room during the first two blocks of the day, when Christina has prep period and then teaches her HSPT class.

Six Functions of the Classroom Setting

Chapter 1 emphasized the wide variety of activities that occurs in classrooms. Although we normally think of the classroom as a place for instruction, it is also a place for making friends, for taking attendance, and passing notes. It is a setting for social interaction, for trying out new roles, and for developing trust, confidence, and a sense of personal identity. Fred Steele (1973) has suggested that physical settings serve *six basic functions:* security and shelter, social contact, symbolic identification, task instrumentality, pleasure, and growth. These six functions provide a useful framework for thinking about the physical environment of the classroom. They make it clear that designing the physical setting is far more than decorating a few bulletin boards.

Security and Shelter

This is the most fundamental function of all built environments. Like homes, office buildings, and stores, classrooms should provide protection from bad weather, noise, extreme heat or cold, and noxious odors. Sadly, even this most basic function is sometimes not fulfilled, and teachers and students must battle highway noise, broken windows, and leaky roofs. In situations like this, it is difficult for any of the other functions to be met. Physical security is a *precondition* that must be satisfied, at least to some extent, before the environment can serve students' and teachers' other, higher-level needs.

Physical security is a particularly important issue in classes like science, home economics, woodworking, and art, where students come into contact with potentially dangerous supplies and equipment. It is essential that teachers of these subjects know about their state's safety guidelines regarding proper handling, storage, and labeling. Sandy goes even further; she tries to anticipate where accidents might occur and to arrange supplies in a way that minimizes risk. For example, when her students are doing a lab that involves two chemicals that are harmful together, she sets one chemical out and keeps one under her control. In this way, students have to ask her for it ("I'm ready for my nitric acid"), and she can double-check that they are following correct lab procedures.

Physical security is also a matter of special concern if you have students in wheelchairs, with leg braces, on crutches, or with unsteady gaits (from muscular dystrophy, for example). Navigating through crowded classrooms can be a formidable and dangerous task. Be sensitive to the need for wide aisles and space to store walkers and crutches when not in use. The physical or occupational therapists working in your school can provide consultation and advice.

Often, school environments provide *physical* security but fail to offer *psychological* security—the feeling that this is a good, comfortable place to be. Psychological security is becoming increasingly crucial as more and more youngsters live in impoverished, unstable, and sometimes unsafe home environments. For them, in particular, schools must serve as a haven.

One way of enhancing psychological security is to make sure your classroom contains some "softness." Many classrooms are examples of "hard architecture" (Sommer, 1974). With their linoleum floors, concrete block walls, and Formica surfaces, they are designed to be "strong and resistant to human imprint" (p. 2). But youngsters (and adults) tend to feel more secure and comfortable in environments that contain items that are soft or responsive to their touch. In elementary classrooms, we sometimes find small animals, pillows, plants, beanbag chairs, and area rugs, but these are generally absent in secondary classrooms. If you are lucky enough to have your own classroom, think about ways to incorporate elements of softness into the environment. Also keep in mind that warm colors, bright accents, and varying textures (e.g., burlap, wood, and felt) can also help to create an atmosphere of security and comfort.

Another way of increasing psychological security is to arrange classroom space so that students have as much freedom from interference as possible. In the crowded environment of the classroom, it is easy to become distracted. You need to make sure that students' desks are not too near areas of heavy traffic (e.g., the pencil sharpener, the bookcase, the front door). This is particularly important for students with attention-deficit hyperactivity disorder (ADHD), a neurobiological disability that interferes with an individual's ability to sustain attention. Students with ADHD have difficulty focusing attention, concentrating, listening, following instructions, and organizing tasks; they may also exhibit behaviors associated with hyperactivity: difficulty staying seated, fidgeting, impulsivity, lack of self-control. You can help students with ADHD by seating them away from high-traffic areas, near well-focused students, and in seats that allow you to make easy eye contact. Although many teachers seat distractible students in the center-front (given a traditional row arrangement), Perlmutter (1994) suggests that the *second* seat from the front in the end rows may be more effective in limiting distractible stimuli.

You can also enhance psychological security by allowing students to select their own seats. Often, students want to sit near their friends, but some individuals have definite spatial preferences as well (e.g., they prefer to sit in a corner, near the window, or in the front row). Donnie, Sandy, and Fred all allow students to sit where they wish—as long as they behave appropriately, of course (and Fred advises his students to "sit next to someone smart"). If you have your own room, you might also set up a few cubicles where students who want more enclosure can work alone, or provide folding cardboard dividers that they can place on their desks. All of us need to "get away from it all" at times, but research suggests that opportunities for privacy are particularly important for youngsters who are distractible or have difficulty relating to their peers (Weinstein, 1982).

Social Contact

Interaction among Students

As you plan the arrangement of students' desks, you need to think carefully about how much interaction you want among students. Clusters of desks promote social contact since individuals are close together and can have direct eye contact with those across from them. In clusters, students can work together on activities, share materials, have small-group discussions, and help each other with assignments. This arrangement is most appropriate if you plan to emphasize collaboration and cooperative learning activities. But it is unwise—even inhumane—to seat students in clusters and then forbid them to interact. If you do that, students receive two contradictory messages: The seating arrangement is communicating that it's okay to interact, while your verbal message is just the opposite!

As a beginning teacher, you may want to place desks in rows until you are confident about your ability as a classroom manager. Rows of desks reduce interaction among students and make it easier for them to concentrate on individual assignments (Axelrod, Hall, & Tams, 1979; Bennett & Blundell, 1983; Wheldall, Morris, Vaughan, & Ng, 1981). This appears particularly true for students who have behavior and learning disabilities. Wheldall and Lam (1987) found that on-task behavior dropped by half and disruptive behavior increased by three times when "behaviourally troublesome" adolescents with moderate learning problems moved from rows to tables.

Rows also direct students' attention toward the teacher, so they are particularly appropriate for teacher-centered instruction. You might also consider putting desks in horizontal rows. (See Figure 3-1.) This arrangement still orients students toward the teacher, but provides them with close "neighbors" on each side.

Figures 3-2 to 3-4 illustrate the way Sandy, Fred, and Christina have arranged their classrooms. As you can see, Sandy's classroom is divided into whole-group instructional areas and laboratory or work areas. For presentations and homework review, students sit in a horizontal row arrangement. An aisle separates clusters of two and three trapezoidal desks (which Sandy hates because they take up so much room). Although she is unhappy that students are packed so closely together, Sandy wants to get as many students as possible in a row, so that all students are relatively close to the front of the room.

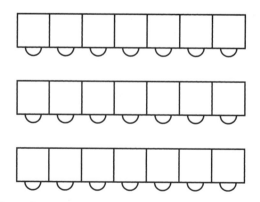

FIGURE 3-1. A horizontal arrangement

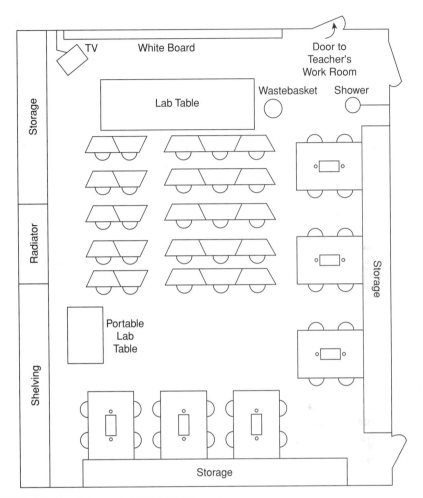

FIGURE 3-2. Sandy's room arrangement

Fred and Christina have chosen to arrange their desks in rows; however, both teachers regularly have students move into other configurations when appropriate. As Christina explains:

I don't like them in rows . . . but it's a functional place to start, especially since I share the room. My philosophy is that I move them based on the activity. [Having the desks in rows] is a good starting point for journal writing, attendance, and whole-group presentations, and then I move them when I want to.

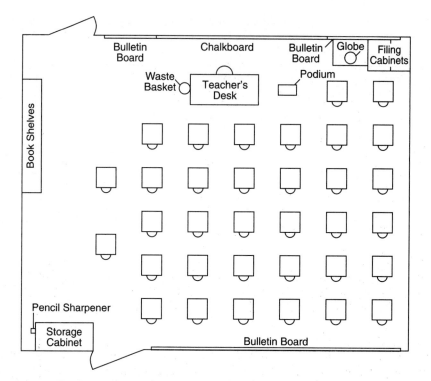

FIGURE 3-3. Fred's room arrangement

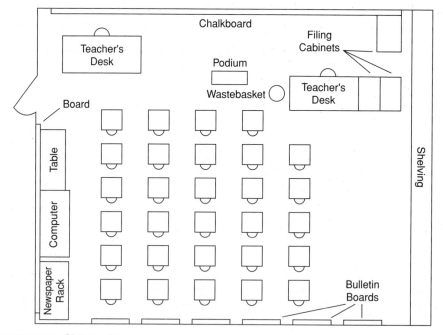

FIGURE 3-4. Christina's room arrangement

36

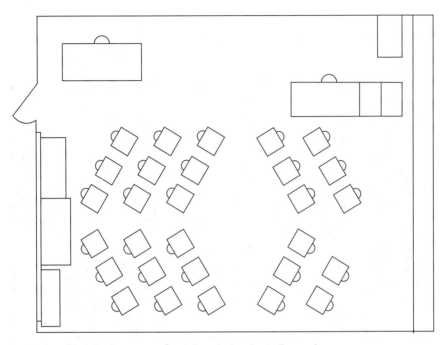

FIGURE 3-5. Christina's arrangement for whole-class discussions

Both Fred and Christina have students rearrange their desks into clusters for small group work, and—when classes are small enough—into a circle for class discussions. This year, Christina's large classes have led to experimentation with a new arrangement for discussion (see Figure 3-5):

> *When we're going to have discussions, I stand in the center of the room, and I tell all the kids to turn their desks to a 45 degree angle, so that they're all facing the center. Then I sit outside the circle; it helps me to keep my mouth shut.*

In Donnie's classroom, the two-person tables are new this year. She has arranged them in groups of two, forming horizontal rows, but continues to try other arrangements (see Figures 3-6 and 3-7). She even allows individual students to move their tables into configurations that they feel are more comfortable. Interestingly, although Donnie's tables are attractive and facilitate small-group work, she actually prefers desks, which are easier to arrange in a horseshoe.

Interaction between the Teacher and the Students

The way students are arranged can also affect the interaction between teacher and students. A number of studies have found that in classrooms where desks are arranged in rows, the teacher interacts mostly with students seated in the front and center of the

Christina's arrangement for class discussions

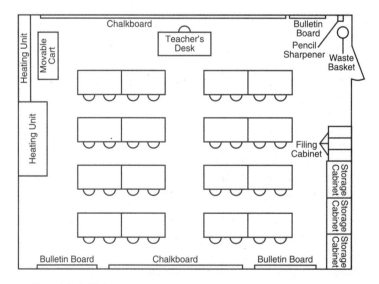

FIGURE 3-6. Donnie's initial room arrangement

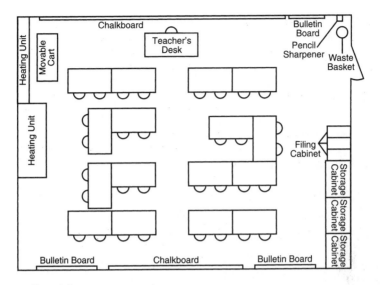

FIGURE 3-7. Donnie's rearrangement

classroom. Students in this "action zone" (Adams & Biddle, 1970) participate more in class discussions and initiate more questions and comments.

Educational researchers have tried to tease out the reasons for this phenomenon. Do students who are more interested and more eager to participate select seats in the front, or does a front seating position somehow produce these attitudes and behaviors? This issue has not yet been fully resolved, but the weight of the evidence indicates that a front-center seat does encourage participation, while a seat in the back makes it more difficult to participate and easier to "tune out." During a discussion with students in Sandy's class, it was clear that they were aware of this phenomenon. As one student said, "When we're all so close to the front, you know that the teacher can see you real easily. That helps keep you awake!"

Christina is also well aware of the influence that seating can have on participation and involvement. On the first day of school, she assigns seats alphabetically so that she can more easily learn students' names. A few weeks later, however, she reassigns seats to maximize students' engagement and participation:

> *I try to evaluate their needs with respect to participation and my needs with respect to management. I look at problem areas; for example, I'll break up areas of too much talking. If students seem to need an extra push to participate, I'll put them in the front. If students are falling out of their chairs trying to participate, it's okay if they're farther back. If I can, I try to avoid seating people in the back corners; that's where they can get lost. But in my class of 29 students, someone has to be in the back corners. I try to remedy this by changing seats every few weeks and by having students reconfigure the seating arrangements for different activities.*

Although research on the action zone has only examined row arrangements, it is easy to imagine that the same phenomenon would occur whenever teachers direct most of their comments and questions to the students who are closest to them. Keep this in mind and take steps to ensure that the action zone encompasses your whole class. Some suggestions are to (1) move around the room whenever possible; (2) establish eye contact with students seated farther away from you; (3) direct comments to students seated in the rear and on the sides; and (4) periodically change students' seats (or allow students to select new seats) so that all students have an opportunity to be up front.

Symbolic Identification

This term refers to the information provided by a setting about the people who spend time there. The key questions are these: What does this room tell us about the students—their classroom activities, backgrounds, accomplishments, and preferences? And what does the classroom tell us about the teacher's goals, values, views of the content area, and beliefs about education?

Too often, classrooms resemble motel rooms. They are pleasant but impersonal, revealing nothing about the people who use the space—or even about the subject that is studied there. This "anonymity" is exacerbated in junior and senior high school when six or seven classes may use the space during the day (and then an adult class uses it in the evening, as in Fred's situation!). Nonetheless, it's important to think about ways of personalizing your classroom setting. Before using wall space or bulletin boards, however, be sure to negotiate "property rights" with the other teachers who are using the room.

All four teachers attempt to personalize their classrooms, within the constraints of their individual circumstances. In Christina's classroom, mobiles of drama masks and literary genres hang from the ceiling. Five brightly colored bulletin boards across the back wall are devoted to various aspects of English. The two nearest the windows contain photographs of famous writers at their desks; quotations describe the ways they approach—and conquer—the agonies of writing. Donnie has the use of only two bulletin boards, but she tries to have them reflect her students' activities and accomplishments. She watches the newspaper and regularly posts stories about her current and former students. One bulletin board is usually devoted to a "Math Honor Roll" (students who have received A's or B's for the marking period). Sometimes, she even takes photographs of the students in her classes and displays them in honor of special events (e.g., when a student does particularly fine work, when a student has had outstanding attendance, etc.).

Sandy also posts photographs of her students conducting laboratory investigations, although never without explicit permission. Occasionally, Sandy also displays students' outstanding work, but she offers words of caution:

> *High school students often don't want their work posted on the bulletin board, because they don't want to "stand out" from their peers in any way. If I do put work up, I make sure to put their names on the back of the paper.*

Sandy's major exception to this rule of thumb is on "Mole Day" (October 23rd) when students decorate the bulletin boards and the walls with poetry, murals, riddles, and recipes—all celebrating the "mole," a basic chemical concept. Begun by a group of chemistry teachers (National Mole Day Foundation, Inc.), Mole Day is intended to promote enthusiasm for chemistry. The impressive exhibits of student work not only suggest that this goal is being achieved, they also serve the function of symbolic identification by providing information about what goes on in Room 234.

In addition to communicating information about students and the subject matter, you can also use the environment to communicate something about *yourself.* In Fred's class, for example, the bulletin board in the rear of the room displays some of his student teacher's favorite quotations: "Study history—or be history," "The best way to make your dreams come true is to wake up" (Paul Valery), and "May the force be with you" (Obi Wan Kenobi). In Sandy's classroom, Millie Mole, a small stuffed animal, often perches on the front lab table, particularly during the Mole Day festivities. Not only does Millie stimulate interest in the study of moles, she allows students to see that Mrs. Krupinksi is a "real" person. Over Christina's desk is a mobile of wooden apples that she made during the summer before her first year of teaching. A teddy bear represents the collection of bears she has at home. On the front chalkboard, a framed poem, written by a former student, begins this way: "This is a poem/about the one who tried to teach us/Though sometimes we all were stubborn/She still managed to reach us."

Task Instrumentality

This function concerns the many ways the environment helps us to carry out the tasks we need to accomplish. Think about the tasks and activities that will be carried out in your classroom. Will students work alone at their desks on writing assignments? Will they work cooperatively on activities and projects? Will you instruct the whole class from the chalkboard? Will you work with small lab groups? Will students do research using the Internet?

For each of these tasks, you need to consider the physical design requirements. For example, if you plan to gather students around you for whole-group instruction before they work individually, you have to think carefully about where to locate the instructional area vis-à-vis the work area. Do you want it near a chalkboard or a bulletin board? In any case, its location should allow all students to see and hear your presentations without being cramped. You also want the work areas to be organized well so that individuals or small groups do not interfere with one another.

Whatever tasks will occur in your classroom, there are a few general guidelines you need to keep in mind:

Frequently used classroom materials should be accessible to students. Materials like calculators, scissors, dictionaries, textbooks, and rulers should be easy to reach. This will minimize the time spent preparing for activities and cleaning up. Decide which materials will be kept in locked or closed cabinets and which will be kept on open shelves. Think about whether materials are accessible to students in wheelchairs or with crutches or walkers.

Shelves and storage areas should be well organized so that it is clear where materials and equipment belong. It is useful to label shelves so that everyone knows where things go. This will make it easier to obtain materials and to return them. You should also have some sort of a system for the distribution and collection of students' work (e.g., in–out boxes).

Pathways throughout the room should be designed carefully to avoid congestion and distraction. Paths to the pencil sharpener, supply closet, and trash can should be clearly visible and unobstructed. These high traffic areas should be as far from students' desks as possible. Are pathways wide enough for students in wheelchairs?

The seating arrangement should allow students to have a clear view of instructional presentations. If possible, students should be able to see instructional presentations without turning their desks or chairs around.

The location of the teacher's desk depends on where you will be spending your time. If you will be constantly moving about the room, your desk can be out of the way, in a corner perhaps. If you will use your desk as a conference area or as workstation, then it needs to be more centrally located. But be careful: With a central location, you may be tempted to remain at your desk for long periods of time, and this cuts down your ability to monitor students' work and behavior. Moreover, if your desk is in a central location, holding student conferences there may be distracting to other students.

Decide where to store your own personal teaching aids and supplies. If you move from room to room, arrange to have a desk drawer or a shelf in a storage cabinet for your own personal use. At the very least, you will probably need storage for pens and markers, paper clips, a stapler, rubber bands, chalk, tape, tissues, attendance forms, and file folders. An alternative strategy is to carry your personal supplies with you, perhaps in one of the plastic carrying bins often used for home cleaning supplies. Some teachers even use a movable cart.

Pleasure

The important question here is whether students and teachers find the classroom attractive and pleasing. To the already overworked teacher preoccupied with covering the curriculum, raising test scores, and maintaining order, aesthetic concerns may seem irrelevant and insignificant (at least until parent conferences draw near). Yet given the amount of time that you and your students spend in your classroom, it is worth thinking about ways to create a pleasing environment. It is sad when students associate education with sterile, uncomfortable, unpleasant places.

The classic study on environmental attractiveness was conducted by Maslow and Mintz (1956). These experimenters compared interviews that took place in an "ugly" room with those that took place in a "beautiful" room. Neither the interviewer nor the subject knew that the real purpose of the study was to assess the impact of the environment on their behavior. Maslow and Mintz found that interviewers assigned to the ugly room complained of headaches, fatigue, and discomfort. Furthermore, the interviews *finished more quickly* in the ugly rooms. Apparently, people in the ugly room tried to finish their task as quickly as possible in order to escape from the unpleasant setting.

Additional studies have also demonstrated that aesthetically pleasing environments can influence behavior. For example, two college-level studies have indicated that attractive classrooms have a positive effect on attendance and feelings of group cohesion (Horowitz & Otto, 1973) and on participation in class discussions (Sommer & Olson, 1980). The classrooms in these studies had specially designed seating, soft lighting, plants, warm colors, and carpeting, hardly the kinds of aesthetic improvements that can be implemented by most secondary school teachers. Nonetheless, it is worth thinking about the kinds of environmental modifications that *are* possible—for example, plants, mobiles, banners, and bulletin board displays.

Growth

Steele's last function is particularly relevant to classrooms, since they are settings specifically intended to promote students' development. This function is also the most difficult to pin down, however. While it's easy to see that environments should be functional and attractive, it's less obvious that they can be designed to foster growth. Furthermore, growth can refer to any number of areas—learning the subject matter, increasing your self-confidence, learning to cooperate. For simplicity, we will restrict our discussion to ways in which the environment can promote students' *intellectual development*.

Psychologists have found that the opportunity to explore rich, stimulating environments is related to cognitive growth. Ideally, your classroom setting should support your instructional program by inviting students to observe, think, investigate, test, and discover. This means that in addition to the standard texts and workbooks, your classroom should contain a wide variety of materials appropriate to the content area. Donnie's math class, for example, contains calculators, rulers, protractors, and compasses; Fred's history classes have access to globes, maps, and other resource materials. In Sandy's chemistry room, students work with balances, Bunsen burners, test tubes, and centrifuges. And Christina's classroom is filled with a variety of texts: novels, literature anthologies, newspapers, dictionaries, and reference materials.

A relatively recent addition to the classroom environment is the microcomputer. Computers can provide opportunities for students to complete practice exercises, to engage in problem solving and exploration through simulations, to access the Internet, and to experience the writing process—to compose, edit, revise, and publish. Unfortunately, in many schools there is only one computer per classroom. This means that teachers have to think carefully about the location of this scarce but precious resource. If students are going to work at the computer in pairs or in small groups, place it in an area where clusters of students can gather round without creating traffic congestion and distraction. Also keep in mind that computer use is often "a social event" (Genishi, 1988); the upright position of the screen invites comment and inquiry from students walking past or sitting nearby. How you feel about this spontaneous interaction should be a factor in your decision about the computer's location.

The Teacher as Environmental Designer

Steele's six functions give you a way of thinking about the environment, but they don't provide you with an architectural blueprint. If you think about the various roles that settings play, you will realize that the functions not only overlap, they may actually conflict. Seating that is good for social contact may be bad for testing, as Donnie can attest: She often prepares two to three versions of a test, since students are sitting so close to one another! Similarly, room arrangements that provide students with privacy may be poor for monitoring and maintaining order. As you think about your room and your own priorities, you will have to determine which functions will take precedence over others. You also need to think about what is possible for you to achieve if you are a "nomad" who must move from room to room or share space with other teachers.

This section of the chapter describes a process that you can follow as you design your classroom.

Think about the Activities and the Students the Room Will Accommodate

The first step in designing a classroom is to reflect on activities your room is to accommodate. For example, if you are teaching a lab science, you may need to accommodate whole-group instruction, "hands-on" lab work, media presentations, and testing. If you are teaching history, you may want to have small group research projects, debates, simulations, and role plays in addition to the standard lecture, recitation, discussion, and seatwork formats. If you are teaching a foreign language, you may want to facilitate conversation among students. List these activities in a column, and next to each activity note if it poses any special physical requirements. For example, computers need to be near electrical outlets and away from chalkboards. For access to the Internet, the location of the computer will also be dictated by hard wiring.

Next, consider which of these activities will *predominate* in your classroom and reflect on the physical arrangement that will be most suitable for the majority of the time. Will students most often be participating in whole-class discussion? If so, you may want to arrange the desks in a large circle. Will you generally be doing presentations and demonstrations at the board? If your answer is yes, then some sort of row arrangement may be best. In addition, consider how the furniture can be rearranged to accommodate the *secondary* activities you will be conducting. For example, Christina has desks arranged in rows, but as soon as students are done with journal writing (the first activity of every period), they move into clusters of four or five to carry out small-group tasks.

Also think about the characteristics of the students who will be using the room. Will you have any students with attentional difficulties who may need seats away from distractions? Will any students have orthopedic problems that require wide aisles or special equipment and furniture? (For example, Sandy has a portable lab table to accommodate a student in a wheelchair.) Will any of your students have full-time aides who accompany them from room to room? If so, the aide may need a desk or chair also, perhaps in close proximity to the student.

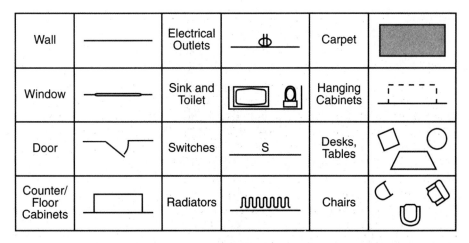

FIGURE 3-8. Drawing a floor plan: some useful symbols

Draw a Floor Plan

Before actually moving any furniture, draw a number of different floor plans and select the one that seems most workable. (Figure 3-8 depicts symbols that may be useful.)

In order to decide where furniture and equipment should be placed, consider the special requirements noted on your list of activities, as well as the room's "givens"—the location of the outlets, the chalkboard, the windows, the built-in shelves, computer wiring, cabinets, or lab tables. Also keep in mind our discussion of psychological security, social contact, and task instrumentality.

It may be helpful to begin by deciding where you will conduct whole-group instruction and the way students will be seated during this time. Think about where the teacher's desk should be, whether frequently used materials stored on shelves or in cabinets are accessible to you and your students, and whether pathways are clear. Remember, there is no one right way to design your classroom. The important thing is to make sure that your spatial arrangement supports the teaching strategies that you will use and the kinds of behaviors you want from your students.

Involve Students in Environmental Decisions

Although a great deal can be done before the start of school, it is a good idea to leave some things undone, so your students can be involved in the design process. Although their suggestions are occasionally beyond the means of the normal public school—planetarium-type ceilings and rope ladders (Hill, 1968)—it is likely that many of their ideas will be reasonable. Listen to Arthur, a student at an inner-city junior high, speaking of his ideal classroom (Coles, 1969):

> *I'd like comfortable chairs, like ones that had cushions so your back doesn't hurt and your bottom either. I'd like us sitting around—you know, looking at*

each other, not in a line, not lined up. I'd like a sink, where you could get
some water to drink, and you wouldn't have to ask the teacher to go down
the hall. . . . There'd be a table and it would be a lot nicer homeroom than it
is now. (pp. 49–51)

If you teach four or five classes in one room, it is obviously impossible to involve everyone in all environmental decisions; however, you might solicit ideas for room design from your various classes, and then select those that seem most feasible. You might also rotate responsibility for some aspect of the environment among your classes (e.g., each class could have an opportunity to design a bulletin board display). Inviting students to participate in environmental decision making not only helps to create more responsive physical arrangements, it also prepares students for their roles as active, involved citizens who possess environmental competence.

Try the New Arrangement, Evaluate, and Redesign

Use Steele's six functions of the environment as a framework for evaluating your classroom design. For example, does the desk arrangement facilitate or hinder social contact among students? Do displays communicate information about the subject matter and students' work? Are frequently used materials accessible to students? Does the room provide pleasure? Does it contain materials that invite students to extend their interests and abilities?

As you evaluate the effectiveness of the classroom setting, stay alert for behavioral problems that might be caused by the physical arrangement. For example, if a student suddenly becomes inattentive when his desk is moved next to the pencil sharpener, it is likely that an environmental change is in order, rather than detention. If the classroom floor is constantly littered despite your appeals for neatness, the underlying problem may be an inadequate number of trash cans.

Improving your room does not have to be tedious and time consuming. In fact, small modifications can bring about gratifying changes in behavior. This was demonstrated by Krantz & Risley (1972), who found that when kindergartners crowded around a teacher who was reading a story, they were inattentive and disruptive. Just spreading the children out in a semicircle markedly improved their attentiveness. In fact, this simple environmental modification was as successful as a complicated system of rewards and privileges that the experimenters had devised!

Some Thoughts on Having to Share Rooms

When we sat down as a group to discuss the role of the physical environment in classroom management, it became clear that Sandy, Christina, and Fred—the three teachers who do not have their own room—feel frustrated by the need to share classrooms. Christina was blunt about having to teach in two different rooms: "I hate it!" Sandy emphasized the difficulties that are created when access to the classroom is limited:

When I'm not in my room, someone else is; that means that I can't get into the room during the school day to prepare labs—and we do six labs a week. I have to prepare labs before or after school, and that's also when I carry out the other responsibilities associated with being a chemistry teacher, like organizing materials, disposing of old chemicals, making sure all the equipment is in working order, and of course, working with kids who are having trouble. Although I'd like to pay attention to creating a more attractive environment, that's got to be a lower priority.

The teachers also expressed irritation over other common problems—for example, inadequate storage space (Christina likes to "hoard" things), inappropriate furniture, and insufficient numbers of desks. They traded war stories about materials that disappear (Fred's gone through three staplers this year) and the lack of personal work areas (it took Sandy three years to get a desk where she could sit during free periods to plan lessons and grade papers; when she finally got one, it was in a storage closet!). They also talked about the problems that arise when the other teachers sharing the room are inconsiderate "roommates" who fail to clean up adequately. Since this was a topic that clearly raised their blood pressure, it seems important to share a few of the lessons they have learned.

Being a Good Roommate

During our discussion, Donnie shared an anecdote that illustrates the kinds of problems that can occur when teachers have to share rooms.

I share the room with a long-term substitute who's supposed to monitor a study hall in my room during second period. He thinks he doesn't really have to watch the kids, so they sit there and write all over the desks. Finally, I couldn't stand it anymore; I took a sponge and cleanser and cleaned all the tables before school began. I taught first period and then turned the room over to him. When I came back third period, the desks were covered with writing again! I was furious!

Given the other teacher's status as a long-term substitute coming in the middle of the year, Donnie's situation was particularly difficult. In general, however, it is helpful to work out an explicit agreement at the very beginning of the year about how the room is to be left. You and your roommate might agree that desks are to be returned to their standard places, boards are to be erased, the floor is to be cleaned, no food is to be in the room, and (of course) no writing is to be on the desks. You also need to agree on a procedure to follow if the agreement is violated, so you don't have to suffer in silence. As Sandy tells us, "It's not enough to have an agreement; you have to follow through. My roommate and I have agreed to hold the kids accountable for the condition of the room. If I come in and find a problem, I tell her about it, and she deals with it the next time she sees those students."

Concluding Comments

Despite the constraints imposed by sharing rooms, all four teachers agreed on the importance of thinking about the physical environment. As Fred commented:

> *Some of the ideas—like the action zone, for example—are important for teachers to know about even if they move from room to room and have little control over the classroom. On the other hand, some of the ideas—like psychological security—are hard to put into practice if you're a nomad like I was. But that's okay; thinking about these issues is important anyway. We need to say to new teachers, "Listen folks, you're going to have to be clever in dealing with this. If you can't add soft, warm fuzzies to your room, then you're going to have to compensate. You're going to have to find other ways of providing psychological security, like making sure your kids feel safe in your classroom because they know they're not going to get hammered."*

As Fred's comments suggest, it is not easy for secondary teachers to create their ideal classroom settings. Nonetheless, I hope this chapter has given you a greater awareness of the physical environment and its impact, along with a realistic sense of how you can use the environment to meet your goals.

Summary

This chapter discussed how the physical environment of the classroom influences the way teachers and students feel, think, and behave. It stressed the need for teachers to be aware of the direct and indirect effects of the physical environment. This awareness is the first step to developing "environmental competence." The chapter suggested ways to design a classroom that will support your instructional goals, using Steele's six functions of the environment as a framework for discussion.

Security and shelter

- Be aware of and implement safety guidelines for dangerous supplies and equipment.
- Be sensitive to the needs of students with physical disabilities and attentional problems.
- Add elements of softness.
- Arrange space for freedom from interference.
- Create opportunities for privacy by adding cubicles or folding cardboard dividers.

Social contact

- Consider how much interaction you want among students.
- Think about whether you are making contact with *all* of your students; avoid a small action zone.

Symbolic identification

- Personalize your classroom space so that it communicates information about you, your students, and your subject matter.

Task instrumentality

- Make sure frequently used materials are accessible to students.
- Make it clear where things belong.
- Plan pathways to avoid congestion and distraction.
- Arrange seats for a clear view of presentations.
- Locate your desk in an appropriate place (off to the side helps to ensure that you will circulate).

Pleasure

- Create an aesthetically pleasing environment through the use of plants, color, and bulletin board displays.

Growth

- Stock your room with a variety of materials relevant to your content area.
- Create relevant bulletin board displays.

Careful planning of the physical environment is an integral part of good classroom management. When you begin to design your room, think about the activities it will accommodate; if possible, invite your students to participate in the design process. Try your arrangement, evaluate it, and redesign as necessary. If you are sharing your room with other teachers, be sure to work out an explicit agreement about how the room is to be left at the end of the period.

Activities

The following activities are intended to help you think about classroom physical environments. The activities are appropriate for inservice teachers with their own classrooms, as well as preservice teachers engaged in pre–student teaching field experiences or student teaching.

1. Visit a junior or senior high classroom, draw a classroom map, and evaluate the physical layout in terms of Steele's six functions of the environment. The following questions, adapted from Bruther (1991), may be helpful.

Security and shelter

a. Does the classroom feel like a safe, comfortable place to be?

b. Does it contain furnishings and materials that are soft or inviting?

c. Do students have freedom from intrusion and interference?

d. Is there any opportunity for privacy?

Social contact

e. Does desk arrangement facilitate or hinder social contact among students? Is this compatible with the explicit objectives?

Symbolic identification

f. Are there displays of students' work in the room?

g. Does the room communicate information about the teacher, students, or the subject matter? What is communicated?

Task instrumentality

h. Are frequently used classroom materials accessible to students?

i. Are shelves and cabinets well organized so that it is clear where materials and equipment are stored?

j. Are pathways clearly visible?

k. Does the seating arrangement allow students to see instructional presentations without difficulty?

Pleasure

l. Are there any amenities present (e.g., plants, bulletin board displays, etc.)?

m. Is the classroom colorful and brightly decorated?

Growth

n. Does the classroom contain a wide variety of materials relevant to the subject matter?

o. Does the classroom contain any computers?

2. Imagine for a moment that you have a classroom of your own: You don't have to change rooms, and you don't even have to share it with any other teacher! Furthermore, you have an unlimited budget to purchase furniture, equipment, and supplies. Using the symbols shown in Figure 3-8, draw a floor plan of this ideal classroom. Be prepared to explain why you are designing the room this way.

3. Consider the following seating arrangements. For each one, think about the types of instructional strategies for which it is appropriate or inappropriate. The first one has been done as an example.

Arrangement	Instructional Strategies for Which This Arrangement Is Appropriate	Instructional Strategies for Which This Arrangement Is Inappropriate
Rows	Teacher or student presentations; audio-visual presentations; testing	Student-centered discussions; small-group work
Horizontal Rows		
Horseshoe		
Small clusters		
Circle		

For Further Reading

Emmer, E. T., Evertson, C., & Worsham, M. E. (2000). Organizing your classroom and materials. Chap. 1 in *Classroom management for secondary teachers.* (5th ed). Boston: Allyn and Bacon.

Lambert, N. M. (1994). Seating arrangements in classrooms. Vol. 9. *The International Encyclopedia of Education.* (2nd ed.) pp. 5355–5359.

Weinstein, C. S., & David, T. G. (Eds.) (1987). *Spaces for children: The built environment and child development.* New York: Plenum Press.

References

Adams, R. S., & Biddle, B. J. (1970). *Realities of teaching: Explorations with video tape.* New York: Holt, Rinehart, & Winston.

Axelrod, D., Hall, R. V., & Tams, A. (1979). Comparison of two common classroom seating arrangements. *Academic Therapy, 15,* 29–36.

Bruther, M. (1991). Factors influencing teachers' decisions about their classroom physical environments. Unpublished doctoral dissertation, Rutgers Graduate School of Education.

Bennett, N., & Blundell, D. (1983). Quantity and quality of work in rows and classroom groups. *Educational Psychology, 3,* 93–105.

Coles, R. (1969). Those places they call schools. *Harvard Educational Review: Architecture and Education, 39*(4), 46–57.

Genishi, C. (1988). Kindergartners and computers: A case study of six children. *Elementary School Journal, 89,* 185–201.

Hill, W. (1968, November). Using students as school design consultants. *School Management,* 81–86.

Horowitz, P., & Otto, D. (1973). *The teaching effectiveness of an alternate teaching facility.* Alberta, Canada: University of Alberta. ERIC Document Reproduction Service No. ED 083 242.

Krantz, P. J., & Risley, T. R. (September, 1972). The organization of group care environments: Behavioral ecology in the classroom. Paper presented at the Annual Convention of the American Psychological Association, Honolulu. ERIC Document Reproduction Service No. ED 078 915.

Maslow, A. H., & Mintz, N. L. (1956). The effects of esthetic surroundings: I. *Journal of Psychology, 41,* 247–254.

Perlmutter, B. F. (1994, August 12). Teaching distractible students: Modifications in seating arrangements and classroom strategies. Paper presented at the Annual Convention of the American Psychological Association, Los Angeles.

Proshansky, E., & Wolfe, M. (1974). The physical setting and open education. *School Review, 82,* 557–574.

Sommer, R. (1974). *Tight spaces: Hard architecture and how to humanize it.* Englewood Cliffs, NJ: Prentice-Hall.

Sommer, R., & Olsen, H. (1980). The soft classroom. *Environment & Behavior, 12*(1), 3–16.

Steele, F. I. (1973). *Physical settings and organization development.* Reading, MA: Addison-Wesley.

Weinstein, C. S. (1982). Privacy-seeking behavior in an elementary classroom. *Journal of Environmental Psychology, 2,* 23–35.

Wheldall, K., & Lam, Y. Y. (1987). Rows versus tables. II. The effects of two classroom seating arrangements on classroom disruption rate, on-task behaviour and teacher behaviour in three special school classes. *Educational Psychology, 7*(4), 303–312.

Wheldall, K., Morris, M., Vaughn, P., & Ng, Y. (1981). Rows versus tables: An example of the use of behavioral ecology in two classes of eleven-year-old children. *Educational Psychology, 1*(2), 171–184.

Chapter Four

Establishing Norms for Behavior

Research on Effective Classroom Management

Defining Your Expectations for Behavior

Planning Rules for General Conduct

Planning Routines for Specific Situations

The First Few Days of School: Teaching Students How to Behave

Concluding Comments

Summary

Secondary teachers sometimes contend that their students know how to behave, since they've been in school for many years. The argument goes like this:

My kids aren't babies. By junior or senior high school, students know the importance of coming to class on time, doing homework, respecting other people's property, and raising their hands to make a comment. Besides, there's so much material to cover, I can't waste time teaching rules to kids who should already know all this stuff.

This reasoning has a certain appeal, particularly for teachers who are enthusiastic about their content area and eager to get started. Yet it's important to recognize that although your students have general notions about appropriate school behavior, they do not know *your specific expectations.* Furthermore, your students probably see five different teachers each day, and specific expectations vary from class to class. A student's first-period teacher may not mind if everyone is milling around the room when the bell rings, while the second-period teacher insists that students be in their seats. In third

53

period, the teacher wants students to put homework in the upper right-hand corner of their desks, but the fourth-period teacher has students drop homework in a basket at the front of the room.

What will *you* expect with regard to basic classroom routines like these—and how will your students know what to do if you don't tell them? It is unfair to keep students guessing about the behaviors you expect. Not knowing the norms for appropriate behavior causes insecurity and misunderstandings, even among "school smart" adolescents. In contrast, *clearly defined classroom rules and routines help to create an environment that is predictable and comprehensible.*

Rules and routines have another major benefit. As Chapter 1 emphasized, classes are crowded, public, unpredictable places in which individuals engage in a variety of activities, often within the time constraints of a 42- or 45-minute period. *Clear rules and routines minimize confusion and prevent the loss of instructional time.* They enable you to carry out "housekeeping" tasks (e.g., taking attendance, distributing materials) smoothly and efficiently, almost automatically. They free you and your students to concentrate on the real tasks of teaching and learning.

This chapter describes research that demonstrates the importance of rules and routines. We then consider some principles to guide you in establishing rules for your own classrooms. We'll also learn how Donnie, Christina, Sandy, and Fred introduce rules and routines to their students and what they think about this central task of classroom management.

Research on Effective Classroom Management

Prior to 1970, teacher preparation programs could offer only limited advice about classroom management to beginning teachers. Teacher educators shared useful "tricks of the trade" (e.g., flick the lights on and off for quiet), stressed the importance of firmness and consistency, and warned prospective teachers not to smile until Christmas. But research identifying the behaviors of effective managers was unavailable, and it was simply not clear why some classrooms function smoothly and others are chaotic.

That situation began to change in 1970, with the publication of Jacob Kounin's study of orderly and disorderly classrooms. You may recall from Chapter 1 that Kounin (1970) set out to compare teachers' methods of responding to misbehavior. To his surprise, he found that the reactions of good classroom managers were not substantially different from the reactions of poor classroom managers. What *did* differ were the strategies that teachers used to *prevent* misbehavior. Effective classroom managers constantly monitored students' behavior. They displayed what Kounin called "withitness": They were aware of what was happening in all parts of the room, and they communicated this awareness to students. They also exhibited an ability to "overlap"—to do more than one thing at a time—certainly a desirable skill in a setting where so many events occur simultaneously! Furthermore, effective managers kept lessons moving at a brisk pace, so that there was little opportunity for students to become inattentive and disruptive.

Kounin's work led researchers to wonder how effective managers began the school year. In the late 1970s, a series of studies was launched at the Research and Development Center for Teacher Education, located at the University of Texas at Austin. One project (Evertson & Emmer, 1982) involved observations of 26 mathematics teachers and 25 English teachers in junior high schools in an urban district. Each teacher was observed teaching two different classes. During the first three weeks of school, researchers observed extensively in each classroom and kept detailed records of what occurred. During the rest of the academic year, each teacher was observed once every three to four weeks (in both of his or her classrooms). On the basis of these latter data, the researchers identified six more and six less effective managers in mathematics and seven more and seven less effective managers in English. They then went back to the information collected at the beginning of the year and compared what the teachers had done during the first three weeks of school. Striking differences were apparent—even on the very first day of school!

Among the major differences documented by Evertson and Emmer was the way teachers handled rules and procedures. Although all of the teachers had expectations for behavior, and they all took time to present or discuss these with students, the more effective managers were more successful in *teaching* the rules and procedures. For example, the more effective teachers were more likely to distribute handouts stating their behavioral expectations or to have students copy them into their notebooks. They were also clearer and much more explicit about behaviors that are likely to cause problems—namely, those that occur frequently and that may vary from teacher to teacher (e.g., call-outs, movement through the room, student–student interaction, hand raising). Interestingly, for behaviors that occur infrequently per period (e.g., tardiness, bringing materials) and are fairly straightforward, no differences between the two groups of teachers were apparent.

Subsequent research has confirmed the importance of explicitly teaching students your expectations for their behavior. Douglas Brooks (1985), for example, videotaped two experienced and two inexperienced junior high school teachers (two in math and two in science) as they met with their classes for the very first time. The contrast between the experienced and inexperienced math teachers is especially vivid.

The experienced math teacher, perceived by students and administrators as exceptionally clear and organized, began her presentation of behavioral expectations by distributing a copy of class rules that students were to keep in their folders. She first discussed schoolwide policies, but spent most of the time on classroom standards—how to enter the class, how to use materials, how to interact with the teacher and other students, what to do in the case of an emergency, and how to exit the class. In general, *she stated a rule, explained the rationale, provided an example of an appropriate behavior, and concluded with the consequences for noncompliance.* Interestingly, she rarely smiled during her presentation of rules and procedures (although she smiled a lot during her later introduction to the course). She spoke in a businesslike tone and continually scanned the classroom; no instances of disruption were observed during her presentation.

In contrast, the inexperienced math teacher was rambling and disorganized. Students were not given a copy of the rules, nor were they encouraged to write them down. Even as the teacher presented rules and procedures about talking in class, she tolerated students talking to each other. In addition, she repeatedly smiled during her presentation of the consequences for misbehavior, a nonverbal behavior that seems incompatible with a discussion of detention and calling home (and might have sent the message that she was not serious about imposing these consequences).

As the following excerpt from the transcript illustrates, the inexperienced math teacher provided few examples or rationales. In fact, she *never* used the experienced teacher's sequence of rule-rationale-example-consequence. Although many of the rules resembled those of the experienced math teacher, she presented rules she could not enforce (wanting students to respect all teachers), and she omitted discussion of some fundamental rules (listening while the teacher is talking). Furthermore, the rules did not appear to be prioritized or organized in any way:

> *OK. I'm just going to tell you a few of my classroom rules. And, ah, so that you'll know these. The first thing I want you to know is I want, that I expect every student will obey any school policies that there are. . . . OK, all the school policies, if you haven't gotten it as of yet you will get it, this yellow sheet. It's got all the school policies on it. It explains everything to you. These apply in school and around school. . . . OK, another thing when you come in that door I expect you to walk through that door being prepared to start class. When you come in don't plan on going back out to get something out of your locker. . . . OK, when you come in you'll have a pencil, your paper, your folders, and a book. . . . OK, if you're fast at working you might bring something extra to do after you finish your work so that you can have something to keep you busy because I don't want any talking. . . . OK, and all times we'll use pencil . . . I don't want any ink on your homework papers or test papers. It should all be done in pencil . . . OK, we'll also have a folder that we'll do and I'll tell you about it later . . . OK, another thing is I expect you to be respectful. First, I want you to respect yourself, at all times respect yourself and then your classmates and also the teachers. Any teacher in the building should be respected by you and each student and if you see one anything they say goes.(pp. 67–68)*

Reading this transcript, it's impossible not to feel sympathy for this inexperienced teacher. After all, most beginning teachers, particularly those being observed, are nervous on the first day of school. But it is precisely *because* of this nervousness that you must (1) think about your expectations ahead of time and (2) plan the way you will present them to your students. Let's look at each of these steps separately.

Defining Your Expectations for Behavior

Before the first student enters your classroom, you need to think about your expectations for behavior. Not only do you need to decide on *rules for students' general conduct,* you also need to identify the *behavioral routines or procedures* that you and your students will follow in specific situations. For example, when students arrive at your classroom door, are they to go immediately to their seats, or may they congregate in small groups and socialize until you tell them to be seated? May they go to the storage cabinet and get the projects they've been working on, or should they wait for you to give out the projects one by one? When students need paper or rulers or protractors for an assignment, will they get them by themselves, will you have students distribute the materials, or will you distribute them yourself? If students have to leave your classroom to go to their lockers or to the library, must they have a pass? When students are working at their seats, may they help one another or must they work individually?

Because these seem like such trivial, mundane issues, it is easy to underestimate their contribution to classroom order. But lessons can fall apart while you try to decide how to distribute paper, and students feel anxious if they're unsure whether answering a classmate's question during an in-class assignment is helping or cheating. As we will see, rules and routines may vary from class to class, but no class can function smoothly without them.

Planning Rules for General Conduct

Rules describe the behaviors that are necessary if your classroom is to be a good place in which to live and work—for example, "bring all needed materials to class," "follow

**Mrs. Mutner liked to go over a few of her rules
on the first day of school.**

FIGURE 4-1. Mrs. Mutner liked to go over a few of her rules on the first day of school. *(CLOSE TO HOME © 1993 John McPherson. Reprinted with permission of UNIVERSAL PRESS SYNDICATE. All rights reserved.)*

directions," "respect others," and "be in your seat and ready to work when the bell rings." In Christina's class, the norms for general conduct are contained in a "newspaper" that Christina writes and distributes on the first day of class. Here are some of her basic rules:

- Respect every member of the class by using appropriate language, by paying attention when another person is speaking, and by raising [your] hand to speak.
- Complete all assignments on time and to the best of your ability.
- Come to class on time and be in your seat when the bell rings.
- Bring a pencil and any other required materials (as assigned by the teacher) to class each day.

As you reflect on rules for your own classroom, there are four principles to keep in mind. (These are summarized in Table 4-1.) First, *rules should be reasonable and necessary.* Think about the age and characteristics of the students you are teaching, and ask yourself what rules are appropriate for them. For example, it would be unreasonable for Sandy to expect her students to work on a chemistry lab without talking to one another. Given adolescents' irresistible desire to interact, creating such a rule would only result in resentment, frustration, and subterfuge. It's far more sensible to establish a rule like "talk quietly," which specifies *how* the talk is to occur.

Also ask yourself whether each rule is necessary. Is there a compelling reason for it? Will it make the classroom a more pleasant place to be? Will it increase students' opportunity to learn? Can you explain the rationale to students, and will they accept it? Sandy stresses the importance of this principle when she comments

Rules have to have reasons. For example, one of my rules is about coming to class on time. Students know they'll get detention if they're late—even once. At the beginning of the year, students think I'm unnecessarily strict about that. But I'm not trying to be mean. I want students there on time

TABLE 4-1. Four Principles for Planning Classroom Rules

Principle	Questions to Think About
1. Rules should be reasonable and necessary.	What rules are appropriate for this grade level?
	Is there a good reason for this rule?
2. Rules need to be clear and understandable.	Is the rule too abstract for students to comprehend?
	To what extent do I want my students to participate in the decision-making process?
3. Rules should be consistent with instructional goals and with what we know about how people learn.	Will this rule facilitate or hinder my students' learning?
4. Classroom rules need to be consistent with school rules.	What are the school rules?
	Are particular behaviors required in the halls, during assemblies, in the cafeteria, etc.?

because I always start class when the bell rings, and if they're not there, they miss important material. After a while, they begin to realize there's a real reason for the rule. I hear them say to their friends, "I have to get to class on time because they'll have started."

Contrast this situation with that of a biology teacher I know who insists that students take notes in black pen only. Although the teacher is able to enforce the rule, she's unable to explain it with any conviction, and her classes perceive it as arbitrary and ridiculous. Similarly, an English teacher insists that students use cursive writing during spelling and vocabulary tests. Even to her student teacher, this seems like a unreasonable rule:

Being a printer myself whose cursive has not improved beyond the third grade, I am not a fan of mandated cursive writing. In the real world whenever I have filled out a form, I have been required to print so the words are legible to the reader. The only time cursive is required is when I sign my name and for vocabulary tests in my cooperating teacher's class. I can see why students are sometimes annoyed with our rules.

It's easier to demonstrate that a rule is reasonable and necessary if it applies to *you* as well as your students. Although some rules may be intended only for students (e.g., raise your hand to speak), others are relevant for everyone (e.g., show respect for other people and their property). Sandy tells us, "If a rule is important for kids, it's important for you too. For example, I make sure that I get to class on time, and if I'm late, I owe them an explanation." Fred echoes this idea when he observes, "I try to make it clear to my students that we *all* have to follow the rules. After all, rules are not about power; they're what make civilized life possible."

Second, *rules need to be clear and understandable.* Because rules are often stated in very general terms ("be polite"), they may be too abstract to have much meaning. When planning your rules, you need to think of specific examples to discuss with students. For example, one of Donnie's basic ground rules is "Be prepared." She makes sure that "preparation" is spelled out in precise, concrete behaviors: "Class preparation consists of having your homework, notebook, pen or pencil, and a covered textbook with you each day."

Some teachers believe that rules are more understandable and more meaningful when students are allowed to participate in the decision-making process. Participation, especially at higher grade levels, may increase students' willingness to "buy into" the rules, may make them more invested in seeing that rules are followed, and may help to prepare students for adult life (Solomon, Watson, Delucchi, Schaps, & Battistich, 1988). On the other hand, allowing students to decide on class rules may result in a different set of rules for each class you teach, surely a confusing situation!

If you decide to include students in the process of deciding on rules, be prepared to receive some suggestions that are silly, sarcastic, or overly harsh ("students who forget homework have to copy 100 pages from the dictionary"). Don't be afraid to veto inappropriate rules, but make sure your reason for rejecting a seriously made sugges-tion is clear to students.

As a beginning teacher, you may feel more comfortable presenting rules you have de-veloped yourself. In fact, despite their years of experience, neither Donnie, Sandy, nor Fred allows students to create classroom rules. Research by Evertson, Emmer, and their colleagues (e.g., Emmer, Evertson, & Anderson, 1980) has demonstrated that these teachers are not alone: Many effective teachers do not allow students to participate in the decision-making process. They do, however, discuss the rationales for the rules they have established, and they solicit examples from students.

A third principle to keep in mind is that *rules should be consistent with instructional goals and with what we know about how people learn.* The first chapter discussed the assumptions underlying this book. One assumption was that the need for order should not supersede the need for meaningful instruction. As you develop rules for your class-room, think about whether they will *facilitate or hinder the learning process.* For ex-ample, in the pursuit of order, some teachers prohibit talking during in-class assign-ments, and others refrain from using cooperative learning activities for fear that students will be too rowdy. Obviously, such restrictions are necessary at times (e.g., you may want students to work alone on a particular assignment so you can assess each student's comprehension of the material). It would be sad, however, if restrictions like this be-came the status quo. Educational psychologists who study the ways children learn stress the importance of children's interaction. Much of this thinking is based on the work of the Soviet psychologist Lev Vygotsky, who believed that children's intellectual growth is fostered through collaboration with adults who serve as coaches and tutors and with more capable peers (Wertsch, 1985). Interestingly, research on the use of small groups indicates that these interactions benefit the *tutor* as well as the person being tutored. Noreen Webb (1985), for example, found that junior high school students who provided explanations for their peers showed increased achievement themselves. Given the im-portant role that interaction plays in young people's learning and cognitive develop-ment, it seems sensible not to eliminate interaction, but to spend time teaching students how to interact in ways that are appropriate. (This topic will be addressed more fully in Chapter 10.)

Finally, *classroom rules need to be consistent with school rules.* The importance of this principle can be illustrated by an excerpt from a student teacher's recent journal entry:

> *The first week of school I ejected a student from the room and told him he couldn't come back into the class until he had a note from his parents. Not only was the student back in class the next day without a note, but I was informed that (1) I was in violation of the school code when I ejected the student, and (2) only homeroom teachers communicate directly with the parents.*

Your school may hold an orientation meeting for new teachers where school rules, policies, and procedures are explained. In particular, find out about behaviors that are expected during assemblies, in the cafeteria and library, and in the hallways. You should also learn about the administrative tasks for which you are responsible (e.g., taking attendance, collecting field trip money, supervising fire drills, recording tardiness). If there is a school handbook, be sure to get a copy and use it as a guide for establishing your own rules and routines.

You also need to know if you are supposed to review the handbook with students. For example, Fred's students receive a booklet explaining "South Brunswick High School's Rules, Regulations, and Policies," and teachers go over it with their first-period class (their homeroom class) on the first day of school. The handbook covers policies and procedures with respect to lateness, absenteeism, smoking, substance abuse, leaving school grounds, bias incidents, use of beepers and pagers, fighting and physical assault, and possession of weapons. After reviewing the handbook, students sign a statement indicating that they agree to abide by the rules. The statement is then returned to the main office.

Reviewing the handbook with his students allows Fred to explain how his classroom rules and routines jibe with those of the school:

OK, as you can see, the school rule is that you have to bring a note when you return to school after an absence. Let's talk about this a little more. When you're absent, it's your responsibility to call someone in class and make up the activity. So before you leave school today, get someone's phone number. [He smiles.] Try to get someone who is as smart or smarter than you. [The students laugh. He continues.] Now the school rule is that if you're out for three days, you have that many days to make up the work. I tend to be a little more lenient than that, but you need to come see me and ask for additional time. Any questions? [There are none.] OK. With respect to lateness, the school rule is "Don't be late." If you're late three times, there's a penalty. I watch the lates pretty carefully, so I'll warn you if I think you're getting in trouble. Now, about cutting. You cut, I'll ask for you to leave my class. Jason, what did I say? [Jason repeats the comment.] Right! I can't teach you if you're not in my class. [He speaks slowly and with emphasis.] If you cut my class, I take it personally. Now I'm a human being. I realize there are times when you need to not be here; you have to go to the bathroom or the library. But you need to come and ask and get a pass. If you don't, that's a cut. And I'm death on that one. So don't cut.

Planning Routines for Specific Situations

So many different activities occur in classrooms that trying to define behavior for specific situations can be daunting. Researchers at the Learning Research and Development Center at the University of Pittsburgh have observed the behavior of effective classroom managers and have categorized the routines they use (Leinhardt, Weidman, & Hammond, 1987). I have adapted their three-category system to provide you with a way of thinking about routines for your own classroom.

Class-Running Routines

These are *nonacademic routines* that enable you to keep the classroom running smoothly. This category of routines includes *administrative duties* (taking attendance, recording tardiness, distributing school notices), *procedures for student movement* (entering the room at the beginning of the period; leaving the room at the end of the period; leaving the room to go to the nurse, the library, or lockers; fire drills; moving around the room to sharpen pencils or get materials), and *housekeeping routines* (cleaning lab tables, watering plants, maintaining storage for materials used by everyone).

Without clear, specific class-running routines, these activities can consume a significant part of the school day. Research on the way time is used in fifth-grade classrooms has indicated that, on the average, these activities (transition, waiting, housekeeping) consume almost 20 percent of the time spent in the classroom—more than the amount of time spent in mathematics instruction (Rosenshine, 1980). This figure is undoubtedly higher in classrooms that are not well managed.

By defining how students are to behave in these specific situations, you can save precious minutes for instruction. You also enable students to carry out many of these routines without your direct supervision, freeing you to concentrate on instruction or other tasks. For example, Christina's students begin each class period by writing in their journals while Christina silently takes attendance. Students know that as soon as they enter the room, they are to get their journals, copy the journal topic from the board, and write silently for the allotted time. On the first day of school, Christina laid the groundwork for the smooth functioning of this activity. In the following vignette, we see her introduce the journals to her basic skills class.

> *Before we start going over what this class is going to be about, I want to give you your journals, which you will keep on a daily basis. . . . Write your name on the cover—but open the journals first so you [can see which way is up and you] won't write your name upside down, which is often a problem. Then write English 3T, Block 2, then my name. [Points to her name on the board.] Open up your journals and write the date on the first page. I'm going to write a journal topic on the board, and I want you to copy it down, and then write a response to that topic. [Writes:* What do you expect from this class?] *When we do journals, you write until I say to stop writing, 5 to 10 minutes. Don't say you don't have anything to write about or that you can't think of anything else to say. If you run out of things to say about the topic I have given you, write about something else. OK, begin now.*

Lesson-Running Routines

These routines directly support instruction *by specifying the behaviors that are necessary for teaching and learning to take place.* They allow lessons to proceed briskly and eliminate the need for students to ask questions like "Do I have to use a pen?" "Should we number from 1 to 20?" and "What do I do if I'm finished?"

Lesson-running routines describe what items students are to have on hand when a lesson begins, how materials and equipment are to be distributed and collected, what kind of paper or writing instrument is to be used, and what should be done with the paper (e.g., folded into eight boxes; numbered from 1 to 10 along the left margin; headed with name, date, and subject). In addition, lesson-running routines specify the behaviors that students are to engage in at the beginning of the lesson (e.g., have books open to the relevant page, silently sit and wait for instructions from the teacher) and what they are to do if they finish early or if they are unable to finish the assignment by the end of the time period.

Clear lesson-running routines are especially important in classroom situations that are potentially dangerous, such as woodworking, auto mechanics, and cooking. When Sandy introduces chemistry labs, for example, she is very careful to specify the special safety procedures:

There are some special safety procedures for this lab. First, before working with the Bunsen burners, make certain that your hair is tied back. Second, make certain that your goggles are on. Third, I'll have a beaker on my desk where you can discard the metals. Everything else you can throw away in the sink. Finally, after you're finished, go to your seat and write the equations. There are reference books up here to help you. You may find that you have to go back and redo part of the lab. That's OK.

Homework procedures can also be included among lesson-running routines, since the pace and content of a lesson often depends on whether students have done their homework assignments. You need to establish routines for determining quickly which students have their homework and which do not, as well as routines for checking and collecting assignments. You also need to have routines for providing assignments for students who have been absent.

Interaction Routines

These routines refer to the *rules for talk*—talk between teachers and students and talk among students themselves. Interaction routines specify *when talk is permitted and how it is to occur.* For example, during whole-class discussions, students need to know what to do if they want to respond to a question or contribute a comment. All four of our teachers, like many others, usually require students to raise their hands and wait to be called on, rather than simply calling out. In this way, the teachers can distribute opportunities to participate throughout the class and can ensure that the conversation is not dominated by a few overly eager individuals. The teachers can also check on how well the class understands the lesson by calling on students who do not raise their hands.

Often it's hard to keep track of which students have had an opportunity to speak. In order to avoid this problem, Donnie sometimes creates a pattern for calling on students, one that is more subtle than simply going up and down rows:

I may start at the back corner of the room and call on students in a diagonal line. Or I might use the alphabetical list of students in my grade book, and alternate between students at the beginning of the list and those at the end. I try not to be obvious, but sometimes students figure out the pattern, and they'll say to me, "You missed so-and-so," or "I didn't get a question," so we'll go back and make sure that person has a turn.

Another way to keep track of which individuals have had a turn is to use the "cup system"—a coffee mug or a box containing popsicle sticks with students' names. Shake the cup, pull out a name, and then place the popsicle stick on the side until you've worked your way through the whole class.

During some lessons, you may want students to respond chorally rather than individually (e.g., during a foreign language drill on verb conjugations). A simple signal can be used to indicate that the rules for talk have changed. For example, Donnie nods and extends her hands, palms up, in a gesture of invitation. Fred, with a background in music, literally conducts the group as if it were a chorus.

Sandy also suspends the normal rules for talk at times, but she adds words of caution for beginning teachers:

If I'm at the board, with my back turned to the class, and a student wants to ask a question, I don't mind if he or she just calls out, "Mrs. K., I don't understand . . ." Or sometimes, during a whole-class discussion, someone will ask a question, and I'll ask other kids to help out. They'll turn to one another and start asking and answering questions as if I weren't even there. I can just stand aside and watch. It's great to see this kind of student–student interaction. But beginning teachers need to be careful about this. If things start to get unruly, I can just say, "Hey guys, use hands," and things settle right down, but I've seen situations like this get out of hand for beginning teachers.

Interaction routines also include *procedures that students and teachers use to gain each other's attention.* For example, if students are busy working, and you need to give additional instructions, how will you signal that you want their attention? Will you say, "Excuse me," the way Donnie does, or will you flick the lights or hold up your arm? Conversely, if you are busy working with a small group or an individual, and students need your assistance, how will they communicate that to you? Will they be allowed to call out your name or leave their seats and approach you?

Finally, you need to think about the rules that will govern *talk among students.* When 20 to 30 students sit so close to one another, it's only natural for them to talk. You must decide when it's all right for students to talk about the television show they saw last night (e.g., before the bell rings) and when their talk must be about academic work (e.g., during cooperative learning activities). You also need to think about times when students may talk quietly (e.g., during in-class assignments), and when you need to have absolute silence (e.g., when you are giving instruction or during a test).

Table 4-2 summarizes the three types of routines we have just discussed.

TABLE 4-2. Summary of Classroom Routines

CLASS-RUNNING ROUTINES: Nonacademic routines that enable the classroom to run smoothly

Administrative routines

    Taking attendance

    Recording tardiness

    Distributing school notices

Routines for student movement

    Entering the room at the beginning of the period

    Leaving the room at the end of the period

    Going to the restroom

    Going to the nurse

    Going to the library

    Fire drills

    Sharpening pencils

    Using computers or other equipment

    Getting materials

Housekeeping routines

    Cleaning chalkboards

    Watering plants

    Storing personal items (book bags)

    Maintaining common storage areas

LESSON-RUNNING ROUTINES: Routines that directly support instruction by specifying the behaviors that are necessary for teaching and learning to take place

    What to bring to class

    Collecting homework

    Recording who has done homework

    Returning homework

    Distributing materials

    Preparing paper for assignment (heading, margins, type of writing instrument)

    Collecting in-class assignments

    What to do when assignments have been completed

INTERACTION ROUTINES: Routines that specify when talk is permitted and how it is to occur

Talk between teacher and students:

    During whole-class lessons

    When the teacher is working with a small group

    When the teacher needs the class's attention

    When students need the teacher's attention

Talk among students:

    During independent assignments

    Before the bell rings

    During transitions

    During loudspeaker announcements

    During cooperative learning activities

    During peer conferencing

    When a visitor comes to speak with the teacher

The First Few Days of School: Teaching Students How to Behave

In order to minimize confusion, you need to *teach students the rules for general conduct,* defining terms clearly, providing examples, and discussing rationales. As I indicated earlier in this chapter, Evertson and Emmer's (1982) research indicates that this is crucial for behaviors that are likely to occur frequently and where the appropriate behavior may be ambiguous (e.g., talking during an independent assignment). You also need to *teach the routines* you want students to follow for specific situations. Such thoroughness is particularly important in new situations, like chemistry laboratories, wood shop, keyboarding, or ceramics studios, where students have had little prior experience.

Let's see what this looks like in action. On the morning of the first day of school, Donnie began by introducing herself to her students and asking them to introduce themselves. Afterwards, she introduced the topic of "ground rules." Note that she also provided information on topics that are sure to be on students' minds—homework, notebooks, grading, and extra help:

> *Today our main concern is to talk about how we're going to operate in here, what I expect of you in terms of behavior and what the consequences might be for some kinds of behavior. I want to discuss my ground rules or codes of behavior. I'll pass these out, and we'll discuss them. If you have any questions or problems, let me know. [She distributes a packet of handouts.] It looks like an awful lot, but it's not really. A lot will be familiar; I'm sure it will be similar to other teachers.*
>
> *OK, let's look at the first page. Here we have my ground rules. The first item on the page deals with general class procedures. I expect you to be in your seat when the bell rings. [She says this slowly and firmly. Her tone is serious but pleasant.] Today several people were tardy. I can understand that. I recognize that today is the first day and you're running around, maybe lost. [She smiles.] But I anticipate that there will be no late arrivals after this. I'll talk about what happens for tardiness in a few minutes.*

Donnie continues to elaborate on the printed statements, answering questions and inviting comments. She reviews the ground rules for notebooks, homework, extra help, paper headings, and participation, and goes on to explain the grading system. She then goes over an assignment sheet that students may use to record assignments and due dates, and elaborates on a checklist she will use to evaluate notebooks.

As this example illustrates, teaching students the rules for conduct doesn't have to be unpleasant or oppressive. In fact, some teachers don't even use the word *rules.* Sandy, for example, prefers to talk about "chemistry classroom guidelines" (see Figure 4-2), but like Donnie, she makes sure her expectations for behavior are explicit. Sandy defines terms ("Late means not being in the room when the bell rings"), provides examples

1. Always be prepared for class. You MUST bring the following items with you each class period.
   a. notebook
   b. pen or pencil
   c. your COVERED textbook
   d. a scientific calculator

2. Be prompt to class. Tardiness will not be tolerated. You are considered late to class if you enter the room after the bell rings.
   a. 1st late 10 minutes after school (with me)
   b. 2nd late 20 minutes after school (with me)
   c. 3rd late 30 minutes after school (with me)
   d. 4th late 7:15 A.M. detention

3. Grades are calculated according to a point system. Every assignment (labs, homework, classwork) and exams (tests and quizzes) are assigned points. Your grade is the number of points received compared to the total number of possible points.

4. Tests and quizzes are based on the information received through class discussions, textbook readings, and lab work. It is imperative that you take notes during class discussions. All tests (with the exception of the midterm and final) are assigned a value of 100 points. Quizzes range in point value from 25–50. A quiz does not have to be announced.

5. Homework is assigned a point value of 10. Homework is always given as a block assignment with a stated due date. Any written work that is assigned will be collected on the stated due date. NO LATE HOMEWORK WILL BE ACCEPTED.

6. If you are absent, it is YOUR responsibility to find out what was missed. Any lab missed due to an absence must be made up within one week of the absence. EXCEPTIONS: (a) If you are absent 3 days or more, more time will be allowed for make-up; (b) If you are absent the day of a test or quiz and you were in class the day before, you will be required to make up that test the day you return to school.

7. THERE WILL BE NO CUTTING!!!!

8. Hats may not be worn in class.

9. NO EXTRA CREDIT POINTS ARE GIVEN IN THIS CLASS!!!

FIGURE 4-2. Chemistry classroom guidelines (Mrs. Krupinski)

wherever necessary, and stresses the reasons for each guideline. She explains why it's important for textbooks to be covered ("so they don't get chemicals on them"); why she has a "disclaimer" in her guidelines reserving the right to give unannounced quizzes ("That's there in case I see you're not doing the reading. But I really don't like to do this; I want kids to do well on tests"); why hats cannot be worn in class (for safety reasons); why she insists on promptness ("I start when the bell rings"); and why she lets them leave when the bell rings—even if she's in the middle of a sentence ("I will not keep you, because you'd be late to the next class and that's not fair to you or to the next teacher. But don't pack up books before the bell rings"). Sandy also discusses course requirements. In particular, she explains how grades are calculated and how homework is assigned and evaluated:

> OK, people, let's talk about homework. Homework is assigned a point value of 10. I always write the homework assignments in this corner of the chalkboard and they're always given as block assignments with stated due dates. For example, your very first assignment is to do pages 3–29, with all the problem numbers. This averages out to five pages plus five problems a night. It's in your best interest to do some every night, instead of waiting

until the very end. Please keep in mind that I will not accept late homework. It doesn't all have to be in the same pen; it doesn't all have to be in the same color. I don't care if you start in blue and finish in black. But it does have to be in at the beginning of the period on the day it's due. Part of the assignment is to get it in on time. I'll give you a reminder when you come in that homework is due, but if you don't hear and then you remember halfway through I don't want it. It's also important for you to understand that homework is not graded based on how correct it is. It's graded on the basis of your effort. Homework is not useless in my class. We go over every single item.

Finally, Sandy stresses the need to come to class (in terms that are amazingly similar to Fred's):

OK, Number 7 is pretty clear ("There will be no cutting"); I don't really think this needs to be discussed. I want you here. I expect you to be here. And I take it personally if you're not.

Like Sandy, Christina also talks about "guidelines" for behavior. On the first day of school she distributes a newspaper that she creates for each class she teaches. Each newspaper begins with a "Letter from the Editor," welcoming students and inviting them to contact her at an e-mail address she has set up specifically for her classes. In addition to listing the "guidelines for student conduct," the newspaper enumerates course objectives, grading policies, penalties for late work and missed assignments, and essential routines regarding notebooks, portfolios, and paper headings. (See Figure 4-3.) Listen as Christina introduces the newspaper to English 10R:

Here's a page of information about this course. On the front page, there's a letter from the editor. That's me; I'm the editor. Read that silently, please. [She gives students a few minutes to read the letter.] There are a couple of things I want to point out. Let's look at the objectives for this class. [She goes over the objectives, clarifying terms and talking about some of the activities they'll be doing to fulfill the objectives.] OK, let's look at the "Guidelines for Student Conduct." [She goes through the list commenting on some of the bulleted points.] We're all working together to make this a positive, comfortable class. I can't do it by myself. There are 29 of you and only one of me. So you have to contribute to the environment—being nice to each other, not using put-downs, using appropriate language. You won't hear me using inappropriate language, so I don't expect you to use it either; I'm very strict about that. . . . "Obtain and complete make-up work." I expect you to be vigilant, to find out what you missed. You have two days to get the work in. "Come to class on time." On time means in your seat, not by someone else's desk. If you need to use the restroom, come to class

English 10 R

January—June 2000   Mrs. C. Vreeland

A letter from the Editor:

Dear Students,

Welcome to tenth grade English. I hope you had a pleasant first semester and are ready for some exciting educational experiences. I am looking forward to working with you this semester.

I have been working hard to plan this course for you and I think you will learn a great deal and have some fun this semester. In order to make this class successful, I must ask for your cooperation. I will ask for your input frequently and if you have any ideas, you may feel free to share them at any time.

Please raise any questions or comments at an appropriate time during class or check my schedule on the classroom door to reach me during the school day. In addition, you can reach me through e-mail if you have access at home. My e-mail address is: Celvreeland@aol.com and this address is designated for student use only, so feel free to use it

whenever you wish.

However, please note that I cannot guarantee immediate response to your e-mail. Therefore, questions or comments that require immediate attention should be addressed before you leave school. "You didn't answer my question on e-mail" is not a valid excuse for not doing your homework!

Please read the rest of this introductory handout carefully and share it with your parents, as it will provide you with an overview of the course. You will learn about rules, procedures, grading policies, and course objectives; all of which will be helpful to you throughout the semester.

I wish you much success this semester and I know that you will achieve your goals and mine if you approach this class with enthusiasm and dedication.

Sincerely,
Mrs. C. Vreeland

Objectives

After successfully completing this course, students will be able to:

1. Recognize the act and importance of listening.
2. Organize, prepare, and present a spoken presentation clearly and expressively.
3. Collaborate by sharing ideas, examples, and insights productively and respectfully.

4. Recognize that reading has many purposes and demonstrate an ability to choose an approach appropriate to the text and purpose.
5. Experience and respond to print and non-print media.
6. Use research skills to access, interpret, and apply information from a variety of print and non-print sources.
7. Compose a variety of written responses for different purposes and audiences.

8. Use a variety of technologies as a tool for learning.
9. Use their language arts skills for decision making, negotiating, and problem solving.
10. Develop a better understanding of themselves, of others, and of the world through literature and through language.

11. Read and respond to a broad range of literature.

Guidelines for Student Conduct

The student will be responsible to:

- Create a positive, comfortable learning environment in the classroom.
- Respect every member of the class, by using appropriate language, by paying attention when another person is speaking, and by raising his/her hand to speak.
- Complete all assignments on time and to the best of his/her ability.
- Obtain and complete make-up work on time — two days for each day absent.
- Listen to and follow all directions given by the teacher, asking for clarification if he/she

does not understand the directions. (NOTE: Refusal to follow directions constitutes interference with the educational process and will result in disciplinary action.)

- Come to class on time and be in his/her seat when the bell rings.
- Bring his/her textbook, notebook, a writing implement, a pen AND pencil, and any other required materials (as assigned by the teacher) to class each day.
- Leave ALL food, drink, and outerwear in his/her locker.
- LEARN and THINK independently as well as cooperatively.

FIGURE 4-3. Christina's introductory newspaper

Penalty Box

Students who do not listen to directions or obtain make-up work will receive a "double F" for all missed assignments. Late work will not be accepted.

Students who are not in their seats when the bell rings will be marked late(three lates equal one cut).

Students who disrupt the learning of others or refuse to follow directions given by the teacher will lose participation credit. If disruption or refusal persists, students will be removed from the classroom. Appropriate disciplinary action will follow.

Grading Policy

There will be three components to your grade at the end of each marking period. Each of the three will be worth one third of your final grade.

<u>Tests</u> — Includes traditional end of unit tests as well as large projects or papers. If an assignment is going to count as a test grade, it will be announced when the assignment is given.

<u>Homework/Classwork/Quizzes</u> — Includes all assignments that receive a letter grade and are completed for homework, classwork, or as a quiz. This may include groupwork. Quizzes may be announced or unannounced.

<u>Participation</u> — Includes a variety of different activities/assignments that are important for you to complete to understand the material or to learn/practice a specific skill that cannot be rated in a traditional A-F format. Participation grades will be assigned weekly and participation will be scored according to a rubric. You will see your participation rubric each week.

Texts

- Selected poetry, short stories, and nonfiction
- <u>A Separate Peace</u> by John Knowles, a novel
- <u>Of Mice and Men</u> by John Steinbeck, a novel
- <u>Ethan Frome</u> by Edith Wharton, a novel
- Selections from *The Legend of King Arthur*
- Sophocles' *Antigone*, a drama
- Shakespeare's *Julius Caesar*, a drama
- Woodbridge Township Research Paper Guide
- Media Center Materials

Procedures

Notebooks

Notebooks must be maintained. Your notebook must be clearly labeled with your name, your homeroom number, the title of the course, block, classroom number, and my name. A three-ring binder type notebook is recommended, as it will accommodate calendars and other handouts that students will be expected to keep at all times.

Notebooks must be divided into the following sections:
- Calendar Section
- Vocabulary Section—daily SAT vocabulary words and vocabulary from literature
- Daily Journal Section—dated with journal topic noted
- Literature Notes Section
- Miscellaneous Section—notes on writing and research as well as project handouts

Journals

Students will maintain daily journals in their notebooks. Journal topics will be provided and students will be expected to begin writing as soon as they enter the classroom. They will continue writing until the teacher signals the end of the journal session. Journal sessions will last approximately 5-10 minutes.

Portfolios

Students will create and maintain portfolios. Portfolios are integral to the class and will receive two test grades each semester (total = four test grades). Details about the portfolio will follow.

Paper Headings & Presentation

Students will be expected to write proper headings on all of their papers. Headings will be written neatly on the right-hand side of the top margin. Headings will include the following:
- Student's Full Name
- Course and Block
- Teacher's Name
- Date

Work will be submitted on clean paper without ragged edges. Work will be written in blue or black ink. Assignments will be clearly labeled on the top line of the paper, noting the title of the assignment and other relevant information, including page numbers. Work that does not meet these minimum requirements will not be accepted.

FIGURE 4-3. *(cont.)*

first, put your books away, and let me know you're here. Then you can go. That way if you're 10 or 20 seconds late, I'll know where you are. Remember that coats, scarves, hats, food, and drink are not allowed in class; that's a school rule so you should all be familiar with that.

[She turns the page over.] Let me point out the penalty box: You get one warning for disruptive behavior and then you're removed from the classroom. Take a minute to look over the texts we'll be using and the grading policy. . . . Read over the section on paper headings carefully.

OK, to make sure that we're all on the same page about rules and procedures, read this paper and then sign it. [She gives out the "Dear Student and Parent/Guardian" page.] Your first homework assignment is to take this home and get your parents to sign it too.

In contrast to Donnie, Sandy, and Christina, Fred introduces rules and routines in a relatively informal way. As we saw earlier, when he reviews the school handbook with his first-period class of sophomores, he uses the school rules as a jumping-off point for a presentation of his class rules. Even here, however, he distributes no handouts, nor does he post rules, and he interjects a degree of humor:

[Fred finishes reviewing the handbook and has students sign the page acknowledging receipt and agreement. He then continues with his own rules for the class.] Do you know what an acronym is? It's letters that form a word and each letter stands for a word. PITA is an acronym. And it's the main rule we have in here: Don't be a PITA. *What's a PITA, Suzanne? [She shakes her head.] You don't know? [He looks around to see if anyone else knows. There's silence.] A PITA is a . . . pain . . . in . . . the . . . neck! [There's some laughter as the class catches on.] I want you to inscribe PITA across your forehead. Don't forget:* Don't be a PITA. *Now, I have one rule for me, too: I must make you laugh once every day. If I don't, I go home in a suicidal mood. [Students laugh.] OK, let's talk about what you'll be learning in U.S. History I.*

With his seniors, Fred prefers an even less systematic approach. On the first day of class, he introduces himself, takes attendance, and immediately launches into a description of the course. During the period, he explicitly teaches his students routines for specific situations that arise (e.g., how to pass in papers), but he does not teach rules for general conduct. Instead, he monitors the class carefully and immediately informs students about behavior he finds unacceptable. His interactions with individual students are watched carefully by the rest—and they quickly learn what he expects. When Fred asks one student to takes off his baseball cap, for example, another hears and takes off his own hat. To a student wearing sunglasses, Fred asks, "Is there is a medical reason for those glasses?" and the student immediately removes them. Later on, when the same student yawns loudly and conspicuously, Fred turns to him and speaks firmly:

> FRED: James, please don't do that.
> STUDENT: I was just yawning.
> FRED: If you have to do that, please transfer to a different class. OK?
> STUDENT: OK. [Fred moves closer to James and continues the discussion.]

At the end of the period, Fred asks James to stay for a minute, a request that is obviously noted by the other students. They speak privately, and then James leaves for his next class. Afterwards, Fred shares what happened:

> *That was clearly a test, but I think I passed it. I told him that yawning like that was clearly inappropriate and that if he couldn't demonstrate the same respect for me that I showed him, then he'd have to find another place to be. I can't operate in an atmosphere of "me against you." He said it was because he hadn't had a cup of coffee. I told him there are no excuses, that it just won't happen in here, that he can't be here if he acts inappropriately. He said OK, and we agreed to chalk it up to a mistake and forget about it. But I'll have to watch him.*

As this incident illustrates, Fred communicates expectations for conduct to older students primarily by providing clear, immediate feedback when behavior is unacceptable. He recognizes that one reason this approach works for him is the reputation he has established during his years at the high school. Reflecting on this reputation, Barry Bachenheimer, Fred's student teacher, observes:

> *Everyone knows that he plays the "dumb old man," but that he's not. He has this incredible relationship with the kids; he knew everyone's name within two days. He works them hard, but he projects warmth, and the kids know he really cares. I've never seen a kid give him lip. One look is enough.*

Concluding Comments

Donnie, Christina, Sandy, and Fred all have well-defined expectations for student behavior, and they make these expectations absolutely clear. Nonetheless, the four teachers have somewhat different expectations, and they introduce rules and routines in different ways. These differences reflect their beliefs about what works best for their own particular students in their own particular contexts. Donnie, Christina, and Sandy teach rules and routines in a systematic, explicit fashion; they all spend considerable time explaining what they expect, and they distribute written copies of the rules for students to keep in their notebooks. Christina goes further: She requires her students to sign a statement that they have read and understood the information regarding "student conduct, penalties, grading policies, and expected class procedures" and to obtain their parents' signatures as well. In contrast, Fred is much more informal. With his sophomores, Fred explicitly teaches rules, but he neither posts them nor distributes copies. With his seniors, he teaches specific routines, but relies primarily on monitoring and feedback to communicate what he expects in terms of general conduct.

As a beginning teacher, you would be wise to adopt a deliberate, thorough approach to teaching rules and routines. Once you've gained experience—and a reputation—you might try a less formal approach with your older students. Also keep in mind that rules and routines are not invented in a single year, polished and fully developed. Instead, they will evolve over time, products of your experience and creative efforts.

✸ Summary

This chapter discussed two important functions of rules and routines in the classroom: (1) to provide a structure and predictability that help students to feel more comfortable; and (2) to reduce the complexity of classroom life, allowing you and your students to concentrate on teaching and learning. I outlined two broad categories of behavioral expectations—rules for general conduct and routines for specific situations—and emphasized the need to teach these explicitly.

When deciding on rules for general conduct, make sure they are:

- Reasonable and necessary.
- Clear and understandable.
- Consistent with instructional goals and with what we know about how people learn.
- Consistent with school rules.

Plan routines for specific situations:

- Class-running routines.
  - Administrative duties.
  - Procedures for student movement.
  - Housekeeping responsibilities.
- Lesson-running routines.
  - Routines governing use and distribution of materials.
  - Routines for paper headings, homework procedures, what to do if you finish early.
- Interaction routines.
  - Routines specifying when talk is permitted and how it is to occur.
  - Routines for students and teachers to use to get each other's attention.

Teach rules and routines explicitly:

- Define terms.
- Discuss rationales.
- Provide examples.

Remember, developing good rules and routines is only the first step. For rules and routines to be effective, you must actively teach them to your students. Time spent on rules and routines at the beginning of school will pay off in increased instructional time throughout the year.

Activities

1. Thinking about rules

   a. Obtain a copy of the school handbook, or talk to the principal or another teacher, to determine the school rules.

   b. Develop a set of rules for your classroom. About five rules should be sufficient. For each rule, list a rationale and examples that you will discuss with students to make the rules more meaningful. Check your rules against the school rules to ensure that there is no conflict.

   c. Think about which rules are most important to you and why.

2. Below is a list of areas for which you will need specific behavioral routines. Use this list to help you think through the ways you expect your students to behave.

   Class-running routines:
   Entering the room at the beginning of the period.
   Going to the lavatories.
   Going to lockers.
   Taking attendance.
   Recording tardiness.
   Fire drills.
   Sharpening pencils.
   Keeping track of work for absent students.
   Cleaning up.
   Leaving the room at the end of the period.
   Lesson-running routines:
   Distributing materials and equipment.
   Heading papers.
   Distributing homework.
   Collecting homework.
   What to do when assignment has been completed.
   Interaction routines:
   Talking during independent assignments.

Hand-raising during whole-class discussions.

Behaving during interruptions (e.g., a visitor comes to the door; an announcement comes over the loudspeaker).

Signaling the teacher for help during an in-class assignment.

Talking during cooperative learning activites.

3. Not all of the routines you thought about in Activity 2 can be taught that first day. You need to decide on priorities and teach routines when it is most appropriate (and most likely to be remembered). Decide which ones are necessary for the first day.

4. If you are teaching or student teaching, keep a reflective journal on developing and teaching rules and routines. Using the routines listed in Activity 2 (or in Table 4-2), note which routines cause the most problems, the nature of the problems, and how you might respond to those problems. Also note which routines work particularly well.

For Further Reading

Evertson, C. M. (1994). Classroom rules and routines. In *International Encyclopedia of Education.* 2nd ed. Oxford: Pergamon Press.

References

Brooks, D. M., (1985). The teacher's communicative competence: The first day of school. *Theory into Practice, 24*(1), 63–70.

Emmer, E. T., Evertson, C. M., & Anderson, L. M. (1980). Effective classroom management at the beginning of the school year. *The Elementary School Journal, 80*(5), 219–231.

Evertson, C. M., & Emmer, E. T. (1982). Effective management at the beginning of the school year in junior high classes. *Journal of Educational Psychology, 74*(4), 485–498.

Kounin, J. S. (1970). *Discipline and group management in classrooms.* New York: Holt, Rinehart and Winston.

Leinhardt, G., Weidman, C., & Hammond, K. M. (1987). Introduction and integration of classroom routines by expert teachers. *Curriculum Inquiry, 17*(2), 135–175.

Rosenshine, B. (1980). How time is spent in elementary classrooms. In C. Denham and A. Lieberman (Eds.), *Time to learn.* Washington, D.C.: U. S. Department of Education.

Solomon, D., Watson, M. S., Delucchi, K. L., Schaps, E., & Battistich, V. (1988). Enhancing children's prosocial behavior in the classroom. *American Educational Research Journal, 25*(4), 527–554.

Webb, N. M. (1985). Student interaction and learning in small groups: A research summary. In R. E. Slavin, S. Sharan, S. Kagan, R. Hertz-Lazarowitz, C. Webb, & R. Schmuck (Eds.), *Learning to cooperate, cooperating to learn.* New York: Plenum.

Wertsch, J. V. (1985). *Vygotsky & the social formation of mind.* Cambridge, MA: Harvard University Press.

Chapter Five

Creating Safer, More Caring Classrooms

Ways of Showing Care and Respect

   Be Welcoming

   Be Sensitive to Students' Concerns

   Welcome Students' Input

   Be Fair

   Be a Real Person (Not Just a Teacher)

   Become Aware of Adolescent Culture

   Share Responsibility

   Be Inclusive

   Search for Students' Strengths

   Develop Communication Skills

   A Note about Touching

Building Caring Relationships among Students

   Ask the Students

   Model the Traits You Want Students to Have

   Provide Opportunities for Students to Get to Know One Another

   Curb Peer Harassment

   Be Alert for Student-to-Student Sexual Harassment

   Use Cooperative Learning Groups

Two Cautionary Tales

Concluding Comments

Summary

Some years ago, I supervised a student teacher named Mollie, who had been placed in a fourth-grade classroom. I had taught Mollie in a course on campus, and I had some concerns about her organizational ability. Nevertheless, I wasn't prepared for what I saw on my first visit to her classroom. Mollie was teaching a lesson on quotation marks. Although it wasn't exactly captivating, it wasn't awful. But her students' behavior *was*. They chatted, rummaged through their desks, and completely ignored the lesson. Furthermore, throughout the period, a steady stream of students walked up to Mollie, asked to go to the restroom, and left the room. I watched in disbelief as a student left about every three minutes; at one point, five or six students were out at the same time. Yet Mollie never asked students to wait until she had finished teaching or until the previous person had returned.

When the period was over and Mollie and I met to discuss the lesson, I asked her to talk about the students' behavior. I wondered how she interpreted the students' lack of interest in her lesson and their obvious desire to leave the room. I also wanted to know why she had never said "no" when a student asked to leave the room. I remember her answer clearly:

I want to show the children that I care about them. I don't want to rule this classroom like a dictator. If I say no when someone asks to go to the bathroom, that would be showing them that I don't respect them.

Mollie never did create the atmosphere of mutual respect she desired; in fact, she never completed student teaching. Her commitment "to care"—which she defined as "never say no"—led to a situation so chaotic and so confused that no learning, teaching, *or* caring was possible.

Over the years, I have thought a lot about Mollie, particularly her definition of caring. And I've heard echoes of Mollie's thinking in other prospective teachers with whom I've worked. Like Mollie, these teacher education students believe that good teachers have to be caring teachers. They also believe they have the capacity to care deeply and to create strong bonds with students. They imagine themselves nurturing students' self-esteem, rejoicing in their successes, and watching over their well-being. They envision classrooms characterized by warmth, affection, and mutual respect.

And then these prospective teachers begin student teaching. Over the weeks, the talk about caring begins to fade away, replaced by talk of control. Talk of empathy and compassion becomes overshadowed by talk of discipline and detention. Students lament the fact that they were "too nice" at the beginning and conclude that they should have been "meaner." Some even seem to believe that caring and order are mutually exclusive.

The tension between wanting to care and needing to achieve order is not uncommon among novice teachers (McLaughlin, 1991; Weinstein, 1998). But caring and order are not irreconcilable goals. Indeed, the two go hand in hand. *When classrooms are orderly, organized environments, caring relationships can flourish.* With clear rules and routines, there is less likelihood of confusion, misunderstanding, and inconsistency—and more likelihood that teachers and students can engage in warm, relaxed interactions. As Christina puts it:

> *I feel like the more organized and the more structured the class is, the more I can show that I'm human, joke around, invite students to tell me things they would like to change. I can let my guard down, because they know what is expected.*

At the same time, *one of the ways teachers create an orderly, productive environment is through acts of caring.* As the secondary students of our four teachers made clear when I spoke with them about classroom management, "dislike = misbehave." (See Chapter 2.) Clearly, *students are more likely to cooperate with teachers who are caring and respectful* (Cothran & Ennis, 2000). A recent study by Davidson (1999) underscores this principle. Interviews with 49 adolescents, representing diverse socioeconomic, cultural, and academic backgrounds, revealed not only students' appreciation and preference for teachers who communicate interest in their well-being, but also students' willingness to reciprocate by being attentive and conscientious. This was particularly evident in the responses of students facing "social borders"—those whose personal worlds were very different from their school worlds. Jamie, an African-American female, put it this way:

> *[Ms. Rocke], she's like another mother . . . I can talk to [her] about everything . . . like if I come to her and ask her, you know, how I feel about this guy and stuff.*
>
> *We owe her something now . . . we can't say "we don't know this" . . . there's no way. We can't just say, "Oh Mrs. Rocke, we sorry," this and that. No way we can say that! We gotta do it [our work], we owe her that you know. (p. 346)*

As Davidson concludes, teachers who communicate caring and interest to students can eliminate the detrimental effects of social borders. Moreover, they "are in a much better position to win [students'] cooperation in academic endeavors" (p. 346).

But gaining cooperation is certainly not the only reason for trying to develop positive relationships with students. If we want adolescents to be seriously engaged in learning, to share their thoughts and feelings, to take risks, and to develop a sense of social responsibility, then we need to organize classrooms so that students feel safe and cared for—emotionally, intellectually, and physically. If we want students to feel a sense of

Calvin and Hobbes

by Bill Watterson

FIGURE 5-1. Calvin's teacher has difficulty gaining his cooperation.
(CALVIN AND HOBBES © Watterson. Reprinted with permission of UNIVERSAL PRESS SYNDICATE. All rights reserved.)

connectedness and trust, then we must work to create classroom communities where students know that they are needed, valued members of the group (Roeser, Eccles, & Sameroff, 2000; Sapon-Shevin, 1999). If we want students to accept and appreciate diversity—ethnic, racial, gender, class, ability/disability—we must model that behavior.

This chapter begins by considering what it really means to show caring and respect for students. We then turn to relationships among students themselves and discuss strategies for creating a "caring community of learners" (Battistich, Watson, Solomon, Lewis, & Schaps, 1999) in which students feel respected, trusted, and supported by one another. As you read, keep in mind the characteristics of classroom groups that were discussed in Chapter 1. Recall that, unlike most other social groups, students do not come together voluntarily. They are a captive audience, often required to work on tasks they have not selected and in which they may have little interest. Remember, too, that classroom groups are formed somewhat arbitrarily; students do not usually choose their peers *or* their teachers, yet they are expected to cooperate with both. Recalling these special characteristics makes it easier to see why teachers must work to create cohesion, cooperation, and a sense of community. (Figure 5-1 illustrates the difficulty Calvin's teacher has in gaining his cooperation.)

Ways of Showing Care and Respect

Be Welcoming

Although teachers are often told not to smile until Christmas, an old Chinese proverb tells us that "a man without a smiling face must not open a shop" (Charles, 2000, p. 39). The proverb was written long ago (note the use of gendered language!), but the sentiment is still applicable—and as relevant to teachers as to shopkeepers. A smile is a simple, effective way to be welcoming.

In addition, you can welcome students by standing at the classroom door and greeting students at the beginning of the period. This not only ensures that students enter the room in an orderly fashion, it also gives you an opportunity to say hello, comment on a new hairstyle, and ask how things are going. If you have students who are not native English speakers, learn a few phrases in their native languages. It can mean a lot to students if you can welcome them to your class each day with a few words from their homeland: Ka hue? ("What's happening?" in Fijian); Apa khabar? ("How are you? in Malaysian); "¿Que tal?" ("How goes it?" in Spanish) (Kottler, 1994).

Most importantly, learn students' names (and any preferred nicknames) as quickly as possible. You also need to learn the correct pronunciation, especially for names that are unfamiliar. In the classes of our four teachers, for example, there are Sriram ("Shreerom"), Hrushita, Yili, Isha ("Eye-sha"), Hamzuh ("Hum-zuh"), Wei Hou ("Wee-how"), and Aisha ("Eye-ee-sha). Christina finds that writing the phonetic pronunciations in her record book is a real help. She has also noted that some Asian American students are reluctant to correct mispronunciation, fearing that it would be disrespectful.

Watch how Donnie and Fred show an interest in students' names as they welcome students on the first day of school:

> *After introducing herself, Donnie asks the students to tell her about themselves in the same way: "Tell me your name, where you got it from or what it means, if you have a nickname you want me to use, and then choose an adjective to describe yourself. I'm going to write these down so I can learn your names as quickly as possible. But please be patient; it might take a little while."*

> *Fred introduces himself to students: "Good morning, ladies and gentlemen, my name is Fred Cerequas, and I'm your homeroom teacher and your first-period teacher. Many students in the past have called me Mr. C. because they've had trouble with my name. You're welcome to call me Mr. C. too. . . . Now let's find out who you are. When I call your name, please indicate your presence here. If I mispronounce your name, please tell me." As Fred calls students' names, he checks on if they have any nicknames they would prefer him to use; occasionally he asks about ethnic origin ("And what kind of a name is that?") and chats about siblings that he has taught.*

Be Sensitive to Students' Concerns

In essence, this means thinking about classroom events and activities from a student's point of view. On the first day of school, for example, Christina assigns seats alphabetically so that she can learn students' names as quickly as possible. Realizing that students may be unhappy about the location of their seats or their particular neighbors, she reassures them that seats will be changed periodically. With a smile, she tells them: "You don't have to worry about getting tired of one another!"

Sensitivity is also demonstrated by keeping grades a private matter between you and an individual student. Most adolescents don't want anyone to know they've gotten a failing grade; public announcements are less likely to increase motivation than to generate resentment. Even if you announce only the A's, you can embarrass students. My daughter was once completely humiliated when her teacher held her test up in front of the whole class and announced that "Laura was obviously the only one who studied!" And what does an announcement like that convey to the student who normally received D's, but studied really hard and earned a C? When Sandy gives students' papers back, she tells them to keep their grades to themselves while they are in the room—"no asking, no telling." If they wish to divulge their grades once they've left the room, that's their prerogative.

Since secondary students have a tremendous need to save face, sensitivity also means discussing inappropriate behavior quietly and privately. (Remember the remarkably public nature of classrooms described in Chapter 1.) Public reprimands are humiliating—and humiliation will surely poison your relationship with students. In order to preserve that relationship, Donnie approaches misbehaving students quietly and sets up a time to meet:

I'll tell them, "I don't want to take up class time and I don't want to embarrass you. Stop by after school so we can talk privately." If that's not possible, we'll meet during lunch or before school. It means giving up some of my own time, but it's much more effective than talking during class in front of everyone.

Sensitivity also means understanding that students' energy levels ebb and flow, and dramatic mood changes from day to day are not uncommon. Football games, Valentine's Day, food fights, and special events can all affect "student weather," and "telling students it makes no difference that the prom is the next day is whistling in the wind" (Gordon, 1997, p. 58).

On an individual level, it's important to notice if someone looks especially edgy, depressed, or angry, and privately communicate your concern. As Donnie puts it:

Sometimes a student will come in and they just don't have the same glow. I'll go over and say, "Is everything OK?" And sometimes they'll say, "No, Miss, I'm having problems at home" or "I'm having trouble with my boyfriend." If they tell me that, I try to respect that and give them some space. I'll go a little easier on them that day, like I won't call on them as much.

It's also important to take students' concerns seriously if they choose to confide in you. From your adult vantage point, breaking up with a girlfriend, having to be home by 1:00 A.M. on a Saturday night, or not making the track team might not be sufficient cause for depression. But Christina emphasizes how important it is to acknowledge the legitimacy of students' concerns:

One of my eleventh-grade students was absent for two days, and when he came back, he was falling asleep, wouldn't talk with anyone, was real cranky. I called him out in the hall while other students were working in small groups and asked him what the problem was. Of course he said, "Nothing." But I told him I was really concerned, and eventually, he told me his girlfriend had broken up with him. Later that day, I arranged for him to see the guidance counselor. She let him stay there, gave him tea. It really meant a lot to him. We can't just blow these things off, even if they don't seem that earth-shattering to us. He needed to know that we noticed and cared about how he was feeling.

Finally, be sensitive to anxiety or difficulty your students may be experiencing with course material or requirements. During a visit to Sandy's class after a severe blizzard that had closed school for several days, I watched students resume a lab activity they had begun before the "vacation." It required them to use pipettes, a new piece of equipment, and several students expressed concern about having forgotten how to use the pipettes.

Sandy acknowledges their concerns: "I know that some of you are worried that you don't remember how to use the equipment. That's a valid concern, since it's been such a long time since you practiced. But don't worry. See if you remember, and if not, just call me over and I'll help you out." Later, when two students express confusion about the lab procedure, she comments: "Your confusion is understandable, because this is the first time we're doing this procedure. Next time we do it you'll know what to do. Remember when we were learning to use the balance, and you were so confused? The first time is always a challenge." At the end of the period, the students express anxiety over an upcoming test: "What if it snows again tomorrow and we don't have a chance to finish the lab, and we're supposed to have the test the next day?" Sandy is reassuring: "If we are in school tomorrow [a Wednesday], then the test will be on Thursday as scheduled. But if we have a delayed opening or no school tomorrow, the test will be on Friday. You've got to see my face for a whole period before the test! However, that doesn't mean you don't have to prepare, so this is what I'm asking you to do.

Welcome Students' Input

Allow students to voice their suggestions and opinions about lessons, assignments, or grouping decisions. Interestingly, all four teachers begin the school year by asking students to write about their expectations for the class. As we saw in Chapter 2, Sandy begins the school year by asking her students to write answers to four questions: (1) How do you learn best? (2) What do you expect to be excited about in chemistry? (3) What do you expect to be nervous about? and (4) What can I do to help? In similar fashion, Fred begins by asking students to share their expectations for the class:

> *It's the first day of school. . . . After the attendance is taken and school rules have been reviewed, Fred gives the first homework assignment. [Students groan until they hear what it is.] "I want to know what your expectations are for me. Write down a few notes and come in tomorrow prepared to tell me what you want from me. Also, what are the expectations you have for yourself?"*

Donnie also solicits students' expectations. On the first day of school, she has students write her a letter, focusing on their attitudes and feelings about mathematics, about the kinds of teaching and managerial strategies they like or dislike, and about their own responsibility in making the classroom a good place to be.

Finally, Christina asks students to write about their expectations and invites their suggestions and feedback on the class:

> *On the first day of school, Christina passes out a "Student Record" form they are to fill out. Meanwhile, she writes the journal entry for the day on the board, "What do you expect from this class?" Students write on that topic for 10 minutes. . . . Afterwards, Christina distributes a two-sided "newspaper" that she has created, with information about the class. She points out behavioral expectations, course objectives, the policy on late work, and then adds an invitation for students to provide her with feedback: "I want you to know that I really welcome your input. I'm sure you have good ideas, and I'm interested in hearing your suggestions for things we can do. Also, if you think something didn't work very well, I welcome your criticism too. For example, you might say, 'I know that you were trying to have a good discussion today, but a lot of people weren't responding because . . .' That kind of feedback would be very helpful." Christina points out her e-mail address and encourages students to use it. Just before the period ends, Christina informs the class there is one more journal entry for the day: "What do you think of this class so far?"*

There is an interesting postscript to my first-day observations of Christina's request for suggestions and criticism. Several months later, it became clear that a few students were disgruntled by the amount of work they had been assigned. Christina tells it this way:

> *It was right after spring break, and there were a couple of kids who seemed upset and complaining about work. So, wondering how widespread it was, I opened up a discussion. It was like opening Pandora's box. Out came all these complaints about how I was giving too much homework, and some*

of it was too difficult for them to do by themselves—they wanted partners. They kept saying it was like college work, and that they were only 15!

I was floored at first, but after everyone had their say, I tried to address their concerns. We made some changes. I postponed some assignments and promised to give them in-class time to work in groups on some of them. I explained why I was giving them challenging work, and I made it clear that I am here every day to work with anybody who needs help. But I also told them that what was most upsetting to me was the fact that they hadn't come to me about all this sooner.

Since the discussion, a lot of kids have been coming in for help, and things really seem to be better. But what I learned is that even if you invite kids to provide input, you still have to go back and check that it's working. You have to teach them that it's really okay to come to teachers and talk about these things. I just assumed my invitation was enough, but it wasn't.

Be Fair

It seems obvious that caring teachers must strive for fairness. For example, issues of fairness often arise in relationship to evaluation and grading. Jeffrey Smith, a colleague who specializes in assessment, emphasizes the need for communication:

If you know the criteria for good work, tell your students. Don't make them guess. Don't withhold information about how you're going to grade, and then play "gotcha." If you're going to count participation and effort as part of the grade, tell students that too, and tell them what you mean by participation.

Christina earnestly follows Jeff's advice. Since she counts participation as one-third of students' grades, she provides her classes with a weekly "participation rubric" that lists the behaviors she expects (see Figure 5-2) and spends considerable time explaining how it works. During one interview, she shared her reasoning:

Most teachers don't use participation as an actual portion of the grade; they use it as a tie-breaker (like if you're trying to decide between an A and a B). But I think it's one of the most important things. Participation is not just raising your hand and speaking out. It's also having your work done, being prepared for class, being engaged, staying on task. I know some kids are going to be more verbal and more confident, but everyone can make some contribution to class.

In this instance, caring and fairness seem to go hand in hand. But it's not always so simple. Indeed, teachers who are trying to treat students well often experience a ten-

Weekly Participation Scoring Rubric			
Name _____			
Week # ____ Beginning Date _____ Ending Date _____			
Criteria	Pts. Avail.	Points Assigned	Total
Attentive to directions	15		
Attentive to class discussion	10		
Contributes to class discussion	15		
Prepared for class	10		
Begins assigned tasks immediately	10		
Completes assigned tasks	10		
Uses time efficiently	15		
Respectful to others	15		
Total for Positive Behaviors	**100**		
Verbally Disruptive	-10		
Physically Disruptive	-10		
Inappropriate Language	-10		
Disrespectful	-10		
Late for class	-10		
Total for Negative Behaviors	**-50**		
Final Weekly Score	**100**		
Grade			

FIGURE 5-2. Christina's participation rubric

sion between two moral orientations (Katz, 1999). Being fair generally involves "making judgments of students' conduct and academic performances without prejudice or partiality" (Katz, 1999, p. 61). In terms of classroom management, this translates into ensuring that rules apply to everyone, no matter what. On the other hand, being fair can also imply a recognition that people may need different, personalized treatment, and being caring certainly seems to demand that we acknowledge students' individuality. From this perspective, treating everyone the same is *unfair.* So what is a teacher to do?

Even experienced, masterful teachers who care deeply about students' well-being may have conflicting positions on this fundamental dilemma. Consider Sandy and Fred. Sandy observes:

> *You can't have community in the classroom unless everyone feels that they'll be treated fairly, whether they're the student congress president or not. You're better off having a class with very few rules that apply to everyone, rather than a lot of rules that apply to only some people.*

Sandy demonstrated this principle not too long ago, when three of her students, including a boy classified as having an emotional disorder, didn't have their homework and asked for permission to turn it in the next day:

> *My answer was no. I don't accept late homework, and they know it. I want them to learn how to budget their time and to prepare. This was a 20-point homework assignment, due on Monday. I reminded them all week, and made a big point of it on Friday. Then they walk in on Monday without it. I said, "I believe you did it; your integrity is not in question. But it's not here." To my horror, Billy (the boy classified as emotionally disturbed) started to cry in front of the whole class. I got him out of the room and talked with him. I told him I understood that other things can interfere with doing homework, but the rule applies to everyone. I know this seems harsh, but I think this was a really significant event. It was important for Billy—and the rest of the class—to see that he has to meet the same expectations.*

From Sandy's perspective, having the rules apply to everyone is both fair *and* caring. But Fred takes a somewhat different position:

> *I try to treat kids fairly in that my decision is always based on what is best for the kid. At times that means you treat everyone the same, and that's the right decision. Other times you may treat everyone differently, and that's the right decision. There's no recipe for being fair that we can all follow. We have to constantly examine our decisions and ask, "Is this in the best interest of the kid?"*
>
> *I gain some things by not always treating everyone the same. I have more flexibility this way. I can say, "This kid is having a really hard time, and I'm not going to give him a zero for the day, no matter what the rule says." I'm just going to throw out that rule. And I've never had a kid say "That's not fair." But I lose some things too—namely, the consistency that comes when everyone knows exactly what's going to happen. So you have people who push the envelope. I have to be more on guard; I have to watch for people who are trying to take advantage.*

In sum, being fair is certainly an essential component of being caring, but it's not always obvious what this means in terms of actual practice. Teaching is messy and uncertain, and we often don't know what the right decisions are until after we've made them. What *is* certain, however, is that teachers need to engage in ongoing reflection about these complex moral issues. (We will return to these issues in Chapter 12, when we discuss fairness and consistency in dealing with inappropriate behavior.)

Be a Real Person (Not Just a Teacher)

On the first day of school, Donnie takes a few minutes to explain how she got the name Donnie, that her husband is the principal of an elementary school in New Brunswick, and that they have a daughter who "is one year short of a quarter of a century." (When students look at her questioningly, she laughs and tells them, "Do your math!") Within the first few minutes of the very first class meeting, she has already communicated an important message: In addition to being a teacher, Donnie Collins is a real person with a life outside of school.

Beginning teachers often puzzle over the extent to which they should share information about their personal lives. I remember having teachers who refused to reveal their first names—as if that would somehow blur the boundary between teacher and student and diminish their authority. On the other hand, there are teachers who are extremely open. In an article on "Building Community from Chaos" (1994), Linda Christensen, a high school English teacher in Portland, Oregon, writes:

> *Students have told me that my willingness to share stories about my life— my father's alcoholism, my family's lack of education, my poor test scores, and many others, opened the way for them to tell their stories. Students have written about rape, sexual abuse, divorce, drug and alcohol abuse. And through their sharing, they make openings to each other. Sometimes a small break. A crack. A passage from one world to the other. And these openings allow the class to become a community. (p. 55)*

As a new teacher, it's probably wise to find a happy medium between these two extremes and to discuss limited aspects of your out-of-school life (Jones & Jones, 1998), such as trips and vacations, cultural and athletic activities, hobbies, or pets. As Chapter 3 discussed, you can also use the physical environment to convey information about your family, cultural background, experiences, and idiosyncrasies. You might want to hang a poster of your favorite music group, display photographs of your family or pets, or exhibit a collection. (I've seen giraffes, penguins, kaleidoscopes, even hubcaps!) All of these "artifacts" communicate the fact that you are a *person* and create opportunities for you to interact with students on a more personal level.

As you gain experience and confidence, you can decide if you want to follow Linda Christenson's example and share more information about your personal life. During an early visit to Christina's classroom, for example, I watched as she introduced a writing assignment on identity. She began by distributing copies of her own identity essay. In it, she reflects on her Puerto Rican father, her "all-American" mother (unable to "recount all of her various nationalities"), her "Asian eyes" (with eyelids that "kept escaping" the blue eyeshadow she tried to use), and the "curious ambiguity" of her skin. Four months later, near the end of the school year, Christina talked about her students' reactions to the essay:

> *I think it helped to build connections with the students. It stimulated all kinds of questions: What do you do for this holiday? Do you go to the Puerto Rican Day parade? They were able to see me as a real person. Just today, it came up again and led to a good discussion about the most appropriate terms for various ethnic and racial groups. It clearly made an impact on them.*

Another way of showing your humanity is to admit when you don't know something. Teachers sometimes feel that they have to be the "sage on the stage," but it can be beneficial for students to see that even "experts" don't know all the answers all the time. The best way to encourage students to take risks in the process of learning is to take risks yourself.

It's also important to apologize if you make a mistake. During another visit to Christina's classroom, she and I chatted in the hallway until the bell rang. When we entered the room, she noticed that students had not begun writing in their journals. Looking at them in surprise, she issued a mild rebuke:

> *"You should all be writing a journal entry. Why are you just sitting there?" Christina turns to the board and realizes she has failed to put one up for the day. "Oops. I didn't put one up. Sorry. OK, we need a journal topic. Who has an idea?"*

Become Aware of Adolescent Culture

Positive relationships with students can be facilitated if you have what Robin Gordon (1997) calls "social insight"—knowledge of popular music, styles of dress, current movies, and other aspects of adolescent culture. In order to acquire this insight, you can watch MTV (at least occasionally), listen to albums of students' favorite music groups, visit students' favorite websites, and attend popular movies. Donnie also finds it helpful to sit quietly and listen to students' chatter right before homeroom:

> *That's when I learn all about the concerts they've attended or the deejays they like. We talk about today's music; I tell them I don't know what the groups are saying these days, and they explain. They also like to hear about the things that I did "back in the old days" and compare it with the things they're doing now.*

As this comment reveals, Donnie understands the importance of understanding adolescent culture—without trying to become a part of it. Gordon puts it this way: "Having an eyebrow pierced will not endear adults to young people and can actually be alienating" (p. 58).

Share Responsibility

Visiting kindergarten classes, I'm always struck by how much more choice and control they have over their day than secondary students do. I see kindergartners making decisions about what they want to do and with whom they want to do it. Ironically, as students advance through the grades, becoming more capable of making decisions and more concerned about having autonomy, we eliminate opportunities for choice.

Think about how you can provide opportunities for students to exercise some autonomy and to make decisions about their own behavior and class events. For example, you might sometimes allow students to choose their own groups for cooperative learning activities. You might give students responsibility for creating assignments, constructing questions for class discussions and tests, leading class activities, and evaluating their own progress and behavior (Ridley & Walther, 1995).

You might also assign "block homework assignments" that require students to develop their own time line for completion. For example, Sandy usually assigns a certain amount of reading and 25 to 30 problems that are due in a week or so. She recommends that students do four or five problems a night, but she does not require them to show her their work on a daily basis. She realizes that this means some students will wait until the last night to do all the problems:

> *High school teachers have to remember that students want to be treated like young adults, not like babies. It's important to give them some responsibility for their own behavior. They might make the wrong decisions and "fall and scrape their knees," but then they can see the consequences. I think they're more likely to take responsibility for their mistakes if teachers don't dictate everything.*

Sharing decision making can be difficult for teachers. When you're feeling pressured to cover the curriculum and to maximize learning time, it's easier to make the decisions by yourself. For example, assigning topics for a term paper is faster than allowing students to decide on their own topic; giving students a particular kind of paper and three paint colors is simpler than helping them to decide on the paper and colors they want to use. Involving students can be messy and time-consuming, and allowing students to make decisions about their own behavior means that they'll sometimes make the wrong decisions. Nonetheless, a "short-term investment of time" can lead to "a long-term gain in decision-making ability and self-esteem" (Dowd, 1997).

Be Inclusive

In recent years, *inclusive education* has been used to refer to the practice of placing students with disabilities in general education classrooms rather than segregating them in special classrooms or schools. But the term can also be used more broadly, to describe classes in which differences related not only to disability, but also to race, class, ethnicity, gender, cultural and linguistic background, religion, and sexual orientation are acknowledged, understood, and respected. As Mara Sapon-Shevin (1999) asserts:

> *The goal of having an inclusive classroom is not to homogenize those differences, pretending that they are not there or do not have an impact on students or their lives. The goal is to acknowledge those differences and create a classroom community that works with those differences (and sometimes around those differences) so that every student can feel a sense of connection and belonging. (pp. 63–64)*

This, of course, is easier said than done. Before we can "create a classroom community that works with differences," we need to recognize that we are often afraid and suspicious of those differences. Sometimes, we deny even *seeing* differences. It is not uncommon, for example, for my European American students to pride themselves on being color-blind, assuming that "to be color-blind is to be fair, impartial, and objective" (Nieto, 1996). Yet, to deny cultural or racial differences is to deny an essential aspect of people's identity—and recognizing those differences does not make us racist. During one conversation, Fred spoke passionately about these issues:

> *So many times I hear teachers say things like, "I don't think of kids as black or Hispanic or Asian—just as kids." But being black or Hispanic or Asian is part of who those kids are—just like being Polish and Russian is part of who I am. . . . A part of the whole community-building thing is acknowledging that these differences exist. We're not all the same . . . To build community we also need to face the fact that racism and bias are part of the real world. People don't want to admit it's there. But it's everywhere; it's part of all of us. The question is not "Are you a racist?" but "How much of a racist are you, and how can you become less so?"*

In addition to *acknowledging* differences, creating inclusive classrooms means learning about disabilities, or cultures, or races, or religions that we've never before encountered. For example, you can't acknowledge, understand, and respect behaviors that have cultural origins if you have no idea that the behaviors are rooted in culture. Teachers may be shocked when Southeast Asian students smile while being scolded if they are unaware that the smiles are meant not as disrespect but as an admission of culpability and an effort to show that there is no grudge (Trueba, Cheng, & Ima, 1993). Similarly, teachers who are not cognizant of the fact that Pacific Islanders value interpersonal harmony and the well-being of the group may conclude that these students are lazy when they are reluctant to participate in competitive activities (Sileo & Prater, 1998). Teachers who are unaware that the culture of most American Indians tends to emphasize deliberate thought may become impatient when those students take longer to respond to questions (Nieto, 1996).

It's unrealistic to expect beginning teachers (or even experienced ones!) to have familiarity with all of the cultures that might be represented in their extremely diverse classrooms. Certainly, developing this kind of "cultural literacy" takes time and effort. Meanwhile, when you encounter behaviors that seem inappropriate and inexplicable, ask yourself whether these behaviors might, in fact, be culturally grounded. Some specific questions to ask yourself are listed in Table 5-1. In addition, think about how you can use your students as a resource. Listen to Fred:

> *If I have kids from other countries in my class, I'll ask about customs there, and how they compare with customs here. Not only do I learn something I didn't know before, but I can just see the "little lights go on." It's like, "Hey,*

TABLE 5-1. Becoming Sensitive to Cultural Differences

In reflecting on your students' cultural backgrounds, it is helpful to ask yourself the following questions:

Family Background

Where did the student come from? Was it a rural or urban setting?

Why did the family move?

How long has the student been in this country?

How many people are in the family?

What are the lines of authority?

What responsibilities does the student have at home?

What are parents' beliefs with respect to involvement in the school and in their child's education? Do they consider teachers to be experts and therefore refrain from expressing differences of opinion?

Is learning English considered a high priority?

Educational Background

If students are new to this country, how much previous schooling have they had?

What kinds of instructional strategies are they used to?

In their former schools, was there an emphasis on large group instruction, memorization, and recitation?

In students' former schools, what were the expectations for appropriate behavior?

Were students expected to be active or passive? independent or dependent? peer-oriented or teacher-oriented? cooperative or competitive?

Student Characteristics

How do students think about time? Is punctuality expected or is time considered to be flexible?

Do students nod their heads to be polite or to indicate understanding?

Do students question or obey authority figures?

Do students put their needs and desires before those of the group or vice versa?

Are expressions of emotion and feelings emphasized or hidden?

Sources: Kottler, 1994; Sileo & Prater, 1998.

here's someone who's interested in my experiences." We don't have to be intrusive about it, but it's important that classrooms be a place where we can learn about one another. I can use my classroom like a textbook.

Just as we must learn to acknowledge and respect racial and cultural diversity, we must also learn to create an accepting classroom environment for other, less visible kinds of differences. As I was working on this chapter, *Newsweek* magazine featured a special report on "Gay today: How the battle for acceptance has moved to schools, churches, marriage, and the workplace." The article on the schools (Peyser & Lorch, 2000) described the efforts of two 17-year-olds, Leslie-Claire Spillman and Martin Pfeiffer, to establish a Gay-Straight Alliance in their Baton Rouge, Louisiana, high school. Like other gays and lesbians, Spillman and Pfeiffer have suffered through years of harassment and hatred. As a result, Pfeiffer had once been suicidal; Spillman dropped out of school, became addicted to heroin, and spent five weeks in "detox." Such problems are all too common among homosexual youth; indeed, some researchers have found that gay and lesbian adolescents are two to three times more likely to attempt suicide than their heterosexual peers; they are also at increased risk for poor school performance, truancy, and dropping out (Nichols, 1999). It is essential that teachers work to create an atmosphere of tolerance for what Anderson (1997) calls the "forgotten children"—those "whose needs have been ignored, whose existence has been whispered about, and whose pain is just beginning to surface" (p. 65). You can take a step toward creating that atmosphere by making it clear that homophobic name-calling is absolutely unacceptable, by respectfully using the words *gay, lesbian,* and *bisexual,* and by referring to spouses or partners rather than husbands or wives (Edwards, 1997).

Search for Students' Strengths

We often think of teaching as a search for deficits—find out what students don't know or can't do, and then try to fix the problems. Certainly, responsible teaching does involve the identification of gaps, misconceptions, and weaknesses. But responsible teaching also involves a search for strengths. In *Teaching to Change the World* (1999), Jeannie Oakes and Martin Lipton argue that when teachers and students have a caring relationship, they work together to find competence: "The student's search is his own discovery of what he knows and how he knows it. The teacher's search—an act of care and respect—is also discovering what the student knows and how he knows it" (p. 252).

I thought of this perspective on caring during one meeting with the teachers, when Sandy talked about her conviction that "everyone needs their 15 minutes of fame":

Chemistry lends itself to a variety of talents—the math problems, the writing, the spatial relations, the mechanical ability. So I can give different people a chance to shine. Take Adam. He's really good at spatial relationships so I know that I can call on him to do diagrams.

When we have student presentations, I always try to think who I want to call on so I can showcase kids' different strengths. For example, I told the class that I was going to randomly choose a lab group to present the lab to the rest of the class. Everyone had to think about how to teach this and to be prepared. It was a nice safe situation—a great opportunity to get these two quiet girls to shine. I knew they had done a good job on the lab. So I wrote their names 12 times and put the slips in a beaker, and had someone pull out a slip. Of course their presentation went very well. But it was important for the girls—and everyone else—to think it was a risky situation, that they had just gotten chosen by chance. When they got a great evaluation, they felt terrific.

Develop Communication Skills

Another way of showing students that you care is by being a good listener. Sandy puts it this way:

How come there are only certain teachers in the school that kids will go to [when they have a problem]? After all, most kids have six teachers a day. It's all about listening. When you're a high school teacher, you have to listen seriously to problems that might not be problems to you, but they are to them. And that's a way of gaining their trust. A kid is not going to come to you and say I want to commit suicide if three weeks earlier you said, "Oh grow up, you'll get over her."

Being a good listener means being attentive, trying to understand students' feelings and concerns, asking appropriate questions, and helping students solve their own problems. Let's briefly examine each of these.

Attending and Acknowledging

Giving a student your complete, undivided attention is the first and most basic task in being helpful (Kottler & Kottler, 1993). It is rare that individuals are fully attentive to one another. Have you ever tried to talk with someone who was simultaneously organizing papers, posting notices on the bulletin board, or straightening rows of desks? Divided attention like this communicates that the person doesn't really have time for you and is not fully paying attention.

Attending and acknowledging involve both verbal and nonverbal behaviors. Even without saying a word, you can convey that you are totally tuned in by orienting your body toward the student, establishing eye contact, nodding, leaning forward, smiling, or frowning. In addition, you can use verbal cues. Thomas Gordon (1974) recommends "empathic grunting"—the little "uh-huhs" and phrases (e.g., "Oh," "I see," "Mmmmm") that communicate, "I'm really listening." Sometimes, when a student needs additional encouragement to talk more, you can use an explicit invitation, what Gordon calls a "door opener": "Tell me more," "Would you like to say more about that?" "Do you want to talk about it?" "Want to go on?"

One of the hardest ideas for teachers to accept is that a person can help another simply by listening. But Kottler and Kottler (1993) remind us that attending can be a powerful helping tool:

> *You would be truly amazed at how healing this simple act can be—giving another person your full attention. Children, in particular, are often so used to being devalued by adults that attending behaviors instantly tell them something is different about this interaction: "Here is a person who seems to care about me and what I have to say." (p. 40)*

Active Listening

Attending and acknowledging communicate that you are totally engaged, but they do not convey if you really *understand*. Active listening takes the interaction one step further by having you reflect back what you think you heard. This feedback allows you to check out whether you are right or wrong. If you're right, the student knows that you have truly understood. If you're off target, the student can correct you, and the communication can continue. Examples of active listening appear in Table 5-2.

If you're new to active listening, you may find it useful to use the phrase, "You feel . . ." when you reflect back what you heard. Sometimes, novices feel stupid, as if they're simply parroting back what the person just said. (In fact, when I was first learning to do active listening, a student became really annoyed and demanded to know why I kept repeating what he had said!) As you gain more skill, however, you are able to *paraphrase* what you hear, and the interaction becomes far more subtle.

Keep in mind that active listening is not easy. Student teachers with whom I work often want to reject it out of hand; they find it unnatural and awkward, and they would much prefer to give advice, not simply communicate that they understand. But knowing that someone really understands can be profoundly important, especially to teenagers who so often feel misunderstood. In addition, active listening provides an opportunity for students to express their feelings and to clarify their problems. It can also help to defuse strong feelings without taking the responsibility away from the student for solving the problem.

Questioning

When people tell us their problems, we often want to ask them questions in order to find out more information. Kottler and Kottler (1993) caution teachers to be careful about this practice:

> *The problem with questions, as natural as they may come to mind, is that they often put the child in a "one down" position in which you are the interrogator and expert problem solver. "Tell me what the situation is and I will fix it." For that reason, questions are used only when you can't get the student to reveal information in other ways. (p. 42)*

TABLE 5-2. Examples of Active Listening

Student:	Wait till my mom sees this test grade. She's gonna flip out.
Teacher:	You think she'll be really mad at you, huh?
Student:	Yeah, she expects me to come home with all As.
Teacher:	Sounds like you're feeling really pressured.
Student:	Well, I am. You'd think that getting a B was like failing. My mom just doesn't understand how hard this is for me.
Teacher:	So you think a B is an OK grade in a tough course like this, but she thinks that you can do better.
Student:	Yeah, she has this thing that if I come home with a B I'm just not working.
Teacher:	That's rough. I can see how that would make you feel like she doesn't appreciate the efforts you're making.
Student:	I can't believe I have to be home at 12:00! It's crazy! All my friends have a later curfew—or they don't have any curfew at all!
Teacher:	So you think your parents are a lot stricter than the other kids' parents.
Student:	Well, they are! I mean, I know it's 'cause they care about me, but it's really a pain to have to be home earlier than everyone else. I feel like a dork. And besides, I think I'm responsible enough to have a later curfew.
Teacher:	So you're not just embarrassed, you're mad because they don't realize how responsible you are.
Student:	All along my boyfriend's been telling me how he'll stick by me if I get pregnant, and then it happens, and he's gone.
Teacher:	You feel really abandoned.
Student:	I don't want to go to School-Base [for mental health counseling]. Only crazy kids go to School-Base!
Teacher:	Going to School-Base is kind of embarrassing . . .
Student:	Yeah. My friends are gonna give me a really hard time.
Teacher:	You think they're going to say you're crazy.
Student:	Yeah. I wanna go, but I don't want people to make fun of me.
Teacher:	I can understand that. It's really rough when people make fun of you.
Student:	I had the worst nightmare last night! I mean, I know it was just a dream, but I just can't get it out of my head. This bloody guy with a knife was chasing me down this alley, and I couldn't get away.
Teacher:	Nightmares can be so scary.
Student:	Yeah, and I know it's babyish, but I just can't shake the feeling.
Teacher:	Sometimes a bad feeling from a nightmare stays with you a long time . . .

Sandy also warns beginning teachers about the use of questions:

I don't ask too many questions. I prefer to let them talk themselves out. Questions can open up situations you're not prepared to deal with. After all, you're not a counselor; you're more like a conduit: You hear about problems and you try to put them in touch with someone who has the knowledge and the skill to help. Twenty-five years ago I didn't realize that.

I was only three or four years older than my students and I thought I could help them solve their problems. But they don't need teachers to solve their problems for them. They need teachers who can help them solve their own problems or who can get them expert help for solving their problems.

If you must ask questions, they should be open-ended—requiring more than a one-word response. Like active listening, open-ended questions invite further exploration and communication, whereas close-ended questions cut off communication. Compare these questions:

What are you feeling right now? versus Are you feeling angry?

What do you want to do? versus Do you want to tell your boyfriend?

Kottler and Kottler point out one notable exception to the rule of avoiding questions whenever possible: that is, when it is important to get very specific information in a potentially dangerous situation, such as when a student is discussing suicide. Then it would be appropriate to ask specific questions: Have you actually tried this? Will you promise not to do anything until we can get you some help?

Problem Solving

Instead of trying to solve students' problems, you can guide them through a process that helps them to solve their *own* problems. In problem solving, students define their problem, specify their goals, develop alternative solutions that might be constructive, narrow the choices to those that seem most realistic, and put the plan into action (Kottler & Kottler, 1993).

Not too long ago, Donnie used a problem-solving approach when a female student told her she was pregnant and asked if she should get an abortion.

First, the student needed to clarify the situation: Was her boyfriend available or not available? Were her parents supportive or not supportive? Was she using drugs or not using? Also, she needed to think about what resources were available to her. All of these factors play a role in making a decision about what to do.

Then, she needed to figure out what her values and priorities were— does she want to go to college? How does she feel about giving the baby up for adoption? Finally, I tried to help her figure out the alternatives— adoption, abortion, staying single and keeping the baby, getting married and keeping the baby.

I don't give advice in situations like this—I wouldn't know what kind of advice to give. But I can try to help kids clarify the situation. They're confused, and as an outside party who can think clearly, I can help them to see alternatives they haven't thought of, to talk about the resources that are available to them. My goal is to help them make the best possible decision for themselves.

A Note about Touching

In recent years, the fear of being accused of sexual harassment and physical abuse has made teachers wary of showing students any physical affection. Although our four teachers share this wariness, they do not want to forgo all physical contact. Listen to Fred:

> *I have colleagues who say they'll never touch a kid at all. I understand, but I think you have to touch people if you're going to be a teacher. There have to be rules, of course. I would never be alone with a kid, because of the appearance of impropriety, but I'll hug kids. . . . It doesn't have to be any big demonstrative thing, but just touching somebody's hand or shoulder can mean a lot. If someone's getting antsy, I'll put my hand on their shoulder, and they'll settle down. If they're hurting, and they need a hug, I'll give them one. What kind of community is it if you can't give someone who's hurting a hug?*

It's important to remember that Fred has been in his district for many years and has a solid reputation. As a new teacher, you are in a very different situation. Speak with your colleagues about the policy in effect in your school; some schools actually direct teachers to "teach but don't touch." Even if there is no explicit prohibition against touching students, you need to be cautious so that your actions are not misconstrued. Give your hugs in front of others. Give "high fives" instead of hugs (Jones & Jones, 1998). When a student stays after school, keep the door open, or make sure that other students or teachers are around.

Building Caring Relationships among Students

A great deal has recently been written on ways of fostering supportive, trusting relationships among students. Unfortunately, much of the advice focuses on elementary classrooms, where teachers generally work with the same group of children for the entire day and there's simply more opportunity to build a sense of connectedness. As Sapon-Shevin (1995) reminds us:

> *Communities don't just happen. No teacher, no matter how skilled or well intentioned, can enter a new classroom and announce, "We are a community." Communities are built over time, through shared experience, and by providing multiple opportunities for students to know themselves, know one another, and interact in positive and supportive ways. Community building must be seen and felt as a process that we're all in together rather than as a task that is important only to the teacher. (p. 111)*

Undoubtedly, the challenge of creating a safe, caring community is more daunting when you teach three or four or five groups of students a day, for 42 or 45 or even 84 minutes. What can secondary teachers possibly do in the limited amount of time—especially when there's so much pressure to cover the curriculum? I posed this question to our four teachers. Here are some of their suggestions, along with others from educational writers interested in students' social and emotional learning.

Ask the Students

In *Beyond Discipline: From Compliance to Community* (1996), Alfie Kohn suggests that teachers begin the school year by asking students about ways of building feelings of safety:

> *A teacher might say, "Look, it's really important to me that you feel free to say things, to come up with ideas that may sound weird, to make mistakes—and not to be afraid that other people are going to laugh at you. In fact, I want everyone in here to feel that way. What do you think we can do to make sure that happens?"*

Model the Traits You Want Students to Have

I once knew a professor of educational psychology who taught about motivation in his courses; he also announced grades while he returned tests—in descending order. Apparently, the professor had not taken to heart the material he taught.

Teachers frequently exhort students to treat one another with respect. Yet exhortation is unlikely to be effective unless teachers themselves are respectful. As Mary Williams (1993) tells us, " 'Do as I say, not as I do' clearly does not work" (p. 22). Williams was interested in learning how respect was taught and learned by students in middle school classrooms (grades six through eight). She found that respect was best taught through modeling. According to students, teachers "have to follow the values themselves" (p. 22). Students resented teachers who told them to be kind and to respect others, yet exhibited favoritism, treated students "like babies," didn't listen, and gave "busywork."

Provide Opportunities for Students to Get to Know One Another

On the first day of school, Christina distributes a handout entitled "Find Someone Who." Students must find one person in the class who fits each of the 36 descriptions (e.g., someone who "has read at least three Stephen King novels," someone who "has the same favorite television show as you do," someone who "is a procrastinator," and someone who "would rather work alone than in groups") and have the person sign his or her name next to the appropriate statement. Students are allowed to sign their names only once per sheet, even if more than one item applies. In the basic skills class, one student laughs loudly at the description "someone who made honor roll," as if no one in that class could have possibly received such recognition. Christina overhears. Knowing that at least one student in the class has, in fact, made the honor roll, she suggests that he check out his assumption. He shortly discovers a girl who can sign his sheet.

Christina's students get to know one another by completing "Find Someone Who."

"Find Someone Who" can be especially useful if you include items relating to race, cultural and linguistic background, and disability and solicit information in addition to a signature. Consider these examples (Sapon-Shevin, 1995):

Find someone who grew up with an older relative. What's one thing that person learned from the older relative?

Find someone whose parents come from another country. What's one tradition or custom that person has learned from his or her parents?

Find someone who has a family member with a disability. What's something that person has learned by interacting with the person with a disability?

In order to build community, we have to create opportunities for students to learn about one another and to discover the ways in which they are both different and similar. There are numerous getting-acquainted activities like the one Christina chose that teachers can use at the beginning of the year:

Guess Who? *Have students write a brief autobiographical statement (family background, hobbies, extracurricular activities, etc.), which they do not sign. Collect the statements, read each description, and ask students to write the name of the individual they believe wrote the description. (You can* *participate too.) After all the descriptions have been read, reread them and ask the authors to identify themselves. Ask students to indicate how many classmates they correctly identified. (Jones & Jones, 1998)*

Two Truths and a Lie *(or **Two Facts and a Fiction**). Have students write down and then share three statements about themselves, two of which are true and one of which is a lie. For example, I might write, "I once played the princess in* Once Upon the Mattress, *and one night during a performance I fell from the top of 15 mattresses and herniated a disk in my back," "I won third prize in the All-Alaska Logging Championship for the rolling pin toss," and "I trekked through Nepal on my honeymoon." Students guess which one is the lie, and then I tell the truth. (I didn't trek through Nepal; I backpacked through Colorado and Wyoming.) The activity can be done as a whole class or in small groups. In either case, since the activity allows students to select what to disclose about themselves, there is little chance of embarrassment. It also provides opportunities for students to discover common interests and experiences and to test assumptions and stereotypes. (No one looking at me today, for example, would ever guess that I had camped on my honeymoon!) (Sapon-Shevin, 1999)*

Little Known Facts about Me. *This is a variation of the previous activity. Students write a statement about themselves that they think others won't know. The papers are folded, collected, put in a box, and shaken. Students take turns drawing a paper and reading the statement aloud. Everyone guesses who wrote the little known fact. (Sapon-Shevin, 1999)*

Lifelines. *Each student draws a line on a piece of paper and then marks six to ten points representing important events in their lives that they are willing to share (e.g., the birth of a sibling, the death of a close family member, the time they starred in the school play, when they moved to this school). Students then get into pairs and share their life stories. Members of each pair could also introduce each other to the rest of the class, referring to points on the lifeline. (Sapon-Shevin, 1999)*

Sometimes, the curriculum itself provides opportunities for students to learn about their classmates and to develop empathy. For example, Linda Christensen (1994), a high school English teacher, had her students read literature that forced them to look beyond their own world and reflect on the experiences of "others." In conjunction with the reading, Christensen paired her native English speakers with students who had emigrated from another country—Vietnam, Laos, Cambodia, Eritrea, Mexico, Guatemala, and Ghana. They interviewed their partner and wrote a profile of the student to share in class. Christensen describes her class's reactions:

Students were moved by their partners' stories. One student whose brother had been killed at the beginning of the year was paired with a student whose sister was killed fighting in Eritrea. He connected to her loss and was amazed at her strength. Others were appalled at how these students had been mistreated at their school. Many students later used the lives of their partners in their essays on immigration. . . . Besides making immigration a contemporary rather than a historical topic, students heard the sorrow their fellow students felt at leaving "home." In our "curriculum of empathy," we forced our class to see these students as individuals rather than the ESL [English-as-a-Second Language] students or "Chinese" students, or an undifferentiated mass of Mexicans. (p. 53)

Curb Peer Harassment

"Boys call me cow." "Boys call one girl popcorn because she has zits." "One time a kid missed the ball. . ., and they called him a f---ing fag." According to Shakeshaft and her colleagues (1997), verbal assaults like these permeate junior and senior high school. Shakeshaft's research team spent three years interviewing more than 1,000 Long Island, New York, students from eight different schools and from all socioeconomic levels. Everywhere they went, they found that "kids made fun of other kids" (p. 22). The primary targets were girls who were unattractive, unstylish, or physically mature and boys who didn't fit the "stereotypic male mold" (p. 23).

Such pervasive, hurtful peer harassment is certainly disturbing, but what is also disturbing is the fact that teachers rarely intervened, leading students to conclude that teachers just didn't care. For example, one girl reported that "in science class, the boys snap our bras. The [male] teacher doesn't . . . say anything. . . . The boys just laugh" (p. 24). When teachers did intervene, their responses were minimal. One student commented,

For name-calling, they'll [teachers] just say, "I don't want to hear that," and then that's it. They really don't do anything else. . . . I wish teachers would stop it right away; even if they hear only one thing. (p. 25)

Another put it this way:

They [teachers] don't take as much control as they should. They say, "Don't do it next time." And when they [the harassers] do it the next time, they [the teachers] keep on saying the same thing. They don't take control. (p. 25)

Shakeshaft and her colleagues argue that adults must take the lead in putting a stop to peer harassment. They recommend that teachers use reflective activities in order to raise awareness. In literature classes, for example, students can read fiction that relates to the topic of harassment and bullying; in math classes, students can conduct surveys and analyze the results; in art classes, students can depict their feelings about name-calling and put-downs. In addition, students and faculty can work together to define the behaviors that are appropriate to inclusive, caring schools. (Peer harassment is also discussed in Chapter 14, "Preventing and Responding to Violence.")

Be Alert for Student-to-Student Sexual Harassment

On the way out of your classroom, a boy pats a girl on her bottom. She gives him an annoyed look and tells him to "quit it." Another girl comes to you in tears because a boy in the class is spreading stories about what they did on a date last weekend. You hear two girls in your class laughing and teasing a boy about what a "stud" he is. Are these instances of sexual harassment? And should you do anything about them?

Sexual harassment is generally defined as *unwanted and unwelcome sexual attention.* This includes a wide range of behaviors:

> *leering, pinching, grabbing, suggestive verbal comments, pressure for sexual activity, spreading sexual rumors, making sexual or sexist jokes, pulling at another student's clothing, cornering or brushing up against a student in a sexual way, insulting comments referring to students' sexual orientation, date rape, sexual graffiti about a student, or engaging in other actions of a sexual manner that might create a hostile learning environment. (Hyman, 1997, p. 318)*

Several studies (AAUW, 1993; Lee, Croninger, Linn, & Chen, 1996; National Council for Research on Women, 1994) have documented the fact that sexual harassment is an all too common occurrence in American high schools. Lee, Croninger, Linn, and Chen (1996), for example, found that 83 percent of girls and 60 percent of boys report unwanted sexual attention in school. Their results also indicate that it's not a simple case of some students being perpetrators while others are victims: Over half of the students report that they have harassed their classmates *and* been harassed themselves. Furthermore, the likelihood of being harassed is strongly influenced by the amount of harassment that surrounds you. Students who perceive high levels of harassment in their schools are very likely to have experienced harassment.

It can sometimes be difficult for you—and your students—to distinguish between harmless flirting and sexual harassment. When you're faced with this situation, it's helpful to keep in mind the fact that whether harassment has occurred is truly in the "eye of the beholder." In other words, the determining factor is "how the person on the receiving end is affected by the behavior, not with what the other person means by the behavior" (Strauss & Espeland, 1992, p. 15). Kissing, touching, and flirting that the recipient likes or wants is *not* sexual harassment (although it may be inappropriate in school!).

Given this emphasis on the recipient's feelings, people can be nervous about giving compliments and having them misunderstood. Strauss and Espeland (1992) suggest asking a few simple questions to guide behavior:

Would I want my comments or behavior to appear in the newspaper or on TV?

Is this something I would say or do if my mother or father, girlfriend or boyfriend, sister or brother were present?

Is this something I would want someone else to say or do to my mother or father, girlfriend or boyfriend, sister or brother?

Is there a difference in power between me and the other person (e.g., in size or social status)?

In recent years, an increasing number of districts have written and distributed sexual harassment policies for both students and school personnel. These generally define sexual harassment, outline the procedures to follow when you learn about an incident of sexual harassment, and spell out the consequences. It's important that you obtain a copy of this policy and follow the specified procedures. Keep in mind that the Supreme Court has ruled that school districts can be found liable if they are "deliberately indifferent" to information about "severe, pervasive, and objectively offensive" harassment among students (Walsh, 1999).

Use Cooperative Learning Groups

Innumerable studies attest to the power of cooperative learning to promote positive interaction and friendship among students who differ in terms of achievement, sex, cultural and linguistic background, and race. There are other social benefits as well: Cooperative learning can facilitate the acceptance of students with disabilities, promote positive attitudes toward class, and increase empathy and social cooperation (Good & Brophy, 2000).

David and Roger Johnson (1999), two prominent researchers in the field of cooperative learning, distinguish among three types of cooperative learning. In *formal cooperative learning,* teachers assign students to small heterogeneous groups that work together on carefully structured tasks; groups may stay together for one class period up to several weeks. In *informal cooperative learning,* students work together in "temporary, ad-hoc groups" that might last from a few minutes to a whole period (Johnson & Johnson, 1999, p. 128). For example, during a whole-class presentation, Donnie frequently tells her students to "turn to your neighbor and talk about how you'd tackle this problem." Finally, *cooperative base groups* are long-term, heterogeneous groups in which students support one another's academic progress and emotional well-being. Members of the base group can collect assignments for absent students and provide assistance when they return, tutor students who are having problems with the course material, check homework assignments, and provide study groups for tests. According to Jones and Jones (1998), it's helpful to have base groups meet several times a week for 5 to 15 minutes: "At the very least, the base group provides a setting in which at least three members of the class are concerned about each student's learning" (p. 133). (See Chapter 10, "Managing Groupwork," for a more detailed discussion of cooperative learning.)

Two Cautionary Tales

Building a caring classroom community is not an easy task, especially for secondary teachers who see students for such a limited amount of time. Nor can it be achieved quickly.

This lesson was brought home to me during a meeting in which Sandy and Fred ruefully described incidents that had just occurred in their classrooms. First, Sandy told this tale:

My kids were going over homework, and they were in groups of three. I picked the groups. In one group, I had a girl who happens to be an honors student and a boy who had to be convinced to take chemistry. They finished reviewing the homework pretty quickly. Another group was in need of assistance, so I suggested that they get help from the first group. Mitchell, one of the kids in the second group, called over to the girl—the honors student—to come and help them. So Ryan—the kid who had to be convinced to take chemistry—says, "Wait a minute. Why did you just ask her, not us? Do you think we're stupid?" Then he turns around to me and says, "See, Mrs. K., that's why I didn't want to take chemistry. Because all the smart kids know who they are and they know who's stupid. They think that kids who haven't done well in school could never do well in chemistry."

I'm standing there thinking, "How do I get out of this one? What do I say?" I had watched it all unfold in front of me. And 24 pairs of eyes are looking at me. Finally I said, "Well, I guess you certainly fooled them." I wish you could have seen it. Ryan's chest puffed up, and he says to Mitchell, "Lucy's not going to help you; I'm going to help you."

Here I thought that there weren't divisions in the classroom, but there were. I thought we had created a cohesive community, and then I find out there are all these little subgroups. The kids have these perceptions of one another, and they become barriers between them. Mitchell's perception was that Lucy would be best at explaining. Ryan's perception was that Mitchell thinks I'm stupid. I've tried hard to break down these barriers. I'm always trying to demonstrate that people have multiple intelligences, multiple talents. I have them working in all these cooperative learning groups, and still, there are these barriers.

Fred was empathetic and, with a grimace, he shared his own story about "cooperative learning":

I put these two guys together in a group. What I didn't realize was that one guy had just slept with the other guy's girl. They wanted to kill each other, and I was completely out of it. Sometime during the class, I realized that they weren't working together very effectively. One was just about to jump the other, when I finally caught on and sent one out.

I add these cautionary tales not to discourage you but to acknowledge just how difficult it is to create a classroom that is *always* safe and caring. When students enter your classroom, they come with "baggage." Maybe someone was just hassled in the hallway;

maybe another received a failing grade in the class before yours. We don't have control over what happens to our students when they're not in our classes, and that makes community building more challenging.

Concluding Comments

Alfie Kohn (1996) suggests that it would be helpful if we all reflected on "what makes school awful sometimes" (p. 114). Then we might be more inclined to make sure that those kinds of experiences and situations don't happen for students in our classrooms. I recently followed his advice. I thought back to my sophomore year in high school, when Friday gym classes were devoted to ballroom dancing. All the boys lined up on one side of the gym, while girls lined up on the other. When the physical education teacher (male) said "OK, go!" the boys rushed across the gym floor to get a dance partner. I tried hard to pretend that I didn't care as more popular, more attractive girls were asked to dance, and I was left standing there. But it was hard to pretend on the one occasion when I was the very last girl standing in line. There was also one boy left, and he was obviously unhappy about having to pair up with me. The teacher approached. The conversation went something like this: "Ask her to dance." "No." "I said, 'Ask her to dance.'" "No!" "Ask her to dance or you get a zero for the day!" He asked me to dance.

I've shared this story with my students—along with my feelings of humiliation—and I've asked them to think about similar experiences. Here are some of their responses to the question, "When was school awful for you?"

As a high school junior, I took Algebra II and Trigonometry. Although I was a good student, the teacher and I did not hit it off for some reason. . . . Midyear, we had an exam on logarithms. I thought I understood it, but I made the same mistake reading the log charts for every problem and I failed the test. I came into class the next day thinking I had done OK on the test. The teacher held up my exam in front of the class and gloated that he had failed me. I hated going to that class for the rest of the year, and I hated that teacher for humiliating me.

When I was a sophomore in high school, one of the girls would follow me around and torment me, call me names, and threaten to hurt me. . . None of my teachers or any authority figure ever helped. I'm still curious why she hated me so much.

The worst was in junior high. . . . I was made fun of by the other girls, girls with whom I had been friends the year before. . . . I was tormented for not having money or clothes and for having a conscience (and by that I mean not breaking the law or hurting other people's feelings). It was the first year I didn't like going to school.

> *School was awful a lot. . . . I outweighed everyone by at least 15 to 20 pounds. I was teased by both the boys and the girls.*

> *School was awful for me when I was switched from second track to first track in Spanish. . . . I wanted to be in that class because I wanted those students to like me and not think I was a dork. However, the guidance counselor went behind my back and called my parents. He did not inform them that I did not want to switch so they said it was OK. I did not even get a chance to talk to them before they switched my schedule. I felt powerless and betrayed.*

For too many students, school is a place where they feel humiliated, threatened, ridiculed, tormented, teased, and powerless. Think about when school was awful for *you*. If you can keep those times in mind and try to ensure that they never happen to your students, you will be well on your way to creating a safer, more caring community.

Summary

This chapter began by discussing the tension that novice teachers often feel between wanting to care and needing to achieve order. I stressed the fact that caring and order are not irreconcilable goals and concluded that it is possible to create a classroom that is not only relaxed and comfortable but also orderly and productive. The chapter then considered ways of showing students that you care about them and ways of building caring relationships among students.

Ways of showing care

- Be welcoming.
- Be sensitive.
- Welcome students' input.
- Be fair.
- Be a real person (not just a teacher).
- Become aware of adolescent culture.
- Share responsibility.
- Be inclusive.
- Search for students' strengths.
- Develop communication skills.

Building caring relationships among students

- Ask the students.
- Model the traits you want students to have.

- Provide opportunities for students to get to know one another.
- Curb peer harassment.
- Be alert for student-to-student sexual harassment.
- Use cooperative learning groups.

For too many students, school is a place where they feel humiliated, threatened, ridiculed, tormented, teased, powerless, and betrayed. Teachers who can "remember when school was awful" are better able to create a safe, caring community for their students.

Activities

1. Interview a few junior or senior high students about their definitions of caring teachers. Ask them to identify the ways in which teachers show caring to students.

2. Think about the teachers you had in junior and senior high school. Select one teacher who showed caring to students and one teacher who did not. Write a paragraph on each teacher, providing details and examples to illustrate what each teacher actually did.

3. Continue your planning for the first week of school. First, plan a way of showing students that you welcome their input. (Will you have students verbally share their suggestions and opinions about rules, lessons, assignments, or grouping? Write a letter to you? Answer specific questions?) Second, plan an introductory activity designed to help students become acquainted.

4. In the following bits of conversation, students have confided in teachers about problems they are experiencing, and the teachers have responded in ways *not* suggested in this chapter. Provide a new response for each case, using the communication skills discussed in this chapter: acknowledging, active listening, asking open-ended questions, and problem solving.

a. *Student:*   *My parents won't allow me to go visit my boyfriend at college for the weekend. They say they trust me, but then they don't show it!*

   Teacher: *Well, I'm sure they have your best interests at heart. You know, you really shouldn't gripe. After all, a lot of kids don't have parents who care about them. I see a lot of kids whose parents let them do anything they want. Maybe you think you'd like that, but I'm sure you wouldn't . . .*

b. *Student:*   *I can't stand my stepmother. She's always criticizing me and making me come home right after school to watch my sister, and making me feel really stupid.*

   Teacher: *Oh, come on now, Cinderella. I'm sure it's not that bad.*

   c. Student: *My parents want me to go to college, but I really want to join the Marines. What do you think I should do?*

     Teacher: *Do what your folks say. Go to college. You can always join the Marines later.*

5. Think about when school was awful for you. Share your experiences with others, either in writing or verbally, and look for commonalities. What themes emerge from these anecdotes?

For Further Reading

Elias, M. J., Zins, J. E., Weissberg, R. P., Frey, K. S., Greenberg, M. T., Haynes, N. M., Kessler, R., Schwab-Stone, M. E., & Shriver, T. P. (1997). Promoting social and emotional learning: Guidelines for educators. Alexandria, VA: Association for Supervision and Curriculum Development.

Kohn, A. (1996). *Beyond discipline: From compliance to community.* Alexandria, VA: Association for Supervision and Curriculum Development.

Nieto, S. (1996). *Affirming diversity: The sociopolitical context of multicultural education.* 2nd ed. White Plains, NY: Longman.

Oakes, J., & Lipton, M. (1999). *Teaching to change the world.* Boston: McGraw-Hill. (See, in particular, Chapter 7, Classroom Management: Caring and Democratic Communities, pp. 234–277).

Stein, N. (1999). *Classrooms and courtrooms: Facing sexual harassment in K-12 schools.* NY: Teachers College Press.

Strauss, S., with Espeland, P. (1992). *Sexual harassment and teens: A program for positive change.* Minneapolis, MN: Free Spirit Publishing.

References

American Association of University Women [AAUW]. (1993). Hostile hallways: The AAUW survey on sexual harassment in America's schools. Washington, DC: AAUW.

Anderson, J. D. (1997). Supporting the invisible minority. *Educational Leadership, 54*(7), 65–67.

Battistich, V., Watson, M., Solomon, D., Lewis, C., & Schaps, E. (1999). Beyond the three R's: A broader agenda for school reform. *The Elementary School Journal, 99*(5), 415–432.

Charles, C. M. (2000). *The synergetic classroom: Joyful teaching and gentle discipline.* New York: Longman.

Christensen, L. (1994). Building community from chaos. In B. Bigelow, L. Christensen, S. Karp, B. Miner, & B. Peterson (Eds.), *Rethinking our classrooms: Teaching for equity and justice.* Milwaukee, WI: Rethinking Schools Limited, pp. 50–55.

Cothran, D. J., & Ennis, C. D. (2000). Building bridges to student engagement: Communicating respect and care for students in urban high schools. *Journal of Research and Development in Education, 33*(2), 106–117.

Davidson, A. L. (1999). Negotiating social differences: Youths' assessments of educators' strategies. *Urban Education, 34*(3), 338–369.

Dowd, J. (1997). Refusing to play the blame game. *Educational Leadership, 54*(8), 67–69.

Edwards, A. T. (1997). Let's stop ignoring our gay and lesbian youth. *Educational Leadership, 54*(7), 68–70.

Good, T. L., & Brophy, J. E. (2000). *Looking in classrooms* (8th edition) New York, Longman.

Gordon, T. (1974). *T. E. T.—Teacher effectiveness training.* New York: Peter H. Wyden.

Gordon, R. L. (1997). How novice teachers can succeed with adolescents. *Educational Leadership, 54*(7), 56–58.

Hyman, I. A. (1997). *School discipline and school violence: The teacher variance approach.* Boston: Allyn and Bacon.

Johnson, D. W., & Johnson, R. T. (1999). The three Cs of school and classroom management. In H. J. Freiberg (Ed.), *Beyond Behaviorism: Changing the Classroom Management Paradigm.* Boston: Allyn & Bacon, pp. 119–144.

Jones, V. F., & Jones, L. S. (1998). *Comprehensive classroom management: Creating communities of support and solving problems.* Boston: Allyn & Bacon.

Katz, M. S. (1999). Teaching about caring and fairness: May Sarton's *The Small Room.* In M. S. Katz, N. Noddings, K A. Strike (Eds.), *Justice and caring: The search for common ground in education.* New York: Teachers College Press, pp. 59–73.

Kohn, A. (1996). *Beyond discipline: From compliance to community.* Alexandria, VA: Association for Supervision and Curriculum Development.

Kottler, E. (1994). *Children with limited English: Teaching strategies for the regular classroom.* Thousand Oaks, CA: Corwin Press.

Kottler, J. A., & Kottler, E. (1993). *Teacher as counselor: Developing the helping skills you need.* Newbury Park, CA: Corwin Press.

Lee, V. E., Croninger, R. G., Linn, E., & Chen, X. (1996). The culture of sexual harassment in secondary schools. *American Educational Research Journal, 33*(2), 383–417.

McLaughlin, H. J. (1991). Reconciling care and control: Authority in classroom relationships. *Journal of Teacher Education, 42*(3), 182–195.

National Council for Research on Women. (1994). Teen-on-teen sexual harassment. *Issues Quarterly, 1*(1), 1–6.

Nichols, S. (1999). Gay, lesbian, and bisexual youth: Understanding diversity and promoting tolerance in schools. *The Elementary School Journal, 99*(5), 505–519.

Nieto, S. (1996). *Affirming diversity: The sociopolitical context of multicultural education.* (2nd ed.). White Plains, NY: Longman.

Oakes, J., & Lipton, M. (1999). *Teaching to change the world.* Boston: McGraw-Hill.

Peyser, M., & Lorch, D. (March 20, 2000). Gay today: The schools. High school controversial. *Newsweek,* 55–56.

Ridley, D. S., & Walther, B. (1995). *Creating responsible learners: The role of a positive classroom environment.* Washington, D. C.: American Psychological Association.

Roeser, R. W., Eccles, J. S., & Sameroff, A. J. (2000). School as a context of early adolescents' academic and social–emotional development: A summary of research findings. *The Elementary School Journal, 100*(5), 443–471.

Sapon-Shevin, M. (1995). Building a safe community for learning. In W. Ayers (Ed.), *To become a teacher: Making a difference in children's lives.* New York: Teachers College Press.

Sapon-Shevin, M. (1999). *Because we can change the world: A practical guide to building cooperative, inclusive classroom communities.* Boston: Allyn & Bacon.

Shakeshaft, C., Mandel, L., Johnson, Y. M., Sawyer, J., Hergenroter, M. A., & Barber, E. (1997). Boys call me cow. *Educational Leadership, 55*(2), 22–25.

Sileo, T. W., & Prater, M. A. (1998). Creating classroom environments that address the linguistic and cultural backgrounds of students with disabilities: An Asian Pacific American perspective. *Remedial and Special Education, 19*(6), 323–337.

Strauss, S., with Espeland, P. (1992). *Sexual harassment and teens: A program for positive change.* Minneapolis, MN: Free Spirit.

Trueba, H. T., Cheng, L. R. L., & Ima, K. (1993). *Myth or reality: Adaptive strategies of Asian Americans in California.* Washington, DC: Falmer Press.

Walsh, M. (June 2, 1999). Harassment ruling poses challenges. *Education Week, 18*(38), 1, 22.

Weinstein, C. S. (1998). "I want to be nice, but I have to be mean": Exploring prospective teachers' conceptions of caring and order. *Teaching and Teacher Education, 14*(2), 153–163.

Williams, M. (1993). Actions speak louder than words: What students think. *Educational Leadership, 51*(3), 22–23.

Working with Families

"His parents actually admitted they can't control him at home, and yet they expect *me* to control him at school!"

"Do you believe they had the nerve to suggest that Sara be allowed to pass the course even if she has a failing average?"

"Joseph hasn't handed in homework for five days, and when I call to talk about it, they tell me it's *my* problem!"

Comments like these can be heard in almost any teachers' room. It's not unusual for preparation periods, lunch time, and after-school meetings to become "gripe sessions" about parents' lack of cooperation, their unrealistic demands, and their irresponsibility.

Similarly, when parents get together, they often voice complaints about their children's teachers:

"How can she teach them anything if she can't even control the class?! She shouldn't be a teacher if she can't make them behave."

"She just doesn't understand what's at stake here. Sara really needs to pass this course so she can graduate. It's not her fault she's failing. I think the teacher just has it in for her."

"He gives way too much homework—it's ridiculous that there should be one hour of homework in just one class!"

As these comments indicate, parents and teachers are often at odds with one another. Indeed, Sara Lawrence Lightfoot (1978) has written: "One would expect that parents and teachers would be natural allies, but social scientists and our own experience recognize their adversarial relationship. . . ." (p. 20).

This "adversarial relationship" is unfortunate. Researchers have documented many advantages of close communication and collaboration between families and teachers. For example, parent involvement in their children's schooling is associated with higher academic achievement, better attendance, more positive student attitudes and behavior, and greater willingness to do homework (e.g., Becher, 1984; Epstein, 1984; Haynes, Comer, & Hamilton-Lee, 1989; Henderson & Berla, 1996).

From a classroom management perspective, there are real benefits to working closely with families. First, *knowing about a student's home situation provides insight into the student's classroom behavior.* Listen to Donnie:

It was the very first day of school—when everyone is still being really good—but this one girl was really loud and hyperactive. It was clear that everyone disliked her. She seemed completely unable to control herself. I checked into her home situation as soon as I had a free period. I found out that her mother had kicked her out of the house; she said she couldn't handle all the kids. The girl had tried to commit suicide, but now she was really trying to get her act together. She had gotten a part-time job, and she was living with an aunt. This girl had really been thrown out into the world, and school is her haven. Actually, when I think about what she's facing, I'm really impressed by how well she's doing.

As Donnie's example illustrates, it's easier to understand why Johnny sits with his head down on his desk if you're aware that he spent the night in a homeless shelter; Carla's belligerence makes sense if you know that her mother just lost her job and her father is absent; and Jana's anxiety about getting all A's is understandable if you appreciate how much her parents pressure her to succeed. Furthermore, insights like these can help you decide what course of action to take when dealing with a student's problems. You're better able to judge if a suggestion that a parent proofread term papers is inappropriate because the parent can't read, or if a note home will lead to benefits or to beatings. (The issue of abuse is discussed in Chapter 13.)

Second, *when families understand what you are trying to achieve, they can provide valuable support and assistance.* Most parents want their children to succeed in school and will do what they can to help. But they can't work in a vacuum. They need to know what you are trying to achieve and how you expect children to behave in your classroom. Familiarizing parents with your curriculum, routines, and policies minimizes confusion, misinterpretations, and conflict. For this reason, Christina requires parents to sign an acknowledgment form at the beginning of the course, indicating that they have read and understood the "newspaper" she sends home describing course objectives, policies, and procedures.

Third, *families can help to develop and implement strategies to change students' behavior.* Working together, parents and teachers can bring about improvements in children's behavior that would be impossible working alone. Fred shares this example:

> I had this kid in my U.S. History II class who wasn't doing any work at all. It was his senior year, and I think he just decided he didn't have to do anything anymore. His parents didn't have a clue about what to do. We all sat down and worked out a plan. They were to call me at 10:30 every Friday morning. If the report on their son was good, he got the car keys, got to go out with his friends, got to go to the ball game. If the report was bad, the weekend did not exist. We told him, "We really care about you and if this is what we have to do to get you through senior year, then so be it." The kid tested the plan once, and there was no weekend for him. After that, he really started to perform and ended up with a B for the year. Plus, there was an additional payoff. His parents were able to give him all kinds of good strokes because he started taking responsibility.

Given the obvious benefits of communication and collaboration between families and teachers, why is the relationship often so detached and distant? Why, at times, is it even strained and distrustful? In the next section of this chapter, we examine three barriers to close working relationships—teacher reluctance to involve parents, parent reluctance to become involved, and the changing nature of families. We then turn to our teachers and to the literature on parent involvement in order to suggest ways that families and schools can work together to educate adolescents.

Barriers to Family–Teacher Cooperation

Teacher Reluctance to Involve Families in Schooling

A primary reason for teachers' reluctance to work with families is the *extra time and energy that are required.* Teaching is physically and emotionally exhausting, and reaching out to parents is sometimes viewed as one more burdensome task. Epstein and Becker (1982) remind us how much time it takes to make just one call home: "If a teacher telephones 30 parents and talks for 10 minutes to each, the teacher spends 5 hours voluntarily on the telephone with parents" (p. 103). And that's for just one class! Since this is obviously in addition to planning lessons and activities, grading papers, organizing cooperative learning groups, and creating tests, it's understandable if teachers wonder whether the extra time required is worth the trouble. Furthermore, there are few external rewards to encourage teachers to spend time working with parents (Epstein & Becker, 1982), and teachers often lament the lack of support from their principals or other teachers. For new teachers, the task of reaching out to parents may seem even more onerous. As Christina admits, "I'm always preparing materials and lessons, grading, or commenting on student papers. It takes time to be creative and effective—and that means there's less time for parent contact than I would like."

In addition, *teachers' perceptions of families* undoubtedly contribute to the reluctance to seek greater parental involvement. Some teachers recognize that time is often a scarce commodity for parents, limited by responsibilities at work, household chores, and caring for other family members. These teachers question whether it is fair to ask already burdened parents to spend time working with their teenage children on academic activities or assisting with behavior problems (Epstein & Becker, 1982). As Sandy told us:

> *Some parents are just overwhelmed. One poor, single mother I know just doesn't have the time or energy to become more involved. She's worried about keeping her job and making ends meet. Her plate is just too full; she can't handle anything else. It's not that she doesn't care. But the fact that her kid is not doing his homework is just not her highest priority right now. Knowing this is important. Once you know you're not going to get parent involvement, you can figure out another approach.*

Other teachers may see parents as too "ignorant" to be a resource (Eccles & Harold, 1993), while still others have been burned by encounters with angry, irresponsible, or apathetic parents. (See Figure 6-1 for a perspective on parental apathy.) They would tend to agree with Anne Walde and Keith Baker (1990), who contend that "far too many parents—and not just disadvantaged ones—simply don't give a damn. For them, school is a free babysitting service" (p. 322). Walde and Baker argue that many parents are not concerned with their child's education, do not want to be involved, or lack the skills needed to support their children. They describe numerous encounters with parents to support their assertion. Here is one example:

TEACHER: John isn't doing his homework.
  PARENT: I know he isn't. He watches TV all the time and doesn't do his homework. I just don't know what to do.
TEACHER: Why don't you turn the TV off?
  PARENT: Oh, he'd never let me do that!

Another reason for teachers' reluctance to involve parents in schooling has to do with *the level of authority and autonomy teachers enjoy within their classrooms.* As public servants, teachers are often exposed to criticism. Parents may blame them for children's

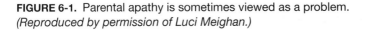

PARENTALAPATHY ? I DON'T KNOW - WE HAVEN'T
THOUGHT MUCH ABOUT IT ONE WAY OR THE
OTHER !

FIGURE 6-1. Parental apathy is sometimes viewed as a problem.
(Reproduced by permission of Luci Meighan.)

problems (Vernberg & Medway, 1981) or question their professional competence
(Power, 1985). It's not surprising that teachers sometimes become guarded and protective of their "turf." Lightfoot (1978) writes:

> *The only sphere of influence in which the teacher feels that her authority is
> ultimate and uncompromising seems to be with what happens inside the
> classroom. Behind the classroom door, teachers experience some measure
> of autonomy and relief from parental scrutiny. (p. 26)*

Lightfoot concludes that teachers who are "more confident of their skills, expertise, and
abilities" (p. 30) will be more likely to reach out to parents, and research supports her con-
tention. In a study of factors that facilitate parent involvement, Hoover-Dempsey, Bassler,
and Brissie (1987) found that *teacher efficacy* (teachers' beliefs that they can teach and
that their students can learn) was the factor most strongly related to parent involvement.

Parent Reluctance to Become Involved in Schooling

It is well recognized that family involvement in schools declines as students move from
elementary to middle school and junior high, and that by high school, it has practically
disappeared (Rioux & Berla, 1993). During one conversation with Donnie, she explained the decline in parent involvement this way:

> *Once kids leave elementary school, parents seem to feel it's time to cut the
> cord. They think the kids need to be on their own more, and that school*

should be the kids' responsibility. Also, they feel they can't help anymore because they don't know the content. They tell me, "I don't know algebra or geometry" or "I don't understand these new ways of teaching math." They're scared off by the content and feel they can't offer assistance.

In addition to this general, pervasive trend, there are more specific reasons why families may resist involvement. Griffith (1998), for example, found that lower socioeconomic status was associated with lower parent participation in schooling. Among the most obvious reasons for this association are the competing demands of work. Low-income households are more likely to have two parents who work full-time, parents who have two or more jobs, parents who have to work evenings and nights, and parents who have jobs with inflexible or unpredictable hours.

Furthermore, some adults have unhappy memories of their own experiences as students. Listen to this father describe his reasons for not participating more fully in his son's schooling:

They expect me to go to school so they can tell me my kid is stupid or crazy. They've been telling me that for three years, so why should I go and hear it again? They don't do anything. They just tell me my kid is bad.

See, I've been there. I know. And it scares me. They called me a boy in trouble but I was a troubled boy. Nobody helped me because they liked it when I didn't show up. If I was gone for the semester, fine with them. I dropped out nine times. They wanted me gone. (Finders & Lewis, 1994, p. 51)

Like this father, some adults remember school as an oppressive institution, not as a "place of hope" for their children (Menacker, Hurwitz, & Weldon, 1988). As sociologist Willard Waller (1932) wrote 70 years ago, "Each generation of teachers pays in turn for the sins of the generation that has gone before" (p. 59).

Other families simply do not see involvement in schooling to be part of their role as parents (Hoover-Dempsey & Sandler, 1997). They may believe that schooling should be "left to the experts" (Greenwood & Hickman, 1991). They may think that they are showing their support for teachers by staying out of the way (Froyen, 1992). They may even suspect that efforts to involve them are attempts to shift responsibility (Froyen, 1992) and resent being asked to do the "teacher's job."

It's important to note that beliefs like these may be culturally influenced. Asian American families, for example, generally hold high expectations for their children's academic success; nonetheless, they tend to view educational matters as the province of the school (Fuller & Olsen, 1998). Similarly, Latinos typically perceive their role as ensuring their children's attendance; instilling respect for the teacher; encouraging good behavior in school; meeting their obligations to provide clothing, food, and shelter; and socializing children to their family responsibilities

(Chrispeels & Rivero, 2000). Becoming involved in school is *not* a key component of this role.

Still others families feel guilty when their teenage children have difficulties in school. They may become defensive and uncooperative when teachers try to discuss their youngster's problem or may be too embarrassed to disclose troubles they are having at home. Rather than deal with the child's problem, these families may try to deny what is occurring and to avoid communication with the teacher (Froyen, 1992).

Finally, some families are unnerved by the "threatening monolith" we call school (Lightfoot, 1978, p. 36). In the main office, high counters serve as barricades to the principal, and there are few spaces in which parents can sit and chat or speak privately with teachers. Overprotective administrators discourage "invading" parents from visiting classrooms or making contact with teachers. If parents are poor, uneducated, or have limited proficiency in English, these barriers to involvement are even more intimidating. Some may find teachers and administrators unresponsive to their requests (Gutman & McLoyd, 2000); others may even fear teachers, viewing them as authority figures who must not be questioned (Lindman, 2001). Immigrant parents may be confused by educational practices that are different from their own; they may not know the words (e.g., "standards," "student-centered," "cum file," "grade equivalence") that would allow them to have a meaningful exchange.

Chrispeels and Rivero (2000) interviewed 11 Latino families about family involvement in schooling. They report that 9 of the 11 felt they had little influence on what happened at school and left decisions in the hands of the teacher. Mrs. Andres was typical:

> *My daughter's report card from fourth grade arrived with all Bs. In third grade she came out with excellence and an A. We waited for the next report card and again she got all Bs. . . . She told me, "My teacher says that she will not give any As because that will make the children who get an F feel bad." My daughter said that in that case she would not try hard because she was not going to get an A. (p. 22)*

Although Mrs. Andres felt this was unfair she did not ask the teacher for an explanation:

> *In a way I felt the teacher could say "Well, who tells you that your daughter deserves an A?" My fear of that comment kept me from going to ask. (p. 22)*

Fear was also a common theme among the Latino parents interviewed by Finders and Lewis (1994). One mother expressed her discomfort this way:

> *Parents feel like the teachers are looking at you, and I know how they feel, because I feel like that here. There are certain things and places where I still feel uncomfortable, so I won't go, and I feel bad, and I think maybe it's just me. (p. 53)*

The Changing Nature of the Family

In 1955, 60 percent of American households consisted of a working father, a homemaker mother, and two or more schoolage children (Hodgkinson, 1985). Teachers sent letters home addressed to "Dear Parents," reasonably confident that two parents would read them, and schools scheduled "Parent Conferences" with the expectation that parents were the primary caregivers of their children.

Times have changed. Consider this entry from the journal of a sixth-grade student teacher:

One boy in my class is very bright . . . but he never turned in assignments or participated in class discussions. He tended to annoy the students around him by doing strange things.

Two weeks ago he missed 2 days of school. Last week he missed 4. Some students saw him playing outside over the weekend, but he wasn't in school at all this week. There were no phone calls, and the social worker had to look into it.

His uncle came to school today and told us that the father dropped him off with the grandparents Monday and hasn't been heard from since. He is officially a "missing person." The mother lives in another state and doesn't want the boy. His parents apparently went through a very messy divorce. Now this boy is tossed around with no one who wants him. And we as teachers were concerned that he didn't do his spelling homework!

Stories like this have become all too common. The typical family of the 1950s now represents less than 10 percent of our households (Cushner, McClelland, & Safford, 2000). Today, almost half of all marriages end in divorce (Swap, 1999), and 50 percent of our children will live in a single-parent family at some point during their childhood (Children's Defense Fund, 1999). In 1999, 32 percent, or nearly 23 million children, were not living with two parents (*Kids Count Data Book*, 1999). Most are growing up with a single parent, but for some, the significant adults in their lives are not their parents at all, but grandparents, aunts, uncles, brothers, sisters, or neighbors. The "stay-at-home" mother is vanishing; indeed, 50 percent of all preschoolers (Children's Defense Fund, 1999) and 70 percent of school-aged children (Swap, 1999) have a mother in the workforce. With a surge in immigration from Central and Latin America, the Middle East, Southeast Asia and the Pacific, and Russia and Eastern Europe, many students come from homes where a language other than English is spoken, and their families are unfamiliar with schools in the United States.

The changing nature of the American family has made communication and collaboration more difficult than ever. Nonetheless, research has found that it is *teachers' attitudes and practices—not the educational level, marital status, or workplace of parents—that determine whether families become productively involved in their chil-*

dren's schooling (Epstein, 1988). In other words, it's the teacher that makes the difference. For this reason, you must not only understand the barriers to parent involvement, you must also be aware of the ways that families and schools can work together.

Overcoming the Barriers: Fostering Collaboration between Families and Schools

Providing cookies for bake sales, attending school plays and athletic events, showing up for parent conferences, signing and returning report cards—these are the traditional ways parents have been involved in their children's schooling. But families and teachers can collaborate in other ways as well. Joyce Epstein and her colleagues at Johns Hopkins University (Epstein, 1984; Epstein & Becker, 1982; Epstein & Dauber, 1991) have studied comprehensive parent involvement programs and have identified different types of family-school collaboration. Four of Epstein's categories provide a framework for our discussion. (These are summarized in Table 6-1.)

Type 1: Helping Families to Fulfill Their Basic Obligations

This category refers to the family's responsibility to provide for children's health and safety, to supervise and guide children at each age level, and to build positive home conditions that support school learning and behavior (Epstein & Dauber, 1991). Schools can assist families in carrying out these basic obligations by providing workshops on parenting skills; establishing parent support groups; holding programs on teenage problems (e.g., drug and alcohol abuse, eating disorders); communicating with families through newsletters, videotapes, and home visits; and referring families to community and state agencies when necessary.

Asking teachers to assume responsibilities for the education of *families*, in addition to the education of *children*, may seem onerous and unfair. Not surprisingly, some teachers hesitate to become "social workers," a role for which they are untrained (Olson, 1990). Others feel resentful and angry at parents who do not provide adequate home environments; in particular, teachers may "write off" parents who are poor and minority, believing that these families cannot or will not assist in their children's education (Olson, 1990).

Although these attitudes are understandable, you need to remember that your students' home environments shape their chances for school success. As the number of distressed, dysfunctional families grows, assisting families to carry out their basic obligations becomes increasingly critical. James Coleman, the late professor of sociology at the University of Chicago, noted:

Traditionally, the school has needed the support and sustenance provided by the family, in its task of educating children. Increasingly, the family itself

TABLE 6-1. Types of Collaboration between Families and Schools

Type	Examples
1. Helping families to fulfill their basic obligations	Inform families about available materials and programs.
	Encourage them to attend parenting workshops.
	Bring transportation problems to the attention of appropriate school personnel.
	Help families to arrange car pools.
	Educate families about relevant community and state agencies.
	Provide families with some perspective on teenagers.
2. Communicating with families	Communicate with families in a timely, respectful manner.
	Avoid educational jargon.
	Communicate with families *before* problems arise.
	Find out how to contact parents or guardians (e.g., are they permitted to get phone calls at work?).
	Be sensitive to cultural differences in communication styles.
	Make an effort to ensure that families will understand communications (e.g., have a translator available for parent-teacher conferences; whenever possible, send notes and memos home in families' native languages; use pictures and simple language when sending notes home to families who may be unable to read fluently).
3. Family involvement in school	Invite parents and guardians to speak to your classes (e.g., about careers, religions, countries of origin).
	Keep in close contact with families of students with disabilities.
4. Family involvement in learning activities at home	Encourage families to monitor their children's schoolwork and provide support.

Source: (Epstein, 1984)

needs support and sustenance from the schools . . . in its task of raising children. (Olson, 1990, p. 20)

Furthermore, research on parent involvement indicates that *most families want to become more effective partners with their children's schools.* Epstein comments: "Our data suggest that schools will be surprised by how much help parents can be if the parents are given useful, clear information about what they can do, especially at home" (Brandt, 1989, p. 27). Although there are certainly a few families who cannot be reached, it appears that most parents are deeply concerned about their children's education; they simply do not know how to help.

What can you, as a teacher, realistically do to assist families in carrying out their basic obligations? Although you will probably not be directly involved in planning parent education workshops, writing newsletters, or creating videotapes, you can play an important, *indirect* role. You can let families know about available materials, motivate and encourage them to attend programs, bring transportation problems to the attention of appropriate school personnel, and help families to arrange car pools (Greenwood & Hickman, 1991).

In Sandy's and Fred's districts, parent support groups are available through Effective Parenting Information for Children (EPIC) (Hayes, Lipsky, McCully, Rickard, Sipson, & Wicker, 1985). EPIC provides parents, teachers, and school support staff with training in ways to help children become responsible adults. It also offers opportunities for families to get together to share concerns and to discuss topics like communicating with adolescents, discipline, resisting peer pressure, and home/school cooperation. A similar program, the Parent Involvement Corps (PIC), was established at Donnie's school some years ago. Designed for parents of ninth-grade students, the program was intended to welcome parents to school, to help them feel comfortable there, to teach parenting skills, and to inform parents of their rights. Although PIC was a one-year, grant-funded program, it led to the creation of a permanent Parent–Teacher Association, which the high school had sorely needed. If programs like EPIC and PIC exist in your school, you can make sure families are aware of them, even if you are not directly involved; if you see a family with special needs, you can alert school personnel involved in these programs about the situation.

You can also educate families about relevant community and state agencies. Donnie, for example, advises families who have no health insurance where they can obtain medical and dental attention. When it became clear that one of her students was bulimic (at prom time!), Donnie worked with the family to find an agency that could provide the necessary psychological and medical assistance.

In addition to playing this indirect assistance role, there are times when it may be appropriate to work *directly* with families. Fred reports that he often needs to provide parents with some perspective on "this unique creature called 'teenager' ": "They haven't had 150 kids, and it's often a revelation for them to learn that they're not the only parents having problems." Similarly, Sandy tells us that a lot of her interactions with parents involve helping them to communicate more effectively with their teenage children:

Many times, I find that my discussions with parents begin with the problems their children are having in chemistry class, but move on to more general problems. You start talking about grades, and the next thing you know you're talking about curfews and dating. Many of the parents have no control over their 15- and 16-year olds. They'll say to me, "I just don't know what to do. He or she is the same way at home. I'm at a loss." I acknowledge their frustration and the difficulty of working with teenagers. (It helps that I have teenagers too!) I tell them, "You're not alone. Many 15- and 16-year-olds behave this way, and many parents feel this way." I try to provide some perspective and give them some tips about communication. I try to encourage them to set some limits. I find that a lot of parents don't like to set limits; they don't want confrontations with their kids, and they need encouragement to monitor what their kids are doing.

Sometimes I encounter overbearing parents who put too much pressure on their kids. Their expectations are unrealistic. Ninety-five on a test is not good enough; they want their child to have the highest test grade in the class. I tell them, "Wait a minute, we both want what's best for your child; we want him to work to his utmost ability, but utmost ability is not perfection on every test." I remember one situation, where a girl in my class was putting out very little effort. She got a 79 on the first test, which was far below her ability. After I spoke with her, she started working a lot harder, and her grade on the next test was 89. I told her how proud I was of her, and said something like, "Your parents must have been delighted." She got this funny look on her face, and I knew something was wrong. I found out that they had made only one comment: "Why wasn't it an A?" They didn't give her any praise at all. I decided I needed to speak with them about the situation. I told them, "Look, your daughter went from doing no work and getting a 79 to working hard and getting an 89, and you didn't even acknowledge the improvement. She's going to figure out that she might as well do no work and get 79s, since working hard and getting 89s doesn't get her any approval." I tried to help them see that as soon as they asked why she hadn't gotten an A, she was absolutely deflated. Parents like this need to understand the importance of acknowledging improvement, instead of holding out for the perfect grade.

If you have students whose families have recently immigrated to this country, you might also help them to understand the expectations and norms of American secondary schools. For example, immigrant parents sometimes view extracurricular activities as distractions from serious study and family responsibilities. Ruth Piatnochka, a colleague who teaches courses in English as a Second Language, shares this story:

My parents, who immigrated from the Ukraine, did not permit me to work on the school paper or yearbook. They did not give my brother permission to play soccer (although he signed the permission slip himself and played). . . . If someone had told my parents that extracurricular activities are really part of the holistic education of their children, I think they would have responded positively.

Tonia Moore, a Student Assistance Counselor at Sandy's school, has similar tales:

I see so many students who are caught between two cultures. At home, they're expected to follow a set of traditional values, but at school they really want to be American teenagers. It's so hard. We hold dances, but we have kids who are going to have arranged marriages. An Indian father wouldn't let his daughter go to Project Graduation [a boat trip the school organizes after graduation so that students will be in a safe, confined space without alcohol or drugs]. He said she couldn't stay out all night. An Iranian girl couldn't go to the prom; her father didn't believe in it. An Asian girl who just got 1400 on her SATs has to spend the summer taking review courses for college achievement tests. Her parents stress the need to achieve, while mainstream American culture stresses the importance of being well-rounded.

Type 2: Fulfilling the Basic Obligations of Schools— Communicating with Families

Epstein's second category of family–school involvement refers to the school's obligation *to communicate about school programs and children's progress.* Communications include report cards and progress reports, memos and notes, open houses and parent–teacher conferences, and phone calls. This is certainly the most commonly accepted way to work with parents, and there is no doubt that these communications are essential. The crucial question, however, is not only whether these communications occur, but *when they occur, whether they are being understood, and whether they lead to feelings of trust and respect or alienation and resentment.*

All of the teachers stress the importance of communicating with parents in a way that promotes a feeling of partnership. Donnie comments:

Sometimes I see parents in the market, or in church, or downtown. When I do, I acknowledge them, and I invite them to call and talk about their children. I tell them, "We've got to work together. We're partners."

Fred echoes Donnie's message:

Sometimes teachers don't invite contact. They'll only call if there is a problem. But some parents need that initial encouragement. If you can make that initial contact, then the parent will usually continue the contact. It's important to make parents understand that you're both working in the best interests of the kid. When you make that clear, even the most irate parent turns into a pussycat. I tell them, "Listen, everything I do is designed to be the best for your kid. But if you're concerned about something, let me know. Feel free to call." I tell my parents: "We need to work together as a team. And your kids need to know we're working together."

Research on family–school communication supports the importance of partnership. A study by Lindle (1989), for example, indicates that maintaining a professional, businesslike manner is not the best way to gain the respect and support of parents. In fact, parents view "professionalism" as *undesirable*; they express dissatisfaction with school personnel who are "too businesslike," "patronizing," or who "talk down to us." Rather than a professional–client relationship, parents prefer an equal partnership, characterized by a "personal touch." (Sometimes, partnership is threatened by the use of educational jargon that parents may find difficult to understand; see Figure 6-2.)

FIGURE 6-2. The use of educational jargon sometimes impedes communication. *(Frank & Ernest reprinted by permission of NEA, Inc.)*

TABLE 6-2. Reaching "Hard to Reach" Parents

Step #1: Try to figure out why parents are hard to reach. Ask yourself (or someone in the school who would know):

Do parents speak English?

Do parents come from cultures that do not identify parent involvement as a priority? Do they come from cultures that believe schooling should be left to the educators?

Do parents have work schedules that conflict with conferences?

Do parents live far from the school? Do they have transportation?

Do parents know where the school is?

Are the parents homeless (and therefore have no good address for receiving written communications from school)?

Step #2: Develop outreach strategies to address the underlying issue. For example:

Make sure that parents receive messages in their native language.

Figure out how to get messages to parents who are homeless.

Schedule conferences at flexible times to accommodate parents with conflicting work schedules.

See if neighbors or friends can be used as a liaison.

Determine if meetings can be held in a more convenient, more familiar, more neutral location.

Arrange for home visits (with appropriate security).

Source: Adapted from Swap, 1993.

It is clear that Donnie, Sandy, Christina, and Fred are able to establish productive partnerships with families, and the next few sections of this chapter describe some of the ways they do this. In addition, Table 6-2 lists some suggestions for communicating with parents who are particularly hard to reach.

Phone Calls

Given the hectic lives that people lead, one of the main problems about telephone calls is making the connection! At the beginning of the school year, all four teachers find out when and how to contact the families of their students. Some businesses have strict policies about employees' receiving phone messages, and a call during work hours may result in a reprimand. Some parents work at night, and a call in the morning will interrupt much-needed sleep; others may not have a phone at all, and you'll need to send a note home asking them to call you. (Donnie and Sandy both send notes home in plain, white envelopes—without the school's return address. This way there is less chance that a wary teenager will remove the letter from the pile of mail before the parent ever sees it!) All of the teachers also let parents know when they can receive telephone calls during the school day. Donnie even gives parents her home phone number; she says that no parent has ever abused the information.

To get the information she needs, Sandy has her students fill out a card with their parents' home and work numbers on the first day of school. She also asks students to indicate if their parents are permitted to get telephone calls at work. In addition, when Sandy has to call a parent, she'll often make a "precall," asking when it would be a convenient time to call and reassuring the parent that there's no earth-shattering problem. She's especially careful about checking the school personnel records to see which parent should be contacted:

A majority of my students come from divorced homes. If the parents are not sharing joint custody, you cannot talk to the noncustodial parent. If the parents are sharing custody, then the record tells which parent the student is residing with, and I call that parent. Sometimes, the records will indicate if calls are to be made to both parents or if written communications are to be done in duplicate for both parents.

Before calling a parent about an academic or behavior problem, Sandy always gives her students notice:

I say something like, "I know you want to be treated like an adult, but sometimes we need to work together with mom or dad to ensure your success. We need some help here. We can't solve this alone." I never use the telephone call as a threat or punishment. And I always wait 24 hours before calling. That way, the student can tell the parent that the call is coming (or about how the 75 they said they got on the test was really a 55!). When I talk with parents, I'm really careful about how I phrase things, so that I don't promote a negative reaction. Instead of saying, "Your son is disrupting the class," I'll say something like "We have to help your son control his behavior so that he can learn some chemistry." If the kid is disrespectful, I'll say, "I'm calling you about this because I know you wouldn't approve of this. I know you'd want to hear." In this way, you're conveying the idea that the parent will be supportive of you and that you don't think the kid comes from a family that would approve of such behavior.

During one meeting, I asked the four teachers to share some of the ideas they have for ensuring that telephone contacts with parents are productive. Here are their responses:

> *When the office receives a telephone call for you from a parent, and you're in class, have the secretary ask when would be a good time to call back.*
>
> *Even if a call comes during your free period, have the office take the message and say you'll call back. That gives you time to shift gears and prepare for the call. You can check your record book so that you are familiar with the student's progress.*
>
> *If a parent is calling with a complaint, try very hard not to get defensive. Listen and try to understand the parent's frustration. Respond by expressing your concern and assuring the parent that you are really committed to finding a solution.*
>
> *If a parent calls to complain that a child is upset about something ("He says you're picking on him" or "She says you're embarrassing her in front of the class"), acknowledge the student's perception. Convey your regret that the student has that perception. For example: "Gee, I'm really sorry that she has that perception. What specifically has she said, so that I can figure out what's going on? Help me to understand, because I don't want her to feel that way." Don't start out defensively: "I don't pick on kids."*
>
> *For chronic callers (parents who call three times a week) make it clear that it's important for you and the child to work the problem out. Explain that the frequent calls are embarrassing the student.*
>
> *If the telephone call is difficult, and there's a danger of your becoming defensive, have another person in the room to help monitor your tone of voice. He or she can tap you on the shoulder or make a face if you begin to get hostile or defensive.*
>
> *If a parent is out of control, suggest that you talk again at a later time, so that you both have a chance to calm down.*
>
> *If parents ask you to call every week with a report on their child's progress, suggest that they call you instead. (After all, you may have 150 students to think about, while they have only one!) Designate a day and time for them to call (e.g., on Fridays, during your prep period).*

A few additional words of caution are in order. First, be careful about using telephone calls to discuss sensitive issues or problems. Talking on the telephone doesn't allow you to "soften" your messages with smiles, gestures, or body language; nor do you have access to parents' nonverbal language in order to judge reactions (Lemlech, 1988). For this reason, telephone calls are more likely to lead to misinterpretations than face-to-face interactions. Second, although it's important to contact parents about serious problems, frequent phone calls about minor misbehaviors can be annoying. Furthermore, the practice can convey the message to both parents and children that the school can't deal with problems that arise; it's like saying, "Wait till your parents find out!"

It's also important to emphasize that phone calls should not be reserved for problems. As Donnie reminds us:

> *Teachers shouldn't just call when there's something bad. It's really important to call parents to give good news, to say "Your kid is really doing well," to tell them about something terrific that happened. Sometimes, when I do that, the student will come in the next day and say, "You called my house! And you didn't say anything bad about me!" And I'll tell them, "I had nothing bad to say!" I'll also let parents know what's coming up, the things that are going on. If you do that, then you've laid the foundation for a good relationship, and parents are more open later on. If you do have to call about a problem, they're less likely to be hostile or defensive.*

Report Cards

Report cards have been the traditional way of communicating with families about a child's progress in school. Unfortunately, they are often not very informative. What exactly does it mean when a student receives a C in Spanish? Is she having problems with vocabulary, with comprehension, or with conversation? Is another student's D in mathematics due to difficulties with problem solving, or is it merely a result of careless computational errors? Since many high schools use computerized report cards, it is not always possible for the teacher to elaborate on grades with a personalized narrative. Donnie tells us:

> *On our report cards, you can pick from nine little statements, like "the student is disruptive," "comes late," "is doing well," "is working at or above grade level," "has missed tests." But you're only allowed to check two! And they're so impersonal, I'm not sure that they really communicate much of anything.*

Another common problem with report cards is timeliness. If you rely solely on report cards to communicate with parents about a student's progress, two months might pass from the time a problem first appears until parents learn about it. In order to avoid this problem, some schools require teachers to send out progress reports midway through each marking period. Specific policies vary from district to district. Sandy explains what happens at Highland Park High School:

> *Progress reports have to be sent out mid–marking period for all seventh- and eighth-graders. In grades 9 through 12, we only have to send home a progress report if a student is in danger of receiving a D or an F for the*

marking period, but I send them out for other reasons too, like attendance or behavior or for commendable progress. I also tell students that I'm sending a progress report home, and I show it to them. I believe that they have the right to know.

Sometimes, showing students the progress reports encourages them to clean up their act. For example, Edward had a 75 average because he had two assignments missing. When I told him I was sending home a progress report, he asked me to just report the 75 average and leave off the part about the two missing assignments. He said his mother "would kill" him if she found out he wasn't doing his homework consistently. He promised he'd never miss another assignment. I decided he was serious, and so I agreed, but I told him that if she asked, I'd have to tell her. He never missed another assignment.

Although Sandy is conscientious about sending home progress reports, she also believes that any serious problem should be dealt with sooner:

Teachers should not rely on progress reports to tell parents about serious problems. Teachers need to contact parents if a problem develops. All of my students' parents know if their child has a D or an F before progress reports. I send progress reports because I have to, but my parents already know. Relying on progress reports is not very smart, since probably 50 percent of the kids take them out of the mail before their parents ever see them!

Back-to-School Night

For many parents, open house or back-to-school night is the first opportunity to meet you and to see the classroom. It's also the first opportunity *you* have to show parents all the great things you've been doing and to tell them about the plans you have for the future. As Fred says,

I always put on a show for back-to-school night. I feel good about what happens in my room, and I want the parents to feel good about what's happening, too. I outline my objectives and the course syllabus; I describe my expectations for kids and for parents, and I talk about what they can expect from me. I usually talk about why I teach history; I give a little propaganda speech about what I'm trying to accomplish and how they can help. But it's always been a fun night. I believe that the parents have to laugh, just like the kids. The bell always rings when I'm halfway through; there's never enough time, but I talk with the parents at the coffee hour afterwards.

If you don't feel quite as enthusiastic as Fred, don't feel bad. Even teachers as experienced as Sandy sometimes feel nervous about back-to-school night. In fact, Sandy tells us:

I hate back-to-school night! The one good thing is that I always get so nervous that I talk really fast and finish early. That leaves plenty of time for people to ask questions.

As these comments suggest, back-to-school night usually involves a brief presentation to groups of parents who move from room to room, following their children's schedules. This is not always the case, however. In Christina's school, for example, teachers remain in their assigned rooms for 90 minutes, while parents visit teachers in any order they wish for brief, individual conferences. Since the time with each parent is so limited, Christina's goals are simply to attach a face to a name, to give parents a general sense of their children's progress, and to invite them to set up a longer conference. She also displays current class projects, so parents can look them over while they are waiting to see her.

Whatever format your school uses, keep in mind that first impressions *do* matter, so you need to think carefully about how you will orchestrate this event. Here are some guidelines that emerged during my discussions with Sandy, Fred, Donnie, and Christina. (Obviously, some of them apply only if you are giving group presentations.)

Greet people at the door, introduce yourself, and find out who they are. *Do not assume that the student's last name is the same as the parents' last name, or that both parents have the same last name.*

Make sure your presentation is succinct and well organized. Parents want to hear about your goals, plans, and philosophy, as well as the curriculum and policies about homework and absences.

If parents raise issues that are unique to their child, let them know in a sensitive way that the purpose of open house is to describe the general program. Indicate that you're more than happy to discuss their concerns during a private conference. You may want to have a sign-up sheet available for this purpose.

Listen carefully to questions that parents have. Provide an opportunity for parents to talk about *their* goals and expectations for their children in the coming school year. This can begin the two-way communication that is so crucial for family–school collaboration.

Provide a sign-up sheet for parents who are able to participate in classroom activities (e.g., as a guest speaker or chaperon on field trips).

Display the books and materials that are used in your courses.

If refreshments are being served after the class meetings, go down and join in conversations with parents. Clustering with the other teachers separates you from parents and conveys the idea that there is a professional barrier.

PREPARE!

Parent-Teacher Conferences

Schools generally schedule one or two formal parent-teacher conferences during the school year. (See Figure 6-3 for Calvin's reaction to the prospect of such a conference.)

Calvin and Hobbes   by Bill Watterson

FIGURE 6-3. Parent-teacher conferences provide a way of communicating with families. *(CALVIN AND HOBBES © Watterson. Reprinted with permission of UNIVERSAL PRESS SYNDICATE. All rights reserved.)*

Interestingly, these meetings are often a source of frustration to both teachers and parents. Parents resent the formality of the situation (Lindle, 1989) and find the limited conference period frustrating. As one mother puts it, "Ten minutes is ridiculous, especially when other parents are waiting right outside the door. I need time to tell the teacher about how my child is at home, too" (Lindle, 1989, p. 14).

Teachers, too, are sometimes unhappy with these formal conferences. They agree with parents that the brief time allotted often precludes meaningful exchange. Furthermore, teachers complain about the lack of attendance: "The parents you *don't* need to see show up, while the ones you desperately *want* to talk with don't come." Interestingly, Donnie doesn't mind that the parents of good students come to parent conferences:

> If there's a real problem, I've already contacted the parents by the time parent conferences come along. We've already met. So I think it's nice to see the ones whose kids are doing well. It's nice to be able to give positive reports. And parents want reassurance that all is going well.

Before a conference, it's important to prepare carefully. For example, Sandy looks over each student's grades, computes a current average, notes any trends in academic performance or behavior, and jots down a few key words to use when she's talking to parents. It's also useful to have a few samples of students' work to show parents.

Conferences can be tense—especially if you're meeting with family members for the first time—so our four teachers begin by trying to put parents at ease. They suggest leading with something positive: "You son is a delight to have in class" or "Your daughter appears to be really interested in the topics we've been studying." Next, problems or weaknesses can be broached—not as character flaws ("she's lazy"), but as problems that need to be solved ("She's having difficulty getting her assignments in on time. What can we do about this?"). Donnie puts it this way:

I might tell parents, "We have a problem. Your son's performance is going down. Can you help me to understand? Is there anything going on that I should know about?" I stress that we have to work together. I explain that if I understand more about the home situation, then I'll know better how to approach the student. Maybe there's been a death in the family, or the father moved out, or a move is imminent. All this helps me to be more effective.

Sandy also tries to enlist parents' assistance in dealing with problems; however, she cautions teachers not to make demands that are impossible for parents to carry out:

Don't say things like, "You have to get your child to participate more in class." Be reasonable. If you're talking about a 17-year-old senior, what are the chances that a parent can do that? On the other hand, you can say, "Joanne is very quiet in class. Is this her normal behavior?"

Although they try to provide parents with substantive information, our teachers emphasize the need *to listen.* All four teachers always allow time for parents to ask questions and to express their concerns, and they solicit parents' suggestions. A conference should be a two-way conversation, not a monologue. *It's also critical not to assume that poor parents, uneducated parents, or parents with limited English proficiency have nothing of value to offer.* One mother in the study by Finders and Lewis (1994) expressed her frustration this way:

Whenever I go to school, they want to tell me what to do at home. They want to tell me how to raise my kid. They never ask what I think. They never ask me anything.

Kottler (1994) stresses the importance of encouraging families whose first language is not English to help you understand their children's educational and cultural background. For example, you might ask about past educational experiences, if their son or daughter is experiencing any cultural conflicts, what their educational goals for their child are, whether English is used at home, and if there are any special needs or customs you need to take into consideration.

You also need to be sensitive to cultural differences in communication styles. Cultures shape the nature of verbal interaction, providing norms for who can initiate conversation, whether it's all right to interrupt, and how long to pause between a question and its answer (Swap, 1993). If these norms are not shared, participants may feel uncomfortable. The following example of conversation between Athabaskan Indians and whites in Alaska illustrates how misunderstanding can arise because of different communication styles:

[A] white speaker often will ask a question, then pause, waiting for the Indian speaker to reply; then, when it appears the listener has nothing to

say, the white speaker will speak again. The Indian, who wishes to reply, but is accustomed to longer pauses between speakers, is not given an adequate opportunity to speak.

On the other hand, when Indian speakers do have the floor, they are interrupted frequently because they take what are perceived by whites to be "lengthy" pauses between thoughts. As an Athabaskan woman said to one of us, "While you're thinking about what you're going to say, they're already talking." Hence, Indian speakers often say very little and white speakers seem to do all the talking. (Nelson-Barber & Meier, 1990, p. 3, as cited in Swap, 1993, p. 91)

In addition, you need to recognize that different cultures hold different views about appropriate classroom behavior. For example, you may encourage students to participate actively in classroom discussions and to voice their opinions, while Hispanic parents may expect their children to be quiet and obedient. Table 6-3, adapted from Scarcella (1990) compares mainstream American teachers' expectations with those of Asian and Hispanic parents.

Finally, our teachers stress the importance of not closing doors to further communication. If a conference is not going well, you might suggest another meeting, per-

TABLE 6-3. Comparing the Expectations of Mainstream American Teachers with Asian and Hispanic Parents

Mainstream American Teachers' Expectations	Asian Parents' Expectations	Hispanic Parents' Expectations
Students should participate in classroom activities and discussion.	Students should be quiet and obedient.	Students should be quiet and obedient, observing more than participating.
Students should be creative.	Students should be told what to do.	Students should be shown what to do but allowed to organize the completion of the task creatively.
Students learn through inquiry and debate.	Students learn through memorization and observation.	Students learn through observation.
Students should state their own opinions, even when they contradict the teacher's.	Students should not contradict the teacher.	Students should not contradict the teacher.
Students need to ask questions.	Students should not ask questions.	Students should not ask questions.

Source: Adapted from Scarcella, 1990.

haps with the department supervisor or a guidance counselor on hand to mediate the discussion.

It should be noted that some schools have started to experiment with three-way conferences that include the teacher, the parent or caretaker, and the student (Davies, Cameron, Politano, & Gregory, 1992; ASCD, 1997). First, all participants, beginning with the student, share their perceptions of the strengths demonstrated in the student's work. They then discuss two areas on which the student needs to work, outline goals for the future, and agree on the kinds of support that each party will provide. Finally, the teacher answers questions and summarizes agreements.

Type 3: Family Involvement in School

At the high school level, most family involvement in school consists of attendance at student performances, athletic events, or other programs. Family involvement may also take place "behind-the-scenes"; for example, parents may engage in fund-raising activities, interview prospective teachers and administrators, prepare breakfast on "Teacher Appreciation Day," participate on committees developing discipline and attendance policies, and chaperon social events.

Participation in classroom activities is far less common, but involving even a few parents can provide considerable support and enrich the curriculum. When Fred's Contemporary World Cultures classes study religions, for example, parents of different faiths come in to explain their religious beliefs; in his Institute for Political and Legal Education (IPLE) class, parents who are lawyers sometimes share their expertise; and his history classes may be visited by survivors of Nazi concentration camps. In Sandy's chemistry classes, parents speak on scientific or environmental issues and parents who are faculty members at Rutgers University have set up tours of the chemistry labs there. Donnie holds a "mini-career day," when successful former students share their career experiences and communicate the message, "You can do this too." In Christina's journalism classes, parents, friends of parents, former students, and local contacts speak about their careers as journalists.

If you decide to invite parents to participate in your classroom, you need to think carefully about how to recruit them. Sometimes parents don't volunteer simply because they're not sure what would be expected or how they could contribute. Back-to-school night offers a good opportunity to make a direct, in-person appeal and to explain the various ways parents can assist.

If you're teaching in a district where there has been little parent involvement in school, special efforts will be needed to change the situation. At New Brunswick High School, a committee has been established to consider ways of making the school more "parent-friendly." As a result of the committee's efforts, teams of teachers have visited neighborhood churches on Sunday mornings to invite parents to the high school. As Donnie puts it,

Parents were complaining that they don't feel welcome. Well, the point of these trips is to say, "We want you to visit. This is your school; come in and see what's going on. If you can, volunteer, work in the library, help kids with homework. We welcome you.

Parents of Youngsters with Special Needs

Since 1975, when Congress enacted Public Law 94-142 mandating that "all handicapped children have available to them . . . a free appropriate public education which emphasizes special education and related services," parents of children with disabilities have had a legal mandate to participate in the planning of their children's educational program. Since then, P. L. 94-142 has been amended and renamed the Individuals with Disabilities Education Act (IDEA), but the essence of the law remains the same. Under IDEA, parents are required to be members of the team that creates the student's Individual Education Plan (IEP), specifying *educational goals, services to be provided* (e.g., physical, occupational, or speech therapy, transportation, counseling), and *placement* (e.g., special school, self-contained special education class in the neighborhood school, general education class, etc.). Parents also have the right to see their children's records, to be informed prior to any change in placement or services, to initiate a due process hearing in the case of a disagreement with the school, and to appeal decisions through the court system.

The IDEA requires children with disabilities to be educated in the "least restrictive environment"—meaning that, whenever possible, they should be in classrooms with their nondisabled peers. In recent years, this principle has gained tremendous momentum. Advocates for "inclusion" have argued that the regular classroom benefits children with disabilities academically because they are held to higher expectations and are exposed to more stimulating content. Advocates also point to the social benefits that occur when students with disabilities can make friends with youngsters from their own neighborhoods and can observe peers behaving in a socially appropriate manner.

Given the trend toward inclusion and the fact that the IDEA mandates parental participation, you are likely to have contact with parents of children with disabilities and, possibly, to be involved in the annual IEP meetings (at which a teacher must be present). But Sandy, who has an emotionally disturbed student in her class this year, cautions teachers not to wait for the formal, mandated meetings, or even for the regularly scheduled parent conferences:

> Anytime I have a student with an IEP, I go to the case manager right away and say, "Tell me about this kid." Then I ask them to set up a time for us to meet with the parents, usually in the first week and a half of school. This shows parents that you're aware of the IEP; it gives them a sense of relief and confidence. They know that the IEP isn't just a piece of paper, that the teacher is already thinking about how to modify the course for the student. It starts you off on the right track, establishes the right tone.

> At our initial meeting, we talk a lot about the IEP. You've got to remember that IEPs are open to interpretation, and that needs to be discussed. For example, an IEP may say that the student can have more time for tests. What does that mean? Is that an indefinite amount of time? Ten minutes? What?

I also want parents to educate me about their kid. This year, with an emotionally disturbed boy, it was important for me to know what sets him off. What will be stressful for him that might result in an outburst? Every kid is different, and I don't like surprises if I can avoid them. Sometimes it's as simple as "don't pair him with another male."

In addition to a meeting like this early in the year, Sandy keeps in close contact with parents throughout the year. Sometimes parents want a weekly report, and Sandy is happy to comply; however, she asks them to take the responsibility for calling: "With so many kids, it's just too hard for me to remember."

Type 4: Family Involvement in Learning Activities at Home

Epstein's fourth type refers to the ways families can assist their children's learning at home (Epstein & Dauber, 1991). At the secondary level, this kind of involvement often creates considerable anxiety for parents. As Donnie mentioned earlier, some parents are scared off by the subject matter. Sandy agrees:

At the elementary level, parents often help with homework, read to their children, and monitor their studying. But at the high school level, the first thing out of a parent's mouth is "I can't do calculus. I can't do chemistry. There's no way I can help."

Parents are not the only ones who wonder how they can help with their teenagers' homework assignments. Some teachers also question whether parents can really be useful, given their "highly variable instructional skills" (Becker & Epstein, 1982, p. 86). Indeed, in a survey of teachers' attitudes toward parental involvement in learning activities at home (Becker & Epstein, 1982) about half of the 3,700 respondents had serious doubts about the success of such efforts. Furthermore, some teachers believe that it's unfair to ask already overworked parents to assume teaching responsibilities.

Although our four teachers acknowledge that parents may not have familiarity with the subject matter, they are convinced that parents can play an extremely important role by monitoring their children's schoolwork, providing support and encouragement, and setting limits. Fred tells us:

I find that parents really want to help their kids, but they often don't have a clue about what to do. They're really receptive to suggestions. Sometimes I suggest that parents help by checking the spelling on their kids' papers. Maybe I'll suggest that they check that the kid has done the homework. Maybe I'll explain the requirements for a research paper, and suggest they check to see the requirements are met. I'll suggest they ask to see the kid's papers. A lot of times kids put their papers in the garbage and never show them to their parents.

Similarly, Sandy tells parents not to worry if they don't know chemistry; they can still help to structure their child's environment:

> *If a kid is having trouble with chemistry, 99 percent of the time, the problem is not with the subject, but with the time spent on the subject. Parents can monitor the time spent on homework. They can say, "Doing chemistry in front of the TV is not working." They can say, "You have to do your homework before you go out." They can suggest that their child call a friend if they're having trouble. They can make sure that their child comes in for help after school. I'll tell them, "I want your child in here two days a week so I can help with the chemistry. But you have to see that they get here."*

It is important to recognize that this view of the parental role may conflict with some families' beliefs about the importance of independence and self-sufficiency. A mother in the study by Finders and Lewis (1994) explains why she stays out of her daughter's schooling:

> *It's her education, not mine. I've had to teach her to take care of herself. I work nights, so she's had to get up and get herself ready for school. I'm not going to be there all the time. She's gotta do it. She's a tough cookie . . . She's almost an adult, and I get the impression that they want me to walk her through her work. And it's not that I don't care either. I really do. I think it's important, but I don't think it's my place. (p. 52)*

As Finders and Lewis (1994) comment, "This mother does not lack concern for her child. In her view, independence is essential for her daughter's success" (p. 52).

Concluding Comments

In 1976, Ira Gordon (1976), a well-known advocate of parent education and involvement, wrote these words:

> *We believe, with good evidence, that virtually all parents want a better life for their children than they have had. . . . We know that parents, when properly approached, want to be involved in the education of their children. . . . We have found that parents, regardless of region, race, or economic status, respond when the school reaches out to them in positive, nonthreatening, nonscolding, nonmanipulative ways. (p. 10)*

This chapter has described different ways that teachers can reach out to families. The suggestions vary considerably in terms of how common they are and how much time and energy they demand. As you get to know your students and their family situations, you will be able to decide which practices are most appropriate and most feasible.

As you consider the various alternatives, remember Gordon's message. This is an age of single parents, of mothers who work outside of the home, of grandparents, aunts, and neighbors who care for children, of increasing numbers of families whose cultural backgrounds differ from that of most teachers. Family–school collaboration has never been more difficult—but it has never been more important.

✴ Summary

This chapter began by discussing the benefits to working closely with families. We then examined the barriers to family–teacher cooperation and stressed that teachers' attitudes and practices—not the educational level, marital status, or workplace of parents—determine whether families become productively involved in their children's schooling. Finally, we presented strategies for overcoming the barriers and for fostering collaboration between families and schools.

Benefits of working closely with families

- Knowing about a student's home situation provides insight into the student's classroom behavior.
- When families understand what you are trying to achieve, they can provide valuable support and assistance.
- Families can help to develop and implement strategies for changing behavior.

Barriers to family–teacher cooperation

- Teachers are sometimes reluctant to involve families in schooling because of

    The extra time and energy that are required.
    Their perceptions that families are too overburdened, apathetic, and irresponsible or that they lack the skills needed.
    The level of authority and autonomy teachers enjoy within their classrooms.

- Parents are sometimes reluctant to become involved in schooling because

    They have unhappy memories of school.
    They believe schooling should be left to the experts.
    They feel guilty if their children are having problems.
    They find schools intimidating and threatening places.

- The changing nature of the family:

    The number of single-parent families has increased.
    The "stay-at-home" mother is vanishing.
    The significant adults in children's lives may not be parents, but grandparents, neighbors, aunts, or uncles.
    Many children come from non-English-speaking homes.

Fostering collaboration between families and schools

- Schools can assist families in carrying out their basic obligations by providing parent education, establishing parent support groups, and referring families to community and state agencies.

- Teachers need to communicate about school programs and students' progress through memos and notes, phone calls, report cards, progress reports, and face-to-face interactions (e.g., back-to-school night, parent conferences).

- Family members can serve as volunteers in classrooms.

- Families can assist their children at home on learning activities:

    Supervising homework.
    Providing encouragement and support.
    Setting limits.

Like Ira Gordon, I believe that most parents will be supportive and helpful if schools reach out to them in welcoming ways. In this age of single parents, mothers who work outside the home, and children who come from diverse cultural backgrounds, meaningful family–school collaboration has never been more difficult, but it has never been more important.

✱ Activities

1. In getting ready for the school year, you have decided to send a letter to the family of each student in your classes. The point of the letter is to introduce yourself, describe the curriculum, highlight a few upcoming projects, and explain your expectations in terms of homework, behavior, and attendance.

    Select a subject that you might actually teach (e.g., American History, Algebra I, Spanish, Home Economics I, World Literature, Physical Education, etc.), and write such a letter. As you write, think about the need to create a warm tone, to be clear and organized, to avoid educational jargon, and to stimulate interest about school.

2. Last week you conducted a parent conference with Mrs. Lewis, Joey's mother. During the conference you described his disruptive behaviors and what you've done to deal with them. You also explained that he is in danger of failing your class because he rarely does homework and has gotten poor grades on most quizzes and tests. Mrs. Lewis seemed to accept and understand the information; however, the next day, an irate *Mr.* Lewis called. He told you that he had never seen his wife so upset and that he wants another conference as soon as possible to get to the bottom of the problem. He also intimated that the problem might be due to a personality conflict between you and his son. Although the phone call caught you off-guard, you scheduled the conference for two days later.

    Consider the following questions:

    a. What will you do to prepare for the conference?

b. How will you structure the meeting so that you can state your information in a productive way without being defensive?

c. What sort of follow-up might you suggest?

3. Anita is extremely "forgetful" about doing homework assignments. She has received innumerable zeros and regularly has to stay for detention to make up the work. You have called her mother to report on this behavior and to ask for assistance, but her mother does not want to get involved. As she puts it, "I've got all I can do to handle her at home. What she does with school work is your responsibility!"

Interview two experienced teachers about what they would do in a case like this, and then formulate your own course of action based on what you learn.

✦ For Further Reading

Dodd, A. W., & Konzal, J. L. (1999). *Making our high schools better: How parents and teachers can work together*. New York: St. Martin's Press.

Fuller, M. L., & Olsen, G. (1998). *Home–school relations: Working successfully with parents and families.* Boston: Allyn & Bacon.

Swap, S. M. (1993). *Developing home–school partnerships: From concepts to practice.* New York: Teachers College Press.

✦ References

Association for Supervision and Curriculum Development (ASCD) (December 1997). Student-involved conferences. Education Update, 39(8), 1, 6.

Becher, R. M. (1984). *Parent involvement: A review of research and principles of successful practice*. Washington, D.C.: National Institute of Education.

Becker, H. J., & Epstein, J. L. (1982). Parent involvement: A survey of teacher practices. *The Elementary School Journal, 83*(2), 85–102.

Brandt, R. (1989). On parents and schools: A conversation with Joyce Epstein. *Educational Leadership, 47*(2), 24–27.

Children's Defense Fund (1999). *The state of America's children yearbook*. Washington, DC: Children's Defense Fund.

Chrispeels, J. H. & Rivero, E. (April 2000). Engaging Latino families for student success: Understanding the process and impact of providing training to parents. Paper presented at the Annual Meeting of the American Educational Research Association, New Orleans.

Cushner, K., McClelland, A., & Safford, P. (2000). *Human diversity in education: An integrative approach.* 3rd ed. Boston, McGraw-Hill.

Davies, A., Cameron, C., Politano, C., & Gregory, K. (1992). *Together is better: Collaborative assessment, evaluation and reporting.* Winnipeg, MB, Canada: Peguis Publishers.

Eccles, J. S., & Harold, R. D. (1993). Parent-school involvement during the early adolescent years. *Teachers College Record, 94*(3), 568–587.

Epstein, J. (1984). *Effects on parents of teacher practices in parent involvement.* Baltimore: Johns Hopkins University, Center for Social Organization of Schools.

Epstein, J. L. (1988). How do we improve programs for parent involvement? *Educational Horizons,* 58–59.

Epstein, J. L., & Becker, H. J. (1982). Teachers' reported practices of parent involvement: Problems and possibilities. *The Elementary School Journal, 83*(2), 103–113.

Epstein, J. L., & Dauber, S. L. (1991). School programs and teacher practices of parent involvement in inner-city elementary and middle schools. *The Elementary School Journal, 91*(3), 289–305.

Finders, M., & Lewis, C. (1994). Why some parents don't come to school. *Educational Leadership, 51*(8), 50–54.

Froyen, L. A. (1992). *Classroom management: The reflective teacher-leader.* 2nd ed. New York: Macmillan.

Fuller, M. L., & Olsen, G. (1998). *Home–school relations: Working successfully with parents and families.* Boston: Allyn and Bacon.

Gordon, I. J. (1976). Toward a home–school partnership program. In I. J. Gordon & W. F. Breivogel (eds.), *Building effective home–school relationships.* Boston: Allyn & Bacon, pp. 1–20.

Greenwood, G. E., & Hickman, C. W. (1991). Research and practice in parent involvement: Implications for teacher education. *The Elementary School Journal, 91*(3), 279–288.

Griffith, J. (1998). The relation of school structure and social environment to parent involvement in elementary schools. *The Elementary School Journal, 99*(1), 53–80.

Gutman, L. M., & McLoyd, V. G. (2000). Parents' management of their children's education within the home, at school, and in the community: An examination of African-American families living in poverty. *The Urban Review, 32*(1), 2000.

Hayes, T. F., Lipsky, C., McCully, T., Rickard, D., Sipson, P., & Wicker, K. (1985). *EPIC—Effective parenting information for children.* Buffalo, NY: EPIC.

Haynes, N. M., Comer, J. P., & Hamilton-Lee, M. (1989). School climate enhancement through parent involvement. *Journal of School Psychology, 27,* 87–90.

Henderson, A. T., & Berla, N. (Eds.) (1996). *A new generation of evidence: The family is critical to student achievement.* Washington, DC: National Committee for Citizens in Education. Eric Document Reproduction Service No. ED 375 968.

Hodgkinson, H. (1985). *All one system: Demographics of education, kindergarten through graduate school.* Washington, D. C.: Institute for Educational Leadership.

Hoover-Dempsey, K. V., Bassler, O. T., & Brissie, J. S. (1987). Parent involvement: Contributions of teacher efficacy, school socioeconomic status, and other school characteristics. *American Educational Research Journal, 24*(3), 417–435.

Hoover-Dempsey, K. V., & Sandler, H. M. (1997). Why do parents become involved in their children's education? *Review of Educational Research, 67*(1), 3–42.

Kids Count Data Book (1999). Baltimore, MD: Annie E. Casey Foundation.

Kottler, E. (1994). *Children with limited English: Teaching strategies for the regular classroom.* Thousand Oaks, CA: Corwin Press.

Lemlech, J. K. (1988). *Classroom management: Methods and techniques for elementary and secondary teachers.* New York: Longman.

Lightfoot, S. L. (1978). *Worlds apart: Relationships between families and schools.* New York: Basic Books.

Lindeman, B. (2001). Reaching out to immigrant parents. *Educational Leadership, 58*(6), 62–66.

Lindle, J. C. (1989). What do parents want from principals and teachers? *Educational Leadership, 47*(2), 12–14.

Menacker, J., Hurwitz, E., & Weldon, W. (1988). Parent-teacher cooperation in schools serving the urban poor. *Clearing House, 62*, 108–112.

Nelson-Barber, S., & Meier, T. (1990, Spring). Multicultural context a key factor in teaching. *Academic Connections*, Office of Academic Affairs, The College Board, 1–5, 9–11.

Olson, L. (April 4, 1990). Parents as partners: Redefining the social contract between families and schools. *Education Week*, 17–24.

Power, T. J. (1985). Perceptions of competence: How parents and teachers view each other. *Psychology in the Schools, 22*, 68–78.

Rioux, J. W., & Berla, N. (1993). Innovations in parent and family involvement. Princeton Junction, NJ: Eye on Education.

Scarcella, R. (1990). *Teaching language minority students in the multicultural classroom.* Upper Saddle River, NJ: Prentice Hall Regents.

Swap, S. M. (1993). *Developing home–school partnerships: From concepts to practice.* New York: Teachers College Press.

Vernberg, E. M., & Medway, F. J. (1981). Teacher and parent causal perceptions of school problems. *American Educational Research Journal, 18*, 29–37.

Walde, A. C., & Baker, K. (1990). How teachers view the parents' role in education. *Phi Delta Kappan, 72*(4), 319–320, 322.

Waller, W. (1932). *Sociology of teaching.* New York: John Wiley and Sons.

Making the Most of Classroom Time

On the first day of school, the academic year seems to stretch out endlessly. If you're a beginning teacher, you may wonder how you'll ever fill all the hours of school that lie ahead—especially if you're not even certain what you're going to do *tomorrow*. And yet, as the days go by, you may begin to feel that there's never enough time to accomplish all you need to do. With assemblies, fire drills, announcements over the intercom, standardized testing, snow days, holidays, and clerical tasks, the hours available for instruction seem far fewer than they did at first. Indeed, by the end of the year, you may view time as a precious resource—not something that has to be filled (or killed), but something that must be conserved and used wisely. (Of course, your students may not share this view—as Figure 7-1 illustrates!)

This chapter discusses issues of time and time management. Guiding the chapter is the premise that the wise use of time will maximize opportunities for learning and

Calvin and Hobbes

by Bill Watterson

FIGURE 7-1. Calvin doesn't agree that time passes quickly in classrooms.
(CALVIN AND HOBBES © Watterson. Dist. by UNIVERSAL PRESS SYNDICATE. Reprinted with permission. All rights reserved.)

minimize opportunities for disruption. First, we look at the amount of school time that is actually available for teaching and learning. Then we consider strategies for using classroom time efficiently, focusing on three complementary approaches—maintaining activity flow, minimizing transition time, and holding students accountable. Finally, we examine block scheduling, a relatively recent reform effort that replaces the traditional 42- or 50-minute period with fewer, longer classes of 85 to 90 minutes.

How Much Time Is There, Anyway?

Although this seems like a straightforward question, the answer is not so simple. In fact, the answer depends on the kind of time you're talking about (Karweit, 1989). Most states mandate a school year of approximately 180 days. Let's suppose that you're teaching in a high school that has divided each of these days into 42-minute periods. This amounts to 126 hours of *mandated time* for each of your classes. But students are absent, and special assembly programs are scheduled; snowstorms cause delayed openings, and parent conferences require early closings. Factors like these immediately reduce the time you have for teaching, so the *time available for instruction* can be substantially less than mandated time. Listen to the reflections of a student teacher who has learned to deal with the constant interruptions and cancelations:

> *"Well, at least you're learning to be flexible!" If I heard that once, I heard it a million times. I believe every teacher that I've had contact with this semester has made this statement to me. A record snowfall, proficiency testing,*

marine biology field trips, half-day inservice days, pep rallies, assemblies ... The actual amount of time I have had a full class of students ... for more than two consecutive days is minimal. Nowhere is the realization that I must be flexible more evident than in my lesson plan book. When I began student teaching, my lesson plans were typed and clipped into a binder [and labeled "Monday," "Tuesday," etc.]. A short time later I began calling each day "Day One," "Day Two," "Day Three," and so on. A short time after that I began writing the lessons in a plan book in pencil. About halfway through my student teaching experience, I began doing my lessons on Post-it paper which I could arrange as needed. I only transferred the lesson to the blocks in the book as I became absolutely sure that they would not be disrupted. I have continued to use this practice with great success and have actually started one of my cooperating teachers on the same method.

Even when school is in session, students are present, and you have your class for the full 42 minutes, some portion of the available class time must be spent in noninstructional activities. This means that only part of the 42-minute period actually constitutes *instructional time*. In *A Place Called School* (1984), John Goodlad reports that the senior high school teachers he studied generally spent about 76 percent of available class time on instruction (teaching and learning), 20 percent on routines, and 1.3 percent on behavior control; the remaining 2.2 percent was spent on socializing. Interestingly, the figures varied by subject area: Foreign language classes ranked first in terms of time spent on instruction (83 percent at the senior high level), while English ranked last (73 percent). School-to-school differences were also apparent, with instructional time varying from 68 percent to 84 percent at the senior high level. There was similar variation at the junior high level. At Crestview Junior High, for example, teachers spent 69 percent of class time on instruction and 25 percent on routines, while Fairfield Junior High teachers spent 87 percent on instruction and only 9 percent on routines.

Even within a school and a subject area, there can be considerable variation from teacher to teacher. In some classes, settling in at the beginning of the period, taking attendance, distributing materials, collecting homework, and reprimanding misbehaving students consume an inordinate amount of time. Karweit (1989) describes a "one-hour" math class, for example, in which the first 10 minutes were typically used to collect lunch money, and the last 10 were used to line up the students for lunch—leaving only 40 minutes for actual instruction.

Situations like this are not unusual in the classrooms of teachers who lack efficient strategies for carrying out routine, noninstructional tasks. Leinhardt and Greeno (1986) provide us with a glimpse into the difficulties encountered by one beginning teacher, Ms. Twain, as she attempted to check homework at the beginning of math class. Ms. Twain had two goals: to identify who had done the homework and to correct it orally. She began by asking, "Who doesn't have their homework?" In response, students did one of three things: They held up their completed work, called out that they didn't have it, or walked over to the teacher and told her whether they had done it or not. Ms. Twain then talked about the importance of homework and marked the results of this check on a posted sheet of paper.

Next, Ms. Twain chose students to give the correct answers to the homework problems:

She called out a set of problem numbers (1–10) and assigned a child to call out the answers as she called the problem number. The student slowly called out the answers in order. (The first child chosen was the lowest in the class, did not have her work done, and was doing the problems in her head.) Thus, for the first 10 problem answers, the teacher lost control of pace and correctness of answer; however, it was only when the child failed on the sixth problem that Twain realized the student had not done her homework. (p. 87)

Ms. Twain continued to call on students to give the answers, while the rest of the class checked their work. The last student chosen went through the sequence of problems quickly, but gave both the problem number and the answer, a situation that caused some confusion (e.g., "24, 27; 25, 64"). Ms. Twain's entire homework check took six minutes—and it was clear to the observers that she was never certain which students had done their homework.

In contrast, Leinhardt and Greeno describe a homework check conducted by Ms. Longbranch, a successful, experienced teacher. Ms. Longbranch first gave a cue, "Okay, set 43," and then began to call the students' names. Those who had done the homework simply responded, "yes." Those who hadn't done the work got up and wrote their names on the chalkboard. In 30 seconds—with a minimum of fuss—Ms. Longbranch was able to determine who had completed the assignment.

The next goal was to correct the work:

The students took colored pencils out and responded chorally with the correct answer, a fraction in lowest terms. As the teacher called the problem, "1/12 + 1/12," they responded "2/12 or 1/6." Time to complete was 106 seconds. (p. 85)

Ms. Longbranch's homework check is not presented as a model to be copied in your classroom; indeed, her procedure may not be appropriate for your particular class. The important point is that Ms. Longbranch has established a routine that enables her to check homework efficiently, almost automatically, while Ms. Twain does not yet have a workable strategy. Although the difference in the time used by the two teachers is only about four minutes, it is probably symptomatic of the ways they managed class time in general.

As you can see, the answer to the question, "How much time is there, anyway?" depends on whether we are talking about the number of hours mandated by the state and district (mandated time), the number of hours your class is actually in session and students are in attendance (available time), or the time actually used for instructional activities (Karweit, 1989). But even when teachers are actually teaching, students are not necessarily paying attention. We must consider still another kind of time—*engaged time* or *time-on-task*.

Let's suppose that while you are teaching, some of your students choose to pass notes about last Saturday night's party, do their homework for the next period, comb their hair, or stare out the window. In this case, the amount of time you are devoting to instruction is greater than the amount of time students are directly engaged in learning. This is not an atypical situation. Research documents the fact that students tend to be "on-task" about 70 percent of the time (Rosenshine, 1980). Again, there are sizable variations from class to class. A study of 30 middle and high school science teachers (McGarity & Butts, 1984) found that some classes had an engagement rate of 54 percent (i.e., the average student was attentive about one-half of the time), while in other classes the engagement rate was 75 percent.

To a large extent, variations like these reflect teachers' ability to manage classroom events and to get students involved in learning activities (McGarity & Butts, 1984). But other factors also come into play—students' attitudes toward school (Marks, 2000), subject matter (Marks, 2000), time of day, and day of week. And some teachers insist that attention falls off (and misbehavior increases) when there is a full moon!

There are also substantial differences in engagement from activity to activity. During independent work, for example, engagement is usually about 70 percent, while discussions led by the teacher yield engagement rates of 84 percent (Rosenshine, 1980). Why should this be so? Paul Gump (1982) suggests that some classroom activities prod students to be involved and "push" them along, while others do not. In a class discussion, external events (i.e., the teachers' questions, the other students' answers, and the teacher's responses) press students to pay attention. In independent work and silent reading, materials (e.g., worksheets, textbooks) are simply made available; students must depend on their own internal pacing to accomplish the task. In other words, students must provide their *own* push—and sometimes the push just isn't there. (This topic is pursued further in Chapter 9.)

The last type of time we need to consider is the *amount of time students spend on work that is meaningful and appropriate.* We sometimes get so caught up in trying to increase students' time-on-task that we overlook the tasks themselves. I once saw students in a ninth-grade general science class spend 15 minutes coloring a worksheet that showed diagrams of flower parts. The students seemed absorbed; indeed, an observer coding time-on-task would have recorded a high engagement rate. But what was the purpose of the activity? In first grade, coloring may be useful for developing children's fine motor skills, but it is hard to imagine why it would be worthwhile in high school. Coloring flower parts is not science, and in this case, one-third of the science period was allocated to a nonscientific activity.

It also makes no sense to have students spend time working on tasks they don't understand and are unable to complete successfully. This was vividly demonstrated in the Beginning Teacher Evaluation Study (BTES), an influential project that examined the use of time in schools (Fisher, Berliner, Filby, Marliave, Cahen, & Dishaw, 1980). BTES researchers created the term *academic learning time* (ALT) to refer to the proportion of engaged time in which students are performing academic tasks with a high degree of success. When students can accomplish a task with relatively few errors, it suggests that the task is appropriately matched to their level of achievement and that the teacher has provided sufficient preparation. (It is important to note, of course, that the BTES focused on the performance of straightforward, routine tasks, not complex, problem-solving tasks.)

This chapter began by asking, "How much time is there, anyway?" Figure 7-2 depicts the answer to this question. The bar at the far left shows the number of hours that a typical 42-minute class would meet in the typical mandated school year—126 (180 days × 42 minutes). For the sake of argument, let's assume that student absences and assembly programs reduce this figure by 10 days or seven hours (10 days × 42 minutes). Thus, the second bar indicates that available time is 119 hours. To be consistent with Goodlad's (1984) findings on the use of available class time, let's also assume that clerical and administrative tasks consume 20 percent of each class, leaving only 34 minutes each day for actual instruction. This yields 96 hours (bar 3). If students pay attention 80 percent of that time, engaged time is 77 hours (bar 4). And assuming that students work on meaningful, appropriate tasks for 80 percent of the time they are engaged, we see that actual learning time is only 62 hours—*about one-half of the "mandated" school time for this typical secondary class* (bar 5).

Obviously, these figures are estimates. As I have stressed, there are substantial variations from subject to subject, school to school, and classroom to classroom (Karweit, 1989). Nonetheless, the graph illustrates the fundamental point: *The hours available for learning are far more limited than they initially appear.*

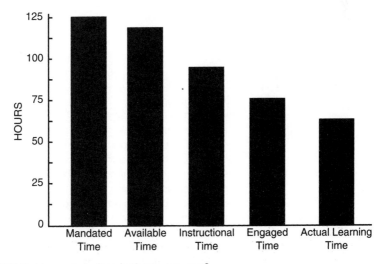

FIGURE 7-2. How much time is there, anyway?

Increasing Opportunity to Learn

In addition to contributing the concept of ALT, the Beginning Teacher Evaluation Study (BTES) also demonstrated the relationship between time and achievement. The findings are not surprising. *As allocated time, engaged time, and academic learning time increase, so does student learning;* of the three, academic learning time is the best predictor of achievement.

The BTES data made time a popular topic for reform-minded educators. In 1983, for example, the National Commission on Excellence in Education declared that we were "a nation at risk" because of "a rising tide of mediocrity" in our educational system. The report advocated a variety of reforms, including recommendations to extend the school day to seven hours and to lengthen the school year to 200 or 220 days. A decade later, the National Education Commission on Time and Learning (1994) also argued the need for more time. The Commission characterized teachers and students as "prisoners of time" and paraphrased Oliver Hazard Perry's dispatch from the War of 1812: "We have met the enemy and they are [h]ours." Acknowledging the "new work of the schools"—education about personal safety, AIDS, family life, driver education, consumer affairs—the Commission asserted the need to relegate the six-hour, 180-day school year to museums, "an exhibit from our education past" (p. 5).

Despite the cogency of the Commissions' reports, the six-hour, 180-day school year is still the norm in the United States. Thus, it is critical for teachers to manage the limited time available with skill and efficiency. The next sections of this chapter will discuss three strategies for increasing students' academic learning time: *maintaining activity flow, minimizing transition time, and holding students accountable.* (See Table 7-1 for a summary.)

Maintaining Activity Flow

Good and Brophy (2000) observe that "four things can happen" when students must wait with nothing to do, and "three of them are bad: (1) students may remain interested and

TABLE 7-1. Strategies for Increasing Students' Learning Time

1. Maintain activity flow	Avoid flip-flopping
	Avoid "stimulus-bounded events": being pulled away from the ongoing activity by an event or object that doesn't really need attention
	Avoid overdwelling and fragmentation
2. Minimize transition time	Prepare students for upcoming transition
	Establish clear routines
	Have clear beginnings and endings: bring first activity to a halt, announce the transition, monitor the transition, make sure everyone is attentive, begin second activity
3. Hold students accountable	Communicate assignments clearly
	Monitor students' progress

attentive; (2) they may become bored or fatigued, losing interest and ability to concentrate; (3) they may become distracted or start daydreaming; or (4) they may actively misbehave" (p. 131). Given the three-to-one odds that waiting will result in undesirable behavior and a loss of valuable learning opportunities, it's essential for teachers to learn how to maintain the flow of classroom activities.

Once again, we turn for guidance to the work of Jacob Kounin (1970). Kounin investigated differences in teachers' ability to initiate and maintain activity flow in classrooms. He then looked for relationships between activity flow and students' engagement and misbehavior.

Kounin's research identified many differences in the ways teachers orchestrated classroom activities. In some classrooms, activities flowed smoothly and briskly, while in others, activities were "jerky" and slow. Kounin even developed a special vocabulary to describe the problems he observed. For instance, he found that some ineffective managers would terminate an activity, start another, and then return to the first activity. Kounin called this *flip-flopping*. It is illustrated by the following situation: A foreign language teacher finishes reviewing homework with the class and tells students to turn to the next chapter in their textbook. She then stops and says, "Wait a minute. How many got all the homework problems right? . . . Very good . . . Okay, now let's talk about the imperfect tense."

Kounin also observed *stimulus-bounded events,* situations in which teachers are "pulled away" from the ongoing activity by a stimulus (an event or an object) that really doesn't need attention. Kounin describes the case of a teacher who is explaining a math problem at the board when she notices that a student is leaning on his left elbow as he works the problem. She leaves the board, instructs him to sit up straight, comments on his improved posture, and then returns to the board.

Sometimes, teachers slow down the pace of activity by *overdwelling*—continuing to explain when students already understand or preaching at length about appropriate behavior. Another type of slowdown is produced when a teacher breaks an activity into components even though the activity could be performed as a single unit—what Kounin called *fragmentation:*

> *The teacher was making a transition from spelling to arithmetic as follows: "All right everybody, I want you to close your spelling books. Put away your red pencils. Now close your spelling books. Put your spelling books in your desks. Keep them out of the way." [There's a pause.] "All right now. Take out your arithmetic books and put them on your desks in front of you. That's right, let's keep everything off your desks except your arithmetic books. And let's sit up straight. We don't want any lazy-bones do we? That's fine. Now get your black pencils and open your books to page sixteen." (p. 106)*

Flip-flops, stimulus-boundedness, overdwelling, fragmentation—these are all threats to the flow of classroom activities. Not only do they result in lost learning time, they can have a significant impact on students' behavior. When activities proceed smoothly and briskly, students are *more involved in work and less apt to misbehave.* Indeed, as Kounin concluded two decades ago, *activity flow plays a greater role in classroom order than the specific techniques that teachers use to handle misbehavior.*

During one visit to Sandy's classroom, I watched the skillful way she maintained the flow of activity in her class. It was the end of October, and students were in the middle of a very intriguing lab that involved the production of silver. As you read the vignette, note how Sandy ensures that there will be no "down time" by preparing the board for the homework review before class begins, by starting class promptly, by having students put homework problems on the board during the lab activity, and by ensuring that students will have something to do if they finish the lab before others.

11:21   Sandy writes the numbers 4 through 11 on the chalkboard, evenly spacing them across the entire width.

11:22   She positions herself by the classroom door to greet students as they enter the room.

11:23   The bell rings. Sandy moves from the door to the front of the room. "Hats off, please. We have a lot to do today. First, we have to finish the lab. You need not wear your goggles. Second, I want to review the chemical equation sheet you did. You'll put the final balanced equations on the board. And third, you'll learn to solve problems associated with the balanced equations. So let's get going."

11:24   The students move to lab tables, get their equipment, and begin working. While students are doing the lab, Sandy moves around the room, assisting, questioning, and monitoring. The atmosphere is very relaxed. Sandy smiles, laughs, and jokes with students about the silver they're producing. While she circulates, she also notes which students are just about done with the lab and selects them to put the homework problems on the board: "Joe, are you finished? You have all your data? Okay, put number four up. Kim, you're done? Please put number five on the board." They leave their lab tables, get their homework, and put their assigned problems on the board. By the time the lab is over, numbers 4 through 11 are up on the chalkboard.

11:33   Sandy notices that students are nearing the end of the lab. She tells them: "When you're finished, take your seats so I know you're finished." One by one, students begin to move back to their seats; they take out their homework and begin to compare their answers to the work on the chalkboard.

11:37   The equipment is all put away, the lab tables have been cleaned, and the class is all seated.

11:38   Sandy introduces the problems on the chalkboard: "OK, let's turn to the equations on the board. Let me preface this by saying that you should not panic if you're having trouble writing formulas. You don't have to be able to write formulas until December. But what you do need to know now is how to balance the equations. All right, let's look at the first one." She turns to the first problem written on the board and begins the review.

12:00   All the problems have been discussed, and Sandy moves to the third activity of the morning. "Now I want you to listen very carefully. Do not take notes. I know this sounds strange, but I want you to be able to watch and listen and think. I'm going to show you a new type of problem." She writes a chemical equation on the board and challenges them to think about it. The students are stuck. Sandy lets them ponder the problem; she asks some easier questions to help them get started, and suggests they use paper if they want to. She walks around the room to see how they're doing, commenting on their efforts, encouraging them to consult with one another.

12:07   The bell rings. Students are still involved in trying to solve the problems. Sandy tells the class, "Think about this tonight, and come back with your ideas tomorrow."

Later, Sandy reflected on the day's lesson and talked about her very deliberate attempts to maintain the flow of activities:

Some people would regard this as obsessive. Many teachers have kids finish the lab, sit down, and then put all the problems on the board. But what do you do when students are sitting there and others are putting things on the board? Even during labs, if they have to boil something for 10 minutes, I'll give them a problem to do. Kids can't just sit and watch something boil for 10 minutes. That's when they'll start squirting water bottles. Maybe I'm strange, but I just can't stand any down time. There's so much to accomplish and so little time.

Minimizing Transition Time

From the perspective of time management, transitions between classes and activities can be very problematic. An analysis by Paul Gump (1982, 1987) helps us to understand the reasons. First, Gump observes, there may be difficulty "closing out" the first activity—especially if students are deeply engaged. (Ironically, the very involvement that teachers strive to achieve makes it more difficult to get students to switch activities!) Second, transitions are more loosely structured than activities themselves (Ross, 1985). Since there's usually more leeway in terms of socializing and moving around the room, there is also more opportunity for disruption. In fact, in a study of 50 classes taught by student teachers, Marshall Arlin (1979) found that there was almost twice as much disruption during transitions (e.g., hitting, yelling, obscene gestures) as during nontransition time.

Third, students sometimes "save up" problems or tensions and deal with them during the transition time (Gump, 1982). They may seek out the teacher to complain about a grade, ask for permission to retrieve a book from a locker, or dump out the contents of their bookbags in search of a lost homework assignment. Although these behaviors are legitimate—and help to protect the adjacent activities from disturbance—they also make transitions more difficult to manage. Finally, there may be delays in getting students started on the second activity (Gump, 1982). Students may have difficulty settling down, or teachers may be held up because they are dealing with individual students' concerns or are busy assembling needed materials.

Gump's analysis suggests that teachers can reduce the potential for chaos by *preparing students for upcoming transitions, by establishing efficient transition routines,* and *by clearly defining the boundaries of lessons* (Ross, 1985). These guidelines are especially important for students with attention-deficit/hyperactivity disorder (ADHD), who have particular difficulty with transitions.

Advance Preparation

Marshall Arlin's (1979) research revealed that transitions were far more chaotic when student teachers failed to warn students about the imminent change of activity. This often occurred at the end of the period because student teachers didn't even realize that time was up:

> *The lesson was still continuing when the bell would ring. Not having reached any closure, the teacher, with some degree of desperation, would say something like "OK, you can go," and pupils would charge out of the room, often knocking each other over. (Sometimes, pupils did not even wait for the signal from the teacher.) The teacher might then remember an announcement and interject to the dispersing mob, "Don't forget to bring back money for the trip!" (p. 50)*

In contrast, other student teachers in Arlin's study were able to prepare students for the upcoming transition. If they were about to dismiss the class, they made sure that desks were in order and that students were quiet and ready to leave. They made announcements while students were still seated and then made sure students left the room in an orderly fashion.

Our four teachers are very diligent "clock watchers." They take care to monitor time and to inform students when the class period is drawing to a close. This is not as easy as it sounds, even for the three very experienced teachers. During one visit to Donnie's class, I watched both teacher and students get caught up in the lesson and lose track of time. When the bell rang, one girl actually blurted out, "Dang! That went fast!" Donnie laughingly agreed, broke off the lesson, and gave the homework assignment. Fortunately, she had taught her students early in the year that *she,* not the bell, dismissed them, so students stayed seated and attentive until she was finished.

In addition to warning students about the end of the period, it's also helpful to prepare them for changes in class activities during the period. In the following example, we see Fred explain to students what they will be doing that day and remind them periodically about how much time is left before they will be changing activities.

The bell rings. Fred tells his students to take out paper and pencil while he distributes an article from Newsweek *magazine regarding human rights and China. "While I meet with people one by one to go over grades, you will read and take notes on this article. You'll have about 12 minutes. At the end of that time, we will discuss these questions: What is the problem we're trying to solve between China and the United States? And is this just a case of Western arrogance? Take good notes—I'm going to collect them— and I will ask you to give an oral presentation of your views."*

As students settle down to read, Fred gets out his grade book and sits at his desk. He quietly signals for individuals to come up to discuss their marking quarter grades. A few minutes later, he checks his watch. "Ladies and gentlemen, you have about seven more minutes to finish reading and taking notes."

Later, he issues another warning about the time: "About two more minutes, so you should be finishing up." At the end of 12 minutes, he gets up from his desk. "Okay, you've had enough time now to read the article and take some notes. At the bottom of the paper, please summarize in 25 words or less what the basic problem is between China and the United States. What is the problem we're trying to solve between China and the United States?"

The Use of Routines

In Chapter 4 we talked about the importance of having clear, specific routines in order to keep the classroom running smoothly. At no time is the use of routines more impor- tant than during transitions (Ross, 1985). Well-established routines provide a structure to transitions that helps to prevent confusion and lost time.

In Christina's class, the routine for entering the room is very clear. Her students come in, take their seats, take out their journals, and begin writing on the journal topic posted on the board. According to Christina, using the journal achieves a number of objectives:

Using this routine allows me to have students engaged in a meaningful activity while I'm taking attendance, checking homework, etc. The journal is a timed writing exercise that encourages fluency in writing. I make it clear that students are not allowed to stop writing until I signal that time is up. . . . It's difficult in the beginning for them to understand that they can't be "finished" with this assignment—that it's timed! However, after a few days of prompting, they get the hang of it. Also, the journal entries are often related to the literature we're studying so they help to introduce or extend the reading. And having a daily journal assignment creates a nice, quiet atmosphere in which I can give instructions for the next activity.

Donnie also has a routine for beginning the period that helps to get students settled quickly. It's the "Do Now," and she uses it once or twice a week.

> *It's period 6 geometry. As students enter the room, they see the "do now" assignment on the board—Pages 57–58, #10–13. Instead of heading for their desks, most of the students go over to the side of the room and get calculators and workbooks. Donnie stands at the side of the room, watching silently. The stragglers notice her standing there; they glance at the board, and then get their materials. When everyone has settled down, Donnie announces, "OK, you have four or five minutes to finish those problems. Then we'll talk about them." While students are working, she takes attendance silently. Then she begins to circulate.*

Clear Beginnings and Endings

Arlin's (1979) study demonstrated that transitions proceed more smoothly if teachers bring the first activity to a halt, announce the transition, allow time to make sure that everyone is attentive, and then begin the second activity. In other words, smooth transitions are characterized by well-defined boundaries.

In the following vignette, we see Christina implement a transition with well-defined boundaries. Watch the way she prepares her students for the transition from small-group work to a whole-class activity.

> *Students are seated in clusters of four or five, working on the poetry lessons they are creating for the rest of the class. Christina is circulating. She checks the clock and then moves to the front of the room. "May I have your attention please? We are ready to move to the next part of the lesson. Please listen carefully to all of my instructions and do not move until I tell you to. First, you will have one member of your group hand in your assignment. This person will check to make sure each person's name is on the paper. Then you will return to your regular seats, take out your notebooks and textbooks and open your books to page 295. Also, have a pen out and on your desk. When you are settled, please begin reading the brief introduction on page 295. Are there any questions? Good. You may move now."*

Later, when I commented on how quickly and efficiently her students had made the transition, Christina observed that it was sometimes difficult to get students to wait patiently for instructions:

> *What I mean is, if the transition will require a series of movements, they want to move as soon as you give them the first direction. If you allow them to do this, they won't hear the rest of the directions. The transition time will actually be longer, since you'll have to spend time repeating everything. I've learned to tell them, "Don't move until I'm finished."*

Holding Students Accountable

Walter Doyle (1983) has commented that students tend to take assignments seriously only if they are held accountable for them. Your own school experiences probably testify to the truth of this statement. Even as adults, it takes a good deal of self-discipline and maturity to put your best effort into work that will never be seen by anyone. And secondary students are *adolescents*. Unless they know that they will have to account for their performance, it is unlikely that they'll make the best use of class time.

Furthermore, students are *unable* to make good use of their time if they are confused about what they're supposed to be doing. Teachers sometimes tell students to "get to work" and are immediately bombarded by questions: "Can I use pen?" "Do I have to write down the questions or can I just put the answers?" "Do we have to show all our work?" "Can I work at the lab table?" When this happens, precious class time has to be spent clarifying the original instructions.

In order to help students use their time wisely, teachers must *communicate assignments and requirements clearly and monitor students' progress* (Emmer, Evertson, & Worsham, 2000). These practices minimize students' confusion and convey the message that schoolwork is important. Let's see what our teachers and the research have to say about these two practices.

Communicating Assignments and Requirements

One finding of the BTES study (Fisher et al., 1980) was that students were more likely to have success on assignments when teachers provided clear, thorough directions. Interestingly, the number of explanations given *in response to students' questions was negatively associated with high student success.* What could account for this curious finding? One possibility is that when many students have to ask about an assignment, their teachers failed to provide sufficient preparation. In other words, the original instructions were not clear or thorough enough.

Before students begin to work, it's a good idea to explain what they'll be doing and why, how to get help, what to do with completed work, what to do when they're finished, and how long they'll be spending on the task. You also need to make sure that students are familiar with your work standards—for example, what kind of paper to use, whether they should use pencil or pen, how to number the page, whether or not erasures are allowed, and what it means to "show all their work." Once you've given your instructions, it's also a good idea to have students explain what they will be doing in their own words and to give students a chance to ask questions. Asking "Does everyone understand?" rarely yields useful information.

Sometimes, in an effort to maintain activity flow, teachers rush into instructions and activities without checking that students are "with them." Arlin (1979) writes: "Several times I noticed over 15 children continuing the previous activity while the teacher was giving directions for the new activity" (p. 50). Needless to say, those teachers then became exasperated when students asked questions about what to do.

On the other hand, Paul Gump (1982) warns that waiting *too* long can cause a loss of momentum. He writes: "Waiting for absolute and universal attention can sometimes lead to unnecessarily extended transition times" (p. 112). Gump reminds us that by keeping the instructional program going, teachers can often "pull in" students whose attention has momentarily wandered.

This lesson was brought home to me on a lovely day in April, as I watched Fred's Contemporary World Cultures class. As soon as the bell rang, Fred scanned the room and then announced that he was going to divide the class into six groups of four or five each (by having students count off). Once students had moved into their groups, Fred distributed paper and atlases, appointed a chairperson for each group, and gave students the following instructions: "Put your name at the top of the page. Turn to page 81 in your atlas—the map of Africa. Your first task is to find the country of Burkina Faso and to write down the names of the countries that surround it." Students immediately started working, and I sat at the side of the room wondering why Fred had not explained why they were doing this and what they would be doing for the rest of the period. Only when students had finished this first task did Fred provide more elaborate instructions:

Ladies and gentlemen, give me your attention so you'll know what we're doing today. You'll remember that after we saw the film on Africa, we talked about how the problems seem so big, so paralyzing. What can an ordinary person do? The situation is just too overwhelming. Well, I found some readings about two ordinary people, Minata in Burkina Faso and Keko in Tanzania. Today, you'll read about these two people and the problems they face. Then I want you to think about the best thing for them to do. What would you do if you were in their shoes? [He distributes the readings.]

Here's how you're going to do it. First read the articles and jot down your own notes to the questions. Then share your reactions in your small group. Then each of you will write out final answers that represent the thinking of the whole group. The chairperson will turn in the notes and the final answers at the end of the period. You already did the first question when you found the countries surrounding Burkina Faso. You'll do the same thing for Tanzania when you read about Keko. Any questions about what you're going to do? [There are a few questions, and he answers them.] This is worth eight points.

Later, I asked Fred why he had started students on the activity *before* explaining what they would be doing for the period and giving general instructions (clearly a departure from "standard operating procedure"). He answered without hesitation:

Look, it's spring, and they're juniors and seniors suffering from spring fever. If I had tried to give instructions when they first came in, half of them wouldn't have been listening, and I would have had to say everything all over again. This way, I got them into groups and got them going on an easy task—finding the countries surrounding Burkina Faso. They got focused, and then I could give instructions and they'd all be listening.

In addition to providing explicit directions for in-class activities, teachers need to communicate homework assignments in a clear, organized manner. This is particularly important if you are working with students who have difficulty remembering what they are supposed to do. Sandy has devised a routine for assigning homework that she first developed to help her learning disabled students. She soon realized, however, that the routine was helpful for everyone:

> *When I first write a homework assignment on the board, I write it really big in the middle of the board and tell students to copy it down* now. *Then I move it to the left-hand corner of the board where it remains until the due date. Periodically, I remind students about it. I'm also really clear about the numbers of the problems that students have to do. For example, if the assignment is to do numbers 1 through 5, and then 7, 9, 11, and 13 through 16, I'll write out one, two, three, four, and five, because some kids (especially my learning disabled students) don't see the difference between the comma and the dash.*

Christina is also very diligent about writing out assignments and directions, especially for big projects. Sometimes, she provides a printed handout with detailed instructions. Other times, she'll have students copy the directions from the board or an overhead projector.

> *Students have been conducting research on various careers. As part of the research, they have conducted interviews and done library research. On Wednesday they will be giving "informative speeches" lasting two to four minutes. Christina reminds them that they are to pretend they work for Career Services; their job is to inform college students about the careers they've researched. Today she reviews the research materials that are due on Wednesday. She turns on the overhead projector; on a transparency are listed the components they are to hand in:*
>
> *5 source cards (4 from library; 1 from interview)*
>
> *16 note cards (12 from library sources, 4 from interviews)*
>
> *list of 10+ interview questions*
>
> *record of interview (tape, video, written record)*
>
> *a work-cited page*
>
> *outline of speech*
>
> *Christina reviews each component and answers questions that students have about the interviews ("What if your interviewee doesn't want to give her last name?"), the speeches, and the written work ("What do we do if there's no author listed?"). When students have no more questions, she tells students to put away their materials so they can begin the next activity.*

After class, Christina and I talked about how explicit her directions had been:

> *Not only does this help to alleviate the number of questions I need to answer—over and over again—it also makes students accountable for the details of the assignment. They can't say, "You didn't tell us we needed five sources" if they've copied it down from the overhead, or "You didn't say to use textual evidence to support our answers" if the written handout states this requirement. I've also learned that doing this is useful for meeting with parents because you have every assignment documented. I save all my handouts and overhead transparencies with the directions. This way, I can prove I stated the requirements to students (and to parents on the rare occasions when I'm questioned). And I also save myself from rewriting directions when I'm using an assignment again.*

Monitoring Student Progress

Once you've given directions for an assignment and your class gets to work, it's important to monitor how students are doing. The BTES study found that teachers with high-achieving classes circulated around the room while students were working at their seats (Fisher, Berliner, Filby, Marliave, Cahen, & Dishaw, 1980). This practice enables you to keep track of students' progress, to identify and help with problems, and to verify that assignments are matched to students' ability. Circulating also helps to ensure that students are using their time well.

Observations of our four teachers revealed that they rarely sit down, unless they're working with a small group.

> *Donnie's class is working with rulers and protractors to "discover" the properties of parallelograms. As students work, Donnie continually circulates. She keeps up a steady stream of comments, questions, and praise: "Very good, Veronica." "Everybody finished with that first question?" "Answer the questions as you go, so you'll have all the answers when you finish." "Anyone need help?" "What does consecutive mean, José?" "Is there anyone who's having problems with the protractor?"*

After class, Donnie talked about the fact that she is constantly on the move:

> *I don't see how a person can teach math and sit down. I just wouldn't feel comfortable sitting down. You have to write on the board, you have to guide students through the problems, you have to see they're on the right track. By walking around the room, I can catch mistakes. I can ask, "What were you doing here? Explain your reasoning." I can talk them through the problem. I have to be up and moving when I'm teaching.*

In addition to circulating while students are working, it's essential to monitor whether students are regularly completing assignments. This requires you to *establish routines for collecting and checking classwork and homework.* For example, at the beginning of class, Donnie has students take out their homework and put it on their tables. While they review the assignment, she circulates around the room and notes in her grade book who has done the homework. The whole procedure takes just a few minutes and there's no loss of instructional time, since the class is simultaneously going over the homework problems.

Sandy uses a different system. She has a folder for each class that she keeps on the front table. Homework assignments are to be placed in the folder at the very beginning of class. She gives a "last call for homework," and then closes the folder. Sometime during the period, Sandy checks the papers to see if any assignments are missing. This allows her to verify immediately that she does not have an assignment from a particular student and to find out what happened. As she puts it, "This way I can avoid the situation where a student says, 'But I *did* do the homework. You must have lost it.' "

It's especially important to *keep track of students' progress on long-term homework assignments.* By establishing intermediate check points, you can help students develop a "plan of attack." For example, if they are writing a research paper, you can set due dates on which they have to submit each stage of the assignment (e.g., the topic; preliminary notes; a list of references; the first draft; the final draft). Not only does this allow you to monitor students' progress, it also helps to lessen the anxiety that adolescents sometimes feel when faced with a large assignment.

Fred tells an ironic story that points out the value of this approach:

Last year, my students did a long research paper. I had them turn in each piece to show me how they were coming along—a working outline, a bibliography, their notes, a rough draft, and then the final copy. I used a point system. The first four parts of the assignment were worth 10 points each; the final copy was worth 60 points.

This year, I decided it was babyish to do this, so I didn't do it. I told my classes, "I'm going to treat you like adults," and they said, "Great. We can do it." Well, they didn't get their papers in. They told me, "We messed up. We let it go, we procrastinated." They asked me to do what I had done last year! I trusted them to be mature, and they said, "We're not."

Finally, you need to *maintain records of what students are accomplishing.* In some districts, teachers can develop their own system for recording students' progress; others require teachers to follow a prescribed format. For example, Donnie's grade book has to reflect her weekly lessons plans and the "quarterly topic plans" she has to submit four times a year; following the district's objectives for her courses, these plans describe what she will be teaching day by day. For each marking period, Donnie must have two grades per week for homework and at least one test grade per objective. If five objectives are to be covered during a particular marking period, then Donnie would have to have at least five test grades.

In contrast, Fred is allowed to develop his own record-keeping system. Fred doesn't even have a regular grade book; instead he records his students' grades on the computer. Nonetheless, like Donnie, he is careful to keep up-to-date records of students' progress. He explained his record-keeping system to students at the very beginning of the year:

> *I want to take a minute or two to discuss grades with you. I don't have a grade book. I keep your grades on the computer. We can go anytime after school and check out your grades. What I use is homework, class work, projects, tests, and quizzes. Each in-class assignment is about four points. A big exam would be worth about five in-class assignments—about 20 points. The total point value for the marking period is 120–130 points. You can always find out what your point total is, what your grade is at any time. . . . It's important to me that everyone in here passes this class and does well. If you need me to get on your case, so you'll do okay in here, let me know. Remember, the grades are yours. You can see them at any time.*

Checking or grading all the work that students do each day is an arduous, time-consuming task. One student teacher in English recently wrote about "the looming mountain of paperwork that a teacher must perpetually climb":

> *Sometimes I'm not sure if I'm a teacher or a certified [public] accountant! However, my experience . . . has enabled me to find ways to reckon with the ponderous load. Simple things like color-coordinated folders for each class, or writing the names of absent students on quiz sheets to keep track of make-up work, are "tricks" that I am extremely grateful to have been shown along the way.*

Like this student teacher, you need to find ways to "make a molehill out of a mountain" (Shalaway, 1989). I asked Sandy, Donnie, Christina, and Fred how they handle the paperwork. Their ideas are listed in Figure 7-3.

The Use of Block Scheduling

Many secondary schools have moved to block scheduling in an effort to maximize time for learning, to encourage the use of varied instructional strategies, and to allow teachers and students to explore topics in depth. There are two common scheduling configurations. On the *4 × 4 block schedule,* four 80- or 90-minute instructional blocks are scheduled each day, instead of the traditional six or seven. Since classes meet every day, a course that would normally last a year can be completed in one semester or 90 days, and students take only four courses at a time. The *A-B or alternating day schedule* also offers four extended periods each day, but classes meet every other day for the entire school year. This means that students still take six or seven courses at one time.

Fred:	Check that students do in-class assignments and routine homework, but don't spend a lot of time reading and grading these. Develop a simple system for keeping track of students' routine assignments (e.g., four points for full credit; 3.5 points for an almost-completed assignment, etc.).
	Spend your time on the assignments that require higher-level thinking. These are harder to grade!
	On tests, create "structured essay" questions. Construct your own answer to the essay. (Know what the essay is "supposed to say.") Look for key words when grading.
	Refuse to grade papers that contain more than three technical errors (spelling, punctuation, etc.). I tell students, "I have 100 of these to grade; it's not fair for me to sit here and correct your spelling mistakes. I'm not here to proofread. . . . Have a smart person proofread your papers before you turn them in."
Sandy:	With homework, grade on attempt/effort, not whether it's right or wrong.
	For the first few assignments, read *everything* really carefully. Go over lab reports with a fine-tooth comb. That way, students come to see that you have really high expectations and that they have to be clear and thorough. Then, later, you can skim the first few pages (objectives, procedures, materials), and spend the bulk of your time on the data section.
	Sometimes, in long labs, have students present their data in table form.
Donnie:	Review homework every day, but have students check their own work. In your grade book, enter a check (as opposed to a grade) to show who has done the assignment.
	Have students grade one homework assignment each week that you record in your grade book.
	Collect one homework assignment each week to grade yourself.
Christina:	Think of "time-spent-grading" as part of your lesson plans. Carefully plan activities and due dates to allow you enough time to grade assignments. For example, after I collect research papers, I plan for students to be primarily engaged in classwork assignments that I can monitor without collecting very much paperwork. This allows me to spend the majority of my grading time on the research papers.
	Use rubrics to provide detailed feedback without having to write the same comments over and over again.
	Instruct students in proper editing, revision, and response procedures so they can provide feedback to one another. For example, I provide detailed response on the first draft of the first section of a long research paper. Then students use a checklist with marking instructions to provide feedback to one another on the second and third sections of the paper.

FIGURE 7-3. Ideas for handling paperwork

Although one 80- or 90-minute block does not actually provide more contact time with students than two 42- or 50-minute periods, advocates of block scheduling contend that the extended class provides more *usable instructional time* (Fleming, Olenn, Schoenstein, & Eineder, 1997). Since classes meet half as many times, the time spent in routine tasks at the beginning of the period (e.g., taking attendance, getting students settled in, distributing materials) and at the end (e.g., talking about homework, getting packed up) is also halved. More importantly, instructional time is less fragmented. As Roger Schoenstein, a Latin and English teacher in Colorado Springs, observes:

[On the old 50-minute schedule,] I'd just get the point across, just get them ready to do something with what we had been learning, . . . and the bell would ring. "Hang onto this stuff, don't forget it, tomorrow we'll practice it—tomorrow we'll do something with it." I said that day after day as they scrambled out the door. When "tomorrow" came, I'd spend 10 to 20 minutes reteaching the same material as the day before, trying to catch my students back up to the point where they were when the bell rang. On the 4 × 4 block I find those minutes given back to me day after day. The students can go right from instruction to application, . . . right from my lecture to cooperative groups to do something with what they've encountered. (Fleming, Olenn, Schoenstein, & Eineder, 1997, p. 14)

At this point, research on the effects of block scheduling on achievement is still sketchy, but results are promising. Preliminary studies in North Carolina, where almost three-quarters of all high schools are on block schedules, indicate that students in the extended classes do just as well on standardized tests or even better than their counterparts on a more traditional schedule (Steinberg, 1999). Similarly, an investigation of block scheduling in Virginia (Shortt & Thayer, 1998/99), where 63 percent of public high schools were on block scheduling by the end of the 1997–98 school year, indicated that both A-B and 4 × 4 block schedules outperformed the single-period schools in both reading and mathematics.

Block scheduling also seems to lead to a more relaxed school climate and a decline in discipline problems—possibly because it also cuts down on hallway traffic (Shortt & Thayer, 1998/99). On the 4 × 4 schedule, teachers have an additional benefit: They generally teach only *three* classes a day instead of four or five, so they are responsible for approximately 75–90 students at a time, rather than 125 or 150. Undoubtedly, this makes it easier to develop more attentive, caring relationships with students.

Despite these advantages, it is clear that block scheduling does not always result in the kind of innovative, varied instruction that proponents had envisioned (Queen, 2000). In an observational study of 48 extended classes (12 each in algebra, biology, English, and U.S. History), Bush and Johnstone (2000) found a predominance of traditional teacher-centered instruction. Teachers in all subject areas spent the majority of time presenting content and monitoring seatwork, while students primarily listened to the teacher, responded to teacher questions, and completed seatwork. There was little individualization of instruction and little groupwork. In other words, although the *structure* of the time had been changed, there was little change in the *use of time.* These findings underscore the comments of one high school senior who observed that an 80-minute class does not necessarily lead to more active learning:

> *Rather, it will simply create more time for students to daydream, scribble in their notebooks or catch up on sleep. A student who is bored in a 40-minute class will not suddenly become interested if the length of the class is doubled. (Shanley, 1999)*

Fred agrees. As he puts it, "Block scheduling with an outstanding teacher is fabulous. Block scheduling with a terrible teacher is pure hell."

Although Christina recognizes the truth of Fred's comments, she is an enthusiastic advocate of JFK's 4 × 4 block schedule. During my visits to her classroom, I was able to observe the effective way she takes advantage of the 84-minute periods. During one class, Christina typically uses a variety of instructional formats—whole-group presentation, small-group work, student-led discussion, writing, student presentations—in order to maintain students' engagement and promote active participation. She may also include a variety of the content areas that comprise "English class." In the following excerpt, we see a class in which students write individually in their journals, work on skill development in small groups, listen to a presentation on the format for a reference or "works cited" page, and act out a play they have been reading:

11:35   Students enter, take their seats, read the journal entry written on the board and begin to write on the day's topic: "Write about how your life would have been changed if one day in your past had come out differently. What actually happened that day?" While students write, Christina silently takes attendance.

11:45   Christina hands out rubric pages with their participation grades for the previous week. She tells them to fill out the page for the coming week. "You should be up to week 14, 12/20 to 12/23." After a few minutes, Christina instructs them to pass the rubric pages forward.

11:50   Christina gives the agenda for the class: "First we're going to do group tasks, and then we'll go over how to create a works-cited page. On Wednesday, you'll be giving your speeches. I'll collect all the written components before you give your speeches, so I want to review what you'll need to turn in. Finally, we'll finish reading *Antigone.*

11:52   Students get into their small groups to do their group tasks. One group is preparing for the High School Proficiency Test by writing a letter on ways to make the community safer. Another group is working on SAT vocabulary study by doing a crossword puzzle that Christina has prepared. A third group is doing "Word Wealth" exercises on prefixes and suffixes. A final group is selecting work to put in their portfolios. While the groups work, Christina circulates and assists.

12:18   Christina announces that the groups have two more minutes to work.

12:20   Students move the chairs back into rows and return to their regular seats. Christina tells them to take out their notebooks and turn to the section on doing research. She moves the overhead projector to the front-center of the room, pulls down the shades, and announces that she wants to explain how to do the "works cited" page for their research papers. She puts an overhead transparency on the projector and reviews the required format. Students are very attentive, taking notes and asking questions.

12:40   "Okay, guys, let's form the Greek Theater so we can finish reading *Antigone.*" Students get into a new configuration, roughly a circle, with the "chorus" at one end and an opening for the entrance to the "stage." "We left off on page 337. Chorus, take your places." Christina reads the stage directions, and students begin acting out *Antigone,* ending with the Queen's death. A boy reads the last speech of the play.

12:58   "All right, everyone, move your desks back to where they belong and listen to what you're going to do next." After students are back in their regular seats, Christina announces the final activity of the period: "Open your journals and open your book. You have four minutes. Write about the last speech you just heard. What does it mean? Why is it important? Do you agree with it?"

1:02   Students finish their journal entries. The bell rings.

Concluding Comments

Tracy Kidder's book, *Among Schoolchildren* (1989), describes one year in the life of Chris Zajac, an elementary teacher who's feisty, demanding, blunt, fair, funny, and hard working. At the very end of the book, Kidder describes Chris's thoughts on the last day of school. Although she is convinced that she belongs "among schoolchildren," Chris laments the fact that she hadn't been able to help all her students—at least not enough:

> *Again this year, some had needed more help than she could provide. There were many problems that she hadn't solved. But it wasn't for lack of trying. She hadn't given up. She had run out of time.*

Like Chris, we all run out of time. The end of the year comes much too quickly, and some students' needs are much too great. Hopefully, the concepts and guidelines presented in this chapter will help you to make good use of the limited time you have.

✦ Summary

This chapter described time as a "precious resource." First, we looked at the amount of school time that is actually available for teaching and learning. Then the chapter discussed three strategies for increasing students' academic learning time. I reviewed research by Kounin demonstrating that activity flow plays a greater role in classroom order than the specific techniques teachers use to handle misbehavior. I stressed the importance of minimizing transition times. Finally, I outlined ways of holding students accountable and helping them to use their time wisely. The last section of the chapter examined the use of block scheduling.

Types of time

- Mandated time: the time the state requires school to be in session.

- Available time: mandated time minus the time lost to absences, special events, half-days.

- Instructional time: the time that is actually used for instruction.

- Engaged time: the time a student spends working attentively on academic tasks.

- Academic learning time (ALT): the proportion of engaged time in which students are performing academic tasks with a high degree of success.

The relationship between time and learning

- As allocated, engaged, and academic learning time increase, so does student learning.

- Of the three, ALT is the best predictor of achievement.

How to increase hours for learning

- Maintain activity flow by avoiding

    Flip-flopping
    Stimulus-bounded events
    Overdwelling
    Fragmentation

- Minimize transition time by

    Defining boundaries to lessons.
    Preparing students for transitions.
    Establishing routines.

- Hold students accountable by:

    Communicating assignments and requirements clearly.
    Monitoring students' progress.
    Establishing routines for collecting and checking classwork and homework.
    Maintaining good records.

Block scheduling

- Types of block scheduling

  4 × 4 block schedule: four 80- or 90-minute instructional blocks scheduled each day for one semester or 90 days; students take four classes at a time.
  A-B or alternating day schedule: 80- or 90-minute instructional periods every other day for the entire school year; students take six or seven courses at a time.

- Advantages

  More usable instructional time.
  Less fragmented instructional time.
  More relaxed school climate.
  Decrease in hallway traffic.
  Opportunities for the use of varied instructional strategies.

- Problems

  Block scheduling does not always result in the innovative, varied instruction that proponents envision.

By using time wisely, you can maximize opportunities for learning and minimize occasions for disruption in your classroom. Think about how much time is being spent on meaningful and appropriate work in your room, and how much is being eaten up by business and clerical tasks. Be aware that the hours available for instruction are much fewer than they first appear!

Activities

1. While you are visiting a class, carefully observe the way the teacher uses the time. Keep an accurate record for a complete period, noting how much of the available time is actually used for *instructional purposes.* For example, let's suppose you elect to observe a 50-minute mathematics class. The *available time* is 50 minutes. But while you are observing, you note that the first five minutes of the period are spent checking to see who does or does not have the homework (a clerical job). In the middle of the period, the teacher asks students to get into groups of four, and moving into groups takes up another five minutes that is not actually spent in instruction. Then an announcement comes on over the loudspeaker, and the class discusses the announcement for another three minutes. Finally, the teacher wraps up class five minutes before the end of the period and gives everyone free time. *Conclusion: Out of 50 minutes of available time, 18 minutes was spent on nonacademic or noninstructional activities, leaving 32 minutes of actual instructional time.*

2. Read the following vignette and identify the factors that threaten the activity flow of the lesson. Once you have identified the problems, rewrite the vignette so that

activity flow is maintained OR explain how you would avoid the problems if you were the teacher.

Mrs. P. waits while her sophomore "A" level students take out the 10 mixed number addition problems she had them do for homework last night. Jack raises his hand. "I brought the wrong book by mistake, Mrs. P. My locker is right across the hall. Can I get my math book?"

"Be quick, Jack. We have 10 problems to go over, and the period is only 50 minutes long." Jack leaves, and Mrs. P. turns back to the class. "OK, this is what I want you to do. Switch papers with your neighbor." She waits while students figure out who will be partners with whom. She scans the room, trying to make sure that everyone has a partner. "OK, now write your name at the bottom of the page, on the right-hand side, to show that you're the checker. When I collect these papers, I want to know who the checkers were, so I can see who did a really accurate, responsible job of checking." She circulates while students write their names at the bottom of the page. "Ariadis, I said the right-hand side." Ariadis erases her name and rewrites it on the right side. "OK, now let's go over the answers. If your neighbor didn't get the right answer, put a circle around the problem and try to figure out what they did wrong so you can explain it to them. OK, number one, what's the right answer?" A student in the rear of the class raises his hand. "Billy?"

"I don't have a partner, Mrs. P. Can I go to the bathroom?"

"Jack will be right back, and then you'll have a partner. Just wait until we finish going over the homework." Jack returns. "Take a seat near Billy, Jack, and exchange homework papers with him."

Jack looks sheepishly at Mrs. P. "It's not in my book, Mrs. P. I must have left it on my desk last night. I was working on it pretty late."

"Class, go over the answers to problems one and two with your neighbors. See if you agree, and if you did the problems the same way. Jack, step outside."

Billy waves his hand again. "Mrs. P., can I please go to the bathroom now?"

"Yes, Billy. Fill out a pass, and I'll sign it. Just get back quickly." Leaving the door open so she can keep an eye on the other students, Mrs. P. follows Jack out of class. "You haven't had your homework done three times in the last two weeks, Jack. What's the problem?"

"Well, Mrs. P., my mother's been . . . " The office intercom phone buzzes.

"Want me to get that, Mrs. P.?" a student calls from the class.

"Yes, tell them I'll be right there."

"They said to just tell you that Billy has to go to the office if he's not doing anything right now."

"Go take your seat, Jack. I'll talk to you after class." Mrs. P. moves to the front of the room again. "I'm sorry, class, let's begin again. Did you all do numbers one and two?" The class murmurs assent. "OK, number three. Let's start with problem three. Joan?"

Joan gives the correct answer. Mrs. P. gets responses and explanations for three more homework problems. As the class reviews the homework, Mrs. P. wanders up and down the rows. As she passes Tanya's desk, she notices a pink slip of paper. "Class, I almost forgot to collect the slips for the Academic Fair. This fair is a chance for us to show how much progress we've made this year in math. How many of you remembered to fill out the slip, describing the project you're going to do?" Students proceed to hunt through their backpacks and flip through their math books. Those who find their pink slips give them to Mrs. P. She reminds the others to return them tomorrow. "OK, let's get back to problem . . . six, no, seven. We were on seven, right? Shakia." Shakia begins to respond. Then Billy returns. A student in a seat by the door reminds Mrs. P. that Billy has to go to the office. "Billy, go to Mr. Wilkins's office."

"Why, Mrs. P.? All I did was go to the john."

"I don't know, Billy. Just go and make it quick. We're trying to have a class." Billy leaves, and Mrs. P. turns to the class. "Pass your papers to the front. I'll check the rest for you and give you credit for your homework. We need to move on to subtraction with fractions. Who can think of a real life problem where you would need to subtract fractions? Missy?"

"Can I go to the nurse, Mrs. P.? I don't feel good."

3. Develop a routine or transition activity for each of the following situations. Remember, your goal is to use time wisely.

   a. Beginning class each day.

   b. Taking attendance.

   c. Checking homework.

d. Collecting papers.

e. Returning papers.

f. Moving from the whole group into small groups.

g. Ending class each day.

h. Students leaving class.

4. You want to have your students do a research report that will be due in four weeks. As you plan this long-term project, you will need to consider how to hold your students accountable. How will you

a. Convey requirements clearly and thoroughly?

b. Monitor student progress?

c. Maintain interest?

5. Observe a class that is on a block schedule. How is the extended time used? What instructional strategies are used (e.g. lecture, cooperative learning, discussion, simulations, etc.)? How long does each instructional strategy last? Does the teacher make use of the entire period? Do students seem able to sustain attention and involvement?

✦ For Further Reading

Fleming, D. S., Olenn, V., Schoenstein, R., & Eineder, D. (1997). *Moving to the block: Getting ready to teach in extended periods of learning time.* (An NEA Professional Library Publication.) Washington, D.C.: National Education Association.

National Education Commission on Time and Learning (1994). *Prisoners of time.* Washington, D.C.: U.S Government Printing Office. [Available online: http://www.emich.edu/public/emu_programs/tlc/toc.html]

✦ References

Arlin, M. (1979). Teacher transitions can disrupt time flow in classrooms. *American Educational Research Journal, 16,* 42–56.

Bush, M. J., & Johnstone, W. G. (2000, April). An observation evaluation of high school A/B block classes: Variety or monotony? Paper presented at the Annual Meeting of the American Educational Research Association, New Orleans.

Doyle, W. (1983). Academic work. *Review of Educational Research, 53*(2), 159–200.

Emmer, E. T., Evertson, C. M., & Worsham, M. E. (2000). *Classroom management for secondary teachers.* Boston: Allyn and Bacon.

Fisher, C. W., Berliner, D. C., Filby, N. N., Marliave, R., Cahen, L. S., & Dishaw, M. M. (1980). Teaching behaviors, academic learning time, and student achievement: An overview. In C.

Denham & A. Lieberman (Eds.), *Time to learn.* Washington, D.C., U. S. Department of Education, pp. 7–32.

Fleming, D. S., Olenn, V., Schoenstein, R., & Eineder, D. (1997). *Moving to the block: Getting ready to teach in extended periods of learning time.* (An NEA Professional Library Publication.) Washington D.C.: National Education Association.

Good, T. L., & Brophy, J. E. (2000). *Looking in classrooms.* 8th ed. New York: Addison Wesley Longman.

Goodlad, J. I. (1984). *A place called school.* New York: McGraw-Hill.

Gump, P. (1982). School settings and their keeping. In D. L. Duke (Ed.), *Helping teachers manage classrooms.* Alexandria, VA: Association for Supervision and Curriculum Development, pp. 98–114.

Gump, P. V. (1987). School and classroom environments. In D. Stokols & I. Altman (Eds.), *Handbook of environmental psychology.* New York: John Wiley & Sons, pp. 691–732.

Karweit, N. (1989). Time and learning: A review. In R. E. Slavin (Ed.), *School and classroom organization.* Hillsdale, NJ: Lawrence Erlbaum.

Kidder, T. (1989). *Among schoolchildren.* Boston: Houghton Mifflin.

Kounin, J. (1970). *Discipline and group management in classrooms.* New York: Holt, Rinehart and Winston.

Leinhardt, G., & Greeno, J. G. (1986). The cognitive skill of teaching. *Journal of Educational Psychology, 78*(2), 75–95.

Marks, H. M. (2000). Student engagement in instructional activity: Patterns in the elementary, middle, and high school years. *American Educational Research Journal, 37*(1), 153–184.

McGarity, Jr., J. R., & Butts, D. P. (1984). The relationship among teacher classroom management behavior, student engagement, and student achievement of middle and high school science students of varying aptitude. *Journal of Research in Science Teaching, 21*(1), 55–61.

National Commission on Excellence in Education (1983). *A nation at risk: The imperative for educational reform.* Washington, D.C.: Government Printing Office.

National Education Commission on Time and Learning (1994). Prisoner of time. Washington, D.C.: Government Printing Office.

Queen, J. A. (2000). Block scheduling revised. *Phi Delta Kappan, 82*(3), 214–222.

Rosenshine, B. (1980). How time is spent in elementary classrooms. In C. Denham & A. Lieberman (Eds.), *Time to learn.* Washington, D.C.: U.S. Department of Education.

Ross, R. P. (1985). Elementary school activity segments and the transitions between them: Responsibilities of teachers and student teachers. Unpublished doctoral dissertation, University of Kansas.

Shalaway, L. (1989). *Learning to teach . . . not just for beginners.* Cleveland, OH: Instructor Books, Edgell Communications.

Shanley, M. (October 22, 1999). Letter to the Editor. *The New York Times,* A26.

Shortt, T. L., & Thayer, Y. V. (1998/99). Block scheduling can enhance school climate. *Educational Leadership, 56*(4), 76–81.

Steinberg, J. (October 10, 1999). Schools find pluses in shift to marathon-length classes. *The New York Times* (Metro Section), pp. 1, 50.

PART III

Organizing and Managing Instruction

Chapter Eight

Enhancing Students' Motivation

Sitting in the teachers' room of a large suburban high school, I overheard a conversation among members of the foreign language department. One ninth-grade teacher was complaining loudly about his third-period class: "These kids don't care about school. I'm not going to waste my time trying to get them motivated. If they can't be responsible for their own learning by now, it's just too bad." As I reflected on the teacher's statement, it seemed to me he was suggesting that motivation is entirely the student's responsibility; to be successful in school, students must arrive motivated, just as they must arrive with notebooks and pens. The statement also suggests that motivation is a stable characteristic, like eye color. From this perspective, some individuals come to school wanting to learn, and some don't. This can be a comforting point of view: If motivation is an innate or unchangeable characteristic, then we don't have to spend time and energy figuring out ways to motivate students.

On the other hand, some educators argue that motivation is an acquired disposition that is amenable to change. It can also be situation-specific, varying with the nature of the particular activity. Thus, students in foreign language classes can be enthusiastic about role playing a visit to a restaurant, but can appear bored and uninterested when it's time to conjugate verbs.

According to this latter perspective, teachers are responsible for stimulating students' engagement in learning activities. It may be gratifying (and a lot easier) when students come to school already excited about learning; however, when this is not the case, teachers must redouble their efforts to create a classroom context that fosters students' involvement and interest. This year, for example, one of Fred's Contemporary World Issues classes has a large proportion of students who, according to Fred, are "just marking time." During one conversation, Fred shared both his frustration and his determination:

These kids are a constant struggle—the toughest kind of kids to work with. They're not dumb; they're not bad; they're just not intrinsically motivated when it comes to school. And they're used to taking it easy; for the last three years of high school, they've found that passive resistance works. They're so passive that teachers just leave them alone. But I refuse to give up on them. I look them in the face and say, "Tell me you want to stay home and be a slug and I'll leave you alone." And nobody's told me that. Actually, I think they're finally getting resigned to the fact that they can't coast in my class. And they can't even be mad at me, because they know that I'm on their side.

As Fred's comment indicates, stimulating students' motivation is easier said than done, especially when dealing with adolescents. The downturn in motivation during the transition years from elementary to secondary school is well documented (Anderman & Maehr, 1994)—and it is often dismaying to beginning teachers, particularly those who are passionate about their subject fields. Consider this entry taken from the journal of a student teacher in English:

I began my student teaching with all of these grand ideas about how I was going to enlighten students to the beauty of literature and unlock all the insight and talent that had been buried. . . . I gave serious, complicated lectures and multitudes of homework assignments, sure that my students would all be grateful when they witnessed the emergence of their intellectual prowess. Somewhere in the middle of the third week, however, the truth came rearing its ugly head: Most of my students did not, and probably never would, approach literature with [as much] enthusiasm [as they feel for] a new computer game.

To assist teachers who find themselves in this all too familiar situation, this chapter focuses on ways to enhance students' motivation. We begin by reflecting on what is realistic and appropriate with respect to motivating secondary students. We then examine the factors that give rise to motivation. Finally, we consider a variety of motivational strategies drawn from research, theory, and the practice of our four teachers.

What Is Realistic? What Is Appropriate?

Many of the teacher education students with whom I've worked believe that teachers motivate students *by making learning fun.* In fact, they frequently mention the ability to design activities that are enjoyable and entertaining as one of the defining characteristics of the "good teacher." Yet, as Jere Brophy (1998) reminds us, "schools are not day camps or recreational centers" (p. xviii), and teachers are not counselors or recreational directors. Given compulsory attendance, required curricula, class sizes that inhibit individualization, and the specter of high-stakes standardized testing, trying to ensure that learning is always fun is unreasonable and unrealistic. Bill Ayers (1993), a professor of education who has taught preschool through graduate school, is even more blunt. Characterizing the idea that good teachers make learning fun as one of the common myths that plague teaching, Ayers writes:

Fun is distracting, amusing. Clowns are fun. Jokes can be fun. Learning can be engaging, engrossing, amazing, disorienting, involving, and often deeply pleasurable. If it's fun, fine. But it doesn't need to be fun. (p. 13)

I would suspect that all of us can remember situations in which we were motivated to accomplish an academic task that was not fun, but that nonetheless seemed worthwhile and meaningful. The example that immediately comes to my own mind is learning French. I have never been very good at languages, and I was anxious and self-conscious whenever I had to speak in French class. I found conversation and oral exercises painful; role-plays were excruciating. Yet, I took three years of French in high school and two more in college, determined to communicate as fluently as possible when I finally got to visit France.

Brophy (1998) refers to this kind of drive as *motivation to learn*—the "tendency to find academic activities meaningful and worthwhile and to try to get the intended learning benefits from them" (p. 12). He distinguishes motivation to learn from *intrinsic motivation,* in which individuals pursue academic activities because they find them pleasurable. At times, of course, you may be able to capitalize on students' intrinsic interests so that the learning activities will be perceived as fun. But it's unlikely that this will always be the case. For this reason, teachers need to consider ways of developing and maintaining students' motivation to learn.

An Expectancy–Value Framework

It is helpful to think about stimulating motivation to learn in terms of an expectancy–value model (Brophy, 1998; Feather, 1982). This model posits that motivation depends on *students' expectation of success* and *the value they place on the task* (or the rewards that it may bring—such as being able to speak fluent French). The two factors work together like a multiplication equation (expectancy × value): If either one is missing (i.e., zero), there will be no motivation.

The expectancy-times-value model suggests that you have two major responsibilities with respect to motivation. First, you need to ensure that students can perform the task at hand successfully if they expend the effort. This means creating assignments that are well suited to students' achievement levels. This may also mean helping students to recognize their ability to perform successfully. Consider the case of Hopeless Hannah (Stipek, 1993). During math class, Hannah frequently sits at her desk doing nothing. If the teacher urges Hannah to try one of the problems she is supposed to be doing, she claims she can't. When the teacher walks her through a problem step by step, Hannah answers most of the questions correctly, but she insists that she was only guessing. Hannah considers herself incompetent, and she interprets her teacher's frustration as proof of her incompetence. She is a classic example of a student with "failure syndrome" problems (Brophy, 1998).

Fortunately, extreme cases like Hannah's are uncommon (Stipek, 1993). But we've probably all encountered situations where anticipation of failure has led to avoidance or paralysis. A lengthy term paper assignment is overwhelming, so we procrastinate until it's too late to do it really well. Calculus is daunting, so we take general mathematics instead. If failure is inevitable, there's no point in trying. And if we rarely try, we rarely succeed.

A second responsibility of teachers is to help students recognize the value of the academic work at hand. For example, Satisfied Sam (Stipek, 1993) is the class clown. He earns grades of C+ and B−, although he's clearly capable of earning A's. At home, Sam spends hours at his computer, reads every book he can find on space, loves science fiction, and has even written a short novel. But he displays little interest in schoolwork. If assignments coincide with his personal interests, he exerts effort; otherwise, he simply sees no point in his school work.

In order to help students like Sam, you need to communicate the value of class activities or the value of the rewards that successful completion or mastery will bring. For example, students may see little value in learning biology, but still recognize that a passing grade is required for college admission.

In accordance with the expectancy-times-value model, Brophy (1987, 1998) has reviewed relevant theory and research and derived a set of strategies that teachers can use to enhance students' motivation. The following sections of this chapter are based on Brophy's work. (See Table 8-1.) We begin with strategies that focus on the first variable in the model—students' expectations of success.

TABLE 8-1. Brophy's Strategies for Enhancing Motivation to Learn

Strategies for Increasing Expectation of Success
- Provide opportunities for success.
- Teach students to set reasonable goals and to assess their own performance.
- Help students recognize the relationship between effort and outcome.
- Provide informative feedback.
- Provide special motivational support to discouraged students.

Strategies for Increasing Perceived Value
- Relate lessons to students' own lives.
- Provide opportunities for choice.
- Model interest in learning and express enthusiasm for the material.
- Include novelty/variety elements.
- Provide opportunities for students to respond actively.
- Allow students to create finished products.
- Provide opportunities for students to interact with peers.
- Provide extrinsic rewards.

As you read, keep in mind *that none of these strategies will be very effective if you have not worked to create and sustain a safe, caring classroom environment* (Chapter 5). Before students can become motivated, they must feel safe from humiliation, understand that it's all right to take risks and make mistakes, and know that they are accepted, respected members of the class. In fact, Brophy considers a supportive environment to be an "essential precondition" for the successful use of motivational strategies (Good & Brophy, 2000, p. 221).

Strategies for Increasing Expectations of Success

Provide Opportunities for Success

If tasks appear too difficult, students may be afraid to tackle them. You may have to modify assignments for different students, make assignments open-ended so that a variety of responses can be acceptable, provide additional instruction, or allow extra time. Fred calls this the "slanty rope theory" of class work: "If we set a rope across a room at four feet, some kids can get over it and some can't. But if we slant the rope, then everyone can find their way over at some point."

When Sandy's classes begin learning the symbols for chemical ions, she doesn't insist that they immediately commit them to memory—a task they would find extremely daunting. Instead, she has them work with the ions and their symbols over a six- to eight-week period—they use them in writing equations, they see them on the chalkboard, and they look them up in their textbook. When it's finally time to have the symbols memorized, students find the task much less formidable.

Christina takes a similar approach when she's teaching her students to write research papers. Instead of assigning a paper that's due in four or five weeks and leaving students on their own, Christina breaks the assignment into small parts—taking notes, constructing a bibliography, creating an outline, writing the introductory paragraph, using parenthetical documentation—and has students turn in each part before writing the final paper. This not only makes the task seem less overwhelming, it also enables Christina to correct mistakes and set students on the right course before it's too late.

Sometimes, it's necessary to go back and reteach material rather than simply plowing ahead. For example, during one class period when Donnie was explaining how to construct and bisect congruent angles, it became apparent that most youngsters were lost. As students labored over their papers, frustrated comments began to be heard from all corners of the room: "I can't do it; you told me not to change the compass, but I had to"; "I need an eraser"; "Huh?"; "How you do this?"; "I don't get this." Circulating around the room, Donnie tried to help individuals who were having trouble. Finally, she moved to the front and center of the room and addressed the class: "Okay, let's start again. I see a lot of people are out in left field." She began to explain the procedure again, very slowly. After every step, she asked, "Does everyone have this?" before moving on to the next step. Students began to respond more positively: "Yeah"; "Uh-huh"; "Okay, we got it." One girl, who had been having particular difficulty, called out, "C'mere, Miss Collins, I wanna show you what I got." Donnie checked her work; it was correct. The girl turned to her neighbor and announced loudly, "You see, all I needed was a little help. Sometimes I gotta work step by step. I got it. I got it."

During one class session with a particularly unmotivated group of seniors, Fred told them to construct a four-sentence paragraph on the following topic: "What do you think about [pause] CELERY?" There was surprised laughter, and then, one by one, students began to write. (Fred sat at his desk and wrote a response too.) After a few moments, Fred asked individual students to read what they had written. The first student rose and read from his paper: "Celery is disgusting. The strings get in your teeth. The only way I like it is with peanut butter. It comes with buffalo wings." After several others had read their responses, Fred moved on to a new topic: Revenge. Once again, students wrote paragraphs and then read them to the class. Afterwards, Fred reflected on the purpose of the lesson:

I'm going to force these kids to succeed—in spite of themselves—because success is a better motivator than anything else I know. This lesson was designed to have them be successful. Anybody can think about celery; it would be hard not to have something to say. And the same with revenge. If a kid writes a good paragraph and can say, "Hey, this is pretty good," they begin to get hooked. I've never met a kid who wanted to grow up to be a bum. If I can get them to feel success, if I can create situations where they have to make the effort and they have to succeed, then maybe I'll be able to get through to them.

Sometimes, providing opportunities for success requires differentiated assignments for students of varying achievement levels. Consider this example from Tomlinson (1999):

Seniors in Mr. Yin's government class are conducting research in groups of three to five. Their goal is to understand how the Bill of Rights has expanded over time and its impact on various groups in society.

Mr. Yin has placed students in groups of somewhat similar readiness (e.g., struggling readers to grade-level readers, or grade-level readers to advanced readers). All research groups must examine an issue such as (1) how one or more amendments in the Bill of Rights became more inclusive over time; (2) societal events that prompted reinterpretation of one or more amendments in the Bill of Rights; (3) court decisions that redefined one or more of the amendments; (4) current interpretations and applications of one or more of the amendments.

Students have a common rubric for the structure and content of appropriate writing, and they will be asked individually to develop a written piece that stems from what they have learned from their group's research. A wide range of print, computer, video, and audio resources are available to all groups.

Mr. Yin has differentiated the work in two major ways. Some research groups will investigate society groups that are more familiar to them, areas where issues are more clearly defined, or areas where there is more information available on a basic reading level. Other groups will examine unfamiliar society groups, issues that are less defined, or issues where the library resources are more complex. In addition, students may choose to write an essay, parody, or dialogue to reflect their understandings. (Tomlinson, 1999, pp. 54–55)

Teach Students to Set Reasonable Goals and to Assess Their Own Performance

Some students think anything less than 100 on a test is a failure, while others are content with a barely passing grade. You may have to help students set goals that are reasonable and obtainable. At the very beginning of each course, Christina has students set the goals they hope to reach. (See Figure 8-1.) Then, based on these goals, students decide the criteria they will use to evaluate their work. They have to include four specific items that Christina requires and eight more that they devise for themselves. Throughout the marking period, students keep their work in a "collection folder," from which they then select work representing their progress in meeting the goals they set. For each selection, students also complete a "reflection sheet," which asks them to explain which goals and criteria the piece represents. The selected work, along with its reflection sheet, gets moved into a portfolio that both they and Christina assess.

Christina also gives her students a rubric that details how each major project will be scored and requires students to score their work before turning it in: "This way, students are aware of the score they will be receiving, and they can make a choice about whether they're happy with that or want to do more." Interestingly, Christina finds that students' self-evaluations are usually within a few points of her own assessments of their work.

I observed another example of helping students set goals when one of Fred's 11th grade students turned in an appalling essay at the beginning of the year. Not only was it short, superficial, and vague, but both the handwriting and spelling were atrocious. When Fred

Goals

Your individual goals should represent what you wish to accomplish in this course. Choose goals that are directly relevant to your expectations for the course. For example, while it is valid to say that you want to be a millionaire, that goal is not specifically relevant to English class. Choose a more specific shorter-term goal.

Once you have chosen your goals, explain your reasons for selecting them on the lines provided. Then, list 2 ways that you think you can reach these goals.

Complete Goals #1–5 at this time. Do not complete the Goal Revisions and Additions sections until you are instructed to do so.

Goal #1 _____
Reason for selection of this goal

_____
_____

2 things you can do to help you reach your goal
#1 _____
#2 _____

Goal #2 _____
Reason for selection of this goal

_____
_____

2 things you can do to help you reach your goal
#1 _____
#2 _____

Goal #3 _____
Reason for selection of this goal

_____
_____

2 things you can do to help you reach your goal
#1 _____
#2 _____

Goal #4 _____
Reason for selection of this goal

_____
_____

2 things you can do to help you reach your goal
#1 _____
#2 _____

Goal #5 _____
Reason for selection of this goal

_____
_____

2 things you can do to help you reach your goal
#1 _____
#2 _____

FIGURE 8-1. Christina's goal-setting handout

Goal Revision/Addition #1

Reason for selection of this goal

2 things you can do to help you reach your goal
#1 _____
#2 _____

Goal Revision/Addition #2

Reason for selection of this goal

2 things you can do to help you reach your goal
#1 _____
#2 _____

FIGURE 8-1. Continued

investigated, he found out that the student had a learning disability; nonetheless, he told the student in no uncertain terms that his performance was inadequate: "Look, you can't write, you can't even print, and you can't spell. But you're not stupid. So what are you going to do to get better? Let's set some goals." With the assistance of the resource room teacher, they devised a plan for the student to learn keyboarding and to use a spell checker. When the next writing assignment was due, the student came to Fred complaining that it was too hard. Fred was sympathetic and supportive—but adamant that the student complete it. He did, and although it was far from adequate, it was a definite improvement over the first assignment. Reflecting on the student's problems, Fred comments:

> *We can all feel sorry for him, but he can't go around like this; he has to be pushed to overcome his deficits. People have allowed him to stay a baby, but it's time for him to grow up. There are ways he can improve. My job is to teach him to set some reasonable goals and then work to achieve them.*

Help Students Recognize the Relationship between Effort and Outcome

Like Hopeless Hannah, some youngsters proclaim defeat before they've even attempted a task. When they don't do well on an assignment, they attribute their failure to lack of ability, not realizing that achievement is often a function of effort. Other students may be overconfident—even cocky—and think they can do well without exerting much effort. In either situation, you have to make the relationship between effort and outcome explicit. Whenever possible, point out students' improvement and help them to see the role of effort: "See, you did all your math homework this week, and it really paid off. Look at how well you did on the quiz!"

The relationship between effort and outcome became painfully clear to a student in Sandy's class who refused to take notes during class. When Sandy first noticed that he wasn't taking notes, she told him to take out his notebook and open it. He did, murmuring, "I'll open my notebook, but you can't force me to take notes." Later, he told Sandy he didn't need to take notes like the other kids, because he had a good memory. She explained that her years of experience had shown her that taking notes in chemistry was absolutely necessary; she suggested he keep his notebook out and open "just in case." When the first test was given, the boy's grade was 40. Sandy told him: "I know it's not because you're unable to do the work. So what do you think? What conclusion do you draw from this?" The boy responded, "I guess I gotta take notes."

Provide Informative Feedback

Sometimes turning in work to a teacher is like dropping it down a black hole. Assignments pile up in huge mounds on the teacher's desk, and students know that their papers will never be returned—graded or ungraded. From a student's perspective, it's infuriating to work hard on an assignment, turn it in, and then receive no feedback from the teacher. But a lack of academic feedback is not simply infuriating. It is also detrimental to students' motivation and achievement. The Beginning Teacher Evaluation Study (Fisher et al., 1980) documented the importance of providing feedback to students:

> *One particularly important teaching activity is providing academic feedback to students (letting them know whether their answers are right or wrong, or giving them the right answer). Academic feedback should be provided as often as possible to students. When more frequent feedback is offered, students pay attention more and learn more.* Academic feedback was more strongly and consistently related to achievement than any of the other teaching behaviors. *(p. 27; emphasis added)*

If you circulate while students are working on assignments, you can provide them with immediate feedback about their performance. You can catch errors, assist with problems, and affirm correct, thoughtful work. In the following vignette, we see Sandy help two girls having problems pouring a solution into a funnel. Only a clear, colorless solution was supposed to come out into the beaker, but the solution was yellow and had particles of the solid in it.

SANDY: Why did this happen?
TANYA: Because I poured too fast and too much.
SANDY: Right. [She calls all the students over to see the problem that the two girls had.] So what happened?
LISA: The yellow stuff got over the filter paper, behind the fold.
SANDY: Okay, so what can you do?
TANYA: Pour it back in, but we're going to lose some.
SANDY: [To the other students] Can they pour it back in?
STUDENT: Yeah.
SANDY: Sure. It was good you washed the beaker.

Sandy monitors the activity of lab groups.

Sometimes you're unable to monitor work while it's being done. In this case, you need to check assignments once they've been submitted and return them to students as soon as possible. You might also decide to allow your students to check their own work. Donnie believes this has numerous educational benefits:

I like to go over the homework in class and have students check their own work. This gives them the chance to see how they're doing, where they're confused. If I just had them turn in the work and I graded it, they'd know which problems were right and which were wrong, but they wouldn't know why. Once a week, though, I do collect the homework and go over it myself. That way I can see for myself how students are doing.

As an English teacher, Christina finds that having students evaluate their own work and that of their peers is not only educational, it also allows them to receive feedback more quickly:

I used to think it was an easy way out to have students grade their own papers or do peer editing, but experienced teachers told me it wasn't so, and I've come to agree. I couldn't have a writing-based classroom if I had to give all the feedback myself. My students write many drafts of their papers, and I simply cannot read them all quickly enough. . . . So I teach them to self- and peer-evaluate before revising. . . . They learn a lot when they do peer editing, and they can get instant feedback.

Whether you correct work while it's being done, at home over a cup of coffee, or together with your students, the important point is that students *need to know how they are progressing.* It's also important to give feedback in terms of *absolute standards or students' own past performance rather than peers' performance* (Brophy, 1998). Thus, instead of saying, "Congratulations! You received the sixth highest grade in the class," you could say, "Congratulations! You went from a 79 on your last quiz to an 87 on this quiz." Similarly, you can point out strengths and weaknesses and add a note of encouragement for further effort ("You've demonstrated a firm grasp of the perspectives of the slaveholders and the abolitionists, but not the slaves themselves. Check the chapter again, and add a paragraph to round out your presentation.")

Provide Special Motivational Support to Discouraged Students

For students with limited ability or learning disabilities, school may be a constant struggle to keep up with classmates and to maintain a sense of enthusiasm and motivation. Such students not only require instructional assistance (e.g., individualized activities, extra academic help, well-structured assignments, extra time), they may also need special encouragement and motivational support. For example, Donnie constantly exhorts students not to get discouraged if they're having trouble and reminds them that people work and learn at different paces. Often, she pairs low-achieving students with those she knows will be patient and helpful and encourages peer-assistance and peer-tutoring. Similarly, Sandy frequently reassures her students that they're in this together:

So many of my students are afraid of taking chemistry, and they find it harder than any subject they've taken. I spend the first five or six weeks of school reassuring them—"You're not alone, there's support, I'm here to help you, we'll do this slowly and systematically. . . . you don't have to learn it in three or four days; it may be a long haul but that's OK. If I can get them to trust me, and I believe they can do it, then eventually they develop more confidence and a sense of well-being.

Sandy also makes sure that she expresses concern and surprise when students don't do well on a test or assignment. She'll ask, "What happened here?" or "What's the problem?" so that student know she's not writing them off:

Too many times teachers will say "good job" to the person who's gotten the A, but nothing to the kid who got the D or F. But if you don't ask what happened, they think you expected it. Sometimes what you don't say is more powerful than what you do say.

Christina finds that students who have failed the High School Proficiency Test (HSPT) are particularly discouraged and anxious. Like Sandy, she makes it clear that she expects them to pass the next time around; at the very least, they will improve their scores. She cheers them on as they take numerous practice tests and analyze their performances. Then she has them think of one thing they will do differently when they take the test again. Responses vary—"I won't fall asleep"; I'm going to read *all* the answer choices before I choose one"; I'm going to figure out what kind of text I'm reading and mark it up"—but simply having a plan seems to help students to be more optimistic. Christina also gives her students granola bars and other healthful snacks the day before the HSPT, an attempt to get them to go to bed early and eat a good breakfast!

Unfortunately, teachers sometimes develop counterproductive behavior patterns that communicate low expectations and reinforce students' perceptions of themselves as failures. Table 8-2 lists some of the behaviors that have been identified.

As Brophy (1998) points out, some of these differences are due to the behavior of the students. For example, if students' contributions to discussions are irrelevant or incorrect, it is difficult for teachers to accept and use their ideas. Moreover, the boundary between *appropriate differentiated instruction and inappropriate differential treatment* is often fuzzy. Asking low achievers easier, nonanalytic questions may make instructional sense. Nonetheless, it's important to monitor the extent to which you engage in these behaviors and to reflect on the messages you are sending to your low-achieving or learning disabled students. If you find that you are engaging in a lot of the behaviors listed in Table 8-2, you may be "merely going through the motions of instructing low achievers, without seriously working to help them achieve their potential" (Brophy, 1998, p. 85).

TABLE 8-2. Ways That Teachers May Communicate Low Expectations

---

1. Waiting less time for low achievers to answer a question before giving the answer or calling on someone else.
2. Giving answers to low achievers or calling on someone else rather than helping the students to improve their responses by giving clues or rephrasing questions.
3. Rewarding inappropriate behaviors or incorrect answers.
4. Criticizing low achievers more often for failure.
5. Praising low achievers less often for success.
6. Paying less attention to low achievers.
7. Seating low achievers farther away from the teacher.
8. Demanding less from low achievers than they are capable of learning.
9. Being less friendly in interactions with low achievers; showing less attention and responsiveness; making less eye contact.
10. Providing briefer and less informative answers to their questions.
11. Showing less acceptance and use of low achievers' ideas.
12. Limiting low achievers to low-level, repetitive curriculum with an emphasis on drill and practice tasks.

Source: Brophy, 1998.

Enhancing the Value of the Task

Recall that the students in the classes of our four teachers stressed the importance of teaching in a way that is stimulating. As one student wrote, "Not everything can be fun . . ., but there are ways teachers can make [material] more interesting and more challenging." (See Chapter 2.) This student intuitively understands that motivation to learn depends not only on success expectations, but also on students' perceptions of the value of the task or the rewards that successful completion or mastery will bring. Remember Satisfied Sam? Seeing no value in his course assignments, he invests little effort in them, even though he knows he could be successful. Since students like Sam are unlikely to respond to their teachers' exhortations to work harder, the challenge is to find ways to convince them that the work has (1) *intrinsic value* (doing it will provide enjoyment), (2) *utility value* (doing it will advance their personal goals), or (3) *attainment value* (doing it will affirm their self-concept or fulfill their needs for achievement, understanding, skill mastery, and prestige) (Brophy, 1998; Eccles & Wigfield, 1985). Let's consider some of the strategies that teachers can use to enhance the perception of value.

Relate Lessons to Students' Own Lives

A study by Newby (1991) of the motivational strategies of first-year teachers demonstrated that students are more engaged in classrooms where teachers provide reasons for doing tasks and relate lessons to students' personal experiences. Unfortunately, *he also found that first-year teachers use these "relevance strategies" only occasionally.* (See Figure 8-2.)

I thought about Newby's study as I read a vignette about a seventh-grade teacher attempting to explain why an oxygen atom attracts two hydrogen atoms (Gordon, 1997). Jesse, a boy in the class, did not find this particularly engaging. However, by phrasing the concept in terms of the fact that two seventh-grade girls were attracted to him, the teacher was able to spark his involvement. As Gordon wryly observes, "metaphors involving sex immediately pique adolescents' interest" and can be particularly useful in

SHOE **By JEFF MACNELLY**

FIGURE 8-2. It's important to point out the relevance of learning activities.
(Reprinted with permission © 93 Tribune Media Service, Inc. All rights reserved.)

generating attention and involvement—"as long as the metaphors do not cross the invisible boundary of propriety" (p. 58).

When students are not from the dominant culture, teachers must make a special effort to relate academic content to referents from the students' own culture. This practice not only helps to bridge the gap between the two cultures, it also allows the study of cultural referents in their own right (Ladson-Billings, 1994). Morrell and Duncan-Andrade (in press), English teachers in a large multicultural, urban school in California, provide a compelling example. Reasoning that "students can be highly motivated to learn when course material is represented in the context of more authentic cultural frames," Morrell and Duncan-Andrade used hip-hop music to develop the critical and analytical skills of their underachieving 12th-grade students. The teachers paired "canonical poetry" (e.g., Coleridge's "Kubla Khan" and Eliot's "Love Song of J. Alfred Prufrock") with rap songs (e.g., "If I Ruled the World" by Nas and "The Message" by Grand Master Flash), divided their class into small groups, and assigned one pair of texts to each group. Students were to interpret their poem and song and analyze the links between them. One group, for example, talked about how both Grand Master Flash and T. S. Eliot view their rapidly deteriorating societies as a "wasteland." Another group pointed out that both John Donne and Refuge Camp use a relationship with a lover to symbolize the agony they feel for society. The curriculum unit that Morrell and Duncan-Andrade designed illustrates the power of what Gloria Ladson-Billings (1994) calls *culturally relevant teaching.*

Our four teachers are well aware of the need to relate academic tasks to youngsters' lives. When Donnie teaches percents, she has students do a project entitled "Buying Your First Car." Students work in small groups to determine how much a car they select will actually cost—a task that involves knowing and using compound interest formulas, calculating depreciation, learning about base prices and shipping fees, and figuring out if monthly payments will fit in their budgets. When students are using graphing calculators to do box-plot graphs, they compare Michael Jordon's scores for a year to the scores of his teammates and calculate how one person's data can change the whole graph. When Christina's basic skills students practice distinguishing between fact and opinion, she uses examples that evoke interest: "Motorcycles are dangerous"; "Forty percent of motorcycle accidents result in head injuries"; "The cafeteria needs a new menu"; "The best chicken sandwich around is at Busy Bee's." When Sandy's students do a lab in which they create silver, she jokes with them about getting rich from their labor: "OK, your last task today is to determine how much silver we made here and to decide if I'm going to get rich. Look up the price of silver on the open market. Was this procedure cost-effective?" When Fred's students study the Bill of Rights, they debate whether wearing a T-shirt with an obscene slogan is protected free speech. When Fred teaches about imperialism and colonialism from 1865 to 1900, he links it to present-day racism and "cultural imperialism"—"how everyone in the world wants to wear clothes like theirs and listen to their music." Reflecting on the need for relevance, he comments:

You don't have to do it every day, but little bits and pieces help. Teachers always have to ask, "So what? What does this material have to do with me?" My brother always said, "If it doesn't make me richer or poorer than don't bother me with it." My brother was not a good student. So whenever I teach anything, I use "my brother Bob test." I ask myself, "So what? How will it make my kids richer or poorer in some way?"

Provide Opportunities for Choice

One of most obvious ways to ensure that learning activities connect to individuals' personal interests is to provide opportunities for choice. Moreover, research has shown that when students experience a sense of autonomy and self-determination, they are more likely to be intrinsically motivated (Ryan & Deci, 2000) and to "bond" with school (Roeser, Eccles, & Sameroff, 2000). Mandated curricula and high-stakes standardized testing thwart opportunities for choice, but there are usually alternative ways for students to accomplish requirements. Think about whether students might (1) participate in the design of the academic tasks; (2) decide how the task is to be completed; and/or (3) decide when the task is to be completed (Stipek, 1993).

To prepare for the state's High School Proficiency Test, Christina's students have to complete various writing tasks, such as a persuasive letter or essay on a controversial topic, a cause/effect essay, and a problem/solution essay, but students often choose their own topics for all of these. When Fred's classes study elections, they decide what candidates they will support. When they have to report on a historical figure, they are instructed to choose the figure who seems most like them (or whom they'd like to be like). Sandy encourages students to find different ways of solving problems. Donnie encourages students to "put their heads together" in small groups to identify the homework problems that caused the most difficulty; those are the ones they then review. And all four teachers sometimes allow students to choose their own groups for collaborative work.

Model Interest in Learning and Express Enthusiasm for the Material

When Fred is about to introduce a difficult concept, he announces: "Now please listen to this. Most Americans don't understand this at all; they don't have a clue. But it's really important, and I want you to understand it." Christina often refers to her love of reading and the fact that she writes poetry. When Donnie gives students complex problems that involve a lot of skills and steps, she tells them, "I love problems like this! This is so much fun!" In similar fashion, Sandy frequently exclaims, "This is my favorite part of chemistry," a statement that usually causes students to roll their eyes and respond, "Oh, Mrs. K., *everything* is your favorite part!"

Include Novelty/Variety Elements

During a visit to Donnie's class, I watched as she introduced the "challenge problem of the day." Donnie distributed a xeroxed copy of a dollar bill and told students to figure out how many $1 bills would be needed to make one mile if they were lined up end to end. The enthusiasm generated by the copies of the dollar was palpable. Fred also used money during one observation to make a point about choosing a more difficult, but more ethical course of action. He moved up an aisle and dropped a $5 bill on an empty chair. Turning to the girl sitting in the next seat, he commented, "You could just stick that in your pocket, walk out the door and go to McDonald's, right? Take the money and run. That would certainly be possible, but would it be right?"

In Christina's basic skills class, I watched as students read and discussed *The Martian Chronicles* by Ray Bradbury. Then Christina explained how they were to create small illustrations of key incidents, which would then be assembled in sequential order on large pieces of butcher paper and mounted in the library. As she assigned the incidents ("Andrew, pages 78 and 79, when Tomas is speaking to Pop at the gas station"; "Natal, pages 92 to 94, when the men take up the collection so he can go on the rocket"), it was clear that incorporating this art activity not only reinforced students' understanding of the story but also generated a great deal of enthusiasm.

Provide Opportunities for Students to Respond Actively

So often the teacher talks and moves, while students sit passively and listen. In contrast, when Donnie reviews a problem involving supplementary and complementary angles, she asks students to suggest a strategy for solving the problem. After each suggestion, she asks, "OK, what do I do next? What's the next step?" When students give the answers, she asks, "How did you get that? Explain your reasoning." Fred also structures lessons so that students must be actively involved. When students in his Institute for Politi-

Fred and his students plan a mock trial.

cal and Legal Education (IPLE) class study the judicial system, they engage in a mock trial. When his Contemporary World Issues class discusses extending "most favored nation" status to China, Fred tells his students: "OK, you're one of our state representatives. How are you going to vote? Take out a piece of paper, write down yes or no, and your reasons." After a few minutes, he announces that the House of Representatives is now in session. He asks a few students to share their opinions and then calls the question.

In Christina's classes, where many students voice an entrenched dislike of poetry, Christina works hard to have students experience poetry in a way that is memorable and personal. She divides the class into groups to design a poetry lesson that requires each student in the class (1) to write a poem that uses a particular literary device (e.g., allusion, metaphor, simile, irony, alliteration, consonance, etc.) and (2) to study a poem. Instructing the groups to use as a model Mr. Keating (the Robin Williams character) from *Dead Poets Society,* Christina encourages students to design lessons that "appeal to the senses," that "are like games or sports with a lot of poetry added in," and that require students "to get up and move around." One group, for example, designed an impossible scavenger hunt for the class to attempt and then explained how the hunt related to Poe's poem "El Dorado."

Allow Students to Create Finished Products

Too much school time is devoted to exercises, drills, and practice. Students practice writing, but rarely write. They practice reading skills, but rarely read. They practice mathematical procedures, but rarely do real mathematics. Yet, creating a finished product gives meaning and purpose to assignments and increases students' motivation to learn.

After a fierce winter blizzard that closed school for seven days and left administrators trying to figure out how to make up the lost time, Fred's students wrote letters to state legislators offering various proposals. Since the task was *real,* the letters had to be suitable for mailing; motivation was far greater than it would have been if the task had been a workbook exercise on writing business letters. Similarly, Sandy's labs are not simply exercises in following a prescribed set of steps leading to a foregone conclusion. They are real investigations into real problems.

As an introduction to a multigenre project, Christina's students wrote children's books. First, a parenting-class teacher spoke with the class about writing for young children (e.g., how many characters would be appropriate; whether fantasy themes or something closer to children's own experiences would be most suitable; the importance of using simple vocabulary). Then students wrote their books, engaging in peer editing and revision. They read each others' books and chose six from each class. These were sent to the art classes, where they were illustrated and bound. Drama classes also got involved: They chose four of the books to act out to first-graders who came to the high school.

Provide Opportunities for Students to Interact with Peers

All four teachers firmly believe that motivation (and learning) are enhanced if students are allowed to work with one another. They provide numerous opportunities for peer interaction (a topic that will be explored further in Chapter 10).

Sometimes, groups are carefully planned; at other times, they are formed more casually. For example, one day I saw Donnie shuffle a deck of cards (admitting that she never learned how to do this really well) and then walk around the room, asking each student to pick a card. She then told students to get up and find the person or persons with the same number or face card that they had. Once students had found their partners, she proceeded to explain the group task.

Christina uses groupwork frequently—particularly for tasks that are not inherently interesting. For example, students intensely dislike their *Word Wealth* book with its tedious lessons on prefixes, suffixes, and root words. In order to make the vocabulary exercises more appealing, Christina has students work in groups. She comments: "They still hate the activities, but at least they like working together (and sometimes they get candy to sweeten the deal even more)!"

Provide Extrinsic Rewards

As Christina's last comment suggests, some effective managers find it useful to provide students with rewards for engaging in the behaviors that support learning (such as paying attention and participating) and for academic achievement. The use of rewards in classrooms is based on the psychological principle of *positive reinforcement:* Behavior that is rewarded is strengthened and is therefore likely to be repeated. Although rewards do not increase the perceived value of the behavior or the task, they link performance of the behavior or successful completion of the task to attractive, desirable consequences.

Rewards can be divided into three categories: social rewards, activity rewards, and tangible rewards. *Social rewards* are verbal and nonverbal indications that you recognize and appreciate students' behavior or achievements. A pat on the back, a smile, a thumbs-up signal—these are commonly used social rewards that are low in cost and readily available.

Praise can also function as a social reward. In order to be effective, however, praise must be *specific and sincere.* Instead of "Good paper," you can try something like this: "Your paper shows a firm grasp of the distinction between metaphor and similes." Instead of "You were great this morning," try, "The way you came into the room, took off your baseball caps, and immediately got out your notebooks was terrific." Being specific will make your praise more informative; it will also help you to avoid using the same tired, old phrases week after week, phrases that quickly lose any impact (e.g., "good job"). If praise is to serve as a reinforcer, it also needs to be *contingent on the behavior you are trying to strengthen.* In other words, it should be given only when that behavior occurs, so that students understand exactly what evoked the praise.

Donnie distributes a lab worksheet that asks students to draw a parallelogram and then work through five activities to "discover" the figure's properties. She stresses that students should write down their observations after each activity and then draw some final conclusions. As students work on the problems, she circulates through the room, helping, correcting, encour-

aging, and commenting. When she sees Shaneika's paper, she tells her: "Shaneika, you are really following directions. You're writing the answers as you go along."

In addition to pats on the back and verbal praise, some teachers institute more formal ways of recognizing accomplishment, improvement, or cooperation. For example, they may display student work, provide award certificates, nominate students for school awards given at the end of the year, or select "Students of the Week." Whichever approach you use, be careful that this strategy of public recognition doesn't backfire by causing students embarrassment. As Sandy reminded us in Chapter 5, secondary students generally do not want to stand out from their peers.

In addition to social rewards, teachers sometimes use *special activities* as rewards for good behavior or achievement. In junior and senior high, watching a video (with popcorn!), listening to music, having free time, or having a night of no homework can be very reinforcing. One way of determining which activities should be used as rewards is to listen carefully to students' requests. If they ask you for the opportunity to listen to music or have a popcorn party, you can be confident that those activities will be reinforcing (at least for those particular students). It's also helpful to observe what activities students engage in when they have free time (e.g., do they read magazines? talk with friends? draw?)

Finally, teachers can use *tangible, material rewards* for good behavior—cookies, candy, key chains, pencils—although such rewards are used less in high school than in elementary school. For example, Donnie goes to a discount supermarket and buys a big supply of candy that she keeps in a back closet; when students have been especially cooperative, she'll break out the Twizzlers for an unexpected treat. Similarly, Fred sometimes gives prizes when students have to review factual information for tests, a task they usually find boring. He may have students play vocabulary bingo, telling them: "I have two prizes in my pocket for the winner—two tickets for an all-expense-paid trip to Hawaii or a piece of candy. You get whichever one I pull out of my pocket first." Every now and then, Fred also uses candy to show his appreciation for good behavior. In his words,

If someone has never given me grief, I may be moved to a spontaneous act of generosity. I'll say, "Here take this," and give them a Sugar Daddy or package of Sweet Tarts. It's amazing; kids go crazy over a little piece of candy.

Problems with Rewards

The practice of providing extrinsic rewards has been the focus of considerable controversy. One objection is that giving students tangible rewards in exchange for good behavior or academic performance is tantamount to bribery. Proponents of this position argue that students should engage in appropriate behavior and activities for their own sake: They should be quiet during in-class assignments because that is the socially responsible thing to do; they should do their homework so that they can practice skills taught during class; they should learn verb conjugations in Spanish because they need to know them. Other educators acknowledge the desirability of such intrinsic motivation, but believe that the use of rewards is inevitable in situations where people are not completely free to follow their own inclinations. Even Ryan and Deci (2000), two psychologists who strongly endorse the importance of self-determination and autonomy, acknowledge that teachers "cannot always rely on intrinsic motivation to foster learning" since "many of the tasks that educators want their students to perform are not inherently interesting or enjoyable" (p. 55).

Another objection to the use of rewards is the fact that they are attempts to control and manipulate people. When we dispense rewards, we are essentially saying, "Do this, and you'll get that"—an approach not unlike the way we train our pets. Indeed, Alfie Kohn, author of *Punished by Rewards: The Trouble with Gold Stars, Incentive Plans, A's, Praise, and Other Bribes* (1993), contends that rewards and punishments are "two sides of the same coin" (p. 50). Although rewards are certainly more pleasurable, they are "every bit as controlling as punishments, even if they control by seduction" (p. 51). According to Kohn, if we want youngsters to become self-regulating, responsible, caring individuals, we must abandon attempts at external control and provide students with opportunities to develop competence, connection, and autonomy in caring classroom communities.

Another major concern is that rewarding students for behaving in certain ways actually *undermines their intrinsic motivation to engage in those behaviors.* This question was explored in an influential study conducted by Lepper, Greene, and Nisbett (1973). First, the researchers identified preschoolers who showed interest in a particular drawing activity during free play. Then they met with the children individually. Some children were simply invited to draw with the materials (the "no-reward" subjects). Others were told they could receive a "good-player" award, which they received for drawing (the "expected-reward" subjects). Still others were invited to draw and were then given an unexpected reward at the end (the "unexpected-reward" subjects). Subsequent observations during free play revealed that the children who had been promised a reward ahead of time engaged in the art activity half as much as they had initially. Children in the other two groups showed no change.

The study by Lepper, Greene, and Nisbett stimulated a great deal of research on the potentially detrimental effects of external rewards. Although the results were not always consistent, this research led educators to conclude that *rewarding people for doing something that is inherently pleasurable decreases their interest in continuing that behavior.* A common explanation for this effect is the *overjustification hypothesis.* It appears to work like this: Individuals being rewarded reason that the task must not be very interesting or engaging, since they have to be rewarded (i.e., provided with extra justification) for undertaking it.

The detrimental effect of extrinsic reward on intrinsic motivation has been—and continues to be—hotly debated. In fact, reviews of the research (Cameron & Pierce, 1994; Deci, Koestner, & Ryan, 1999) have reached contradictory conclusions about the effects of expected tangible rewards. According to Cameron and Pierce, it's all right to say, "If you complete the assignment accurately, you'll get a coupon for something at the school store at the end of the period" (reward contingent on completion and level of performance), but it's *not* all right to say, "Work on the assignment and you'll get a coupon for something at the school store at the end of the period" (noncontingent reward). In contrast, Deci, Koestner, and Ryan contend that expected "tangible rewards offered for engaging in, completing, or doing well at a task" are *all* deleterious to intrinsic motivation (p. 656). With respect to verbal rewards and unexpected tangible rewards, the two reviews are more consistent: Both sets of researchers conclude that verbal praise can enhance intrinsic motivation and that unexpected tangible rewards have no detrimental effect.

At the present time, caution in the use of external rewards is clearly in order. As you contemplate a system of rewards for your classroom, keep in mind the following suggestions:

Use verbal rewards to increase intrinsic motivation for academic tasks. It seems clear that praise can have a positive impact on students' intrinsic motivation. But remember that teenagers may be embarrassed by public praise, and they are good at detecting phoniness. In order to be reinforcing, praise should be specific, sincere, and contingent on the behavior you are trying to strengthen.

Save tangible rewards for activities that students find unattractive. When students already enjoy doing a task, there's no need to provide tangible rewards. Save tangible rewards for activities that students tend to find boring and aversive.

If you're using tangible rewards, provide them unexpectedly, after the task performance. In this way, students are more likely to view the rewards as information about their performance and as an expression of the teacher's pleasure rather than as an attempt to control their behavior.

Be extremely careful about using expected tangible rewards. If you choose to use them, be sure to make them contingent upon completion of a task or achieving a specific level of performance. If you reward students simply for engaging in a task, regardless of their performance, they are likely to spend less time on the task once the reward is removed.

Make sure that you select rewards that students like. You may think that animal stickers are really neat, but if your high school students do not find them rewarding, their behavior will not be reinforced.

Keep your program of rewards simple. An elaborate system of rewards is impossible to maintain in the complex world of the classroom. The fancier your system, the more likely that you will abandon it. Moreover, if rewards become too salient, they overshadow more intrinsic reasons for behaving in certain ways. Students become so preoccupied with collecting, counting, and comparing that they lose sight of why the behavior is necessary or valuable.

Motivating Underachieving and Disaffected Students

Finding ways to enhance students' motivation is particularly daunting when students are disaffected, apathetic, or resistant. As Brophy (1998) observes, such students find academic tasks relatively meaningless and resist engaging in them although they know that they could be successful. Some may even be fearful that school learning "will make them into something that they do not want to become" (p. 205). This fear is apparent in some African Americans and other students of color who equate academic achievement with "acting white." In a now classic paper, Fordham and Ogbu (1986) describe how bright black students may "put brakes" on their academic achievement by not studying or doing homework, cutting class, being late, and not participating in class:

> *This problem arose partly because white Americans traditionally refused to acknowledge that black Americans are capable of intellectual achievement, and partly because black Americans subsequently began to doubt their own intellectual ability, began to define academic success as white people's prerogative, and began to discourage their peers, perhaps unconsciously, from emulating white people in academic striving. . . . (p. 177)*

Motivating resistant, underachieving, or apathetic students requires "resocialization" (Brophy, 1998, p. 203). This means using the strategies described in this chapter in more sustained, systematic, and personalized ways. Extrinsic rewards may be especially useful in this regard (Hidi & Harackiewicz, 2000). By triggering engagement in tasks that students initially view as boring or irrelevant, "there is at least a chance" that real interest will develop (p. 159).

An inspiring example of motivating the academically unmotivated comes from an account by Linda Christensen (1994), a high school teacher in Portland, Oregon. In *Building Community from Chaos,* Christensen writes about her fourth block senior English class, a tracked class where most of the students were short on credits to graduate but long on anger and attitude. Convinced that English class was a waste of time, her students made it clear that they didn't want "worksheets, sentence combining, reading novels and discussing them, writing about 'stuff we don't care about' " (p. 51). Christensen knew she needed to engage them "because they were loud, unruly, and out of control" (p. 51), but she didn't know how. She eventually decided to use the novel, *Thousand Pieces of Gold,* by Ruthann Lum McCunn, a book normally read by her college-level course in Contemporary Literature and Society:

> *Students weren't thrilled with the book; in fact they weren't reading it. I'd plan a 90 minute lesson around the reading and dialogue journal they were supposed to be keeping, but only a few students were prepared. Most didn't even attempt to lie about the fact that they weren't reading and clearly weren't planning on it.*

In an attempt to get them involved in the novel, I read aloud an evocative passage about the unemployed peasants sweeping through the Chinese country side pillaging, raping, and grabbing what was denied them through legal employment. Suddenly students saw their own lives reflected back at them through Chen whose anger at losing his job and ultimately his family led him to become an outlaw. Chen created a new family with this group of bandits. Students could relate: Chen was a gang member. I had stumbled on a way to interest my class. The violence created a contact point between the literature and the students' lives.

This connection, this reverberation across cultures, time and gender challenged the students' previous notion that reading and talking about novels didn't have relevance for them. They could empathize with the Chinese but also explore those issues in their own lives. (pp. 51–52)

Concluding Comments

A while back, a professor of educational psychology told me that learning about classroom management would be unnecessary if prospective teachers understood how to enhance students' motivation. Although I thought his argument was naive and unrealistic, I understood—and agreed with—its underlying premise; *namely, that students who are interested and involved in the academic work at hand are less likely to daydream, disrupt, and defy.* In other words, management and motivation are inextricably linked.

As you contemplate ways to increase your students' expectations for success and the value they place on academic tasks, remember that motivating students doesn't happen accidentally. Fred emphasizes this point when he contends that "how I will motivate my students" should be an integral component of every lesson plan. Fortunately, the motivational strategies discussed in this chapter are consistent with current thinking about good instruction, which emphasizes students' active participation, collaborative group-work, and the use of varying assessments (Brophy, 1998).

Finally, remember the suggestions in Chapter 5 for creating a safer, more caring classroom. Rogers and Renard (1999) contend that "students are motivated when they believe that teachers treat them like people and care about them personally and educationally" (p. 34). Research by Kathryn Wentzel (1997, 1998) confirms this assertion. In two recent studies, Wentzel demonstrated that when middle-school students perceive their teachers as caring and supportive, they are more likely to be academically motivated, to engage in classroom activities, and to behave in prosocial, responsible ways. As Brophy (1998) observes: "You can become your own most powerful motivational tool by establishing productive relationships with each of your students" (p. 254).

✿ Summary

Although teachers are responsible for enhancing motivation, this chapter began by questioning the belief that "good teachers should make learning fun." I argued that such a goal is unrealistic and inappropriate given the constraints of the secondary classroom—compulsory attendance, required curricula, class sizes that inhibit individualization, and the specter of high-stakes standardized testing. A more appropriate, realistic goal is to stimulate students' *motivation to learn,* whereby students pursue academic activities because they find them meaningful and worthwhile.

An expectancy–value framework

- Motivation depends on (1) students' expectation of success and (2) the value they place on the task (or the rewards that it may bring).
- If either factor is missing, there will be no motivation.

Strategies for increasing expectations of success

- Provide opportunities for success.
- Teach students to set reasonable goals and to evaluate their own performance.
- Help students recognize the relationship between effort and outcome.
- Provide informative feedback.
- Provide special motivational support to discouraged students.

Strategies for enhancing the value of the task

- Relate lessons to students' own lives.
- Provide opportunities for choice.
- Model interest in learning and express enthusiasm for the material.
- Include novelty/variety elements.
- Provide opportunities for students to respond actively.
- Allow students to create finished products.
- Provide opportunities for students to interact with peers.
- Provide extrinsic rewards:

    Keep in mind the different types of rewards:
    Social rewards
    Special activities
    Tangible rewards
    Be aware that rewarding people for doing something they already like to do may decrease their interest in continuing that behavior.
    Think carefully about when and how to use rewards:
    Use verbal rewards to increase intrinsic motivation for academic tasks.
    Save tangible rewards for activities that students find unattractive.

Provide tangible rewards unexpectedly (after the task performance).

Provide expected tangible rewards only for completion of a task or for achieving a specific level of performance.

Select rewards that your students like.

Keep your reward program simple.

By working to ensure that students are engaged in learning activities, you can avoid many of the managerial problems that arise when students are bored and frustrated. Management and motivation are closely intertwined.

Activities

1. Design a "slanty rope assignment" in your content area that will enable students of varying achievement levels to experience success. For example, the task might vary in complexity; it might be open-ended, allowing a variety of acceptable responses; it might require the use of different reference materials; or it might allow students to choose the format in which they demonstrate their understanding (e.g., a report, poster, or role-play). (Use the example of Mr. Yin in this chapter as an example.)

2. Select a topic in your content area and design a lesson or activity that incorporates at least one of the strategies for enhancing perceived value. For example, you might relate the material to students' lives, provide opportunities for choice, allow students to work with peers, or produce a final product.

3. In the following two vignettes, the teachers have directed the activity. Think about ways they could have involved students in the planning, directing, creating, or evaluating. Rewrite each vignette to show this more student-centered approach.

   a. Mrs. Peters felt that the unit her seventh-grade class completed on folk tales would lend itself to a class play. She chose Paul Bunyan and Pecos Bill as the stories to dramatize. The students were excited as Mrs. Peters gave out parts and assigned students to paint scenery. Mrs. Peters wrote a script and sent it home for the students to memorize. She asked parents to help make the costumes. After three weeks of practice, the play was performed for the elementary classes and the parents.

   b. Mr. Wilkins wanted his 10th-grade World Civilization class to develop an understanding about ancient civilizations. He assigned a five-part project. Students had to research four civilizations (Egyptian, Mesopotamian, Indus Valley, and Shang); write a biography of Howard Carter, a famous archaeologist; describe three pyramids (step, Great Pyramid, Pyramid of Sesostris II); outline the reigns of five kings (Hammurabi, Thutmose III, Ramses II, David, and Nebuchadnezzar); and make a model of a pyramid. He gave the class four weeks to complete the projects and then collected them, graded them, and displayed them in the school library.

4. Interview an experienced, effective teacher about the motivational strategies he or she finds particularly effective with disaffected, resistant students.

✦ For Further Reading

Brophy, J. (1998). *Motivating students to learn.* Boston: McGraw-Hill.

Burden, P. R. (2000). *Powerful classroom management strategies: Motivating students to learn.* Thousand Oaks, CA: Corwin Press.

Kohn, A. (1993). *Punished by rewards: The trouble with gold stars, incentive plans, A's, praise, and other bribes.* Boston: Houghton Mifflin Company.

Stipek, D. J. (1993). *Motivation to learn: From theory to practice.* 2nd ed. Boston: Allyn and Bacon.

Tomlinson, C. A. (1999). *The differentiated classroom: Responding to the needs of all learners.* Alexandria, VA: Association for Supervision and Curriculum Development.

✦ References

Anderman, E. M., & Maehr, M. L. (1994). Motivation and schooling in the middle grades. *Review of Educational Research, 64*(2), 287–309.

Ayers, W. (1993). *To teach: The journey of a teacher.* New York: Teachers College Press.

Brophy, J. (1998). *Motivating students to learn.* Boston: McGraw-Hill.

Brophy, J. (1987). Synthesis of research on strategies for motivating students to learn. *Educational Leadership, 45,* 40–48.

Cameron, J., & Pierce, W. D. (1994). Reinforcement, reward, and intrinsic motivation: A meta-analysis. *Review of Educational Research, 64,* 363–423.

Christensen, L. (1994). Building community from chaos. In B. Bigelow, L. Christensen, S. Karp, B. Miner, & B. Peterson (Eds.), *Rethinking our Classrooms: Teaching for Equity and Justice* (A special edition of *Rethinking Schools*). Milwaukee, WI: Rethinking Schools.

Deci, E. L., Koestner, R., & Ryan, R. M. (1999). A meta-analytic review of experiments examining the effects of extrinsic rewards on intrinsic motivation. *Psychological Bulletin, 125*(6), 627–668.

Eccles, J., & Wigfield, A. (1985). Teacher expectations and student motivation. In J. Dusek (Ed.), *Teacher expectancies* (pp. 185–226). Hillsdale, NJ: Erlbaum.

Feather, N. (Ed.) (1982). *Expectations and actions.* Hillsdale, NJ: Erlbaum.

Fisher, C. W., Berliner, D. C., Filby, N. N., Marliave, R., Cahen, L. S., & Dishaw, M. M. (1980). Teaching behaviors, academic learning time, and student achievement: An overview. In C. Denham & A. Lieberman (Eds.), *Time to learn.* Washington, D.C.: U. S. Department of Education, pp. 7–32.

Fordham, S., & Ogbu, J. U. (1986). Black students' school success: Coping with the "burden of 'acting white.'" *The Urban Review, 18*(3), 176–206.

Good, T. L., & Brophy, J. E. (2000). *Looking in classrooms.* 8th ed. New York: Addison Wesley Longman.

Gordon, R. L. (1997). How novice teachers can succeed with adolescents. *Educational Leadership, 54*(7), 56–58.

Hidi, S., & Harackiewicz, J. M. (2000). Motivating the academically unmotivated: A critical issue for the 21st century. *Review of Educational Research, 70*(2), 151–179.

Kohn, A. (1993). *Punished by rewards: The trouble with gold stars, incentive plans, A's, praise, and other bribes.* Boston: Houghton Mifflin.

Ladson-Billings, G. (1994). *The dreamkeepers: Successful teachers of African American children.* San Francisco: Jossey-Bass.

Lepper, M., Greene, D., & Nisbett, R. E. (1973). Undermining children's intrinsic interest with extrinsic rewards: A test of the "overjustification" hypothesis. *Journal of Personality and Social Psychology, 28,* 129–137.

Morrell, E., & Duncan-Andrade, J. (in press). What they do learn in school: Using hip-hop as a bridge between youth culture and canonical poetry texts. In J. Mahiri (Ed.), *What they don't learn in school: Literacy in the lives of urban youth.* New York: Peter Lang.

Newby, T. (1991). Classroom motivation: Strategies of first-year teachers. *Journal of Educational Psychology, 83,* 195–200.

Roeser, R. W., Eccles, J. S., & Sameroff, A. J. (2000). School as a context of early adolescents' academic and social–emotional development: A summary of research findings. *The Elementary School Journal, 100*(5), 443–471.

Rogers, S., & Renard, L. (1999). Relationship-driven teaching. *Educational Leadership, 57*(1), 34–37.

Ryan, R. M., & Deci. E. L. (2000). Intrinsic and extrinsic motivations: Classic definitions and new directions. *Contemporary Educational Psychology, 25,* 54–67.

Stipek, D. J. (1993). *Motivation to learn: From theory to practice.* 2nd ed. Boston: Allyn and Bacon.

Tomlinson, C. A. (1999). *The differentiated classroom: Responding to the needs of all learners.* Alexandria, VA: Association for Supervision and Curriculum Development.

Wentzel, K. R. (1997). Student motivation in middle school: The role of perceived pedagogical caring. *Journal of Educational Psychology, 89*(3), 411–419.

Wentzel, K. R. (1998). Social relationships and motivation in middle school: The role of parents, teachers, and peers. *Journal of Educational Psychology, 90*(2), 202–209.

Managing Independent Work

Chapter 1 discussed the assumption that the tasks of classroom management vary across different classroom situations. I pointed out that the classroom is not a "homogenized glob" (Kounin & Sherman, 1979) but is composed of numerous "subsettings" such as opening routines, homework routines, teacher presentations, transitions, and whole-class discussions. How order is defined in each of these subsettings is likely to vary. For example, during transitions students may be allowed to sharpen pencils and talk with friends, but these same behaviors may be prohibited during a whole-group discussion or a teacher presentation.

Variations in behavioral expectations are understandable, given the fact that subsettings have different goals and pose different challenges in terms of establishing and maintaining order. To be an effective manager, you must consider the unique characteristics of your classroom's subsettings and decide how your students need to behave in each one in order to maximize opportunities for learning.

This chapter focuses on the subsetting known as *independent work,* the situation in which students are assigned to work at their desks with their own materials, while the teacher is free to monitor the total class—to observe students' performance, provide support and feedback, engage in mini-conferences, and prepare students for home-work assignments. Independent work is often used to provide students with the chance to practice or review previously presented material. For example, in "direct instruc-tion" or "explicit teaching" (Rosenshine, 1986), the teacher reviews previous material, presents new material in small steps, and then gives students the opportunity to prac-tice, first under supervision ("guided practice") and then independently ("independent practice").

To be honest, this chapter almost didn't get written. Independent work is also referred to as *seatwork,* and this term has very negative connotations, particularly among educa-tors who promote students' active participation and collaboration. Indeed, when I sat down with Donnie, Sandy, Fred, and Christina to discuss their views, I found heated dif-ferences of opinion on this particular subsetting. On one hand, Fred argued that seatwork could be a valuable activity:

> *I use seatwork to give kids the opportunity to practice skills like making predictions, valid inferences, generalizations. . . . Intellectual skills like these benefit from practice just like a backhand stroke in tennis. If I have 27 kids doing an assignment in class, I can walk around, see immediately what they're doing, give individual critiques, catch them if they're having a problem. I can't give that individual, immediate feedback if the work is done as homework.*

On the other hand, Sandy was vehemently negative: "I hate seatwork," she told us. "As far as I'm concerned, it's just a way of killing time." Similarly, Donnie claimed that she never used seatwork. I pointed out that I had frequently observed her using a pattern of direct instruction, beginning class with a review of the homework, then introducing a small segment of the new lesson, and having students do one or two problems at their seats while she circulated throughout the room. Donnie readily acknowledged her use of "guided practice," but argued that this was not seatwork:

> *It's not like elementary school, where you have different reading groups, and you have to find a way for kids to be busy for long periods of time while you're working with a small group. Most of my instruction is done with the whole group, so there's no need for all the kids to be sitting there quietly working on worksheets.*

Finally, Christina admitted some ambivalence. She acknowledged that whenever she heard the word *seatwork,* she immediately thought of "bad teachers who sit at their desks grading papers, writing lesson plans, or even reading the newspaper, while their students do boring work designed to keep them in their seats and quiet." But she also recognized that independent work was sometimes useful:

> *Realistically, there are times when I need to conference with individuals, so I need the rest of the class to be meaningfully occupied. Or I might want*

students to do something in class so I don't have to give them additional homework (especially if they're already working on a long-term assignment). Or I might want the work to be preceded by some instruction and to be followed by an interactive activity. This necessarily situates the seatwork in the middle of the class period, rather than for homework. But because I'm so leery about seatwork, I always try to ask myself, "Does this work need to be done in the classroom, or should it be done as homework?"

We debated, we moralized, and we shared anecdotes about the awfulness or the usefulness of seatwork. Eventually, we came to realize that there was no fundamental difference of opinion among us. We all agreed that teachers sometimes need to assign work that provides students with the opportunity to practice. We also agreed that seatwork didn't have to mean silence; in fact, all the teachers felt strongly that students should generally be allowed to help one another. But we also agreed that seatwork is too often busywork, that it frequently goes on for too long, and that too many teachers use it as a substitute for active teaching. As Donnie put it:

Some teachers think of seatwork as "give them something to do all period so I can do something else." They'll teach for 10 minutes, then give their students 30 minutes of seatwork, and sit down. That's not seatwork—that's a free period.

This chapter begins by discussing the problems that occur when independent work is misused—when teachers do not reflect on ways to organize the work so that it is appropriate and meaningful for students. We then go on to consider the ways Donnie, Sandy, Fred, and Christina try to avoid, or at least minimize, these problems. The intent is *not* to encourage you to spend large amounts of time in seatwork activities, but rather, to provide you with a way of thinking about seatwork so that you can make better decisions about when and how to use it. Throughout the discussion, the two terms—*independent work* and *seatwork*—are used interchangeably.

What's Wrong with Seatwork?

As Christina points out, the term *seatwork* conjures up images of bored, passive students doing repetitive, tedious worksheets while teachers sit at their desks calculating grades or reading the newspaper. Consider the following description of a typical seatwork situation. It was observed by Robert Everhart (1983), who spent two years conducting fieldwork in a junior high school. His book, *Reading, Writing and Resistance: Adolescence and Labor in a Junior High School,* is a chronicle of the daily routine experienced by students, and to some extent, by teachers. This scene takes place in Marcy's English class, where students are supposed to be learning about the proper form of business letters.

First, Marcy asked the class to turn to the chapter on business letters in their grammar books and read that section. After five minutes Marcy asked the class, "How many have not yet finished?" Initially about one-third of the class raised their hands. Roy, sitting in the rear near where I was sitting, nudged John. John then spoke up, "I'm not finished."

"I ain't finished either," Roy added, smiling. Needless to say, they both had finished; I had seen them close their books a few minutes earlier and then proceed to trade a Mad *magazine back and forth.*

"Well, I'll give you a few more minutes, but hurry up," said Marcy. Those not finished continued reading while the rest of the class began engaging in different activities: looking out the window, doodling, and pulling pictures from their wallets and looking at them. Roy then pulled a copy of Cycle *magazine from beneath his desk and began leafing through it. After a few minutes Marcy went to the blackboard and began outlining the structure of the business letter.*

"Ok, first thing we do is to place the return address—where, class?"

"On the paper," said one boy slouched in his chair and tapping his pencil.

"All right, comedian, that's obvious. Where else?"

"On the front side of the paper."

"Come on class, get serious! Where do you place the return address? Larry?"

Marcy eventually gets through a description and explanation of the form of the business letter. She then informs students that they will be writing their own business letters, which will be due at the end of the following week. Today, they are to write the initial paragraph:

After about 10 minutes of writing, Marcy asked, "How many are not finished with their paragraph?" About six students raised their hands. "OK, I'll give you a few minutes to finish up. The rest of you, I want you to read your paragraphs to each other because I want you to read them to the class tomorrow and they'd better be clear; if they aren't clear to you now they won't be clear to the class tomorrow."

One of the students at the back of the room seemed somewhat surprised at this. "Hey, you didn't say anything about having to read these in front of the class."

"Yeah, I don't want to read mine in front of the class," added Phil.

Marcy put her hands on her hips and stated emphatically, "Now come on, class, you'll all want to do a good job and this will give you a chance to practice and improve your paragraphs before they're submitted for grades. And you all want to get 'A's', I'm sure." There was a chorus of laughs from most of the class and Marcy smiled.

"I don't care," I heard one girl say under her breath.

"Yeah, I don't care either, just so I get this stupid thing done."

After saying that, Don turned to Art and said, "Hey, Art, what you writing your letter on?"

"I am writing the Elephant Rubber Company, telling them that their rubbers were too small."

"Wow," Ron replied.

"Don't think I'll write that letter though. Marcy will have a bird."

"For sure," Art replied.

The students continued talking to each other, which finally prompted Marcy to get up from her desk and say, "Class, get busy or some of you will be in after school."

Analysis of this scenario allows us to identify five problems that are frequently associated with seatwork. (These are summarized in Table 9-1.) First, it is clear that *the assignment is not meaningful to students.* Don calls the business letter a "stupid thing," Art jokes about writing to the Elephant Rubber Company, and an unnamed girl mumbles that she doesn't care about getting an A. In Fred's terms, Marcy has given her students the kind of "garbage assignment" that is responsible for seatwork's bad reputation. "Garbage assignments" are not only a waste of precious learning time, they also foster

TABLE 9-1. The Problems with Seatwork

ALL TOO OFTEN:
1. Assignments are not meaningful, educationally useful, or motivating.
2. Assignments are not matched to students' achievement levels.
3. Directions are not clear and thorough.
4. Teachers do not circulate and monitor students' comprehension and behavior.
5. Some students finish early, while others do not finish.

Calvin and Hobbes
by Bill Watterson

FIGURE 9-1. Calvin's response to seatwork that is too difficult for him.
(CALVIN AND HOBBES © Watterson, Dist. by UNIVERSAL PRESS SYNDICATE. Reprinted with permission. All rights reserved.)

boredom, alienation, and misbehavior. Clearly, if students do not perceive the value of a seatwork assignment, they are unlikely to become invested in it. That's when teachers have to resort to threats about detention or extrinsic incentives like grades. Recall Marcy's words. First she tells her class, "And you all want to get 'A's,' I'm sure." Later she warns, "Class, get busy or some of you will be in after school."

Second, it appears that Marcy's assignment *does not match students' varying achievement levels.* (Figure 9-1 depicts Calvin's rather special strategy for dealing with seatwork that is too difficult for him.) For some students, the reading assignment seems too easy; they finish reading quickly and fill their time by doodling, looking out the window, and reading magazines. Others seem to find the reading more difficult and need "a few more minutes." Similarly, writing one paragraph in 10 minutes doesn't seem like a particularly challenging assignment for most of Marcy's students, yet six students indicate they are not finished when Marcy checks their progress. (Of course, it's possible that they have just been wasting time.)

Assigning work that does not match students' achievement levels is typical of the behaviors exhibited by the less effective managers studied by Carolyn Evertson and Ed Emmer (1982; see Chapter 4 for a fuller description of this study). You may recall that Evertson and Emmer observed mathematics and English teachers at the junior high level and identified those who were more effective managers and those who were less effective. The observations led Evertson and Emmer to conclude that the more effective teachers had greater awareness of students' entering skills:

An example of an activity showing low understanding was an assignment in one of the lower achieving English classes to "Write an essay from the perspective of an inanimate object." The problem was compounded by an unclear explanation of the term, perspective. Narratives noted more instances of vocabulary beyond some of the students' comprehension. As a consequence of being more aware of student skills. . ., the more effective teachers' classes had more success in participating in class activities and completing assignments. (p. 496)

A third problem is that Marcy *does not provide her students with clear, complete directions.* At the beginning of the period, Marcy tells the students to read the chapter on business letters, but she says nothing about why they are to read the chapter, how long they have, or whether they should take notes. In other words, she merely tells them to "do it"— without explaining the purpose for reading or suggesting strategies that might be used. Nor does Marcy explain that they will be writing their own letters later in the period. It is only after reviewing the form of the business letter that Marcy instructs her students to write the initial paragraph, and once again, she neglects to tell them what will be coming next— namely, that they will be reading the paragraphs aloud the following day. (Marcy might have made this decision at the last minute, in order to provide an activity for students who finished early.) Not surprisingly, some of the students react with displeasure. One complains, "Hey, you didn't say anything about having to read these in front of the class," while another protests, "Yeah, I don't want to read mine in front of the class."

Marcy's lack of clarity and thoroughness is reminiscent of the less effective managers studied by Evertson and Emmer (1982). In addition to differing in their awareness of students' entering abilities, teachers also differed in terms of skill in communicating information. More effective English teachers were clearer in giving directions and stating objectives than less effective teachers. (Interestingly, this difference did not appear in comparisons of more and less effective math teachers.) According to Evertson and Emmer, more effective managers

were better able to segment complex tasks into step-by-step procedures and to help students understand their tasks, and how to accomplish them. When students knew what to do and had the skills to do it, they were more likely to stay on task. (p. 496)

A fourth problem evident in Marcy's class is her *lack of monitoring.* Although the vignette doesn't explicitly describe what Marcy is doing while her students are reading and writing, the last paragraph does state that Marcy gets up from her desk to admonish students who are talking. Furthermore, Marcy not only has to ask how many students have not yet finished, she also seems unaware that students in the rear of the room are reading *Mad* magazine. These are sure signs that Marcy is not circulating through the room, checking on students' progress, helping them with problems, and providing feedback. If Marcy is not going to provide this supervision and support, she might as well have her students do the assignment at home.

Finally, Marcy does not really plan for the fact that *students work at different paces.* They may *begin* seatwork at the same time, but they never *finish* at the same time. "Ragged" endings can upset a schedule that looked beautiful on paper. Students who cannot complete assignments in the allotted time may have to do the assignment for homework. Students who complete their work earlier than you expected need something to keep them occupied; if they must sit and wait with nothing to do, they may distract students who are still working. In Marcy's class, students who finish earlier than their peers are actually quite well behaved: They read *Mad* and *Cycle* magazines, look out the window, doodle, and look at pictures from their wallets. Nonetheless, they are wasting time that could be spent on more profitable activities.

Implications for Classroom Practice

Analysis of Marcy's seatwork sheds light on the special problems associated with this particular subsetting of the classroom. In this section of the chapter, we consider ways to avoid or at least minimize these problems. (See Table 9-2.)

Assign Work That Is Meaningful and Relevant to Students

Secondary textbooks generally have questions, activities, and exercises at the end of each chapter, and some come with supplemental study guides, workbooks, or activity sheets. Since these materials may not always be meaningful and relevant to students, it is essential that you evaluate the activities you assign. As Fred observes:

> *The typical seatwork assignment is not well thought through. It's mindlessly designed and mindlessly done. "Read and answer the questions on page 287." "Fill in the blank." "Read and outline the chapter." What's really scary is when the kids don't even think assignments like that are so bad! That tells me that they're so used to that kind of thing, they don't realize it's a waste of time.* But seatwork doesn't have to be that way.

In order to be sure that the independent work they assign is not *"that way,"* Donnie, Christina, Sandy, and Fred carefully evaluate the tasks they give students to complete during class. Here are some of the questions they ask themselves:

What is the purpose of the task?

Does the task relate to current instruction? Are students likely to see the connection?

Are students likely to see the task as something worth doing or something boring and unrewarding?

TABLE 9-2. Guidelines for Minimizing the Problems with Seatwork

1. Provide assignments that are meaningful and relevant.
2. Match assignments to students' varying achievement levels.
3. Make sure written and oral directions are clear and thorough.
4. Monitor behavior and comprehension.
5. Plan for ragged endings.

Does the task provide students with an opportunity to practice important skills or to apply what they are learning?

Does the task provide students with the opportunity to think critically or to engage in problem solving?

Does the task require reading and writing, or does it simply ask students to fill in the blank, underline, or circle?

Does the task require higher-level responses or does it emphasize low-level, factual recall and "drill and kill" practice of isolated subskills?

Is there a reason the task should be done in school (e.g., the need for coaching by the teacher) rather than at home?

Many teachers prefer to create their own assignments rather than to rely on commercially prepared materials. In this way, they are better able to connect the tasks with students' backgrounds and experiences, target particular problems that students are having, and provide greater individualization. For example, when Fred wants students to become familiar with the resources in the library, he asks them to do tasks like these:

List three facts on one topic that interests you using the electronic database *Facts on File.*

Use an almanac to find a country that begins with the first letter of your last name and tell the population of that nation.

Use *The New York Times* electronic database (Internet or CD-ROM) to identify an important event that occurred on your last birthday.

Locate a biography about a person whose last name begins with the same letter as your first name.

According to Fred, this simple way of individualizing the assignment has a very positive effect on students' motivation. (And there's an added bonus: Students have to do their own work.)

Fred acknowledges that he can't always "be creative and wonderful five days a week, week after week," but he always tries to ensure that the independent work he assigns has a valid purpose. It's worth keeping his comments in mind:

Look, I'm human . . . There are times when I'll give kids seatwork assignments that are less than wonderful, assignments that I'm not especially proud of. But I really try to make that the exception, not the rule, and to come up with seatwork that's meaningful to kids and educationally useful.

Match the Work to Varying Achievement Levels

Fred also likes to use open-ended assignments that allow students working on a variety of levels to complete the work successfully. For example, when his students read a chapter in their texts, Fred often forgoes the end-of-chapter questions (which often have one correct answer); instead, he may ask students to create their own questions. At other times, he asks a question that is broad enough to allow a variety of responses. When students discussed a terrorist attack on a U.S. warship (October 2000), for example, Fred asked them to read an article from *Newsweek* and "tell how and why you would vote on a Senate resolution granting the president support for a retaliatory strike against the terrorist leader." Almost everyone in his extremely diverse class was able to respond—in some fashion—to this question, although answers obviously varied in terms of length, substance, and coherence. As I mentioned in Chapter 8, Fred calls this the "slanty rope theory":

> *If we set a rope across a room at four feet, some kids can get over it and some can't. But if we slant the rope, then everyone can find their way over at some point. I firmly believe that people don't all want to go over at the lowest level. We can encourage kids to stretch—and once you teach kids to stretch, you've taught something more important than the subject matter.*

In the following example (Tomlinson, 1999), we see how a foreign language teacher has created a "slanty rope assignment" that allows her heterogeneous class to pursue the same general topic, but at varying levels of difficulty and sophistication:

> *Mrs. Higgins's German 1 class is studying the formation of past-tense verbs. One group of students will work with pattern drills in which much of a German sentence is supplied. However, each sentence uses an English verb, and students must supply the correct form of the past-tense German verb. Mrs. Higgins has ensured that the missing verbs are regular.*
>
> *A second, more proficient, group has a similar activity. But they will encounter a greater number and complexity of missing words, including a few irregular verbs. Another group of students works with the same sentences as the second group, but virtually all of the sentences are in English and must be translated into German. Two or three students don't need the skill drill at all; they are given a scenario to develop, with instructions about the sorts of grammatical constructions that must be included. (pp. 51–52)*

For more about ways of differentiating assignments and responding to the needs of all learners, see Tomlinson (1999).

Make Sure That Written and Oral Directions Are Clear

It is important to check that instructions provided in a text or on a worksheet are clear and precise. If you don't, you may encounter situations like this one, related by a student teacher in a foreign language class:

> *I decided to use this worksheet that listed in random order 10 statements from a short story we had read (e.g., "The gardener reported that the*

dandelions were growing furiously"). Underneath the list were 10 lines, numbered from 1 through 10, and students were instructed to put the statements or events in sequential order. A lot of the students thought that the numbers (1–10) referred to the order of events, so next to each number, they wrote the number of the statement. (So "1–7" was meant to indicate that the first thing that happened in the story was the seventh item in the list). Other kids figured that the 1 through 10 referred to the number of the statement. When they put "1–7," they meant that the first statement in the list occurred seventh. Needless to say, lots of kids "failed" the assignment! I couldn't understand how it could be, until we went over the papers. Then I realized how confusing it was. I learned a good lesson. Don't assume that everything printed on an "official" worksheet is clear!

Having had a number of experiences like this one, Christina now makes it a point to rewrite directions she thinks are confusing. For example, one districtwide assignment she gives requires students to read a book and write their reflections in a journal with at least 10 entries. Students are provided with 10 guiding questions, but it's not clear from the directions if students have to answer *one* question or *all* the questions for each journal entry. Actually, they have to do neither. So Christina adds a sentence specifying that students have to address each question *somewhere* in the journal, but not in any specific order and not in every entry.

Sometimes teachers think they don't have to explain orally what students are to do since there are written instructions in the textbook or on the worksheet. It's certainly important for students to read written instructions, but don't assume that they'll do this automatically; this may be a skill you'll have to teach. Consider the lesson learned by this student teacher:

These kids don't instinctively read something when it is given to them: They wait to have it explained . . . I know that I'm supposed to state all the objectives and explain things carefully, but there are times when I want them . . . to be curious enough to take a look at what's in front of them. I try to pepper my handouts with cartoons and some of my own spectacular drawings just to make them more attractive and engaging. I'm so used to the college mentality—something is passed out and you read it rather than listen to it being explained. I have to remember it's usually the opposite in high school.

In addition to checking written directions for clarity, make sure your oral directions are clear and complete (Chilcoat, 1990). Recall that one of the problems with Marcy's letter-writing activity was that she didn't tell students why they were to read the chapter on business letters or how long they would have; nor did she explain that they would be writing their own letters later in the period. Contrast this with the way Donnie introduces a brief seatwork assignment on rearranging equations to solve for different variables. Even though the assignment will take just a few minutes, she explains what students are to do, how much time they will have, and what they will be expected to do when they're finished:

What I need you to do now is turn to page 178. Get out some paper and a pencil or pen. We're going to look at the chapter review, up through #15. I'm going to begin by making an assignment to each person. Problem #1, Ernest; Problem #2, Damika; Problem #3, Latoya; Problem #4, Jerome. [She continues until everyone has been assigned a problem to do.] Now I want you to solve the problem you were assigned. These are just like the homework problems we just reviewed. You're going to be rearranging equations to solve for the different variables. . . . I'll give you approximately two minutes to do this. When we come back, make sure you can give us the answer and explain the problem to the rest of the class.

Marcy also failed to tell students that they would be reading their paragraphs aloud the following day, an omission that upset a number of her students ("Hey, you didn't say anything about having to read these in front of the class."). This is a situation that Christina tries hard to avoid, especially since English class often involves having students write about personal experiences and feelings:

Christina distributes copies of her own personal essay, which deals with her ethnic background. She explains that students should read her essay and then begin to jot down ideas and write a draft of their own personal essay on the topic of identity. They will have a total of 30 minutes. She cautions them to "select something that you will feel OK to share in small groups, and keep in mind that I'll be picking the groups." A girl in the front row nods and comments, "So we should write something we can share with anyone."

When you're presenting directions for seatwork assignments, you also need to make it clear whether or not students can ask peers for assistance. In some classes, teachers encourage students to work collaboratively, while in other classes giving or receiving help is tantamount to cheating (Rizzo, 1989). This latter situation can present a real dilemma for students. On one hand is their need to follow the teacher's directions and to stay out of trouble. On the other hand is their need to complete the assignment successfully and to assist friends who are having difficulty (Bloome & Theodorou, 1988).

In general, all of our four teachers not only allow, they *encourage* students to help one another. As Donnie puts it, "I can't possibly get around to everybody. The kids would constantly be calling me to come over and help them. For my own sanity, I have to have students help one another. But I think they learn better that way anyway." Christina agrees. When she circulates around the room monitoring students' progress, she'll frequently refer students who are having problems to individuals she's already assisted:

I do this for a few reasons. First, it's nice for the students I just helped to know that I now consider them to be "experts." Second, I think that having students teach others helps them to remember what I just explained. Third, it saves me having to repeat the same explanations. And finally I think it builds a helping community. But I always try to go back to the kids and check if the helpers were able to explain clearly and if the "helpees" now understand. I don't want kids to think I'm just pushing them off on others because I don't want to be bothered.

It's important to note that all of the teachers work hard to explain what "helping" really means. They take pains to explain to students that simply providing the answer or doing the task for someone else is not helping, and they stress the futility of copying. Donnie says she has "parasites" in her geometry class who don't want to do anything on their own; they just want someone to give them the answer. (This often irritates more diligent students, as Figure 9-2 illustrates.) In order to prevent this from happening, she'll sometimes assign different problems to students sitting next to each other; this allows them to help each other, but not to copy.

Although all the teachers firmly believe in the value of peer assistance, there are also times when they do *not* allow students to help one another. In these situations, they are careful to explain that the ground rules are different. Listen to Sandy:

Most of the time, I stress that scientists do not work in isolation, that it's necessary to look at everyone's data and ask, "Did anyone else get these results?" But four or five times a year, I run "quiz labs" where students are individually responsible for listening to instructions, carrying out the procedures, and drawing conclusions. This is my way of making certain that every single person knows how to light the Bunsen burner, handle the equipment, etc. These are not discovery or inquiry lessons, but opportuni-

Calvin and Hobbes   by Bill Watterson

FIGURE 9-2. Sometimes students don't like to help classmates who haven't tried to do the assignment on their own.
(CALVIN AND HOBBES © Watterson, Dist. by UNIVERSAL PRESS SYNDICATE. Reprinted with permission. All rights reserved.)

ties for students to apply what has been learned in class. During these lab activities, students cannot speak to one another. This is a real departure from regular lab activities, so I have to make it really clear that they are not to consult with one another—that the norms are different.

Monitor Behavior and Comprehension

Observers of classroom life have noted that students' engagement during independent work is often lower than their engagement during teacher-directed activities. Why should this be so? Apparently, even when they do find the activity meaningful and comprehensible, seatwork requires students to pace themselves through assignments. Since there are no external signals such as teachers' questions to push students along (Gump, 1982), they may begin to doodle, pass notes, comb their hair, and sharpen pencils—until the teacher reminds students to get back to work. In fact, research has shown that engagement in seatwork often follows a predictable cycle (deVoss, 1979): Students begin their assignments; attention wanes; the noise level increases; the teacher intervenes; the students return to the assignment. This cycle can repeat several times, until a final spurt when students rush to complete their tasks before the time is over.

In order to avoid the "mad rush" problem, Christina gives students a breakdown of the time that should be spent on each part of an assignment and periodically reminds students where they should be. She also monitors their behavior carefully by circulating around the room. In fact, none of our four teachers sits down while students are working, unless they are having individual conferences. In the following example, also taken from Donnie's lesson on rearranging equations, we see the way she circulates throughout the room while students are working. Notice how she is able to "overlap" (Kounin, 1970)—to monitor the behavior of students doing seatwork while she also works with an individual.

Students are working on the problems Donnie has just assigned. She walks around the room, peering over students' shoulders, commenting, helping, prodding them along. Then she heads over to three students who were absent and are making up the assignment that everyone else did the day before. She checks what they are doing, and helps one girl who is having particular difficulty. While she is working with this student, she periodically looks up and scans the room to monitor the rest of the class. One boy appears to be doing nothing. "Jerome, are you finished with your problem?"

The purpose of circulating is not simply to monitor behavior. Roving around the room allows you to monitor students' *understanding of the assignment.* Clearly, it's not enough for students to remain busy and on-task. They must also understand what they are supposed to do and carry out their tasks successfully. This requires monitoring. Sandy comments:

When I give a seatwork assignment, I never sit at my desk doing paper- work. I give an assignment for an instructional reason, not just to keep kids

Donnie circulates while students are working so that she can provide immediate feedback and assistance.

busy while I grade papers. This means that I need to be moving around, seeing what they're doing. For example, at the end of the period, I might say, "Let's try problems 1, 2, and 3." I walk around and help. If I see that students are doing all right, then I know I can have them complete 4 through 6 for homework.

Plan for Ragged Endings

Although it's essential to plan activities for students who finish early, you need to think carefully about the approach that you will take. In Marcy's class, Roy and John both reported that they hadn't finished reading the chapter, when they had. Obviously, they wanted time to read *Mad* rather than move on to a new assignment about business letters. And behavior like this isn't limited to school-smart teenagers; even very young students learn to dawdle if they know that they'll only be given more (uninteresting) work to do when they finish. Jones and Jones (1986) report the following anecdote:

During a visit to a second-grade classroom, a student in one of our courses reported observing a child who was spending most of his time staring out the window or doodling on his paper. The observer finally approached the child and asked if she could be of any assistance. Much to her surprise, the child indicated that he understood the work. When asked why he was staring out the window rather than working on his assignment, the boy pointed to a girl several rows away and said, "See her? She does all her work real fast and when she's done she just gets more work." (p. 234)

In the classrooms of our four teachers, ragged endings are rarely a problem, since class activities are structured so that students rarely finish early. Listen to Sandy:

Not only do students have to understand what to do and why they're doing it, they need to know what's expected upon completion. If you don't do this, some kids may rush through, thinking I'll finish real fast and then I'll have time to do my homework. If they know they'll have a follow-up related assignment, they keep going. I never make it a closed assignment. I'll say, "Today you're going to do an analysis of knowns. Once you've completed the analysis, formulate the flow chart for your unknowns." I know it usually takes a complete double period to do this. When time is about to run out, I'll say, "If you're not done, do it tonight." If they know at the beginning that it's a homework assignment, they may relax, figure they'll just do it for homework. So I never let them know that they won't be able to finish. If they see that they have a lot to do, they'll say, "Wow, I really need to work." If it's a 10-minute task, they may drag it out. I suggest that teachers predict how long something will take and then tack on a related assignment.

Fred takes a similar approach. He tells us:

I make sure that my seatwork assignments will more than fill the period so kids can't get done early. At the end of the period, I'll say, "You can either hand this in now for partial credit, or you can take it home and finish it in order to get full credit. It's up to you."

Christina finds that ragged endings are a special challenge when students are doing creative writing assignments:

Some kids will say "I'm done" after only a few minutes. I tell them they can stop writing if they think they are finished, but they have to reread the paper over and over again until the end of the allotted time. And during their rereading, they have to keep a pen poised over the paper. This encourages students to revise, edit, and extend their writing.

Concluding Comments

This chapter has highlighted the pitfalls and problems associated with independent work and has provided suggestions for avoiding, or at least minimizing, these problems. Keep these in mind as you decide on the kinds of activities students will do during seatwork time, the way you will introduce assignments, and the rules and procedures you will establish to guide behavior.

It is important to note that the chapter focused almost exclusively on the situation in which the work is assigned to the entire class while the teacher circulates and assists students in accomplishing the tasks. But this is only one way that seatwork can be used. Another option is to assign seatwork to the majority of the class while you work with individuals who need additional help or a more challenging assignment.

This use of seatwork is common at the elementary level. Most of us recall our primary teachers meeting with the "Cardinals," the "Butterflies," or the "Tigers," while the rest of the class worked independently. But independent seatwork combined with small-group instruction is far more unusual at the high school level, where instruction often tends to be conducted in a large group.

Research (Anderson, 1985; Fisher, Filby, Marliave, Cahen, Dishaw, Moore, & Berliner, 1978) suggests that *elementary students spend far too much time doing seatwork assignments that have questionable value, so I am certainly not suggesting that you replicate this situation at the secondary level.* Nonetheless, there are times when it may be appropriate to have the majority of students work on an independent assignment, while you meet with individuals. This format may be particularly useful if you have an extremely heterogeneous class. But take heed: If you are going to be unavailable for circulating and assisting, your assignments need to be even clearer and more meaningful than usual. You also need to hone the skill of overlapping. This is a situation that truly requires you to have "eyes in the back of your head."

✸ Summary

This chapter examined the subsetting known as independent work or seatwork, the situation in which students work individually on a given task at their own desks. Seatwork provides teachers with the opportunity to observe students' performance, to provide support and feedback, to engage in mini-conferences with individuals, and to prepare students for homework assignments. But it can also be misused. Too often, seatwork is synonymous with images of bored, passive students doing repetitive, tedious worksheets, while teachers sit at their desks calculating grades or reading the newspaper.

Problems with seatwork

- The assignment is not meaningful to students.
- The assignment does not match students' varying achievement levels.
- The teacher does not provide students with clear, complete directions.
- The teacher does not monitor what students are doing.
- Students work at different paces, so that some finish early, while others do not finish.

Guidelines for minimizing the problems

- Provide assignments that are meaningful and relevant.
- Match the work to varying achievement levels.
- Make sure written and oral directions are clear.
- Monitor behavior and comprehension.
- Plan for ragged endings.

This chapter focused almost exclusively on the situation in which seatwork is assigned to the entire class, but it may sometimes be appropriate to give an assignment to the majority of the class while you work with individuals who need additional help or a more challenging assignment. This use of seatwork is rare at the secondary level; however, it may be a useful strategy if you need to work with small groups (e.g., if you have an extremely heterogeneous class). But be careful: If you are going to use seatwork this way, you truly need to have "eyes in the back of your head."

Activities

1. Obtain a workbook (preferably in your content area), and select three pages to examine closely. For each page, note the topic, describe the format of the worksheet, identify the skill being practiced or extended, and generate an alternative activity that would accomplish the same goal. An example is provided.

Topic	Description of Worksheet	Skill	Alternative
Who fired the first shot at Lexington and Concord?	Three accounts by individuals who observed or participated in events at Lexington and Concord; students are to determine point of view for each account	Identifying point of view and bias	Choose two of the following characters (a British officer, an American militiaman, a French reporter, the minister's wife at Lexington, a maid at the inn in Concord) and tell the story of the events at Lexington and Concord from their respective points of view.

2. Select a workbook page or a handout (preferably in your content area). Examine it, using the following questions as a guide. Suggest ways to improve the page.

Question	Response	Suggested Improvement
Are the directions clear?		
How does the page organization facilitate or hinder students' understanding of the task?		
To what extent does the activity reinforce the intended skill?		
How meaningful is the task?		
If there are illustrations, to what extent do they help or distract?		

3. Interview two to four high school students to learn their perceptions about seatwork. If possible, select students who vary in terms of achievement level. Include the following questions in your interview:

In what classes is seatwork used most? Least?
To what extent is seatwork used in your academic classes?
Under what circumstances is seatwork useful/useless? Interesting/boring?
What do your teachers generally do when the class is doing seatwork? Are there consistent differences among teachers in this regard?
Are you generally allowed to ask for help from peers or do you have to work alone?

✴ For Further Reading

Tomlinson, C. A. (1999). *The differentiated classroom: Responding to the needs of all learners.* Alexandria, VA: Association for Supervision and Curriculum Development.

✴ References

Anderson, L. (1985). What are students doing when they do all that seatwork? In C. W. Fisher and D. C. Berliner (Eds.), *Perspectives on instructional time.* New York: Longman, pp. 189–202.

Bloome, D., & Theodorou, E. (1988). Analyzing teacher–student and student–student discourse. In J. E. Green & J. O. Harker (Eds.), *Multiple perspective analyses of classroom discourse.* Norwood, NJ: Ablex, pp. 217–248.

Chilcoat, G. W. (1990). How to make seatwork more meaningful. *Middle School Journal, 21*(4), 26–28.

deVoss, G. G. (1979). The structure of major lessons and collective student activity. *Elementary School Journal, 80,* 8–18.

Emmer, E. T., Evertson, C. M., Clements, B. S., & Worsham, M. E. (1994). *Classroom management for secondary teachers.* Boston: Allyn and Bacon.

Everhart, R. B. (1983). *Reading, writing, and resistance: Adolescence and labor in a junior high school.* Boston: Routledge and Kegan Paul.

Evertson, C. M., & Emmer, E. T. (1982). Effective management at the beginning of the school year in junior high classes. *Journal of Educational Psychology, 74*(4), 485-498.

Fisher, C. W., Filby, N. N., Marliave, R. S., Cahen, L. S., Dishaw, M. M., Moore, J. E., & Berliner, D. C. (1978). *Teaching behaviors, academic learning time and student achievement. Final report of Phase III-B, Beginning Teacher Evaluation Study.* San Francisco: Far West Laboratory for Educational Research and Development.

Gump, P. V. (1982). School settings and their keeping. In D. L. Duke (Ed.), *Helping teachers manage classrooms.* Alexandria, VA: Association for Supervision and Curriculum Development.

Jones, V. F., & Jones, L. S. (1986). *Comprehensive classroom management: Creating positive learning environments.* Boston: Allyn and Bacon.

Kounin, J. S. (1970). *Discipline and group management in classrooms.* New York: Holt, Rinehart & Winston.

Kounin, J. S., & Sherman, L. (1979). School environments as behavior settings. *Theory into Practice, 14,* 145–151.

Rizzo, T. A. (1989). Friendship development among children in school. Norwood, NJ: Ablex.

Rosenshine, B. V. (1986). Synthesis of research on explicit teaching. *Educational Leadership, 43*(7), 60–69.

Tomlinson, C. A. (1999). *The differentiated classroom: Responding to the needs of all learners.* Alexandria, VA: Association for Supervision and Curriculum Development.

Chapter Ten

Managing Groupwork

The Pitfalls of Groupwork

Designing Successful Groupwork

Four Specific Approaches to Cooperative Learning

Concluding Comments

Summary

Keep your eyes on your own paper.

Don't talk to the person sitting next to you.

Pay attention to the teacher.

If you need help, raise your hand.

Do your own work.

For most of us, these are familiar instructions. We have heard them time and time again, spoken by teachers trying to instill the norms of the traditional classroom. (See

Figure 10-1.) Phrases like these are so much a part of the way we view classrooms that four-year-olds who have never even attended kindergarten use them when playing school.

As these instructions suggest, students in traditional classrooms work either alone or in competition. There are few opportunities for students to interact, to assist one another, or to collaborate on tasks (Gerleman, 1987; Goodlad, 1984; Graybeal & Stodolsky, 1985); in some classrooms, helping may even be construed as cheating. This lack of interaction is unfortunate. Letting students work together in pairs or small groups has many advantages. Donnie and Christina alluded to one advantage in Chapter 9: If students can help one another during classwork, they are less likely to "get stuck," to have to sit and wait for the teacher's assistance, and to become uninvolved and disruptive.

There are other benefits to groupwork. Working with peers on tasks can enhance students' motivation. Groupwork can also have a positive effect on achievement. In fact, according to a recent review in the *Harvard Education Letter* (Walters, 2000),

hundreds of studies over more than three decades show a positive correla-tion between cooperative learning [a form of groupwork] and achievement. Research has been done in every subject, at all grade levels, in all kinds of

"This class will stimulate your ideas and thoughts. And remem-ber — no talking."

FIGURE 10-1. Students are rarely allowed to work together.
(Reprinted with permission.)

schools. And there is widespread consensus that students benefit when they can help one another learn instead of having to work apart from—or against—one another. (pp. 3–4).

One reason for the benefits is that cooperative learning allows students to take an active role in their own learning—to ask questions, to allocate turns for speaking, to evaluate the work of others, to provide encouragement and support, to debate, and to explain—and some of these behaviors have clear academic payoffs. For example, research has consistently demonstrated that providing explanations to peers is beneficial to achievement (Webb & Farivar, 1994); in other words, the more students explain, the more they learn.

Opportunities for interaction also have social payoffs. When students work in heterogeneous groups, they can develop relationships across gender, racial, and ethnic boundaries (Slavin, 1991). Groupwork can also help to integrate individuals with disabilities into the general education classroom (Johnson & Johnson, 1980; Madden & Slavin, 1983). As our school-age population becomes increasingly diverse, fostering positive intergroup relationships grows more and more important.

Given all these benefits, why is there so little groupwork in secondary classrooms? Part of the answer has to do with the teacher's responsibility for keeping order and covering curriculum. In the crowded, complex world of the classroom, it's easier to keep order and cover curriculum when teachers do the talking, and students do the listening. Futhermore, if the school culture equates orderly classrooms with quiet classrooms, teachers may feel uncomfortable when groupwork raises the noise level. Consider this student teacher's journal entry:

Every time I read about groupwork it sounds so great I'm ready to use it everyday. Then I attempt it in the classroom and I start having second thoughts. I love the learning that comes out of it, but I never feel in control when it is happening. The part that really upsets me is that I really do not mind if the class gets loud. It's the other teachers and the principal I worry about. There have been a few times when I was using cooperative learning and someone has come in to ask if I need any help or they will take it upon themselves to tell my class to be quiet. This really makes me angry. I feel like the only acceptable noise level is no noise at all.

Finally, like seatwork, groupwork has its own set of "built-in hazards" (Carter, 1985) that can make it particularly difficult for teachers to manage. This chapter examines those special pitfalls. It then discusses ways they can be minimized, drawing on the experiences of our four teacher, as well as the research and scholarly literature on groupwork. In the last section of the chapter, four specific approaches to groupwork are described—Student Teams–Achievement Divisions (STAD), Jigsaw and Jigsaw II, Group Investigation, and the structural approach to cooperative learning.

The Pitfalls of Groupwork

Let's begin by considering the recent experience of Ralph, a student teacher in social studies. During a recent meeting, Ralph recounted his first attempt to use groupwork with his third-period U.S. History I class:

We were working on sectional differences—the period from 1800 to 1850, when the Northeast, the West, and the South were like three different countries. I wanted my kids to research the views that each section of the country had on three topics—tariffs, slavery, and the role of the federal government. I didn't want to just lecture, or have them read out of the textbook and then discuss the material, and it seemed like this could be a great cooperative learning activity. My kids haven't had much experience working in groups, but my cooperating teacher is really good about letting me try new things, and he said, "Sure, go ahead and see what happens."

I decided to do this over two days. On the first day, I planned to divide the class into the three sections of the country and have each group learn about its section's position on the three topics. I only have 20 kids in this class, so I figured that would be about six or seven kids in each group, which seemed about right. At the end of the first day, they were supposed to pick someone to be their section's spokesman—Daniel Webster from the Northeast, John C. Calhoun from the South, and Henry Clay from the West. The second day, these three spokesmen would debate the issues.

So I come into class all fired up about this great thing we're going to do. It didn't seem important to have the groups be absolutely equal in size, and I figured if the kids could choose their own section they'd be more motivated. So I told them they could decide what section of the country they wanted to study. I told them, "If you want to do the Northeast move to this corner, and if you want to do the South move to that corner, etc. Ready, move." Well, it didn't work out. First of all, most of the kids wanted to be the West or the South—there were like nine people in the West and six people in the South and only four people in the Northeast. Plus—I couldn't believe it—the West was all girls (white and Asian American), the South was this really juvenile group of white boys (I just knew they would never get anything done), and the Northeast was my three African American kids and Rick Moore, this white basketball player! And this really quiet, insecure kid just kind of stood there in the middle of the room, not knowing where to go. I had to start asking people to switch and they weren't very happy about that and started making comments about how I didn't know what I was doing and when was Mr. M going to come back and do some "real teaching."

Well, I finally got some of the girls from the West to move into the Northeast group so the sections were about the same size, and I explained what they were going to do. I told them to use their text, and I showed them all the resource materials I had gotten from the library, and told them to use them too. I explained that they were all supposed to help one another research their section's views on tariffs, slavery, and the role of the federal government. Then they were to work together to write a position paper outlining these views and choose someone to be Webster, Calhoun, or Clay for tomorrow's debate. By this time there's only about 25 minutes left, so I tell them to get to work right away. Well, most of them just sat there and stared and kept saying things like, "I don't understand what we're supposed to do." A few kids got up and went back to their desks to get their textbooks and pencils (of course, I had forgotten to tell them to take their books and stuff with them when they moved), and I went around giving out paper, but a lot of the kids just sat there.

I kept going around and trying to get them to work. When I'd come over, they'd begin to jot down notes, but I think they were really just acting like they were working, to get me off their back. Finally, some of the kids in the West and the Northeast began looking up stuff in their texts and taking notes, but they weren't helping each other much. I just could not get them to work together! And some of the kids never did anything—they just sat and let the other kids do it. I even heard comments like, "Let Allison be Clay—she's the smartest one in history." Meanwhile, the guys in the South spent most of the time fooling around and laughing. And they kept putting each other down, saying things like, "He's too dumb to be Calhoun. . . . We don't have any smart kids in this group, " and yelling, "Hey Mr. G, we need some smart kids in this group." I kept asking them to be quiet and get to work but they just ignored me.

At the end of the period I told them they'd have to finish looking up their section's views for homework. Then I told them to decide on their spokesman, and of course nobody wanted to do it. In the West, they decided that this one kid who's really conscientious should do it. In the South, they fooled around a lot and then finally this real wise-guy says OK, he'll do it. Well, he was absent the next day, so there was no Calhoun, which they seemed to think was really funny.

All in all, these were two of the worst days of my student teaching experience. After reading all these education theorists who say that cooperative learning is such great stuff, I had been real excited, but now I'm not so sure. Maybe if your class is really motivated to begin with, it would work, but my class is not all that great (the really smart kids are in Honors History), and maybe they just can't work together like this.

Unfortunately, Ralph's story is not unusual. It illustrates all too vividly what can happen when teachers don't understand the problems associated with groupwork and don't work to prevent them from occurring. Let's take a closer look at four of these problems.

First, as Ralph discovered, allowing students to form their own groups often leads to *segregation* among students in terms of gender, race, and ethnicity. Have you ever had lunch in the cafeteria of a desegregated school? One glance is enough to see that members of each ethnic and racial group tend to sit together (Slavin, 1985). It is important to recognize that strong forces operate against the formation of cross-ethnic friendships; left to their own devices, most students will choose to be with those they perceive as similar. An even greater barrier to friendship exists between students with disabilities and their nondisabled peers (Slavin, 1991). Public Law 94-142, passed in 1975 and reauthorized as The Individuals with Disabilities Education Act (IDEA, Public Law 101-476), encourages the inclusion of students with disabilities in general education classrooms, but mere physical presence is not enough to ensure that these individuals will be liked, or even accepted.

A second problem of groupwork is the *unequal participation of group members.* Sometimes, this is due to the "freeloader" phenomenon, where one or two students in the group end up doing all the work, while the others sit back and relax. We saw this happen in Ralph's class, when only a few of the students took the research assignment seriously, and one group decided to let Allison, the "smartest" history student, be her group's spokesperson. Although this might be an efficient approach to the task, it's not exactly a fair distribution of responsibility. And those who were freeloading were unlikely to learn anything about sectional differences.

Unequal participation can occur for other, more poignant, reasons as well. In a study of students' perceptions of doing mathematics in a cooperative learning group (King, Luberda, Barry, & Zehnder, 1998), Brett, an average achiever, reported that he often failed to understand the task; consequently, he either withdrew from participation or engaged in distracting, off-task behavior. Similarly, Peter, a low achiever, "was aware that the other students seldom asked for his ideas and if he suggested ideas they never listened to him" (p. 8). In order to save face, he engaged in "silly," "weird" behaviors.

Brett and Peter are good examples of the "discouraged" and "unrecognized" categories in Catherine Mulryan's (1992) typology of passive students (outlined in Table 10-1). It is worth keeping these categories in mind. Although a desire to freeload may be at the root of some students' passivity, it is also possible that uninvolved students are feeling discouraged, despondent, unrecognized, bored, or superior.

TABLE 10-1. Six Categories of Passive Students

Category	Description	Typical Achievement Level
Discouraged student	The student perceives the group task to be too difficult and thinks it better to leave it to others who understand.	Mostly low achievers
Unrecognized student	The student's initial efforts to participate are ignored or unrecognized by others, and he/she feels that it's best to retire.	Mostly low achievers
Despondent student	The student dislikes or feels uncomfortable with one or more students in the group and does not want to work with them.	High or low achievers
Unmotivated student	The student perceives the tasks as unimportant or "only a game," with no grade being assigned to reward effort expended.	High or low achievers
Bored student	The student thinks the task is uninteresting or boring, often because it is seen as too easy or unchallenging.	Mostly high achievers
Intellectual snob	The student feels that peers are less competent and doesn't want to have to do a lot of explaining. Often ends up working on the task individually.	High achievers

Source: C. Mulryan, 1992.

Just as some individuals may be passive and uninvolved in the group activity, others may take over and dominate the interaction (Cohen, 1994a, 1994b). Frequently, the dominant students are those with high "academic status" in the classroom—those who are recognized by their peers as successful, competent students. At other times the dominant students are those who are popular because they are good athletes or are especially attractive. And sometimes dominance simply reflects the higher status our society accords to those who are white and male. Indeed, research has shown that in heterogeneous groups, males often dominate over females (Webb, 1984), while whites dominate over African Americans and Hispanics (Cohen, 1972; Rosenholtz & Cohen, 1985).

A third pitfall of groupwork is *lack of accomplishment.* In Ralph's class, a significant amount of instructional time was wasted while students formed groups, and most people didn't get much done even once the groups had formed. A number of students, particularly those in the group doing the South, seemed to view the opportunity to interact as an opportunity to fool around and socialize. (Mulryan, 1992, calls these the "social opportunists.") Their behavior undoubtedly distracted students who were trying to work. Furthermore, the disruption was upsetting to Ralph, who repeatedly asked students to quiet down—without success.

Finally, a fourth problem associated with groupwork is students' *lack of cooperation* with one another. Ralph tells us that the students tended to work alone, and the boys in the "juvenile" group spent a lot of time "putting each other down." Although these kinds of behavior are certainly disappointing, they are not surprising. As we have pointed out, most students have little experience working in cooperative groups, and the norms of the traditional classroom are dramatically different from the norms for successful groupwork (Cohen, 1994a):

Ask peers for assistance.

Help one another.

Explain material to other students.

Check that they understand.

Provide support.

Listen to your peers.

Give everyone a chance to talk.

Students who are used to keeping their eyes on their own papers may find it difficult to follow these new norms. Those who are used to asking the teacher for help may be reluctant to turn to their peers, perhaps because they don't want to appear "dumb" (Newman & Schwager, 1993). Some may have difficulty giving clear, thorough explanations to their peers (O'Donnell & O'Kelly, 1994; Webb & Kenderski, 1984). Those who are not "effective speakers" may lack the skills needed to obtain assistance (Wilkinson & Calculator, 1982). Students whose cultural backgrounds have fostered a competitive orientation may have difficulties functioning in cooperative situations (Kagan, Zahn, Widaman, Schwarzwald, & Tyrrell, 1985). And students who are used to being passive may be unwilling to assume a more active role (Lazarowitz, Baird, Hertz-Lazarowitz, & Jenkins, 1985). As Elizabeth Cohen (1994a) reminds us, it is a mistake to assume that individuals (children *or* adults) know how to work together in a productive, collegial manner.

The next section of this chapter considers some general strategies for managing groupwork. Remember, *successful groupwork will not just happen.* If you want your students to work together productively, you must plan the groups and the tasks carefully, teach students the new norms, and provide opportunities for them to practice the behaviors that are required. As Sandy comments:

Sometimes, when beginning teachers do groupwork, they think, "I'll divide my students into groups and that's it. That's all I have to do." They don't plan the groups and they don't plan the groupwork. That's where they get into trouble. You not only have to think about how you're going to get your kids into groups, but what you're going to do after they're in the groups. You have to plan it so carefully, and it's not an easy thing to do.

Designing Successful Groupwork

Decide on the Type of Group to Use

Students can work together in a variety of ways. Susan Stodolsky (1984) has identified five different types of groupwork: helping permitted, helping obligatory, peer tutoring, cooperative, and completely cooperative. The first three types of groups can be considered "collaborative seatwork" (Cohen, 1994a). All of them involve students assisting one another on individual assignments. In a *helping permitted* group, individuals work on their own tasks, and they are evaluated as individuals; however, they are allowed—but not required—to help one another. *Helping obligatory* situations differ only in that students are now *expected* to offer mutual assistance. In *peer tutoring,* the relationship between the students is not equal: An "expert" is paired with a student who needs help, so assistance flows in only one direction. In recent years, peer tutoring has been recommended as a particularly useful way of meeting the needs of students from culturally and linguistically diverse backgrounds (Webb & Palincsar, 1996).

Cooperative groups differ from these helping situations in that youngsters now share a common goal or end, instead of working on completely individual tasks. In a *simple cooperative group,* some division of responsibilities may occur. For example, a group researching the Civil War might decide that one student will learn about the causes of the war, while another learns about famous battles, and a third learns about important leaders. Tasks are carried out independently, but everyone's assignment has to be coordinated at the end in order to produce the final joint product.

More complex is a *completely cooperative group.* Here, students not only share a common goal, there is little or no division of labor. All members of the group work together to create the group product. This was the type of groupwork that Ralph used when he directed his history students to research their section's views on tariffs, slavery, and the role of the federal government and then develop a position paper. (Of course, his students could have decided to divide up the research assignment, and then coordinate their findings, but Ralph did not direct them to do so.)

It is important to keep these distinctions in mind as you plan groupwork. *Different types of groups are suitable for different types of activities, and they require different kinds of skills.* (See Table 10-2.) In helping situations, for example, students are ultimately responsible for completing individual tasks. Although these students need to know how to ask for help, how to explain and demonstrate (rather than simply providing the right answer), and how to provide support and encouragement, they do not need the more complex skills required in truly cooperative situations where they share a common goal.

TABLE 10-2. Different Types of Groups

Type of Group	Skill Required	Example of an Activity

Helping permitted
Helping obligatory
	How to ask for help
	How to explain
	How to provide support and
	    encouragement
		Creating clay sculptures:
		    Students ask each
		    other for assistance and
		    opinions, but everyone
		    completes an
		    individual sculpture

Peer tutoring	How to ask for help
	How to explain
	How to provide support and
	    encouragement
		Tutor helps tutee to
		    complete a set of
		    chemistry problems

Cooperative group	Divide group task into
	    individual tasks
	Coordinate individual efforts
	    to produce final group
	    product
		Survey on what students
		    do after school: Each
		    group member
		    interviews students at
		    one grade level, then
		    pool figures to make a
		    group graph

Complete cooperative	Take turns
	Listen to one another
	Coordinate efforts
	Share materials
	Collaborate on a single task
	Solve conflicts
	Achieve consensus
		Determining political party
		    affiliation: As a group,
		    decide if hypothetical
		    person is Democrat or
		    Republican

As an example of a helping situation, let's consider the following activity that I observed in Christina's class:

Christina's students are working in small groups on various tasks designed to develop and assess skills—Word Wealth (prefixes), SAT vocabulary study, HSPT preparation, and portfolios. Students in the portfolio group sit around the rectangular table in the front of the room, sorting through work in their "collection folders," selecting items to include in their portfolios, and completing "portfolio selection sheets," where they explain why they chose that particular assignment and which criteria it demonstrates. Some of the talk is commentary on progress, not directed to anyone in particular: "I'm going to choose this piece. I finally understood the difference between metaphors and similes." "I love the alliteration in this poem." But there are also requests for assistance and opinions: "Which of these two would you choose?" "How many things are we supposed to select?" "Do you like this one or this one?" "I don't understand what it means here . . ."

In contrast to helping situations, cooperative groups require skills beyond requesting and giving appropriate assistance. Students must be able to develop a plan of action; they must be able to coordinate efforts toward a common goal; they must be able to evaluate the contributions of their peers and give feedback in a constructive way; they must monitor individuals' progress toward the group goal; they must be able to summarize and synthesize individual efforts. Consider the following example, provided by Donnie:

In my basic skills class, I work on collecting, analyzing, and depicting data. I have the students work in groups of four. Each group has to create a survey designed to learn what high school kids do after school—for example, how much they watch TV, just hang around, play basketball, have an after-school job, do homework. Then, each group has to interview 80 students in the high school, and each person in the group is responsible for interviewing 20 students at one grade level (in other words, one person interviews all freshmen, one interviews all sophomores, and so on). Each person has to collect his or her own information, but then they have to come together to make a group graph showing how people at all four grade levels manage their time. Kids know that they can't complete the project unless everybody does their part, so they really get on each other's case if somebody isn't working.

Completely cooperative groups with no division of labor present even greater challenges. Not only must students be able to take turns, listen to one another carefully, and coordinate efforts, but they must also be able to collaborate on a single task, reconcile differences, compromise, and reach a consensus. During one visit to Fred's class, I observed a good example of a completely cooperative group activity. The class was divided into groups of four or five to consider profiles of eight hypothetical Americans (e.g., "A union member working in an automobile plant in one of the large factories located in the Industrial Belt that includes Buffalo, Cleveland, Toledo, Detroit, Chicago, and Milwaukee. He is a college graduate"; "A bank executive in a small county seat in Colorado. She is concerned about her career, is unmarried, and is about to buy her own home"). For each profile, students had to determine the probable party affiliation (or lack of one), the kinds of issues that would be important to the individual in a campaign, and whether the individual was likely to be a voter or a nonvoter. Although students were required to carry out individual tasks, they had to coordinate their individual efforts if the groups were to be successful:

Fred hands out the worksheet describing the eight hypothetical American voters (or nonvoters). He explains that students will first do the task individually, taking notes for each profile. When everyone is finished, he divides the class into groups of four or five. Fred explains that students are to share their opinions, being sure to provide their reasoning. He encourages the groups to work toward consensus on each hypothetical voter and suggests that a different person serve as recorder for each voter. Each group will be expected to report on their results to the rest of the class.

Students begin to go through the eight profiles, sharing their responses. Fred circulates, asking students to explain their reasoning ("Why do you think he's a Democrat?"), commenting on their responses ("I can't believe how confident you people are!"), and checking on group process ("What number are you on? Has everyone had a chance to be a recorder for at least one profile?").

When the groups have finished, Fred announces that Group B will be the first group to report out. The four members of Group B stand in the front of the room. Sandra reports on the group's opinions about the first two profiles: "We think he's a Democrat. He definitely votes. We think he cares about auto safety." The reports continue, with Fred interjecting questions and comments.

Although this activity first required students to think through their responses as individuals, they then had to work together to construct a group report. They had to decide who would be the recorder and reporter for each profile, take turns explaining the reasons for their ideas, listen respectfully to one another, reject ideas without being destructive, and reach consensus on what to report. These are not easy skills to learn—even for adults.

As these three examples illustrate, the more interdependent students are, the more skills they need to cooperate successfully. It's a good idea to use simpler types of groups when you are just starting out. In Ralph's case, we can see that he began with the most complex kind of groupwork. He set up a situation in which students who were not even used to helping one another were expected to cooperate completely.

Decide on the Size of the Group

To some extent, the size of the group you use depends on the task you assign. Pairs are appropriate when foreign language students are drilling one another on vocabulary words, or when home economics students are reviewing weights and measures in preparation for a test. Groups of two maximize students' opportunity to participate (Webb, 1989). They are also easier for beginning teachers to manage (Johnson, Johnson, Holubec, & Roy, 1984), and teachers of younger or less mature students often prefer pairs over larger groups that require more elaborate social skills (Edwards & Stout, 1989/90). Even with senior high school students, Sandy makes sure to provide students with experiences in pairs before using cooperative groups.

In the following vignette, we see Donnie use pairs of students in a helping situation:

Donnie is reviewing problems that involve different kinds of angles (supplementary, complementary, and vertical). After going through a number of problems on the board, Donnie announces that students will be doing the next set by themselves. She explains: "Please listen to what you're going to do next. On this assignment, you may confer with one other person. You're going to count off: one, two, three. [The students do so.] If you are a number one, you will start with problem number 19, and then go up by 3's (22, 25, 28, 31, 34, and 37). If you are a number two, your problems will start with 20, and go up by 3's. If you are a number three, your problems will start with 21, and go up by 3's. Pair yourself up with someone who has the same number that you have. Your job is to help one another understand the problems. You have 20 minutes to do these. Please have them ready to be passed in at the end of the period."

In situations where the task is an ambitious one that requires a division of labor (e.g., the survey on what high school students do after school), it makes sense to form groups larger than two. Groups of three are still relatively easy to manage, but you need to make sure that two students don't form a coalition, leaving the third isolated and excluded (Cohen, 1994a).

In general, educators recommend cooperative groups of four or five (Cohen, 1994a), and six is usually the upper limit (Johnson, Johnson, Holubec, & Roy, 1984). Keep in mind that as group size increases, the "resource pool" also increases; in other words, there are more heads to think about the task and more hands to share the work. It is also true, however, that the larger the group, the more difficult it is to develop a plan of action, allocate turns for speaking, share materials, and reach consensus.

Assign Students to Groups

In addition to deciding on the type and size of your groups, you must think carefully about group composition. As I mentioned earlier in this chapter, groupwork allows students to develop relationships with those who differ in terms of gender and ethnicity. Groupwork also helps to integrate students with disabilities into the general education classroom. For these reasons, groups should be heterogeneous with respect to gender and ethnicity, and students with disabilities should be included in groups with their nondisabled peers.

You also need to consider whether groups will be homogeneous or heterogeneous with respect to ability level. At times, homogeneous groups can be useful; for example, you may want to form a helping group of several students who are all working on a particular mathematics skill. In general, however, educators recommend the use of heterogeneous groups (Cohen, 1994a; Johnson, Johnson, Holubec, & Roy, 1984; Slavin, 1991). One reason is that they provide more opportunities for asking questions and receiving explanations (Johnson, Johnson, Holubec, & Roy, 1984; Webb, 1985).

Just how heterogeneous your groups should be is still not clear. Research by Noreen Webb and her colleagues (1985) has shown that in junior high math groups composed of high-, medium-, and low-achieving students, those of medium ability tend to get left out of the interaction. In fact, Webb (1989) argues that two-level groups (high-medium or medium-low) are most beneficial for all students. In contrast, other proponents of cooperative learning (e.g., Slavin, 1991) recommend that four-person teams consist of a high achiever, a low achiever, and two average achievers.

Another variable you need to consider when deciding on group composition is social skill. After observing a completely cooperative learning activity in Sandy's class, she and I talked about how she had decided on the groups. Her comments emphasized the importance of considering more than ability:

> When I form groups, I consider kids' personalities more than their ability, although I do try not to put just one bright kid in a group. (If I do, the others expect that person to tell them what to do.) I think about how they interact with other people and try to think about where they'll feel comfortable and where they'll work best. For example, I try to pair Steven [a student with an emotional disorder] with Jeremy, because Jeremy's unusually patient and mature, and he can deal comfortably with the outrageous things that Steven sometimes says. In the same way, I would never pair Kahlil and Michael. Michael is impulsive—he blurts out the first thing that comes into his mind— while Kahlil is very deliberate and careful. He would retreat into himself and not say a word if I put him in a group with Michael. So I put Kahlil with Laura. Laura is kind of insecure and quiet. But Kahlil draws her out. During today's lesson, he said to her, "What's the matter? Why are you so quiet?" She said, "I'm thinking," and he said, "Well say something—we need to work together." He was really showing good leadership, but he would never have done that with Michael. On the other hand, I was able to put Michael with Nathan. When Michael blurts out, Nathan says, "Wait a minute. Slow down."

As Sandy's comments indicate, groups work better when students' personalities and social skills are taken into consideration. Some students have difficulty working with others—they may be unusually volatile, or angry, or bossy—and it makes sense to distribute them across the groups. On the other hand, some students have unusual leadership abilities; others are particularly adept at resolving conflicts; still others are especially alert to injustice and can help to ensure that everyone in the group has a chance to participate. When forming groups, it generally makes sense to disperse students like these too, so that each group has the benefit of their talents. All four teachers follow this practice; however, Sandy and Donnie occasionally find it useful to put all of the leaders in one group. Donnie explains:

> At first, the kids in the other groups say, "Oh, we don't have anybody good in our group. This isn't fair." They sort of sit there aimlessly, wondering what to do. But with encouragement, they begin to get their act together. It doesn't always work, of course, but sometimes this creates a chance for new leaders to emerge.

Teachers develop different systems for assigning students to groups. Some teachers of academic subjects write each student's name on a note card, along with information about achievement and interpersonal relationships (e.g., with whom the student doesn't get along). Then they rank students in terms of achievement level and assign a top-ranked student and a bottom-ranked student to each of the groups. Next, the average students are distributed, keeping in mind the need to balance the groups in terms of gender, ethnicity, and social skill. Having each student's name on a note card allows you to shuffle students around as you try to form equivalent groups that will work well together.

Fred has developed a different system. Like Sandy, he focuses more on social skills and personalities than on academic ability:

> *First I think about who can't be in the same group, and I say, "Okay, he goes in Group 1, and she goes in Group 2, etc." Then I think about who the nicest people in the class are—the people who can get along with everybody—and I spread them out too. Then I separate the loudmouths—the kids who are not good listeners and who tend to talk a lot. Finally, I think about the kids who need "special handling." Maybe somebody who doesn't speak English, or maybe someone who's very sensitive or shy. I think, "Which group will not destroy this person?" and I try to put that kid in a group that will be most supportive.*

Since group composition is so important, it is risky to allow students to select their own groups. On the other hand, a brief group activity might not warrant lengthy reflection on group composition. One approach is to use a random assignment strategy, like having students count off by fours. As I mentioned in Chapter 7, I once observed Donnie take a deck of playing cards from her desk, walk toward a student, and ask him to help her shuffle:

> *"I've never been very good at this. I never learned how." [A few students tease her about her inability to shuffle.] After the cards are shuffled, Donnie moves from student to student, directing each one to "pick a card." As she makes her way around the room, the students and I wonder what she is up to. When everyone has a card, Donnie tells the students to pay close attention. "Now, I need you to find the people with the same number or face card that you have. When you find your partners, choose a table and sit down in a group. Then I'll tell you what you're going to do and pass out the materials." The students get up and walk around the room to find their partners. Once the groups have all formed, Donnie proceeds to give directions for the problem-solving activity they are to do as a group.*

After class, Donnie and I talked about this strategy for forming groups:

> *This was the first time I ever tried this. My main reason was to get them talking and working with people other than their normal neighbors. They're in seats they chose on the first day, and some of them are very quiet and shy. They don't like to move around or interact with new people. This made them get up and form some new groups.*

Christina, Fred, and Sandy also use random assignment every now and then. Christina particularly appreciates the opportunity to observe interactions among students she would not have grouped, but she's careful to use this strategy only for brief activities that won't have a large impact on students' grades. Fred is also cautious; in general, he doesn't use this strategy until later in the school year when he knows his students well.

Finally, there are times when Donnie, Fred, Sandy, and Christina allow their students to form their own groups, but only for certain kinds of tasks, and not until the students have had substantial experience working in various kinds of groups with almost everyone in the class. For example, Christina allows students to form their own groups for long-term assignments that require work to be done at home. As she comments, "It's just too difficult for students to get together with people other than their friends outside of school."

Structure the Task for Positive Interdependence

If you want to ensure that students cooperate on a task, you have to create a situation in which students perceive that they need one another in order to succeed. This is called *positive interdependence,* and it's one of the essential features that transforms a group-work activity into true cooperative learning (Antil, Jenkins, Wayne, & Vadasy, 1998).

One simple strategy for promoting interdependence is to require group members to *share materials* (Johnson, Johnson, Holubec, & Roy, 1984). If one member of a pair has a page of math problems, for example, and the other member has the answer sheet, they need to coordinate (at least a little) if they are both to complete the problems and check their answers. By itself, however, sharing materials is unlikely to ensure meaningful interaction.

Another way to encourage interdependence is to create a *group goal.* For example, you might have each group produce a single product, such as a report, a science demonstration, a poem, or a skit. When Christina's students studied the play *Antigone,* she had students individually read Henry David Thoreau's essay, "Resistance to Civil Government," and then meet in groups to (1) define civil disobedience in their own words; (2) explain the purpose of civil disobedience; (3) list three to five real-life examples of civil disobedience; and (4) predict how the issue of civil disobedience is important in the play. Christina explained how group members were to discuss each part of the assignment, combine their ideas, and turn in one paper from the whole group. Similarly, Donnie sometimes has groups turn in just one solution to a challenging problem, with the names of all group members on the page. Although requiring a group product increases the likelihood that students will work together, both teachers recognize that this strategy is not foolproof: In both situations, one person in the group could do all the work while the others remain uninvolved.

A stronger way to stress the importance of collaborating is to give a *group grade or group reward.* For example, suppose you want to encourage students to help one another with the symbols for chemical ions. You can do this by rewarding groups on the basis of the total number of ions correctly supplied by all the members of the group. You can also give bonus points to every group in which all students reach a predetermined level of accomplishment. Some teachers give each group member a number (e.g., one to four) at the beginning of class, and then spin a numbered spinner or toss a die to select the number of the group member whose homework or classwork paper will be graded (Webb & Farivar, 1994). Then everyone in the group receives that score. Such a practice clearly increases the pressure on group members to make sure that everyone's homework or classwork is complete and well done.

Another way of promoting collaboration is to structure the task so that students are dependent on one another for *information* (Johnson, Johnson, Holubec, & Roy, 1984). In Donnie's lesson on collecting and displaying information, for example, group members had to pool their individual data on adolescents' after-school activities. Since each student was responsible for collecting data on one grade level, they needed each other in order to construct a graph depicting the activities of freshmen, sophomores, juniors, and seniors.

You can also foster interdependence by creating rich, complex tasks that require *multiple abilities* (e.g., reading, writing, computing, role playing, building models, spatial problem solving, drawing, creating songs, public speaking). By convincing your students that *every* member of the group is good at *some* of these and that *no* member of the group is good at *all* of them, you can reduce the differences in participation between high- and low-status students and enable those who are often left out to contribute (Cohen, 1994a, 1994b, 1998). Listen to Donnie:

> *I have one girl who is not very good in math, but she's a great artist. When we were doing group projects on baking cookies, I put her in a group that I knew would be receptive and sensitive, and I structured the activity so there would be a need for artwork. I try to show them that we're not all good at the same things, but that we bring different strengths and weaknesses to the table.*

Finally, you can assign *different roles* to group members, requiring each role to be fulfilled if the group is to complete the task. For example, Fred sometimes designates a recorder, a timekeeper, an encourager (to facilitate participation), a taskmaster (to keep people on track), a summarizer (to report out at the end of the group session), and an observer (to monitor group process). At times, the roles that Fred assigns are integral to the activity itself. In a social studies simulation on reconstruction, students form "Presidential Advisory Committees" to advise President Andrew Johnson on a program for the South after the Civil War. Groups have to provide guidance on weighty issues:

Are the southerners who lately rebelled against us citizens? Shall they have the same rights and privileges as other loyal Americans?

What shall we do with the leaders of the rebellion, especially General Lee and President Davis?

How can I make sure that the South is governed by leaders loyal to the United States?

Are the soldiers who fought against us traitors?

What shall we do about the former slaves? Should they be given citizenship? Should they be allowed to vote? Should we pay former slave owners for the loss of their slave "property?"

Each Presidential Advisory Committee is composed of characters with very different backgrounds and points of view. Here are a few examples:

The Reverend Harry (Harriet) Stone, 43 years old, deeply religious, attended college in Virginia, not very active in the Abolition Movement. Believed slavery is immoral but felt John Brown took things "too far."

William (Mary) Hardwick, 52, a rich mill owner from Delaware, two sons fought in the war, the youngest was killed in the Wilderness while serving under Grant. Manufactures shirts and has profited from government war contracts, which have been canceled since Lee's surrender at Appomattox. Southern distributors still owe you $40,000 for purchases made before the war began.

Having a variety of roles ensures that everyone has a role to play and that all students have to participate if the group is to succeed.

Ensure Individual Accountability

As I discussed earlier in the chapter, one of the major problems associated with group-work is unequal participation. Sometimes individuals refuse to contribute to the group effort, preferring to "freeload." Sometimes more assertive students dominate, making it difficult for others to participate. In either case, lack of participation is a genuine problem. Those who do not actively participate may not learn anything about the academic task; furthermore, the group is not learning the skills of collaboration.

One way to encourage the participation of all group members is to make sure that everyone is held responsible for his or her contribution to the goal and that each student's learning is assessed individually. *Individual accountability* is the second essential feature of cooperative learning—and it is one that teachers most often neglect (Antil, Jenkins, Wayne, & Vadasy, 1998).

There are several ways to establish individual accountability. You can require students to take individual tests on the material and receive individual grades; you can have each student complete an identifiable part of the total group project; or you can call on one or two students from each group to answer a question, explain the group's reasoning, or provide a demonstration. One morning in May, I watched Sandy explain that students were going to be working on understanding the idea of equilibrium. She divided the class into groups of three, explained the task, and reminded students that they needed to work together to discover the operative principle. Before she allowed them to begin work, however, she stressed that a group should not consider itself through until all group members understood, since everyone would eventually be taking an individual quiz. In other words, Sandy made it very clear that every student would be accountable for explaining the process of equilibrium.

In addition to planning tasks so that individuals are held accountable, you need to monitor students' effort and progress during groupwork time. Christina, Donnie, Fred, and Sandy continually circulate throughout the room, observing each group's activity. In this way they can note problems, provide assistance, and keep students on task. During the cooperative learning activity on equilibrium, Sandy was especially vigilant because she knew that the task was difficult and that students might become frustrated:

> *Students are working in groups of three, trying to predict the molecular behavior of three chemical systems. Sandy notices that one group is particularly quiet. She moves over and places her hand on one boy's shoulder. He looks up and tells her: "I don't know what I'm doing." Sandy responds: "Why don't you talk to your group members?" He moves closer to the other individuals. As Sandy approaches another group, a girl indicates that she's "got it." Excitedly, she tries to explain the process to her group and to Sandy, but then collapses in confusion. "I'm just babbling," she says. Sandy decides it's time to intervene: "Okay, let's go back to the question. You have to understand what the question is asking first. What's the question?" In another group, a boy doesn't like the idea offered by a teammate: "I don't want to argue, but I don't think that's right." Sandy reaffirms his behavior: "That's okay. You're supposed to question one another." At one point, Sandy divides one group and sends its members to temporarily join two adjacent groups. "Mrs. K. says I should ask you my question," one boy says to his new group. While Sandy is working with a group on one side of the room, two groups on the other side begin to fool around. One boy has a bottle of correction fluid that he is tossing into the air with one hand and trying to catch with the other (which is behind his back). Sandy notices the disruption: "Excuse me, I don't think you're done, are you?" One group finally discovers the principle that is involved and erupts in a cheer. A girl in another group expresses frustration: "We're clueless over here and they're cheering over there." A few minutes later, Sandy joins this group to provide some assistance.*

After class, during her free period, Sandy reflected on the importance of monitoring cooperative learning activities:

> *Since this was a difficult activity, I expected that there would be some frustration, so it was really important to keep close tabs on what the groups were doing. You can tell a lot just by watching students' physical positions. If kids' heads are down, or if they're facing away, those are good signs that they're not participating or interacting with other group members. Today, I could tell that Richard was going to try the problem as an individual; he was off by himself—until he got frustrated and joined the other students.*

But that group never really worked well. I thought that Sylvia would help the group along, but she never got completely involved.

I also try to listen closely to what they're saying to one another in terms of group process. Like Mark—he wasn't sure it was OK to disagree. I was glad I heard that so I could reassure him that he's supposed to do that. What's neat is to see how some kids begin to function as really good group leaders. For example, Sivan is really quiet, but she really listens, and she was able to bring in the other two boys she was working with.

You also have to monitor students' progress in solving the problem and try to prevent them from getting completely off track. Today I could see that one group got stuck; the kids were really in a rut, saying the same words over and over. So I split the group up and sent the kids to explain what they were thinking or to ask their questions to two other groups. Sometimes having them talk to other kids can help to move them forward. In this case, it seemed to work. By interacting with a different group, Roy got out of the rut and then he was able to go back and help the kids in his own group.

Sandy assists a small group during a lab activity.

Occasionally, the four teachers also build in "progress checkpoints." For example, after two days of having his students try to rewrite South Brunswick's Human Dignity and Affirmative Action policies, Fred stopped the groups' activity and asked students to report on what they had accomplished and what problems they were having. Similarly, you can divide large assignments into components that are due every few days (see the section on monitoring student progress in Chapter 7). This allows you to keep track of how well groups are functioning.

Teach Students to Cooperate

Recently, I read the following entry in a reflective paper written by a student teacher in English:

> *I have tried to use cooperative learning activities as much as possible but I'm not at all sure it's been beneficial. It seems to me that instead of facilitating students' learning—as my education professors claim—these group activities have generally been a waste of time. Students spend more time socializing, goofing off, arguing, and procrastinating than getting anything done. I guess I'm not convinced that cooperative learning can work unless (1) students are mature enough to work without a teacher breathing down their necks and (2) they have the social skills to interact with peers. Given these criteria, I am skeptical about using cooperative learning with freshmen.*

This student teacher has come to understand the fact that students' social skills can make or break a groupwork activity. What he fails to understand, however, is the role of the teacher in teaching these skills. David and Roger Johnson (1989/90), two experts on cooperative learning, warn teachers not to assume that students know how to work together. They write:

> *People do not know instinctively how to interact effectively with others. Nor do interpersonal and group skills magically appear when they are needed. Students must be taught these skills and must be motivated to use them. If group members lack the interpersonal and small-group skills to cooperate effectively, cooperative groups will not be productive. (p. 30)*

As the classroom teacher, *it is your responsibility to teach students to work together.* This is not a simple process; students do not learn to cooperate in one 45-minute lesson. Indeed, we can think about the process in terms of three stages: learning to value cooperation, developing group skills, and evaluation. Let's consider each of these briefly.

Valuing Cooperation

Before students can work together productively, they must understand the value of cooperation. Sandy introduces cooperative groupwork early in the year by setting up a situation that students are unable to do alone:

I tell the kids that they are to solve a particular chemical problem (it's different every year), and that they should go to the lab tables and get started. They look at me as if I'm crazy. They say, "But Ms. Krupinsky, you didn't tell us what procedure to use." I tell them I forgot to write out the procedure for them. I say, "Let's see if you can come up with the procedure. You'll get five extra points if you can figure out a procedure by yourself. If you do it in pairs, you'll split the five points, etc." They all start out working alone—they want that five points for themselves. But as the period goes on, they begin to work in groups. They realize that they need each other, that they can really help one another and they don't care about the points. At the end of the period, I say, "Let's talk about what happened here. Why did you start out by yourself?" They tell me, "I wanted the five points, but I had to ask for help because I didn't know enough." We talk about how helpful it is to work together when you're learning something new, and how the points don't matter.

When students are going to work in the same groups over a period of time, it's often helpful to have them engage in a nonacademic activity designed to build a team identity and to foster a sense of group cohesion. One idea is to have each team create a banner or poster displaying a group name and logo. In order to ensure that everyone participates in creating the banner, each group member can be given a marker of a different color; individuals can only use the marker they have been given, but the banner must contain all the colors.

Group Skills Training

Teaching a group skill is much like teaching students how to balance equations or use a pipette. It requires systematic explanation, modeling, practice, and feedback. *It's simply not enough to state the rules and expect students to understand and remember.* And don't take anything for granted: Even basic guidelines like "don't distract others" and "speak quietly" may need to be taught.

It's helpful to begin by analyzing the groupwork task you have selected in order to determine the specific skills students need to know (Cohen, 1994a). Will students have to explain material? Will they have to listen carefully to one another? Will they have to reach a consensus? Once you have analyzed the task, select one or two key behaviors to teach your students. Resist the temptation to introduce all the required group skills at once; going too far too fast is sure to lead to frustration.

Next, explain to your students that they will be learning a skill necessary for working in groups. *Be sure to define terms, discuss rationales, and provide examples.* Johnson and Johnson (1989/90) suggest that you construct a "T-chart" on which you list the skill and then—with the class—record ideas about what the skill would look like and what it would sound like. Figure 10-2 shows a T-chart for "encouraging participation."

Finally, you need to provide opportunities for students to practice the skill and to receive feedback. You might have students role play; you might pair the skill with a familiar academic task so that students can focus their attention on using the social skill

Encouraging Participation	
Looks Like	**Sounds Like**
Make eye contact. Look and nod in person's direction. Gesture to a person to speak. Make sure everyone's chair is in the cluster (no one is physically left out).	What do YOU think? We haven't heard from you yet. Do you agree? Anyone else have something to say? I'd like to know what you think? Let's go around to see what each person thinks.

FIGURE 10-2. A T-chart for encouraging participation

(Carson & Hoyle, 1989/90); or you might have students engage in exercises designed to teach particular skills. (Elizabeth Cohen's book, *Designing Groupwork,* 1994, contains cooperative exercises, such as "Master Designer" and "Guess My Rule," which focus on helping and explaining, and Epstein's "Four-Stage Rocket," designed to improve group discussion skills.)

Donnie sometimes teaches group skills in a more "devious" way. She secretly assigns individuals to act out different roles: the dictator, the nonparticipant, the person who tears down everybody else, and the facilitator who encourages participation and listens well. Students engage in some sort of nonacademic activity—perhaps the task of building a tower with pins and straws—and then debrief, sharing their reactions about the group process. An activity like this serves to heighten students' awareness of group skills—and they have fun at the same time.

Regardless of the type of practice you provide, you need to give students feedback about their performance. Fred has found that it's helpful to designate a "process person" or "observer" for each group. This individual is responsible for keeping track of how well the group is functioning; for example, he or she may monitor how many times each person speaks. At the end of the groupwork session, the process person is able to share specific data that the group can use to evaluate its ability to work together.

Evaluation

In order to learn from their experiences, students need the chance to discuss what happened and to evaluate how successful they were in working together. Ross (1995) demonstrated the power of feedback in a study that audiotaped seventh-grade mathematics students in cooperative learning groups, gave students edited transcripts of their discussions, and trained them in how to interpret them. Students then devised an improvement plan to increase the frequency of requesting help, giving help, and being on task. According to Ross, after the feedback, both the frequency and quality of help seeking and help giving improved. For example, students became more aware of the needs of lower-ability students and felt more obligated to help. Consider the following exchange, recorded before the feedback. Here, Sharon has fallen behind the other members of her group, but they will not wait, and they exclude her from the discussion of the answers:

SHARON: Hey, what about me?
 CURTIS: You're not in it.
SHARON: Hey, you guys, what about me? . . . How come you guys won't let me do none?
 GWEN: Because you're not even here yet.
SHARON: I'm on number 15.
 GWEN: Yeah, I know, but we're on number 16. (p. 135)

In a session recorded after the feedback, group members continue to treat Sharon rather impatiently when she has fallen behind; nonetheless, they are now more willing to wait for her:

 CURTIS: We have to wait for her. We have to wait for her.
 GWEN: Come on, Sharon. You know we are waiting.
SHARON: You guys were going ahead and you weren't supposed to.
 GWEN: I know; we won't. We won't do the answers.
 CURTIS: We won't look at the answers. We'll wait for you. (p. 135)

Obviously, it's impossible to provide this kind of elaborate, detailed feedback on a regular basis. But an extensive evaluation session can be instructive when norms for groupwork are first being established. For example, during one visit to Fred's classroom early in the year, I observed a lesson on U.S. policy toward Haiti. Students were working in groups of four or five, trying to reach consensus on a number of politically sensitive questions: Should the United States maintain a military presence in Haiti as a training cadre for the Haitian military and the paramilitary police? Should the United States continue to finance and monitor elections in Haiti? In the event of a right-wing coup d'etat, should U.S. troops intervene? Would your group favor a U.S. takeover of the electoral process in Haiti if the Haitians are unable to establish free and open elections? Before students began to work, Fred explained that students were to discuss each question and prepare a report for a special envoy advising the President on Haitian policy. The chairperson of each group was responsible for compiling the report and seeing that all members had an opportunity to participate. Fred made it clear that groups would not be evaluated solely on their reports, but also on how well they worked together— specifically, how quickly they got to work; how involved and engaged they looked; how well group members listened to each other; if members conducted themselves with maturity and decorum; and if all group members had a chance to express their views. During the activity, Fred roamed the room, watching and listening; in addition, the school's media specialist videotaped the entire class.

The following day, Fred spent about half the period evaluating the group activity his students had done. First, Fred talked about how difficult it is to work in groups and told a few "horror" stories about groups in which he had worked. Then he asked students to

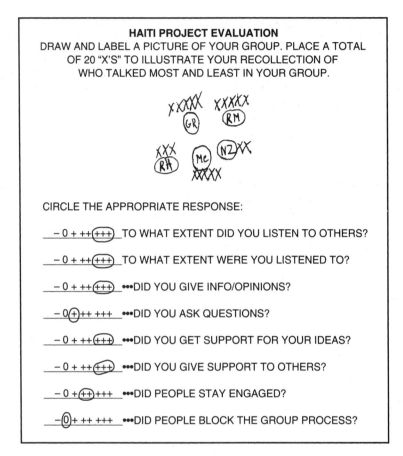

FIGURE 10-3. One student's evaluation of the groupwork activity.

complete a self-evaluation of their group's interaction. (See Figure 10-3 for one student's evaluation.) Finally, he played the videotape, commenting on the things he had noticed:

[The tape shows students getting into groups, getting organized, and getting to work.] The first thing I did was watch you getting started. I actually timed you, from the moment you entered class to the time the last group was seated and working. It was less than three minutes. I think that was pretty good. [The camera zooms in on each group.] I also looked at how people were seated. [The tape shows a group where four people are clustered and one person is sitting away.] Your physical placement in the group is very important; if you have someone sitting outside the group, it's a good bet that person's not participating. I also tried to watch the way you took turns participating. Look at this. [William's group is shown on the

tape.] William was a very organized chairperson. He went around to each person, asking "What do you think? What do you think?" It was very orderly, and everyone got a chance to speak. But what's a drawback? A drawback is you might be disengaged when you're not talking. [Camera shows Frank's group.] Now Frank here ran a more free-wheeling group. There was more arguing back and forth. What's a drawback here? [Student responds.] Yeah, someone can easily get left out. Now take a look at Jan's group. Jan really made an effort to draw people in. . . . I also tried to look at whether any people were dominating the discussion. It really ticks people off if you dominate the group. I'll say that again. It ticks people off. Now what did you people think about the composition of the groups? [Students comment.] I tried to put one person in each chair's group who I thought the chair could relate to. Instead of separating all the friends, I though it might make it easier to chair. Did it? What do you think about having friends in the group?

A far simpler approach to evaluation is to ask students to name three things their group did well and one thing the group could do better next time (Johnson & Johnson, 1989/90). You can also have students consider more specific questions, such as

Did everyone carry out his or her job?

Did everyone get a chance to talk?

Did you listen to one another?

What did you do if you didn't agree?

A simple checklist, like the ones in Figure 10-4, can be helpful.

After individual groups have talked about their experiences, you might want to have them report to the whole class. You can encourage groups to share and compare their experiences by asking, "Did your group have a similar problem?" "How many groups agree with the way they solved their problem?" "What do you recommend?"

Instead of using a form or checklist, Christina sometimes has students write letters to members of their group, noting the group's strengths and weaknesses, each member's contributions, and what areas need improvement. Afterwards, students pass the letters around their group, read what everyone has written, and briefly discuss the sentiments that were expressed. They then respond in writing to Christina.

Sometimes this process can be very encouraging for individuals. One very bright senior, for example, was gratified to learn that her less-proficient peers appreciated her patience, encouragement, and explanations. On the other hand, the process can sometimes lead to rancor. During one observation, I saw Christina meet with four students to discuss how they felt about having Nathan—who was now working by himself—rejoin their group. I was curious about what had happened, and after class, Christina explained:

About a week ago, I had the students write letters to their group. Nathan's was really offensive; it was racist, sexist, and vulgar. The other kids were

Group rating for younger or less mature students:

1. Did we get to work promptly?
2. Did we stick to the point?
3. Did we work quietly?
4. Did we all contribute?
5. Did we ask for help as soon as we needed it?

What did we accomplish?

Self-rating for younger or less mature students:

1. Was I prepared?
2. Did I follow directions?
3. Did I make good use of my time?
4. Did I work without disturbing other groups?
5. Did I listen to the other people in my group?
6. Did I contribute to my group's task?

My chief contribution to my group was:

Self-rating for older or more mature students:

1. Did I assume the responsibility the group wished?
2. Did I listen alertly?
3. Did I willingly express my own point of view?
4. Did I try to understand the viewpoint of others?
5. Did I attempt to assess the strengths and weaknesses of all opinions expressed?
6. Did I encourage those who seemed reluctant to speak?
7. Did I help maintain a friendly, businesslike atmosphere?
8. Did I keep the discussion moving pruposefully?

My greatest contribution to the group was:

FIGURE 10-4. Checklists for evaluating group skills
Source: Adapted from Stover, L. T., Neubert, G. A., and Lawlor, J. C. (1993). *Creating interactive environments in the secondary school.* New York: National Education Association.

really upset, for good reason. He said it was all a joke, of course, but he got ISS [in-school suspension] for one day. I also removed him from the group for one week, and I told him we would then discuss whether or not he would go back. I know he's afraid to go back to the group. He knows they're mad. He asked me to check out how they feel about having him come back. They wanted to write their responses to me. Two said they don't want him, and two said they don't care. He's really bright and knows the material, but he's always telling everyone how great he is, and distracting everyone, and the kids get annoyed with him. And of course the letter was the last straw. But he's not learning any social skills sitting there by himself. I think I'm going to put him back in the group for a trial period and see what happens.

Obviously, this process can be very sensitive and cause a lot of hard feelings. Things like this don't usually happen, though, because students know that I'm going to collect the letters and that I expect them to give constructive criticism.

Four Specific Approaches to Groupwork

Several structured approaches to cooperative learning have been developed to avoid the problems characteristic of groupwork and to encourage norms of effort and mutual support. Designed for use at any grade level and in most school subjects, all of these cooperative learning strategies are characterized by heterogeneous groups working together to achieve a common goal (Slavin, 1985). This section of the chapter briefly examines four of these strategies: STAD, Jigsaw and Jigsaw II, Group Investigation, and the structural approach to cooperative learning. You can learn more about these by referring to the references listed in "For Further Reading."

Student Teams–Achievement Divisions (STAD)

STAD is a cooperative learning method developed and studied at Johns Hopkins University by Robert Slavin and his colleagues. It is particularly appropriate for routine tasks with "right answers," such as simple mathematics problems, spelling, vocabulary, and grammar.

In STAD, the teacher presents a lesson, and students then work within their teams on an academic task. In other words, students help one another with the assignment instead of doing it individually. Suppose the task is to translate a set of English sentences into Spanish. Students may do the sentences individually and then compare answers, or work together on each one. Their objective is to ensure that all team members complete the task successfully. Team members are told that they are not finished studying until everyone on the team feels confident about knowing the material.

Following team practice, students take individual quizzes on which they receive individual scores. In addition, a *team score* is calculated, based on team members' *individual improvement over their own past performance*. This is an extremely important feature: Using improvement scores prevents low-achieving students from being rejected because they cannot contribute to the team. In STAD, the student whose quiz scores go from 57 to 67 contributes as much as the student whose scores go from 85 to 95. Finally, teams that earn a designated number of points receive certificates or other rewards.

As you can see, STAD clearly reflects the two conditions essential to cooperative learning. Positive interdependence and individual accountability are induced by having students receive a group reward based on every member's individual quiz score.

Jigsaw and Jigsaw II

In Jigsaw, one of the earliest cooperative learning methods (Aronson, Blaney, Stephan, Sikes, & Snapp, 1978), heterogeneous teams work on academic material that has been divided into sections. Jigsaw is particularly appropriate for narrative material, such as a social studies chapter, a biography, or a short story. Each team member reads only one section of the material. The teams then disband, and students reassemble in "expert groups" with other people who have been assigned the same section. Working together, they learn the material in these expert groups and then return to their home teams to teach it to their teammates. Since everyone is responsible for learning all the material, successful task completion requires students to listen carefully to their peers. Jigsaw also includes team-building activities and training to improve communication and tutoring skills.

Consider the following example (Hintz, 1995):

Time constraints in literature classes often negate assigning more than one work by a writer. As a result, students are assigned a "typical" work and are expected to understand the writer based on only an isolated piece. A jigsawed reading activity may be constructed instead. [For example,] several short stories by O. Henry can be used. Each member of the small groups is assigned a different short story ("The Gift of the Magi" "The Cop and the Anthem," and "After Twenty Years") and is asked to consider the writer's style, theme, point of view, and use of literary devices in his/her assigned story. After students complete their individual tasks, the small groups meet to share information. By combining their knowledge, the groups are able to develop an overall profile of O. Henry. Again, "expert" groups of the students who read the same short story may meet first to share ideas and be sure everyone has accurate information to provide the small groups. (pp. 306–307)

Jigsaw II (Slavin, 1985) is a modification developed by the researchers at Johns Hopkins to induce a greater sense of individual accountability. It differs from the original Jigsaw in that all students of a team read the entire assignment. Then they are assigned a particular topic on which to become an expert. Like STAD, Jigsaw II uses individual quizzes and team scores based on individual improvement.

Group Investigation

Group Investigation, developed by Shlomo Sharan and his colleagues at the University of Tel Aviv (Sharan & Sharan, 1976, 1989/90) places students in small groups to investigate topics from a unit being studied by the entire class. Each group further divides their topic into individual subtopics and then carries out the research. Students work together to find resource materials, to collect and analyze information, and to plan and present a report, demonstration, play, learning center, or exhibition for the class. Evaluation focuses on both learning and affective experiences; assessment procedures may include comments from peers, students' self-evaluations, and questions submitted by groups for a common test, as well as evaluation by the teacher.

The Structural Approach to Cooperative Learning

The structural approach was developed by Spencer Kagan, a former psychology professor at the University of California, Riverside, and director of Kagan Publishing and Professional Development. According to Kagan (1989/90), teachers can make cooperative learning a part of any lesson by using "structures"—content-free ways of organizing social interaction among students. Structures usually involve a series of steps, with prescribed behavior at each step. A traditional classroom structure, for example, is the "whole-class question–answer" situation. In this structure, the teacher asks a question, students raise their hands to respond, and the teacher calls on one person. If that person answers the question incorrectly, the other students get a chance to respond and to win the teacher's praise. Thus, students are often happy if a classmate makes a mistake, and they may even root for one another's failure.

Kagan has developed a number of simple cooperative structures that can be used at a variety of grade levels and in many content areas. He emphasizes the need for teachers to select the structures that are most appropriate for their specific objectives. Some structures are useful for team building or for developing communication skills, while others are most suitable for increasing mastery of factual material or for concept development.

"Numbered Heads Together" is a good example of a structure that is appropriate for checking on students' understanding of content. (It also provides a cooperative alternative to "whole-class question–answer.") In Numbered Heads, students "number off" within teams (e.g., one through four). When the teacher asks a question, team members "put their heads together" to make sure that everyone on the team knows the answer. The teacher then calls a number, and students with that number may raise their hands to answer. This structure promotes interdependence among team members: If one student knows the answer, everyone's chance of answering correctly increases. At the same time, the structure encourages individual accountability: Once the teacher calls a number, students are on their own.

Another structure is "Timed Pair Share," in which students pair up to share their responses to a question posed by the teacher. First Student A talks for a minute, and then Student B has a turn. As Kagan points out, this simultaneous interaction allows all students to respond in the same amount of time that it would have taken for just two students if the teacher had used the more traditional "whole-class question–answer" structure (Walters, 2000).

Some of Kagan's other structures are listed in Table 10-3.

Concluding Comments

Although this chapter is entitled "Managing Groupwork," we have seen that there are actually a number of different groupwork situations, each with its own set of uses, procedures, requirements, and pitfalls. As you plan and implement groupwork in your classroom, it's important to remember these distinctions. Too many teachers think that

TABLE 10-3. Some of Spencer Kagan's Cooperative Structures

Name	Purpose	Description	Functions
Round-Robin	Team building	Each student in turn shares something with teammates.	Expressing ideas and opinions. Getting acquainted.
Match Mine	Communication	Students try to match the arrangement of objects on a grid of another student using oral communication only.	Vocabulary building. Communication skills. Role-taking ability.
Three-Step Interview	Concept Development	Students interview each other in pairs, first one way, then the other. Students then share information they learned with the group.	Sharing personal information such as hypotheses, reactions to a poem, conclusions from a unit. Equal participation. Listening.
Inside-Outside Circle	Multifunctional	Students stand in pairs in two concentric circles. The inside circle faces out; the outside circle faces in. Students use flash cards or respond to teacher questions as they rotate to each new partner.	Checking for understanding. Review. Tutoring. Sharing. Meeting classmates.

Source: Adapted from Kagan, S. (1989–1990). The structural approach to cooperative learning. *Educational Leadership, 47*(4), p. 14.

cooperative learning is putting students into groups and telling them to work together. They select tasks that are inappropriate for the size of the group; they use heterogeneous groups when homogeneous groups would be more suitable (or vice versa); they fail to build in positive interdependence and individual accountability; they fail to appreciate the differences between helping groups and cooperative learning. The following example, taken from O'Donnell and O'Kelly (1994), would be funny—if it weren't true:

> One of our colleagues recently described an example of "cooperative learning" in his son's school. The classroom teacher informed the students that [they] would be using cooperative learning. His son was paired with another student. The two students were required to complete two separate

parts of a project but were expected to complete the work outside of class. A grade was assigned to each part of the project and a group grade was given. In this instance, one child received an "F" as he failed to complete the required part of the project. The other child received an "A." The group grade was a "C," thus rewarding the student who had failed to complete the work, and punishing the child who had completed his work. In this use of "cooperative learning," there was no opportunity for the students to interact, and the attempt to use a group reward (the group grade) backfired. Although this scenario is not recognizable as cooperative learning to most proponents of cooperation, the classroom teacher described it as such to the students' parents. (p. 322)

This example illustrates the need for teachers to acquire an understanding of the intricacies of groupwork in general and cooperative learning in particular. No three-hour class, no one-shot in-service workshop, and no chapter can adequately meet this need. Nonetheless, I hope that this chapter has sensitized you to some of the problems that can arise with groupwork and has provided you with some strategies for minimizing these problems. Despite the pitfalls, groupwork should be an integral part of secondary classrooms. Like Donnie, Christina, Fred, and Sandy, I believe that students must learn to work together and that students can learn from one another. As Sandy puts it:

Having students do cooperative group activities takes a lot longer than just getting up there and telling them the material. But I really believe that this is the best way. When they've worked through the material in a group, they really understand.

Sandy's reflections focus on the academic benefits of groupwork. But as I mentioned at the beginning of the chapter, groupwork has social payoffs as well. It's important to remember that the classroom is not simply a place where students learn academic lessons. It's also a place where students learn *social lessons*—lessons about the value of helping one another, about relationships with students from other racial and ethnic groups, about accepting individuals with disabilities, and about friendship. As a teacher, you will determine the content of these lessons. If planned and implemented well, groupwork can provide students with opportunities to learn lessons of caring, fairness, and self-worth.

Summary

This chapter began by talking about the potential benefits of groupwork and about some of the special challenges it presents. It then suggested strategies for designing successful groupwork. Finally, the chapter described some structured programs of cooperative learning.

Benefits of groupwork

- Less idle time while waiting for the teacher to help.
- Enhanced motivation.
- Greater achievement.
- More involvement in learning.
- Decreased competition among students.
- Increased interaction across gender, ethnic, and racial lines.
- Improved relationships between disabled students and their nondisabled peers.

Some common pitfalls

- Segregation in terms of gender, ethnicity, and race.
- Unequal participation.
- Lack of accomplishment.
- Lack of cooperation among group members.

Challenges of groupwork

- Maintaining order.
- Achieving accountability for all students.
- Teaching new (cooperative) behavioral norms.
- Creating effective groups.

Designing successful groupwork

- Decide on the type of group to use (helping permitted, helping obligatory, peer tutoring, cooperative, completely cooperative).
- Decide on the size of the group.
- Assign students to groups.
- Structure the task for interdependence (e.g., create a group goal or reward).
- Ensure individual accountability.
- Teach students to cooperate.

Structured programs of cooperative learning

- STAD.
- Jigsaw I and II.
- Group Investigation.
- The structural approach to cooperative learning.

Groupwork offers unique social and academic rewards, but it is important to understand the challenges it presents and not to assume that, just because a task is fun or interesting, the lesson will run smoothly. Remember to plan groupwork carefully, prepare your students thoroughly, and allow yourself time to develop experience as a facilitator of cooperative groups.

Activities

1. For each of the following types of groupwork, give an example of an activity from your own content area.

   a. Helping permitted

   b. Helping obligatory

   c. Peer tutoring

   d. Cooperative group

   e. Completely cooperative group

2. Choose a topic from your own content area and create a completely cooperative activity. As you design the activity, keep in mind the following questions:

   How will you assign students to groups?
   How will you structure the activity to foster positive interdependence?
   What roles will you assign, if any?
   What forms of individual accountability will you build in?
   What are the social skills you need to teach, and how will you teach them?
   How will you monitor the groupwork?
   How will you provide an opportunity for students to evaluate the group process?

3. Choose two topics from your own content area. For each one, select an approach discussed in this chapter (STAD, Jigsaw, Group Investigation, or one of Kagan's cooperative structures). Briefly describe how you would use the cooperative learning strategy you selected. Use a different strategy for each topic.

4. Observe a cooperative learning activity. In what ways has the teacher tried to promote positive interdependence and individual accountability?

For Further Reading

Cohen, E. G. (1994). *Designing groupwork: Strategies for the heterogeneous classroom.* 2nd ed. New York: Teacher College Press.

Johnson, D. W., Johnson, R. T., & Holubec, E. J. (1993). *Circles of learning: Cooperation in the classroom.* 4th ed. Edina, MN: Interaction.

Kagan, S. (1989). *Cooperative learning resources for teachers.* San Juan Capistrano, CA: Resources for Teachers.

Pedersen, J. E., & Digby, A. D. (1995). *Secondary schools and cooperative learning: Theories, models, and strategies.* New York: Garland.

Slavin, R. (1995). *Cooperative learning: Research, theory, and practice.* 2nd ed. Boston: Allyn and Bacon.

Webb, N. M., & Palincsar, A. S. (1996). Group processes in the classroom. In D. Berliner and R. C. Calfee (Eds.). *Handbook of Educational Psychology.* New York: Macmillan, pp. 841–876.

✵ References

Antil, L. R., Jenkins, J. R., Wayne, S. K, & Vadasy, P. F. (1998). Cooperative learning: Prevalence, conceptualizations, and the relation between research and practice. *American Educational Research Journal, 35*(3), 419–454.

Aronson, E., Blaney, N., Stephan, C., Sikes, J., & Snapp, M. (1978). *The Jigsaw classroom.* Beverly Hills, CA: Sage.

Carson, L., & Hoyle, S. (1989/90). Teaching social skills: A view from the classroom. *Educational Leadership, 47*(4), p. 31.

Carter, K. (March–April, 1985). Teacher comprehension of classroom processes: An emerging direction in classroom management research. Paper presented at the annual meeting of the American Educational Research Association, Chicago, IL.

Cohen, E. G. (1972). Interracial interaction disability. *Human Relations, 25,* 9–24.

Cohen, E. G. (1994a). *Designing groupwork: Strategies for the heterogeneous classroom* (2nd ed.). New York: Teacher College Press.

Cohen, E. G. (1994b). Restructuring the classroom: Conditions for productive small groups. *Review of Educational Research, 64*(1), 1–35.

Cohen, E. G. (1998). Making cooperative learning equitable. *Educational Leadership, 56,*(1) 18–21.

Edwards, C., & Stout, J. (1989/90). Cooperative learning: The first year. *Educational Leadership, 47*(4), 38–41.

Gerleman, S. L. (1987). An observational study of small-group instruction in fourth-grade mathematics classrooms. *The Elementary School Journal, 88,* 3–28.

Goodlad, J. I. (1984). *A place called school.* New York: McGraw-Hill.

Graybeal, S. S., & Stodolsky, S. S. (1985). Peer work groups in elementary schools. *American Journal of Education, 93,* 409–428.

Hintz, J. L. (1995). Putting the pieces together—together. In J. E. Pedersen & A. D. Digby (Eds.), *Secondary schools and cooperative learning: Theories, models, and strategies.* New York: Garland.

Johnson, D. W., & Johnson, R. T. (1980). Integrating handicapped students into the mainstream. *Exceptional children, 47*(2), 90–98.

Johnson, D. W., & Johnson, R. T. (1989/90). Social skills for successful groupwork. *Educational Leadership, 47*(4), 29–33.

Johnson, D. W., Johnson, R. T., Holubec, E. J., & Roy, P. (1984). *Circles of learning: Cooperation in the classroom.* Alexandria, VA: Association for Supervision and Curriculum Development.

Kagan, S. (1989/90). The structural approach to cooperative learning. *Educational Leadership, 47*(4), 12–15.

Kagan, S., Zahn, G. L., Widaman, K. F., Schwarzwald, J., & Tyrrell, G. (1985). Classroom structural bias: Impact of cooperative and competitive classroom structures on cooperative and competitive individuals and groups. In R. Slavin, S. Sharan, S. Kagan, R. Hertz-Lazarowitz, C. Webb, & R. Schmuck (Eds.), *Learning to cooperate, cooperating to learn.* New York: Plenum Press, pp. 277–312.

King, L., Luberda, H., Barry, K., & Zehnder, S. (1998). A case study of the perceptions of students in a small-group cooperative learning situation. Paper presented at the Annual Conference of the American Education Research Association. San Diego, CA.

Lazarowitz, R., Baird, J. H., Hertz-Lazarowitz, R., & Jenkins, J. (1985). The effects of Modified Jigsaw on achievement, classroom social climate, and self-esteem in high-school science classes. In R. Slavin, S. Sharan, S. Kagan, R. Hertz-Lazarowitz, C. Webb, & R. Schmuck (Eds.), *Learning to cooperate, cooperating to learn.* New York: Plenum Press, pp. 231–253.

Madden, N. A., & Slavin, R. E. (1983). Cooperative learning and social acceptance of mainstreamed academically handicapped students. *Journal of Special Education, 17,* 171–182.

Mulryan, C. M. (1992). Student passivity during cooperative small groups in mathematics. *Journal of Educational Research, 85*(5), 261–273.

Newman, R. S., & Schwager, M. T. (1993). Students' perceptions of the teacher and classmates in relation to reported help seeking in math class. *The Elementary School Journal, 94*(1), 3–17.

O'Donnell, A., & O'Kelly, J. (1994). Learning from peers: Beyond the rhetoric of positive results. *Educational Psychology Review, 6*(4), 321–349.

Rosenholtz, S. J., & Cohen, E. G. (1985). Status in the eye of the beholder. In J. Berger & M. Zelditch, Jr. (Eds.), *Status, rewards, and influence.* San Francisco: Jossey Bass.

Ross, J. A. (1995). Effects of feedback on student behavior in cooperative learning groups in a grade 7 math class. *The Elementary School Journal, 96*(2), 125–143.

Sharan, S. (1990). The group investigation approach to cooperative learning: Theoretical foundations. In M. Brubacher, R. Payne, & K. Rickett (Eds.), *Perspectives on small group learning.* Oakville, Ontario: Rubicon.

Sharan, S. & Sharan, Y. (1976). *Small-group teaching.* Englewood Cliffs, NJ: Educational Technology Publications.

Sharan, Y., & Sharan, S. (1989/90). Group investigation expands cooperative learning. *Educational Leadership, 47*(4), 17–21.

Slavin, R. (1985). An introduction to cooperative learning research. In R. Slavin, S. Sharan, S. Kagan, R. Hertz-Lazarowitz, C. Webb, & R. Schmuck (Eds.), *Learning to cooperate, cooperating to learn.* New York: Plenum Press, pp. 5–15.

Slavin, R. (1991). *Student team learning: A practical guide to cooperative learning.* 3rd ed. Washington, DC: National Education Association.

Slavin, R. E. (1989/90). Guest editorial: Here to stay or gone tomorrow? *Educational Leadership, 47*(4), p. 3.

Stodolsky, S. S. (1984). Frameworks for studying instructional processes in peer work groups. In P. L. Peterson, L. C. Wilkinson, & M. Hallinan (Eds.), *The social context of instruction.* New York: Academic Press, pp. 107–124.

Walters, L. S. (2000). Putting cooperative learning to the test. *Harvard Education Letter, 16*(3), 1–6.

Webb, N. M. (1984). Sex differences in interaction and achievement in cooperative small groups. *Journal of Educational Psychology, 76,* 33–44.

Webb, N. M.(1985). Student interaction and learning in small groups: A research summary. In R. Slavin, S. Sharan, S. Kagan, R. Hertz-Lazarowitz, C. Webb, & R. Schmuck (Eds.), *Learning to cooperate, cooperating to learn.* New York: Plenum Press, pp. 147–172.

Webb, N. M. (1989). Peer interaction and learning in small groups. *International Journal of Educational Research, 13,* 21–41.

Webb, N. M., & Farivar, S. (1994). Promoting helping behavior in cooperative small groups in middle school mathematics. *American Educational Research Journal, 31*(2), 369–395.

Webb, N. M., & Kenderski, C. M. (1984). Student interaction and learning in small-group and whole-class settings. In P. L. Peterson, L. C. Wilkinson, & M. Hallinan (Eds.), *The social context of instruction.* New York: Academic Press, pp. 153–170.

Webb, N. M., & Palincsar, A. S. (1996). Group processes in the classroom. In D. Berliner and R. C. Calfee (Eds.), *Handbook of Educational Psychology.* New York: Macmillan, pp. 841–876.

Wilkinson, L. C., & Calculator, S. (1982). Effective speakers: Students' use of language to request and obtain information and action in the classroom. In L. C. Wilkinson (Ed.), *Communicating in the classroom.* New York: Academic Press, pp. 85–100.

Managing Recitations and Discussions

Much of the talk that occurs between teachers and students is unlike the talk you hear in the "real world." Let's consider just one example (Cazden, 1988). In the real world, if you ask someone for the time, we can assume that you really need to know what time it is and will be grateful for a reply. The conversation would probably go like this:

"What time is it?"

"2:30."

"Thank you."

In contrast, if a teacher asks for the time during a lesson, the dialogue generally sounds like this:

"What time is it?"

"2:30."

"Very good."

Here, the question is not a request for needed information, but a way of finding out what students know. The interaction is more like a quiz show (Roby, 1988) than a true conversation: The teacher asks a question, a student replies, and the teacher evaluates the response (Mehan, 1979). This pattern of interaction (initiation-response-evaluation or I-R-E) is called *recitation,* and several studies (e.g., Stodolsky, 1988) have documented the substantial amount of time that students spend in this subsetting of the classroom.

The recitation has been frequently denounced as a method of instruction. Critics object to the active, dominant role of the teacher and the relatively passive role of the student. They decry the lack of interaction among students. They condemn the fact that recitations often emphasize the recall of factual information and demand little higher-level thinking. (See Figure 11–1 for an example of this kind of recitation.)

An additional criticism focuses on the public evaluation that occurs during recitation. When the teacher calls on a student, everyone can witness and pass judgment on the response. In fact, as Phil Jackson (1968) comments, classmates are sometimes encouraged to "join in the act":

Sometimes the class as a whole is invited to participate in the evaluation of a student's work, as when the teacher asks, "Who can correct Billy?" or "How many believe that Shirley read that poem with a lot of expression?" (p. 20)

Questions like these exacerbate the "negative interdependence" among students that recitations can generate (Kagan, 1989/90). In other words, if a student is unable to respond to the teacher's question, the other students have a greater chance to be called on and to receive praise; thus, students may actually root for their classmates' failure.

Finally, critics observe that the format of the recitation is incompatible with the cultural background of some students. A vivid illustration comes from Susan Philips (1972), who wondered why children on the Warm Springs Indian Reservation in Oregon were so reluctant to participate in classroom recitations. Her analysis of life in this Na-

Mr. Lowe is conducting a "discussion" about Macbeth in his 12th-grade English class. Students have just finished reading the first act.

MR. LOWE: OK, let's talk about the first act of this play. In the very first scene—which is very brief—three witches are on stage. What's the weather like, Sharon?

SHARON: It's thundering and lightning.

Mr. Lowe: Right. What are the witches talking about, Larry?

LARRY: How they're going to meet Macbeth.

MR. LOWE: Good. When are they going to meet him? Jonathan?

JONATHAN: When the battle's done.

MR. LOWE: Right. Okay, let's jump to the third scene. The battle's done, and the three witches tell us that "Macbeth doth come." So we meet Macbeth and Banquo, two generals in the King's army. They've just returned from the battle. Who were they fighting? Missy?

MISSY: Cawdor.

MR. LOWE: Very good. Now we know that Cawdor was a traitorous rebel, right? Who was he rebelling against, Tanya?

TANYA: King Duncan.

Mr. Lowe: Good. What country is Duncan king of? Melissa?

MELISSA: Scotland.

MR. LOWE: Yes. Now, when the witches first speak to Macbeth, what do they call him? Eric?

ERIC: Thane of Glamis.

MR. LOWE: Right. That's his own title, so that makes sense. But then what do they call him?

SUSAN: Thane of Cawdor.

MR. LOWE: Right! So we know that Macbeth is going to be named the new thane of Cawdor. What happens to the old thane of Cawdor? Paul?

PAUL: He's killed.

MR. LOWE: Yes, he's put to death.

FIGURE 11–1. An example of a poor recitation: *Macbeth* as quiz show

tive American community disclosed a set of behavioral norms that conflict with the way recitations are conducted. As I have noted, recitations permit little student–student interaction, but Warm Springs children are extremely peer oriented. During recitations, the teacher decides who will participate, while Warm Springs traditions allow individuals to decide for themselves if and when to participate in public events. Recitations involve public performance and public evaluation—even if a student has not yet mastered the material—but Warm Springs children are used to testing their skills in private before they choose to demonstrate them in public. Understanding these disparities helps us to see why the children would find recitations unfamiliar and uncomfortable.

Despite the validity of these criticisms, recitations remain an extremely common feature of secondary classrooms. What is there about this instructional strategy that makes it so enduring in the face of other, more highly touted methods (Hoetker & Ahlbrand, 1969)?

I thought hard about this question during one visit to Fred's classroom, and my observation of a recitation session that he conducted provided some clues. Students had just read an article from *Newsweek* magazine on whether the United States should renew China's most-favored-nation status. Fred then told them he wanted to hear what they thought about the basic issue described in the article:

> FRED: OK, I'm going to call on people, and I want to hear what you people think about the basic issue described in this article. Ms. Harnett, would you start, please?
>
> HARNETT: I was really confused about this article. . . . I think it was talking about how in China there are a lot of political prisoners . . . and we don't like that . . . so we're trying to get them to change . . . Oh, I don't know, it was confusing.
>
> FRED: You really understand more than you thought. Let's hear from someone else. Jenny.
>
> JENNY: Well, like the United States doesn't like it that China has all these political prisoners . . . but China says leave us alone, our people are doing OK.
>
> FRED: OK, so China's saying that you have to look at the whole picture. You have to look at it from *their* perspective. [He calls on a student whose hand is raised.] Philip.
>
> PHILIP: The Chinese are saying we keep talking about the dissidents, but they want to look at everyone. And like there's different ideas about human rights.
>
> FRED: Hmmm. Let's talk about that. Let's talk about what we value as basic human rights in the United States. What are some of our basic human rights?
>
> STUDENT: Equality.
>
> FRED: What does that mean, equality? Come over here, Sally. [She comes up and stands next to him.] Are you my equal? Is she my equal?
>
> STUDENT: Well, she's not as big as you are [laughter], and she's probably not as strong, but she's equal in terms of rights.
>
> FRED: Hmmm. So we're not equal in terms of size or strength. Are we equal economically? [Murmurs of "No . . ."] Probably not. Are we equal in terms of power? You bet we're not. [More laughter.] But we have *legal* equality; we've got equal rights under the law. What are some of those rights?
>
> STUDENT: Freedom.
>
> FRED: To do what?
>
> STUDENT: To speak . . . freedom of speech.
>
> FRED: OK. What else?
>
> STUDENT: Freedom of religion.
>
> STUDENT: Freedom to vote.
>
> FRED: OK. In the United States, human rights means *individual* rights. We emphasize personal freedoms—the right of individuals to follow their own religion, to vote for who they want. But in China, the *group* is the focus of human rights.

Fred leads a whole-class discussion.

Fred's question-and-answer session helped me to identify five very useful functions of classroom recitations. First, the recitation allowed Fred to assess students' comprehension of the reading and to check their background knowledge on the issue of human rights and most-favored-nation status. Second, by asking intellectually demanding questions (e.g., "What do we mean by equality in the United States?"), Fred was able to prod his students to do some critical thinking and to guide them to some fundamental understandings (Good & Brophy, 2000). Third, the recitation permitted Fred to involve students in the presentation of material—what Roby (1988) calls "lecturing in the interrogatory mood." Instead of telling students directly about most-favored-nation status and the debate over human rights, Fred brought out the information by asking questions. Fourth, the recitation provided the chance to interact individually with students, even in the midst of a whole-group lesson. In fact, my notes indicate that Fred made contact with eight different students in just the brief interaction reported here. Finally, through his questions, changes in voice tone, and gestures, Fred was able to maintain a relatively high attention level; in other words, he was able to keep most of his students "with him."

Later, Fred reflected aloud on some other useful functions of recitations:

> *I'll use recitation a lot at the beginning of the year because it's a good way to get to know kids' names and to see how they handle themselves in class. It's also a tool for building self-confidence in a new class. They have a chance to speak in class, and I can provide them with opportunities for success early in the year. It's generally a pretty nonthreatening activity;*

since it doesn't ask for as much higher-level thinking as discussions, it's easier. I also try to emphasize that it's OK not to know, *that we can figure out this stuff together. That's what education* is.

As we can see, Fred's recitation session was hardly a "quiz show" in which passive students mindlessly recalled low-level, insignificant facts. On the other hand, both the pattern of interaction (I-R-E) and the primary intent (to assess students' understanding of the reading) set it apart from another type of questioning session: the *discussion*. (Table 11–1, adapted from Dillon, 1994, summarizes the differences between recitation and discussion.)

In order to make the distinction clear, let's consider another example from Fred's class. Here, students had been asked to read brief descriptions of hypothetical voters and determine if they were likely to be Democratic or Republican. (See Chapter 10 for a fuller description of this activity.) In this excerpt from the class, Fred was soliciting students' thoughts about the case of a retired school teacher living in New Jersey and dependent upon Social Security:

FRED: What are the indicators that the retired school teacher is left of center? Jeremy, what do you think?

JEREMY: She's from New Jersey.

FRED: Why would that affect her political views?

JEREMY: Well, New Jersey generally votes Democratic.

TABLE 11–1. Differences between Recitations and Discussions

Dimension	Recitation	Discussion
1. Predominant speaker	Teacher (2/3 or more)	Students (half or more)
2. Typical exchange	Teacher question; student answer; teacher evaluation (I-R-E)	Mix of statements and questions by mix of teachers and students
3. Pace	Many brief, fast exchanges	Fewer, longer, slower exchanges
4. Primary purpose	To check students' comprehension	To stimulate variety of responses; encourage students to consider different points of view; foster problem solving and critical thinking; examine implications
5. The answer	Predetermined right or wrong; same right answer for all students	Not predetermined right or wrong; can have different answers for different students
6. Evaluation	Right/wrong, by teacher only	Agree/disagree, by student and teacher

STUDENT: [Jumping in.] Wait a minute—we just elected a Republican governor.

JEREMY: Yeah, but there's a lot of diversity here, and like, I don't know, but I think people tend to be more liberal here.

FRED: What do other people think about this issue? Do you think living in New Jersey is an indicator that she's probably Democratic?

STUDENT: Well I know this is going to sound dumb, but everybody I know around here is a Democrat, so I think if she's from New Jersey, she's probably Democratic.

FRED: Anything else here to indicate she might be liberal?

STUDENT: She's a teacher, so she's well educated.

FRED: Hmmmm . . . why would education be a factor that makes you more liberal?

STUDENT: Well it just seems like the more you know the more you understand about other people.

FRED: What other indicators might make you think that she's liberal?

STUDENT: Since she's a teacher, she probably cares about social issues. So that probably makes her more liberal.

STUDENT: Yeah, but she's older and she's retired. I think that would make her more conservative.

FRED: Let's consider that. Would age tend to make her more conservative?

STUDENT: Yeah. That happens.

FRED: Why? Why would age make her more conservative?

STUDENT: Older people are more set in their ways.

FRED: OK, I tend to be more skeptical because I've been around more. I've been dumped on more. But of course, we've got to remember that these are generalizations. I'm going to bring in an older guy who's a far left liberal and a young guy who's real conservative, just to defy the generalizations. OK, what other indicators are there that she's conservative?

STUDENT: She's living on Social Security, so she's probably real concerned about money.

FRED: So she's concerned about money. Why would that make her conservative?

STUDENT: She might vote against social programs that would cost her.

STUDENT: Yeah, like she'd probably vote against the school budget.

STUDENT: I don't agree with that. As a retired teacher, I can't see that she'd ever vote against a school budget.

Later in the interaction, after Fred and the students had decided that the retired teacher was probably a Democrat (but conservative on issues "close to the pocketbook"), Fred stressed the fact that there could be no right answers in this exercise:

Are we right? I don't know. All we can make are informed generalizations. If there's a right answer here, it's that there's no right answer. But this is not just an exercise in futility that we did. Lots of times in politics, people are given tasks where they are required to make judgments and they don't have enough data to know the right answer. But people can make better judgments—in the absence of complete data—by being more attuned to the indicators. The indicators are useful for making predictions, which is really important in politics. And if it turns out your predictions are right, you're considered a brilliant strategist; if you're wrong, you're fired.

As in the recitation presented earlier, Fred was still very much in charge of this interaction. In fact, we can characterize this as a *teacher-led discussion,* since Fred set the topic, posed the questions, and called on students to speak. Nonetheless, there are some obvious differences. In the discussion, Fred generally initiated the questions and students replied, but he often dispensed with an evaluation of their responses. Thus, the predominant pattern was not I-R-E, but I-R, even I-R-R-R. Furthermore, students occasionally initiated questions of their own, both to Fred and to each other, and sometimes they commented on or evaluated the contributions of their peers. Finally, the purpose of this interaction was not to "go over material" or to "elaborate on a text" (Good & Brophy, 2000). Rather, the teacher-led discussion was intended to stimulate a variety of responses, to encourage students to consider different points of view, to foster problem solving, to examine implications, and to relate material to students' own personal experiences (Good & Brophy, 2000).

Although educational critics frequently decry the use of recitation and promote the use of discussion, both types of interaction have a legitimate place in the secondary classroom—if done well. As Good and Brophy (2000) write: "The operative question about recitation for most teachers is not whether to use it but when and how to use it effectively" (p. 387).

This chapter begins by examining the managerial hazards associated with recitations and teacher-led discussions. Like seatwork and groupwork, these subsettings of the secondary classroom have their own set of "built-in hazards" (Carter, 1985): unequal participation; loss of pace, focus, and involvement; and the difficulty of monitoring comprehension. Next, we consider what our teachers and the research have to say about minimizing these problems. The final section of the chapter takes a brief look at yet another type of questioning session—the student-centered discussion—and offers some guidelines for managing this third pattern of interaction.

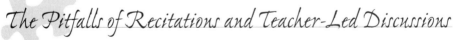

The Pitfalls of Recitations and Teacher-Led Discussions

Unequal Participation

Imagine yourself in front of a class of 25 students. You've just asked a question. A few individuals have their hands up, conveying their desire (or at least their willingness) to be called on. Others are sitting quietly, staring into space, their expressions blank. Still others are slumped down as far as possible in their seats; their posture clearly says, "Don't call on me."

In a situation like this, it's tempting to call on an individual whose hand is raised. After all, you're likely to get the response you want—a very gratifying situation! You also avoid embarrassing students who feel uncomfortable speaking in front of the group or who don't know the answer, and you're able to keep up the pace of the lesson. But selecting only those who volunteer or those who call out may limit the interaction to a handful of students. This can be a problem. Students tend to learn more if they are actively participating (Morine-Dershimer & Beyerbach, 1987). Furthermore, since those who volunteer are often high achievers, calling only on volunteers is likely to give you a distorted picture of how well everyone understands. Finally, restricting your questions to a small number of students can communicate negative attitudes and expectations to the others (Good & Brophy, 2000): "I'm not calling on you because I'm sure you have nothing to contribute." Negative attitudes like this can be communicated even if you have the best of intentions. Listen to Sandy recall a situation in which she made a practice of not calling on a student who seemed painfully shy:

> *It was my second year of teaching, but I still remember it clearly. My kids did course evaluations at the end of the year, and one kid said I didn't care about students. I was devastated. I tracked her down and asked her why she thought I didn't care. She said it was because I hadn't required her to participate in class discussions. Here I had been trying to avoid causing her embarrassment. She seemed so afraid to talk, so I left her alone. And she interpreted my behavior as saying I didn't care. That taught me a good lesson!*

Losing It All: Pace, Focus, and Involvement

In the early 1960s, a popular television program capitalized on the fact that *Kids Say the Darndest Things*. The title of the show aptly describes what can happen during a recitation or discussion. When you ask your question, you might receive the response you have in mind. You might also get answers that indicate confusion and misunderstanding, ill-timed remarks that have nothing to do with the lesson (e.g., "There's gum on my shoe" or "When are you going to give back the lab reports?"), or unexpected comments that momentarily throw you off balance. All of these threaten the smooth flow of a recitation or discussion and can cause it to become sluggish, jerky, or unfocused.

Threats like these require you to make instantaneous decisions about how to proceed. It's not easy. For example, if a student's answer reveals confusion, you need to determine how to provide feedback and assistance without losing the rest of the class. During recitations and discussions, you are frequently confronted with two incompatible needs: the need to stay with one person to enhance that individual's learning and the need to move on to avoid losing both the momentum and the group's attention. Donnie reflects on this common situation:

> *There always seems to be one person who doesn't understand! While you're trying to help that student, the rest of the class begins to mumble things like, "Why are we still doing this? We know this stuff already." They become really restless. Of course, they want you to stay with them when*

they *don't understand, but they get disgusted if you spend too long on someone else.*

When "kids say the darndest things" during a recitation or discussion, you also need to determine if the comment is genuine or if it is a deliberate ploy to get you sidetracked. Fred has had firsthand experience with this particular hazard:

I'll have kids try to get me off on a tangent by asking a question that's out of the blue. It's especially true with sharp kids. When that happens, I'll say, "What a great question. It's not what we're dealing with today, but I'd really like to discuss that with you. Is 2:30 OK or how about tomorrow?"

Sometimes, questioning sessions get sluggish because ambiguity in the teacher's question makes it difficult for students to respond. For example, Farrar (1988) analyzed a social studies lesson in which the teacher asked a yes–no question: "Did you read anywhere in the book that Washington's army was destroyed?" When students responded, "No," and "Uh-uh," he rejected their answers. The result was confusion and a momentary breakdown of the recitation. In retrospect, it appears that the teacher was not really expecting a yes or no answer, but wanted a restatement of information that had appeared in the reading. Students responded to his *explicit* question, while he was waiting for the answer to his *implicit* question: "What happened to Washington's army?"

Questioning sessions can also become bogged down if the teacher has not developed a set of verbal or nonverbal signals that communicate to students when they are to raise their hands and when they are to respond chorally. Without clear signals, students are likely to call out when the teacher wants them to raise their hands, or to remain silent and raise their hands when the teacher wants them to call out in a choral response.

Difficulties in Monitoring Students' Comprehension

Recitations and discussions provide an opportunity for teachers to check students' comprehension, but doing so is not always easy. Recently, a fifth-grade teacher talked about a lesson taught by her student teacher, Rebecca. The class had been studying the human body, and halfway through the unit, Rebecca planned to give her students a quiz. On the day of the quiz, she conducted a brief review of the material by firing off a series of questions on the respiratory and circulatory systems. Satisfied with the high percentage of correct answers, Rebecca then asked "Before I give out the quiz, are there any questions?" When there were none, she added, "So everybody understands?" Again, there was silence. Rebecca told the students to close their books and distributed the quiz papers. That afternoon, she corrected the quiz. The results were an unpleasant shock—a large number of students received D's and F's. During a postlesson conference with her cooperating teacher, she wailed, "How could this happen? They certainly knew the answers during our review session!"

This incident underscores the difficulty of gauging the extent to which all members of a class really understand what is going on. As we mentioned earlier, teachers sometimes get fooled because they call only on volunteers—the students most likely to give the correct answers. In this case, Rebecca's cooperating teacher had kept a "map" of the verbal interaction between teacher and students and was able to share some revealing data: During a 15-minute review, Rebecca had called on only 6 of the 19 children in the class, and all of these had been volunteers. Although this allowed Rebecca to maintain the smooth flow of the interaction, it led her to overestimate the extent of students' mastery. Moreover, as Rebecca's cooperating teacher pointed out to her, questions that try to assess comprehension by asking "Does everyone understand?" are unlikely to be successful. There's no accountability built into questions like this; in other words, they don't require students to demonstrate an understanding of the material. In addition, students who do not understand are often too embarrassed to admit it. (They may not even realize they don't understand!) Clearly, you need to find other ways to assess if your class is "with" you.

Strategies for Managing Recitations and Teacher-Led Discussions

Recitations and teacher-led discussions pose formidable challenges to teachers. You need to respond to each individual's learning needs, while maintaining the attention and interest of the group; to distribute participation widely, without dampening the enthusiasm of those who are eager to volunteer; to assess students' understanding without embarrassing those who don't know the answers; to allow students to contribute to the interaction, while remaining "on course."

This section of the chapter considers six strategies for meeting these challenges. As in previous chapters, research on teaching, discussions with the four teachers, and observations of their classes provide the basis for the suggestions. Although there are no foolproof guarantees of success, these strategies can reduce the hazards associated with recitations and teacher-led discussions. (Table 11–2 provides a summary of the suggestions.)

Distributing Chances to Participate

Early in the school year, I watched Fred introduce the topics that his Contemporary World Issues class would be studying during the coming year. He explained that students would be examining a variety of cultures, looking at how people make a living in each culture.

> *OK, let's think about what goes into making a living. Make a list of the five most important elements in our economic system that have a bearing on your own life. I'm going to do this too. [Students begin to write. After a few minutes, Fred continues.] OK, let's see if we can develop a good answer, a consensus. Let's go around the room and each person give one thing.*

In this situation, Fred chose to use a "round-robin" technique, which allowed him to give everyone a chance to participate. Since he didn't have to deliberate each time he called

TABLE 11–2. Strategies for Managing Recitations

Strategy	Example
Distribute chances to participate	Use patterned turn taking Pick names from a cup Check off names on a seating chart
Provide time to think	Extend wait time to three seconds Tell students you don't expect an immediate answer Allow students to write a response
Stimulate and maintain interest	Inject mystery and suspense Inject humor and novelty Challenge students to think
Provide feedback to students	When answer is correct and confident, affirm briefly When answer is incorrect, but careless, make a simple correction When answer is incorrect but student could get answer with help, prompt or backtrack to simpler question If student is unable to respond, don't belabor the issue
Require overt responses	Have students write answers, physically display answers with manipulative materials, respond chorally
Use a steering group	Observe the performance of a sample of students (low and average achievers) in order to know when to move on

on someone, this strategy also enabled him to keep the pace moving. Watching him, I recalled a study by McDermott (1977) of first-grade reading groups. McDermott found that turn taking in the high-achievement group proceeded efficiently in round-robin fashion, with little time lost between readers. In the low-achievement group, however, the teacher allowed the students to bid for a turn, and so much time was devoted to deciding who would read next that students spent only one-third as much time reading as students in the top group.

Sometimes, teachers prefer to use a pattern that is more subtle than the round-robin, so that students do not know exactly when they will be called on. Donnie often uses this approach (described earlier in the section on interaction routines in Chapter 4):

After a review of solving equations with two unknowns, Donnie tells her students to open their textbooks to the oral exercises on page 351. She tells them: "Everyone in here will get a chance to answer a problem. OK,

Kevin has his hand raised, so let's start with him. Decide if the ordered pairs are solutions to the equation." [She goes through the oral exercise, rapidly calling on students.]

After class, when I discussed this lesson with Donnie, I asked her if she had used some system for calling on students. She explained:

I used a pattern. I started with Kevin, and then went diagonally to the back of the room, then across, and down. I find that using a pattern like that helps me to keep track of who I call on, and it helps me make sure I get to everyone. And it's less obvious than just going up and down the rows. This way, kids are not so aware of who I'm going to call on next. So they don't sit there and try to work out the answer to the problem they know they're going to get. Sometimes, they'll try to figure out the pattern, and they'll say, "Wait a minute, you missed me," but it's like a game.

Instead of a pattern, some teachers use a list of names or a seating chart to keep track of who has spoken. Christina, for example, often records the names of all students who participate during a recitation or discussion, using tick marks to indicate how many times they contribute. Other teachers use a "coffee mug technique," pulling students' names from a coffee mug, and placing the slips of paper or Popsicle sticks on the side after the student has responded. Whichever system you choose, *the important point is to make sure that the interaction is not dominated by a few volunteers.*

It's also important to make sure that males and females have equal opportunity to participate. A review of the literature (Grossman & Grossman, 1994) reports that "teachers demonstrate a clear bias in favor of male participation in their classes":

Teachers are more likely to call on a male volunteer when students are asked to recite; this is also true when they call on nonvolunteers. When students recite, teachers are also more likely to listen to and talk to males. They also use more of their ideas in classroom discussions and respond to them in more helpful ways. . . . This pattern of giving more attention to males is especially clear in science and mathematics classes. (p. 76)

Similarly, *How Schools Shortchange Girls* (1992), a study commissioned by the American Association of University Women (AAUW), reports that males often demand—and receive—more attention from teachers. In one study of 10 high school geometry classes (Becker, 1981), for example, males called out answers to teacher questions twice as frequently as females. The same result was obtained in a study of 30 physical science and 30 chemistry classes (Jones & Wheatley, 1990): Whereas the female students appeared "self-conscious and quiet," the males were "more aggressive in calling out responses and tended to use louder tones of voice when seeking the teacher's attention" (p. 867).

Why would teachers allow male students to dominate classroom interaction by calling out? Morse and Handley (1985) suggest three possible reasons: (1) the behavior is so frequent that teachers come to accept it; (2) teachers expect males to be aggressive; and (3) the call-outs may be perceived by teachers as indicators of interest. Whatever the reasons, Morse and Handley's study of junior high science classes found that the trend toward male dominance became even greater as students moved from seventh to eighth grade.

Sandy is one science teacher who does not allow the boys to "grab the floor":

I find that the boys are often faster at responding than the girls. Boys will call out the answers even if they're not sure, while the girls will sit and think before they give an answer. I really have to stay aware of that and make sure that the girls get an opportunity to respond.

The following vignette illustrates one strategy that Sandy uses to ensure that girls have the opportunity to participate:

SANDY: Listen really carefully. [She writes an equation on the board. Pointing to the equation, she turns to the class and continues.] A student was asked to produce 30 grams of O_2 gas. How many grams of $KClO_3$ must the student use to do this? [There is no response.] Can I say that if the student needs to produce 30 grams of O_2 gas she would need to start with 30 grams of $KClO_3$?

STUDENTS: [in chorus] No-o-o.

SANDY: Why not? [Students raise their hands. A few boys start to call out.] Wait, raise your hand. [She calls on a girl who has not raised her hand.] Janice.

JANICE: Because oxygen is different. [Several boys start to call out again. Sandy shakes her head to indicate that they should wait.]

SANDY: Okay, Janice. Because O_2 is a different chemical, but what is the relationship between moles of O_2 and moles of $KClO_3$?

JANICE: [She shrugs. Again, boys start to call out.]

SANDY: Look back at the board. Does the equation reveal anything to you about the relationship?

JANICE: [Her eyes light up.] It's a two-to-three ratio.

SANDY: Super!

Although greater participation by males may be a common phenomenon, it does not hold true across all contexts. In the urban high school where Donnie teaches, for example, it's not considered "cool" for a boy to act too smart or too interested in learning:

The boys may try to "take over" in basic skills, but not in the more advanced math classes like algebra or geometry. In these classes, it's the girls who want to respond. As you get to 11th or 12th grade, there are fewer and fewer boys in these classes and they're not the leaders. We're really losing a lot of our males.

Whatever the pattern, teachers need to be sensitive to gender differences in participation and use strategies to ensure that both males and females have opportunities to participate. Sometimes these are very straightforward. Listen to Christina:

In one of my classes, the boys really dominate the conversation if I let them. This is something I've pointed out to them, but they still grab the floor whenever they can. So sometimes I'll just say, "For the next five minutes, boys can't talk. I want to hear only from the girls."

Sometimes, distributing participation is difficult because students are reluctant to speak and there are too *few* volunteers. At other times, distributing participation is problematic because there are too *many* volunteers. The more teachers stimulate interest in a particular lesson, the more students want to respond. This means greater competition for each turn (Doyle, 1986), and "bidding" for a chance to speak can become loud and unruly.

One useful strategy is to allow several students to answer one question. In the following interaction, we see Christina increase participation by not "grabbing" the first answer and moving on to a new question. She has just focused students' attention on a passage from Edith Wharton's *Ethan Frome,* in which Ethan looks at a cushion his wife Zeena had made for him when they were engaged—"the only piece of needlework he had ever seen her do"—and then flings it across the room.

CHRISTINA: He throws it across the room. What does this suggest about his feelings for her?

STUDENT 1: I think it shows that he really did hate her.

STUDENT 2: I think he was fed up, but I don't think he hated her. He had a lot of opportunities to leave her and he didn't.

STUDENT 3: I think he just felt so guilty. Guilt overpowered the hate. That's why he didn't leave her.

STUDENT 4: He wouldn't know how to react to the freedom. I think he's afraid to leave.

CHRISTINA: Good point. Is he not leaving because he's used to the farm, or because of Zeena, or because he's afraid to be alone?

STUDENT 5: Now that you said that, it made me think, maybe it's not Zeena who has the problem. Maybe it's Ethan. And maybe it would happen again with Mattie. . . .

STUDENT 6: Yeah. He needs someone to rely on. First he relied on Zeena and his parents. Now she's getting sicker, and he can't rely on her, so he's turning to Mattie.

STUDENT 7: But if he relied on her when he needed it, why can't she rely on him now that she needs it?

STUDENT 8: He could slip something into her drink and get rid of her and marry Mattie.

STUDENT 9: I don't think he hates her enough. He's just fed up with her.

During one visit to Donnie's class, I watched her distribute participation widely by specifying that each student should give only one possible answer to the problem:

DONNIE: Today we start a new adventure—equations with two variables. Our answers are going to be ordered pairs. I'm going to put this up here, $x + y = 3$. [She writes the equation on the board.] Now, if I ask you to give me all the possible answers, what would you say? [There are lots of hands up.] Okay, give me *one,* Shameika.

SHAMEIKA: (0, 3).

DONNIE: [She writes that on the board.] Okay, give me another. Sharif.

SHARIF: (1, 2).

DONNIE: Another. Tayeisha.

TAYEISHA: (2, 1).

Another strategy is to have each student write a response and share it with one or two neighbors. This allows everyone to participate actively. You might then ask some of the groups to report on what they discussed.

One final thought: While you're thinking about ways to distribute participation, keep in mind the suggestions made in Chapter 3 for counteracting the action zone phenomenon: (1) move around the room whenever possible; (2) establish eye contact with students seated farther away from you; (3) direct comments to students seated in the rear and on the sides; and (4) periodically change students' seats so that all students have an opportunity to be up front.

Providing Time to Think without Losing the Pace

Envision this scenario: You've just asked a well-formulated, carefully worded, higher-level question designed to stimulate critical thinking and problem solving. And you're met with total silence. Your face begins to feel flushed, and your heart beats a little faster. What to do now?

One reason silence is so uncomfortable is that it's hard to interpret: Are students thinking about the question? Are they asleep? Are they so muddled they're unable to respond? Silence is also troubling to teachers because it can threaten the pace and momentum of the lesson (Arends, 1988). Even a few seconds of silence can seem like eternity. This helps to explain why many teachers wait less than *one second* before calling on a student (Rowe, 1974). Yet research demonstrates that if you extend *"wait time"* to three or four seconds, you can increase the quality of students' answers and promote participation. After all, if you're asking a thought-provoking question, you need to give students time to think.

Sometimes it's helpful to tell students that you don't expect an immediate answer. This legitimates the silence and gives students an opportunity to formulate their responses. During a visit to Fred's class, I saw him indicate that he wanted everyone to think for a while before responding:

> We're been talking about how you can use indicators to decide if a person will be a liberal or conservative, a Republican or a Democrat, and some people came to me after school and said they thought that maybe I was encouraging you all to make stereotypes. I'm really glad they brought that up. You should not do an assignment in an unthinking, unquestioning way. So let's talk about this. First, these people obviously thought it was bad to

stereotype people. Why? Why is it bad to stereotype people? Before you answer, think. *[There's a long pause. Fred finally calls on a student to respond.]*

Allowing students to write an answer to your question is another way of providing them with time to think. Written responses also help to maintain students' engagement, since everyone has to construct a response. In addition, students who are uncomfortable speaking extemporaneously can read from their written papers. In the following example, we see Sandy use this strategy:

Sandy is introducing the concept of chemical equilibrium. She has drawn a diagram on the board showing the relative concentrations of A + B and C + D over time. She asks, "Where is equilibrium established? At Time 1, Time 2, or Time 3? Jot it down and write a sentence explaining why you chose T1, T2, or T3." She walks around the room, looking at students' papers. With a little laugh, she comments: "I see a lot of correct answers, and then the word because.*"*

During our conversation about her lesson, Sandy recalled an incident that underscored the value of having all students write a response to a question:

I had this girl in my honors class, who came to see me about the second week of school. She was obviously upset about how she was doing; she wanted to drop the class. She started to cry. "Everyone is so much smarter than I am." I asked her how she had come to that conclusion, and it was clear that she was equating response time with ability. I find that a lot of the girls do that. She says, "I'm just in the middle of figuring it out, and the other kids are already answering." She says, "I like it when you ask us to write our answers down first. But when I have to respond orally I'm intimidated."

Once you have selected someone to respond, it's also important to provide that student with an opportunity to think. This is another kind of wait time, and research has documented that here, too, teachers often jump in too soon (Rowe, 1974). Sometimes they provide the answer themselves or call on another individual. This is particularly tempting if other students are waving their hands. Watch the way Donnie deals with this situation during a lesson on linear measurement:

DONNIE: Okay, so how are you going to figure this out? Eugene.

EUGENE: You have to know how many inches are in a mile.

DONNIE: And how are you going to figure *that* out? [Eugene is silent, but Ebony is waving her hand.]

EBONY: Ooh, ooh, Miss, I know, I know how to do it.

DONNIE: [very softly] Wait a minute, Ebony, give him a chance. Let him think.

Stimulating and Maintaining Interest

In previous chapters, we have discussed Kounin's classic study (1970) of the differences between orderly and disorderly classrooms. One finding of that study was that students are more involved in work and less disruptive when teachers attempt to involve non-reciting individuals in the recitation task, maintain their attention, and keep them "on their toes." Kounin called this behavior "group alerting." Observations of our four teachers reveal that they frequently use group-alerting strategies to stimulate attention and to maintain the pace of the lesson. For example, watch how Christina tries to generate interest in "parenthetical documentation"—a lesson that has the potential to be really deadly:

> *Today we're going to be talking about the next step in doing the research paper—how to cite sources in the body of the paper using MLA format. It's called parenthetical documentation. Now some of you have been asking why you have to learn this. Well, here's an example of a paper using parenthetical documentation. [She puts an excerpt from a paper on the overhead.] This is an excerpt from a 60-page paper [she waves it in the air] written by a friend of mine who works for a sales corporation. The paper doesn't have anything to do with literary analysis; it's a profitability analysis of one of my friend's $2.5 million clients. She's not in English, but we went to high school together, and we learned how to do this there, just like you're learning how to do it now. This is a skill that you'll use in lots of different situations, not just writing a literary analysis for English 10R.*

Students' interest can also be stimulated and maintained if you inject some humor or novelty into the recitation itself. During a lesson on the difference between third-person limited narration and third-person omniscient narration, Christina uses Michaela, a student in the class, as an example:

CHRISTINA: Let's say that Michaela comes into the room, goes to her seat, does her journal entry, and then does her group task. We don't know anything at all about how she's feeling inside. That's an example of third-person, limited narration. All we know is what the narrator can *see.* Now, here's another version: Michaela comes into the room feeling tired, but then she sees the journal topic on the board and gets really excited. She enjoys writing her journal entry, and then enthusiastically moves to her group task. What would that be?

STUDENT: A fairy tale! [Everyone laughs.]

Challenges to students can also be a way of encouraging students to think and to pay attention. Here are a few examples:

FRED: Please listen to this now . . . most Americans don't understand this at all; they don't have a clue. I want you to understand this.

DONNIE: You need to fix this in your minds because we're going to use this later. . . . Now this is not really a trick question, but you'll have to think.

SANDY: This usually isn't covered in a first-year chemistry course. As a matter of fact, it's a problem that I asked on my honors chemistry test. But I know you guys can do it. I have confidence that you can do it. Just take it apart, step by step.

These challenges are reminiscent of the behavior of "Teacher X," one of the subjects in Hermine Marshall's (1987) study of three teachers' motivational strategies. Marshall found that Teacher X frequently used statements designed to challenge students to think: "I'm going to trick you, " "Get your brain started . . . You're going to think," "Get your mind started," "Look bright-eyed and bushy-tailed" (stated, according to Marshall, "with enthusiasm and a touch of humor"). This frequent use of statements to stimulate and maintain student attention was in sharp contrast to the typical statements made by the other two teachers in the study (e.g., "The test will be on Thursday" or "Open your books to page 382"). In fact, Teacher Y and Teacher Z *never* used the strategy of alerting students to pay attention, and they rarely challenged students to think. The vast majority of their directives were attempts to *return* students to the task *after* attention and interest had waned.

Another way of engaging students is to make room for personal knowledge and experience. Bracha Alpert (1991) studied students' behavior during classroom recitations

Donnie challenges students to think during a lesson on triangles.

and discussions in three high school English classrooms. She found that in two classrooms, students tended to be resistant: They mumbled, refused to answer, and argued. In the third classroom, no signs of student resistance were apparent; instead, students in this class actively participated in discussions. Alpert concluded that the resistance was created by the teachers' tendency to emphasize factual, formal, academic knowledge, without any attempt to relate students' personal life experiences to what was being taught. She provides some examples of this approach: "What's the significance of the dream [in the poem]?" "What is the tone of the poem?" or "What's being implied [by the author] in that scene?" In sharp contrast, the third teacher encouraged students to relate their personal experiences to the literary works they read. For example, when discussing why the literary character is so angry, he asked students to think of things that made them angry. He also asked them questions that promoted their involvement with the literary works—for example, "Do you feel sorry for any of the characters?" "Do you want Eliza to marry Freddy?"

Although it may be easier to do this in subjects like English and social studies, observations indicate that Sandy and Donnie also try to relate topics to students' own personal experiences. For example, when Sandy is introducing acids and bases, she'll begin by inviting students to tell her everything they already know about the topic. Her invitation usually leads to a discussion about fish tanks and pools, and once, they talked about what could happen if a child for whom you were babysitting drank Drano (a base) and why you couldn't use vinegar (an acid) to neutralize it! Similarly, when Donnie teaches about circles in geometry, she talks in terms of bicycles; each spoke of the tire is a radius, and the place where the chain touches the gear is the point of tangency.

Providing Feedback without Losing the Pace

As we discussed in Chapter 8, the Beginning Teacher Evaluation Study (Fisher, Berliner, Filby, Marliave, Cahan, & Dishaw, 1980) documented the importance of providing feedback to students:

> *When more frequent feedback is offered, students pay attention more and learn more. Academic feedback was more strongly and consistently related to achievement than any of the other teaching behaviors. (p. 27)*

But how can you provide appropriate feedback while maintaining the pace and momentum of your lesson? Barak Rosenshine (1986) has reviewed the research on effective teaching and has developed a set of guidelines that may be helpful. According to Rosenshine, when students give correct, confident answers, you can simply ask another question or provide a brief verbal or nonverbal indication that they are correct. If students are correct but hesitant, however, a more deliberate affirmation is necessary. You might also explain *why* the answer is correct ("Yes, that's correct, because . . .") in order to reinforce the material.

When students provide an incorrect answer, the feedback process is trickier. If you think the individual has made a careless error, you can make a simple correction and move on. If you decide that the student can arrive at the correct answer with a little help, you can provide hints or prompts. Sometimes it's useful to backtrack to a simpler question that you think the individual can answer, and then work up to your original question step by step. Watch Sandy:

Students are stuck on the question: "Given the following balanced equation, what volume of hydrogen gas can be produced from the decomposition of two moles of H_2O?" Their faces are blank, and there's absolute silence. Sandy asks: "Well, what is the volume of one mole of any gas at STP [standard temperature and pressure]?" All hands shoot up. Sandy calls on a student to respond. "22.4 liters." Sandy continues: "Do you know the relationship between moles of H_2O and moles of hydrogen gas produced?" Again, there are lots of hands, and a student replies: "It's a one-to-one relationship. The equation shows you that." Suddenly there is a lot of handwaving, and students begin to call out, "Ooh, I see." "Oh, I got it." With a smile, Sandy motions for them to calm down and wait: "Okay, hold on, let's go back to the original question. Given the following balanced equation, what volume of hydrogen gas can be produced from the decomposition of two moles of H_2O?"

There are times when students are simply unable to respond to your question. When that happens, there's little point in belaboring the issue by providing prompts or cues; this will only make the recitation or discussion sluggish. Donnie sometimes allows students in this situation to "pass." This practice not only helps to maintain the pace, it also allow students to "save face." Meanwhile, she makes a mental note that she needs to reteach the material to the individuals having difficulty.

Donnie is reviewing homework problems on the Pythagorean theorem. "Okay, moving on to number 14." She moves over to Edward and looks as though she's going to call on him. He signals that he doesn't want to answer that question. "Don't call on you? Okay. I'll come back." She moves away and calls on someone else.

The most problematic situation for teachers is when students' answers are clearly incorrect. Saying "No, that's not right" can be uncomfortable, yet students deserve to have accurate feedback. As Sandy emphasizes: "It's really important to be clear about what's correct and what's not. The students have to know that the teacher will not leave them thinking the wrong thing." Rather than directly correcting students, however, Sandy prefers to help them discover their own errors:

I have difficulty saying "Your answer is wrong," but I usually don't have to. I can ask them to explain their reasoning. Or I can take the part of the answer that is correct and work with it. I can ask a question about their response. "How does the graph show that?" "So you're saying it would have to be like this . . ." I like students to find their own mistakes and correct them.

Similarly, Donnie will ask, "How did you arrive at that answer?" And Fred will tell students: "That answer doesn't make sense to me. How did you figure it out?" Sometimes, he compliments students on making a "really good mistake": "I love mistakes. That's how we all learn."

Monitoring Comprehension: Requiring Overt Responses

A simple way to determine how well your students understand the material is to have them respond overtly to your questions. Earlier, we saw how Sandy had her students write down their responses to her question, so she could circulate and see what they were writing. Fred and Donnie also use this strategy:

Fred's students have just read an article about the "Nacirema" people. [They later learn that the Naciremas are Americans—spelled backwards.] When the students are finished reading, Fred asks them to make 10 valid inferences about these people, providing supporting evidence for each inference. "Now, before you begin, I want to see if you understand what to do or if you're clueless about this assignment. Take this piece of paper and write down: 'In Nacirema culture, kids cry when they lose their [rac].' Now this is a valid inference. Write down one, two, or three pieces of evidence for this valid inference." He circulates throughout the room and checks to see what students are writing.

Donnie's students have been learning about the properties of circles. At the end of the period, Donnie tells her students to take out a piece of unlined paper, a compass, a ruler, and a pencil. She tells the students: "Now this is to check on your ability to apply the terms that we've been going over, not just regurgitate the definitions. I will repeat the directions two or three times. This also checks your ability to listen and follow directions. [One boy calls out, "My worst quality," and everyone laughs.] Draw a circle with a radius of two inches. [She pauses to give the students the chance to do so.] Call the center of the circle point P. . . . From the center, going due south, draw radius PA. Label it. . . . The next thing you're going to do is draw a chord, but listen, the chord you're going to draw is going to bisect PA and go in an east-west direction."

Another way of quickly assessing students' comprehension is to ask them to put their thumbs up or down to indicate agreement or disagreement with a particular statement. You can also assess students' comprehension by having them respond chorally rather than individually. This allows you to scan the room and see who's having difficulty. This can be particularly helpful in a drill situation.

Monitoring Comprehension: Using a Steering Group

Another way of checking on students' understanding is to observe a "steering group." This is a sample of students whose performance is used as an indicator that the class is "with you" and that it's all right to move on to a new topic (Lundgren, 1972). Be careful, however, about choosing students for the steering group. If you select only high achievers, their performance may lead you to overestimate the comprehension of the class as a whole.

During one discussion with Donnie, she explained that a boy in her algebra class was a key member of her steering group:

I have this one boy who's average in ability. He generally sits in the back of the room, and when he doesn't understand, he gets a certain look on his face. I can tell he's confused. But when he does understand, the "light goes on." When I see the light is on with him, I can be sure most of the other kids understand.

Moderating Student-Centered Discussions

Thus far, the chapter has examined three major problems associated with recitations and teacher-led discussions and has provided some suggestions for avoiding these problems. We have considered these two subsettings together because they share a number of features. In both the recitation and the teacher-led discussion the teacher is in charge, determining the content, the participants, and the pacing. Now we turn to a third type of verbal interaction, the *student-centered discussion*. Here, students have an increased opportunity to interact directly with one another, while the teacher acts as a facilitator or moderator.

Consider this example observed in Fred's Institute for Legal and Political Education (IPLE) class. The topic was budget deficits, and Hope had just asked a key question: "Why can't the government just print more money to pay off a debt?" Fred noted that this was an important question, and he attempted to provide an explanation. Hope wasn't convinced. Other students joined in:

SUSAN: I think I got it now. You know how they say that everyone can't be a millionaire. There's got to be some poor people? It's like that.

JOHN: Yeah, like when I play monopoly. I buy every property, so I go into bankruptcy. So I take out a loan, and I'm ruining the game because I'm not playing with the money I'm supposed to have. It's like cheating.

LORIE: Yeah, that money doesn't really exist.

HOPE: What do you mean? If the government prints the money, it does exist. [A number of students begin talking at the same time.]

FRED: Hold on. Stuart, then Roy, then Alicia.

STUART: The money's worth a lot because there's only a little. If there were a lot, it would only be worth a little.

HOPE: I still don't understand. So what, if it's only worth a little.

ROY: Pretend there's this gold block sitting in Fort Knox and it's worth $10, but there's only one $10 bill. Now if we make up 10 $10 bills, each will only be worth $1.

HOPE: So what? I can still use it to buy stuff. [A few students start to jump in, but
        Fred intervenes.]
FRED: Alicia hasn't had her chance to talk.
ALICIA: I think I got it now. Let me try. There's this diamond, and we both want it. . . .
        [She continues to explain, but Hope is still confused.]
FRED: Let's see if I can help out here. . . .

As we can see from this excerpt, Fred essentially stays out of the interaction, except for making sure that students have an opportunity to speak when the interaction gets excited. In contrast to the recitation, or even many teacher-led discussions, students speak directly to one another. They comment on one another's contributions, they question, they disagree, and they explain.

Providing opportunities for student–student discussions means that teachers have to give up their role as *leader* and assume the role of *facilitator*. This can be difficult for teachers who are used to dominating or at least directing the conversation. Even Fred, who encourages and values student-centered discussions, sometimes feels frustrated at not playing a larger role in the conversation:

> *I really like having kids asking other kids questions, asking one another for supporting evidence, debating issues directly. But even so, sometimes I really get ticked off that I can't get a word in. During some discussions, I'm dying to say something. Sometimes, I'll just say, "Teacher prerogative," and jump in.*

Acting as a facilitator rather than a leader does not mean abdicating responsibility for guiding the interaction. This became very clear during a conversation with Fred, when he described some of the problems that he tries to anticipate and avoid:

> *First of all, a discussion like this can be an opportunity for some kids to show how smart they are and to get air time, so it's important to watch out that kids don't pontificate and monopolize. Second, you have to listen carefully and ask yourself, "Where is this going?" I often have an end goal in mind, and I try to make sure that the discussion doesn't get too far afield. Occasionally, I'll jump in and say something like, "I think we're losing the focus here" or "I think you're arguing over semantics." Also, a lot of times kids state opinions as fact, and I think it's important not to let them get away with that. I'll interject and ask them to provide supporting evidence. Or I'll ask for clarification: "Is that what you meant to say?"*

Because student-centered discussions can be so difficult for both students and teachers, Christina has developed a strategy she calls "Post-It Note discussions." When students read an assigned text, they choose a passage that especially interests them—it can be a few words, a few pages, or anything in between. They place a Post-It Note near the passage they've chosen, and write responses to questions that Christina constructed (e.g., Why did you choose this passage? What does it mean? What does it tell you about the rest of the text? What issues are raised here?) Then they take a second Post-It Note and write a question for discussion. The following exchange is from a Post-It Note discussion on *Ethan Frome:*

STUDENT 1: My passage is on page 95, beginning with "His impulses . . ." [Students turn to page 95, and she reads the paragraph aloud, while everyone follows along.] I chose this passage because I think it's the most important in the chapter. It shows how Ethan is finally deciding to tell Zeena how he feels, but then he begins to change his mind and he's thinking he can't do it. My question is, why do you think Ethan is having such a hard time about leaving Zeena?

STUDENT 2: I think he feels it's wrong to leave her because she's sick and she's relying on him.

STUDENT 3: I also think he's worried about the money, but it wouldn't stop him.

STUDENT 4: But I *do* think it would stop him. He can't even afford the train ticket to leave her.

STUDENT 3: But in the next sentence, he says he's sure he's going to get work.

STUDENT 5: He's worried he won't be able to support Mattie.

STUDENT 6: He wants to leave but he's afraid of change. . . .

As we can see, the students' role is to pose the discussion questions and to call on classmates to respond—not a role to which students are accustomed. During the previous discussion, in fact, a girl asked her question and then seemed paralyzed in the face of her peers' raised hands. When she turned to Christina for assistance, Christina quietly reminded her, "You're in charge, Renata." The girl laughed, "I'm not used to this!"

Being "in charge" is certainly an unfamiliar role for students, but one that students gradually learn to assume with the Post-It Note strategy. After class, Christina shared her thoughts on the importance of having students take responsibility for class discussions:

During my field experiences and student teaching, I often saw class "discussions," where the teachers did almost all the talking. I worried that I wouldn't be able to run an effective discussion because even the most experienced and talented teachers I observed were struggling to involve their students. It seemed like it would be torture to stand in front of a class and get no response. So I started thinking about how I could get students to take more responsibility for the discussion. I always write in the margins of my books when a passage interests me, but obviously kids can't do that with the school's books. So I hit upon the idea of Post-It Notes. I think it's working pretty well, and students' reactions have been overwhelmingly positive. This way, students really "own" the discussion. They talk about what interests them, rather than just what I think is important. They have to prepare for the discussion by putting their thoughts into writing, and that almost always makes it a better discussion. And all the students have to participate, at least to read their passage and ask their question. I think the students really like it too. The hardest part is being quiet. I purposely sit on

1. Carefully formulate the discussion question (making sure that it is not in a form that invites a yes/no or either/or answer), along with subsidiary questions, embedded questions, follow-up questions, and related questions.

2. Create a question outline, identifying at least three subquestions and at least four alternative answers to the main question.

3. Present the discussion question to the class, writing it on the chalkboard or on an overhead transparency or on paper distributed to the class. After reading the question aloud, go on to give the sense of the question, identifying terms, explaining the relevance of the question, connecting it to a previous discussion or class activity, and so on. End with an invitation to the class to begin addressing the question.

4. Initially, help the class focus on the question, rather than giving answers to it. For example, invite the class to tell what they know about the question, what it means to them.

5. DO NOT COMMENT AFTER THE FIRST STUDENT'S CONTRIBUTION. (If you do, the interaction will quickly become I-R-E.) In addition, do not ask, "What does someone else think about that?" (If you do, you invite statements of difference or opposition to the first position, and your discussion turns into a debate.)

6. In general, do not ask questions beyond the first question. Instead use nonquestion alternatives: statements (the thoughts that occurred to you in relation to what the speaker has just said; reflective statements that basically restate the speaker's contribution; statements indicating interest in hearing further about what the speaker has just said; statements indicating the relationship between what the speaker has just said and what a previous speaker has said); signals (sounds or words indicating interest in what the speaker has said); even silence. (Dillon acknowledges that deliberates silence is the hardest of all for teachers to do. To help teachers remain quiet, he recommends silently singing "Baa, baa, black sheep" after each student's contribution.)

7. Facilitate the discussion by

Locating: "Where are we now? What are we saying?"

Summarizing: "What have we accomplished? agreed on?"

Opening: "What shall we do next?"

Tracking: "We seem a little off track here. How can we all get back on the same line of thought?"

Pacing: "Just a minute, I wonder whether we're not moving a little too fast here. Let's take a closer look at this idea. . . ."

8. When it is time to end the discussion, help students to summarize the discussion and identify the remaining questions.

FIGURE 11–2. Guidelines for leading discussions
Source: Based on Dillon, 1994.

the outside of the group, so I'm less likely to dominate, but I still have to remind myself a lot to stay out of it as much as possible.

As Christina's comments suggest, it's not easy to conduct a good discussion, particularly for teachers who are used to dominating verbal interaction in the classroom. Dillon (1994) provides some extremely helpful guidelines for preparing and conducting discussions (see Figure 11–2). In addition, keep in mind three basic suggestions (Gall & Gillett, 1981):

1. *If possible, limit the size of the group:* It's difficult to have a student-centered discussion with a large number of participants. Fred's IPLE class has only 12 students, so group size wasn't too much of a problem here, but in a class like

Christina's, opportunities to speak are more limited. In his larger classes, Fred sometimes uses the "fishbowl" method, in which five or six students carry on the discussion in the middle of the room, while the rest of the class sits in a large circle around them and acts as observers and recorders. Another solution is to divide the class into small discussion groups of five, with one student in each group acting as a discussion leader.

2. *Arrange students so they can make eye contact.* It's very difficult to speak directly to someone if all you can see is the back of a head. If at all possible, students should move their desks into an arrangement that allows them to be face-to-face.
3. *Teach discussion skills.* Just as you need to teach students the skills for working in small groups, it is important to prepare students for participating in a student-centered discussion. Gall and his colleagues (1976; cited in Gall & Gillett, 1981) have developed a list of skills that you may have to teach explicitly:

   • Talk to each other, not just to the moderator.
   • Don't monopolize.
   • Ask others what they think.
   • Don't engage in personal attack.
   • Listen to others' ideas.
   • Acknowledge others' ideas.
   • Question irrelevant remarks.
   • Ask for clarification.
   • Ask for reasons for others' opinions.
   • Give reasons for your opinions.

Concluding Comments

This chapter has focused on three different patterns of verbal interaction: recitations, teacher-led discussions, and student-centered discussions. It's important not to get them confused—to think that you're leading a discussion when you're actually conducting a recitation.

Teachers often say that they use discussion a great deal, when in fact they are conducting recitations. For example, in a provocative article entitled "What Teachers Do When They Say They're Having Discussions of Content Area Reading Assignments," Alvermann, O'Brien, and Dillon (1990) found that although 24 middle school teachers reported using discussion, only 7 could actually be observed doing so; the others were using recitation or lecture interspersed with questions. These findings are consistent with observations of 1,000 elementary and secondary classrooms across the country, in which discussion was seen only 4 to 7 percent of the time (Goodlad, 1984). It is clear that real discussion is very rarely used in classroom. As Sandy comments:

A lot of beginning teachers get these two mixed up. They've been told they're supposed to ask a lot of questions, so they do, but often the questions are yes/no questions or questions that elicit short answers without a lot of depth: What do all atoms have in common? How many protons are in this atom? In discussions, the majority of the questions are critical thought questions, and the response time is longer. You're trying to develop an idea or draw a conclusion. You're not just reviewing; you're working toward a conceptual goal.

Also keep in mind the criticisms that have been leveled against recitations, and reflect on how frequently you dominate the verbal interaction in your classroom. Ask yourself whether you also provide opportunities for student-centered discussion, during which you serve as a facilitator (rather than a questioner) and encourage direct student–student interaction. Reflect on the level of thinking that you require from students. The classroom recitation can serve a number of useful functions, but *overuse* suggests that your curriculum consists largely of names, dates, facts, and algorithms (Cazden, 1988).

🧩 Summary

This chapter began by examining some of the major criticisms of recitation, as well as the useful functions it can serve. It then distinguished recitations from teacher-led discussions and considered the hazards these two subsettings present to teachers. Next, the chapter suggested a number of strategies for using recitations and teacher-led discussions successfully in your classroom. Finally, we looked at two examples of a student-centered discussion and briefly considered a number of guidelines for managing this type of verbal interaction.

Characteristic pattern of a recitation

- I-R-E (teacher initiation, student response, teacher evaluation).
- Quick pace.
- Used to review material, to elaborate on a text.

Criticisms of recitation

- The teacher plays a dominant role, the student a passive one.
- There is a lack of interaction among students.
- Recall is emphasized over higher-level thinking skills.
- Recitation promotes public evaluation that can lead to negative interdependence.
- Recitation format sometimes conflicts with students' cultural background.

Five functions of recitation

- Provides opportunity to check on students' comprehension.
- Offers an opportunity to push students to construct more complete responses.

- Involves students in presentation of material.
- Allows for contact with individuals in a group setting.
- Helps to maintain attention level.

Characteristics of a teacher-led discussion

- I-R (or even I-R-R-R).
- Student-initiated questions.
- Student comments on contributions of peers.
- Slower pace.
- Intended to stimulate thinking, to foster problem solving, to examine implications.

Three hazards of recitations and teacher-led discussions

- Unequal participation.
- Losing the pace and focus.
- Difficulty in monitoring comprehension.

Strategies for successful use of recitations and teacher-led discussions

- Distribute chances for participation.
  Use some type of patterned turn taking.
  Ensure that males and females have equal opportunity to participate.
- Provide time to think about answers before responding.
- Stimulate and maintain interest by
  Injecting mystery/suspense elements into your questions.
  Using humor, novelty.
  Making room for personal knowledge and experience.
- Provide feedback without losing the pace.
- Monitor comprehension by requiring overt responses.
- Monitor comprehension by observing a steering group.

Moderating student-centered discussions

- Act as facilitator rather than questioner.
- Ensure that some students don't monopolize.
- Make sure the discussion stays on track.
- Ask students to provide supporting evidence for opinions.
- Limit group size.
- Arrange students so they have eye contact.
- Teach discussion skills.

When planning your lessons, think about the extent to which you use recitations, teacher-led discussions, and student-centered discussions in your classroom. Think about the level of the questions that you ask: Are all of your questions low-level, factual questions that can be answered with a word or two, or are your questions designed to stimulate thinking and problem solving? Ask yourself if you consistently dominate the interaction, or if you also provide opportunities for real discussion among students.

Activities

1. Visit a classroom and observe a recitation. On a seating chart, map the verbal interaction by placing a check in the "seat" of each student who participates. Analyze your results and draw conclusions about how widely and fairly participation is distributed in this class.

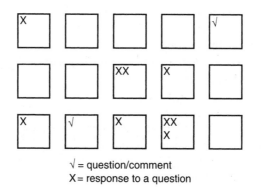

√ = question/comment
X = response to a question

2. Your colleague has asked you to help him figure out why his students are not paying attention in class. He would like you to observe him and offer feedback. What follows is a session you observed. Using what you know about distributing participation, stimulating and maintaining interest, and monitoring comprehension, identify the trouble spots of his lesson and provide three specific suggestions for improvement.

   When you enter the class, Mr. B. is perched on a stool in front of the room with the science book in his hand.

   MR. B.: Who remembers what photosynthesis is? [No response.] Do you remember yesterday when we looked at green plants and we discussed how a plant makes its own food? [Mr. B. notices that Thea is nodding.] Thea, do you remember about photosynthesis?

   THEA: Yeah.

   MR. B.: Well, can you tell the class about it?

   THEA: It has something to do with light and chlorophyll.

MR. B.: Good. Tom, can you add to this? [Tom was drawing in his notebook.]

TOM: No.

MR. B.: Tom, Thea told us that photosynthesis had to do with light and chlorophyll. Do you recall our discussion from yesterday when we defined photosynthesis?

TOM: Sort of.

MR. B.: What do you mean? Didn't you write down the definition with the rest of the class? Look in your notebook and tell me the definition. [Tom starts to page through his notebook. Many of the students have begun to whisper and snicker. Some are looking in their notebooks.] How many of you have found the page where we defined photosynthesis? [Seven students raise their hands.] Good. Would somebody read to me that definition? Thea.

THEA: Photosynthesis is the process of forming sugars and starches in plants from water and carbon dioxide when sunlight acts upon chlorophyll.

MR. B.: Excellent. Does everyone understand? [A few students nod.] Good. Tomorrow we will be having a quiz about plants and photosynthesis. Tom, will you be ready for the quiz?

TOM: Sure, Mr. B.

MR. B.: Okay, now let's all turn to page 135 in our science texts and read about the uses of plants.

3. Monitoring students' comprehension is sometimes problematic. Choose one of the following topics (or think of one in your own content area) and suggest two different ways a teacher could elicit overt participation in order to determine student understanding.

   a. Main characters and their traits.

   b. Characteristics of parallelograms.

   c. Symbols for chemical ions.

   d. Types of woodworking joints.

   e. Foreign language vocabulary words.

   f. Longitude and latitude.

   g. States and capitals.

   h. Types of clouds.

   i. Fat content of various products.

4. We know that recitations and discussions are often confused. Observe and record 10 minutes of a class "discussion." Then, using the following checklist, see if the verbal interaction actually meets the criteria for a discussion or if it is more like a recitation.

- Students are the predominant speakers.
- The verbal interaction pattern is not I-R-E, but a mix of statements and questions by a mix of teacher and students.
- The pace is longer and slower.
- The primary purpose is to stimulate a variety of responses, to encourage students to consider different points of view, to foster problem solving, and the like.
- Evaluation consists of agree/disagree, rather than right/wrong.

✦ For Further Reading

Brookfield, S. D., & Preskill, S. (1999). *Discussion as a way of teaching.* San Francisco: Jossey-Bass.

Dillon, J. T. (1994). *Using discussion in classrooms.* Philadelphia: Open University Press.

✦ References

The AAUW Report: How schools shortchange girls. (1992). Washington, DC: The AAUW Educational Foundation and National Education Association.

Alvermann, D., O'Brien, D., & Dillon, D. (1990). What teachers do when they say they're having discussions of content area reading assignments. *Reading Research Quarterly, 25,* 296–322.

Alpert, B. (1991). Students' resistance in the classroom. *Anthropology and Education Quarterly, 22,* 350–366.

Arends, R. I. (1988). *Learning to teach.* New York: Random House.

Becker, J. R. (1981). Differential treatment of females and males in mathematics classes. *Journal for Research in Mathematics Education, 12*(1), 40–53.

Carter, K. (March–April 1985). Teacher comprehension of classroom processes: An emerging direction in classroom management research. Paper presented at the annual meeting of the American Educational Research Association, Chicago.

Cazden, C. B. (1988). *Classroom discourse: The language of teaching and learning.* Portsmouth, NH: Heinemann.

Dillon, J. T. (1994). *Using discussion in classrooms.* Philadelphia: Open University Press.

Doyle, W. (1986). Classroom organization and management. In M. C. Wittrock (Ed.), *The handbook of research on teaching* (3rd ed.). New York: Macmillan, pp. 392–431.

Farrar, M. T. (1988). A sociolinguistic analysis of discussion. In J. T. Dillon (Ed.), *Questioning and discussion—A multidisciplinary study.* Norwood, NJ: Ablex.

Fisher, C. W., Berliner, D. C., Filby, N. N., Marliave, R., Cahen, L. S., & Dishaw, M. M. (1980). Teaching behaviors, academic learning time, and student achievement: An overview. In C. Denham & A. Lieberman (Eds.), *Time to learn.* Washington, D.C., U.S. Department of Education.

Gall, M. D., & Gillett, M. (1981). The discussion method in classroom teaching. *Theory Into Practice, 19,* 98–103.

Good, T., & Brophy, J. E. (2000). *Looking in classrooms* (8th ed.). New York: Addison Wesley Longman.

Goodlad, J. (1984). *A place called school.* New York: McGraw-Hill.

Grossman, H., & Grossman, S. H. (1994). *Gender issues in education.* Boston: Allyn and Bacon.

Hoetker, J., & Ahlbrand, W. P., Jr. (1969). The persistence of the recitation. *American Educational Research Journal, 6,* 145–167.

Jackson, P. W. (1968). *Life in classrooms.* New York: Holt, Rinehart and Winston.

Jones, M. G., & Wheatley, J. (1990). Gender differences in teacher–student interactions in science classrooms. *Journal of Research in Science Teaching, 27,* 861–874.

Kagan, S. (1989/90). The structural approach to cooperative learning. *Educational Leadership, 47*(4), 12–15.

Kounin, J. S. (1970). *Discipline and group management in classrooms.* New York: Holt, Rinehart & Winston.

Lundgren, U. (1972). *Frame factors and the teaching process.* Stockholm: Almqvist and Wiksell.

Marshall, H. H. (1987). Motivational strategies of three fifth-grade teachers. *The Elementary School Journal, 88*(2), 135–150.

McDermott, R. P. (1977). Social relations as contexts for learning in school. *Harvard Educational Review, 47,* 198–213.

Mehan, H. (1979). *Learning lessons: Social organization in a classroom.* Cambridge, MA: Harvard University Press.

Morine-Dershimer, G. & Beyerbach, B. (1987). Moving right along. . . . In V. Richardson-Koehler (Ed.), *Educators' handbook, A research perspective.* New York: Longman, pp. 207–232.

Morse, L. W., & Handley, H. M. (1985). Listening to adolescents: Gender differences in science classroom interaction. In L. C. Wilkinson & C. B. Marrett (Eds.), *Gender influences in classroom interaction.* Orlando, FL: Academic Press.

Philips, S. (1972). Participant structures and communicative competence: Warm Springs children in community and classroom. In C. Cazden, V. John, & D. Hymes (Eds.), *Functions of language in the classroom.* New York: Teachers College Press.

Roby, T. W. (1988). Models of discussion. In J. T. Dillon (Ed.), *Questioning and discussion—A multidisciplinary study.* Norwood, NJ: Ablex, pp. 163–191.

Rosenshine, B. V. (1986). Synthesis of research on explicit teaching. *Educational Leadership, 43*(7), 60–69.

Rowe, M. B. (1974). Wait-time and rewards as instructional variables, their influence on language, logic, and fate control: Part 1: Wait time. *Journal of Research in Science Teaching, 11,* 291–308.

Stodolsky, S. S. (1988). *The subject matters: Classroom activity in math and social studies.* Chicago: University of Chicago Press.

PART IV

Coping with the Challenges

Chapter Twelve

When Prevention Is Not Enough: Protecting and Restoring Order

Concluding Comments

Summary

Not too long ago, I read an entry in the journal of a student teacher whose fourth- and fifth-period English classes were giving her a hard time. It was the middle of November, and Sharon was feeling frustrated by the disrespectful and disruptive behavior of her students. "They just won't sit still long enough to hear directions," she wrote. "I am spending more and more time on telling people to 'Shhh.' I don't understand why they are so rude, and I just don't know what to do."

As I read more, it became clear that this student teacher's problem was not due to an absence of clear rules and routines or to boring, tedious instruction:

> *On the first day that I took over, we reviewed the rules my cooperating teacher had established (just like you suggested!): Come to class on time, don't call out, treat each other with respect, etc. They were really cooperative; I thought this was going to be great, but I guess they were just "psyching me out." Now they argue with me all the time. I say "quiet" and they say, "But I was just telling him . . ." I say, "Put the newspaper/comic book/photo album away," and they say "Just let me look, I have to see . . ." There doesn't seem much else to do except repeat myself. Sometimes it works, sometimes it doesn't. . . . I'm really at my wit's end. If I can't gain some control, there's obviously no way I can teach anything. Sometimes I think I'd be better off if I just forgot about trying to have interesting discussions, projects, small groups, etc., and just gave out worksheets every day, lectured, and didn't allow any talking. That's a far cry from the kind of classroom I wanted to have. I wanted to respect my students, to treat them like adults, but I found I can't. I've always gotten along great with kids, but not now. All these kids seem to understand is discipline referrals and detention.*

This student teacher had learned a sad fact of classroom life: Having clear, reasonable rules and routines doesn't automatically mean that everyone will follow them. At the beginning of the school year, students work hard at "figuring out the teacher"—determining teachers' expectations and requirements, the amount of socializing they will tolerate, and how far they can be pushed. Most students will pursue their agendas within the limits the teacher sets, but they need to know those limits. This underscores the importance of communicating your behavioral expectations to students (the topic of Chapter 4)—and then *enforcing those expectations.* In other words, just as it's part of the students' role to push, it's part of the teacher's role to communicate that students can't push too far. Listen to Sandy:

It's crucial to hold high school students to the expectations you set. In the beginning of the year, they'll try different things to see how much they can get away with. They're constantly testing you. Knowing that, I don't overlook anything in the first few weeks of school; I try to be on top of everything. That way students learn that they can't put one over on you.

Donnie also recognizes that students are busy figuring her out during the first few days of school. She comments:

New teachers should not be fooled by the good behavior that students exhibit at the very beginning of school. I usually find that on the first day of school, everyone is really subdued. They're checking you out. It isn't until the second week that they really start testing. That's when the problems start!

In this chapter, we consider ways of responding to the problems that you may encounter—from minor, nondisruptive infractions to chronic, more serious misbehaviors. Before going any further, however, let's consider what these problems are likely to be.

What's in Store

In the late 1990s, a series of horrific school shootings seized the nation's attention. Newspaper headlines about murderous rampages and television footage of terrorized students conveyed the image of schools as "blackboard jungles." In districts all across the country—whether large or small, rural, urban, or suburban—school personnel agonized over the same question, "Could it happen here?" (Richard, 1999). Fearing the answer, many schools installed metal detectors, banned book bags, and did away with lockers. Yet the vast majority of problems are not nearly so frightening. Survey results suggest that tardiness, class cutting, and tobacco use are the three most serious problems faced by high schools (National Center for Educational Statistics, 1998). (See Table 12-1.)

On a day-to-day basis, teachers must also cope with a host of other frustrating problems (Doyle, 1986, 1990)—socializing at inappropriate times, not having homework done, calling out, daydreaming, forgetting to bring supplies and books, teasing, and name calling. Even if behaviors like these are not seriously disruptive, they can be aggravating, discouraging, and wearing. Furthermore, inappropriate behavior *threatens classroom order by interrupting the flow of instructional activity.* Lessons cannot proceed smoothly and efficiently if students have not brought their homework, and giving instructions is a waste of time if no one is listening.

TABLE 12-1. Principals' Perceptions of Discipline Problems in High Schools

Problem	Percentage of High Schools
Tardiness	67%
Absenteeism/cutting	52
Tobacco use	48
Student drug use	36
Student alcohol use	27
Verbal abuse of teachers	20
Physical conflicts among students	17
Robbery or theft of items greater than $10.00	15
Vandalism	13
Sale of drugs	10
Gangs	9
Racial tensions	7
Possession of weapons	2

Source: National Center for Educational Statistics. (1998). *Violence and discipline problems in U.S. public schools: 1996–97, NCES 98-030.* Washington, DC: U.S. Department of Education, Office of Educational Research and Improvement.

Principles for Dealing with Inappropriate Behavior

There is little research on the relative effectiveness of disciplinary strategies (see Emmer & Aussiker, 1990), but four principles guide our discussion. First, *disciplinary strategies must be consistent with the goal of creating a safe, caring classroom environment.* You need to achieve order, but you also need to choose strategies that support your relationship with students, help them to become self-regulating, and allow them to save face in front of their peers. Curwin and Mendler (1988), authors of *Discipline with Dignity,* put it this way:

> *Students will protect their dignity at all costs, even with their lives if pushed hard enough. In the game of chicken, with two cars racing at top speed toward a cliff, the loser is the one who steps on the brake. Nothing explains this bizarre reasoning better than the need for peer approval and dignity.* (p. 27)

In order to protect students' dignity, it is important to avoid power struggles that cause students to feel humiliated and ridiculed. (Remember our discussion of "when school was awful" in Chapter 5.) Consider this incident, related by a student teacher in an English class:

> *In our remedial writing lab, a student left to get a drink of water and was gone too long. Upset that the student took too long to get a drink, and upset that the student had failed to write his name on an in-class essay, the teacher proceeded to write the student's essay on the board for all to see.*

A few moments later, class was interrupted by a fire alarm. Again the student returned later than he was expected to return—between 30 seconds and a minute—and my teacher proceeded to yell and yell loudly right up in the kid's face. The student asked to speak but his request was denied. After the exchange, my teacher went to the board and proceeded to rip apart the student's essay. The student reminded him that he was not done and that the class was told that they could work on their essays today. The teacher said that this essay was going nowhere, even if given an extra day. I watched the student's face while his essay was being critiqued, and I realized firsthand how vulnerable and powerless students can be. Here is a group of students who lack confidence in writing, who do not dare to take risks with their writing—and this is how we treat them.

In contrast to this teacher, Fred, Donnie, Sandy, and Christina all make a real effort to speak with misbehaving students calmly and quietly. They don't bring up past sins. They take care to separate the youngster's *character* from the specific *misbehavior;* instead of attacking the student as a person ("You're lazy"), they talk about what the student has done ("You have not handed in the last two homework assignments"). When more than a brief intervention is necessary, they try to meet with students privately.

During the first week of school, I witnessed a good example of disciplining with dignity in Sandy's classroom. Even though it was early in the school year, some students had already begun to test Sandy's adherence to the rules she had distributed a few days earlier:

Sandy stands by the door, greeting students as they come in. The bell rings; Sandy begins to close the door, when William breathlessly rushes up. "You're late," she tells him quietly. "Does that mean I have to come after school?" he asks. "I'll talk to you later," she replies and moves to the front of the room to begin the lesson.

Later in the period, students are working in small groups on a lab experiment. Sandy circulates through the room, helping students with the procedure. She goes over to William and pulls him aside. She speaks softly: "You owe me 10 minutes. Today or tomorrow?"

"What's today?"

"Tuesday."

"Uh-oh." William looks worried.

"Is it better for you to come tomorrow?" Sandy asks.

"Yeah—but will you remind me?"

"I certainly will," she says with a rueful smile. Sandy goes over to her desk, makes a note in her grade book, and then continues circulating. A few minutes later, she stands beside William again, helping him with a problem and encouraging his progress.

In this vignette, we see how Sandy tried to avoid embarrassing William by speaking with him privately; how she demonstrated concern for William by offering him a choice about when to come for detention; how she avoided accusations, blame, and character assassination; and how she showed William that she held no grudge by helping with the lab a few minutes later. In short, the vignette demonstrates the way a teacher can communicate clear expectations for appropriate behavior while preserving a student's dignity.

Another way of disciplining with dignity is to structure opportunities for students to assume some responsibility for regulating their own behavior. In Chapter 5, I talked about the importance of sharing responsibility and decision-making authority. This chapter continues that theme by discussing strategies that involve students in solving the problems that arise in classrooms.

The second principle for dealing with misbehavior is that it is essential to *keep the instructional program going with a minimum of disruption.* Achieving this goal requires a delicate balancing act. On one hand, you cannot allow inappropriate behavior to interrupt the teaching–learning process. On the other hand, you must realize that disciplinary strategies themselves can be disruptive. As Doyle comments, interventions are "inherently risky" because they call attention to misbehavior and can actually pull students away from a lesson (1986, p. 421). In order to avoid this situation, you must try to anticipate potential problems and head them off; if you decide that a disciplinary intervention *is* necessary, you need to be as unobtrusive as possible.

Watching the four teachers in action, it is clear that they recognize the importance of protecting the instructional program. In the following incident, Christina sizes up a potentially disruptive situation and is able to maintain the flow of her lesson:

Christina is reviewing the difference between first-person and third-person narrative. In the back of the room, students are passing some photographs around. Christina continues to talk about narrative while she moves up the aisle. In between sentences, she gives the students a quizzical look, as if to say, "What are you folks doing?" Everyone returns the photographs to a girl who puts them in her backpack.

The third principle is that *whether or not a particular action constitutes misbehavior depends on the context in which it occurs* (Doyle, 1986). There are obvious exceptions to this notion—punching another person and stealing property are obvious violations that always require a teacher response. But other behaviors are not so clear cut. For example, in some classes, wearing a hat, sitting on your desk, chewing gum, and talking to neighbors are all misbehaviors, while in other classes these are perfectly acceptable. What constitutes misbehavior is often a function of a particular teacher's tolerance level or the standards set by a particular school (Cairns, 1987). Even within a class, the definition of misbehavior is dependent upon the context. A teacher may decide that talking out of turn is acceptable during a class discussion, as long as students' comments contribute to the lesson and the situation doesn't turn into a free-for-all; at other times, this same teacher may feel that a more structured lesson is needed.

When determining a course of action, you need to ask yourself, "Is this behavior disrupting or benefiting the ongoing instructional activity? Is it hurtful to other children? Does it violate established rules?" If the answer to these questions is no, disciplinary interventions may not be necessary.

> *"I've got no control today," Fred announces with a grin. A glance around the room seems to confirm his assessment. Some students are sitting on their desks; others are standing in the aisles, leaning over other students who are writing. In the back of the room, four students are turned around in their seats and are having an animated discussion. One girl is standing by Fred's desk, loudly debating with a girl seated nearby. Just about everyone is talking. After a few moments, the topic of all this heated conversation becomes clear. Because of severe winter storms, the South Brunswick school district has exceeded the normal allotment of snow days. In order to meet the state mandate for 180 days of school, the board of education must now decide whether to eliminate spring break or extend the school year. Fred has seized the opportunity to teach a lesson on political activism. His students are to think about the issue, consider whether there should be a waiver from the 180-day mandate, and write to their state legislators. Today's assignment is to construct the first draft of the letter. After class, Fred thinks about the atmosphere in the class: "I know I could have exerted a lot more control over the situation. I could have told them to sit quietly, to jot down ideas, and then silently write a first draft. But what would I have gained?"*

Finally, the fourth principle emphasizes the importance of *making sure the severity of the disciplinary strategy matches the misbehavior you are trying to eliminate.* Research (e.g., Pittman, 1985) has indicated that some teachers think about misbehavior in terms of three categories: *minor misbehaviors* (noisiness, socializing, daydreaming); *more serious misbehaviors* (arguing, failing to respond to a group directive); and *never tolerated misbehaviors* (stealing, intentionally hurting someone, destroying property). They also consider whether the misbehavior is part of a pattern or an isolated event.

When deciding how to respond to a problem, it is useful to think in terms of these categories and to select a response that is congruent with the seriousness of the misbehavior. This is easier said than done, of course. When misbehavior occurs, teachers have little time to assess its seriousness, decide if it's part of a pattern, and select an appropriate response. And too often, the situation is ambiguous: Since misbehavior often occurs when the teacher is looking somewhere else, it may not be absolutely clear who is doing what to whom. Nonetheless, you don't want to ignore or react mildly to misbehavior that warrants a more severe response; nor do you want to overreact to behavior that is relatively minor.

With these four principles in mind—preserving a safe, caring classroom environment; protecting the instructional program; considering the context; and selecting a disciplinary strategy that matches the misbehavior—we turn now to specific ways of responding to inappropriate behavior.

Dealing with Minor Misbehavior

As I mentioned in Chapter 4, Jacob Kounin's (1970) classic study of orderly and disorderly classrooms gave research support to the belief that successful classroom managers have eyes in the back of their heads. Kounin found that effective managers knew what was going on all over the room; moreover, *their students knew they knew,* because the teachers were able to spot minor problems and "nip them in the bud." Kounin called this ability *"with-it-ness,"* a term that has since become widely used in discussions of classroom management.

How do "with-it" teachers deal with minor misbehavior? How do they succeed in nipping problems in the bud? This section discusses both nonverbal and verbal interventions and then considers the times when it may be better to do nothing at all. (Suggestions are summarized in Table 12-2.)

Nonverbal Interventions

A while back, an 11-year-old I know announced that she could be a successful teacher. When I asked why she was so confident, she replied: "I know how to make *the look.*" She proceeded to demonstrate: her eyebrows slanted downward, her forehead creased, and her lips flattened into a straight line. She definitely had "the look" down pat.

The "teacher look" is a good example of an unobtrusive, nonverbal intervention. Sandy points out one benefit of this strategy when she comments: "In a science class, it's really important not to raise your voice a lot. If my students get used to yelling, I won't be able to get their attention in an emergency lab situation. So I give *looks* instead." Making eye contact, using hand signals (e.g., thumbs down; pointing to what the individual should be doing), moving closer to the misbehaving student, and lightly touching a shoulder are other nonverbal ways of communicating with-it-ness. All of these convey the message, "I see what you're doing, and I don't like it," but since they are less directive than verbal commands, they encourage students to assume responsibility for getting back on task.

Nonverbal strategies are most appropriate for behaviors that are minor but persistent: frequent or sustained whispering, staring into space, calling out or walking around the room, putting on makeup, and passing notes. The obvious advantage of using nonverbal cues is that you can deal with misbehaviors like these without distracting other students.

TABLE 12-2. Dealing with Minor Misbehavior

Strategy	Advantages
1. Nonverbal interventions:	Allow you to prompt appropriate behavior without
Facial expressions	disrupting lesson
Eye contact	Encourage students to assume responsibility for
Hand signals	changing behavior
Proximity	
2. Verbal interventions:	
Direct commands	Straightforward
Stating student's name	Brief, unobtrusive
Rule reminders	Reinforce desired behavior
Calling on student to participate	Gets student back on task without even citing
Incorporating student's name into lesson	misbehavior; maintains flow of lesson
Use of gentle humor	Prompts a smile along with appropriate behavior
I-messages	Minimize negative evaluations and preserve relationships
	Point out consequences of behavior
	Promote student's autonomy and responsibility for actions
3. Ignoring the misbehavior	Unobtrusive; protects the flow of the lesson

In short, nonverbal interventions enable you to protect and continue your lesson with minimum disruption.

> *Donnie is at the board demonstrating how to construct congruent segments and congruent angles. Students are supposed to be following along, constructing congruent segments with rulers and compasses. Instead of working, two boys sit twirling their rulers on their pencils. Donnie notices what they are doing, but continues with her explanation. While she's talking, she gives the two boys a long, hard stare. They put down the rulers and get to work.*

A nonverbal cue is sometimes all that's needed to stop a misbehavior and get a student back "on task." In fact, a study of six middle school teachers (Lasley, Lasley, & Ward, 1989) found that the *most successful responses to misbehavior were nonverbal.* These strategies stopped misbehavior 79 percent of the time; among the three "more effective managers," the success rate was even higher—an amazing 95 percent.

Verbal Interventions

Sometimes you find yourself in situations where it's just not possible to use a nonverbal cue. Perhaps you can't catch the student's eye, or you're working with a small group, and it would be too disruptive to get up and walk across the room to the misbehaving individual. Other times, you're able to use a nonverbal cue, but it's unsuccessful in stopping the misbehavior.

In cases like this, you might use a *nondirective verbal intervention*. These allow you to prompt the appropriate behavior, while leaving the responsibility for figuring out what to do with the misbehaving student. For example, *simply saying the student's name* might be enough to get the student back on task. Sometimes it's possible to *incorporate the student's name* into the ongoing instruction:

> *Donnie's algebra class is reviewing homework. In the front row, a girl leans over and starts playing with the hand of the girl seated across the aisle from her. Without breaking stride, Donnie says, "So added together, that would be 4y, right, Ismara?" The girl straightens up and turns to her homework.*

> *Shaheed is slouching down in his seat and appears inattentive. As Fred talks about respect for the elderly in China, he moves closer to him. "Let's say Shaheed was my son, and I beat him up because he was getting a failing grade in class. What happens to me?" Shaheed sits up and "tunes in."*

If the misbehavior occurs while a group discussion or recitation is going on, *you can call on the student to answer a question*. Consider the following example:

> *The class is going over homework on isosceles triangles. As Donnie calls on students to do the problems, she walks through the room. "OK, we need someone to do number 14." Hands begin to go up. Donnie notices a girl in the back of the room who is gazing off into space. "Dominica, please do number 14." Dominica "comes back" from wherever she was, looks at the book, and answers correctly. Donnie smiles, "Good!"*

Calling on a student allows you to communicate that you know what's going on and to capture the student's attention—without even citing the misbehavior. But keep in mind what we said earlier about preserving students' dignity. If you are obviously trying to "catch" students and to embarrass them, the strategy may well backfire by creating resentment (Good & Brophy, 1994). One way to avoid this problem is to alert the student that you will be calling on him or her to answer the *next question:* "Sharon, what's the answer to number 18? Taysha, the next one's yours."

The *use of humor* can provide another "gentle" way of reminding students to correct their behavior. Used well, humor can show them that you are able to understand the funny sides of classroom life. But you must be careful that the humor is not tinged with sarcasm that can hurt students' feelings.

> *It's near the end of the year, and Fred's students obviously have a case of "senioritis." They have just entered the room, and Fred is trying to get them*

to settle down. "Ladies and gentlemen, I know it's almost the end of the year, but could we make believe we're students now?"

Donnie's class is about to do the challenge problem of the day. She tells the students that they may work together, but then announces with a smile that Zelia, a very talented math student, is getting a "handicap." She won't be allowed to talk, although she may work with other students. Zelia moans, but there's a big smile on her face. As the students work, it is clear that Zelia finds it hard to restrain herself. She quickly works the problem, and she wants to tell her groupmates how to do it. When Donnie begins to question students about their thinking, Zelia jumps up and calls out, "I know, Ms. Collins." Then she catches herself, laughs, and sits back down. Later, Donnie explains that Zelia often dominates class discussion by calling out the (correct) answers and telling her peers what to do. In an effort to give other students a chance to think for themselves, Donnie occasionally gives Zelia a "handicap." This helps to remind Zelia that other students need a chance to work the problems, but it's more fun than constantly saying things like, "Zelia, other people need a chance too. Please, Zelia, don't call out."

An *"I-message"* is another way of verbally prompting appropriate behavior without giving a direct command. I-messages generally contain three parts. First, the teacher *describes the unacceptable behavior in a nonblaming, nonjudgmental way*. This phrase often begins with "when": "When people talk while I'm giving directions . . ." The second part describes the *tangible effect on the teacher:* "I have to repeat the directions and that wastes time . . ." Finally, the third part of the message states the *teacher's feelings* about the tangible effect: "and I get frustrated." Consider these examples of I-messages:

"When you come to class without your supplies, I can't start the lesson on time, and I get really irritated."

"When you leave your book bag in the middle of the aisle, I can trip over it, and I'm afraid I'll break a leg."

Although I-messages ideally contain all three parts in the recommended sequence, I-messages in any order, or even with one part missing, can still be effective (Gordon, 1974). I've witnessed the four teachers use "abbreviated" I-messages. For example, Fred communicates how strongly he feels about paying attention when he tells his class: "If you pass notes while I'm lecturing, I'll become suicidal." To a student who called him by his first name, he says, "I really feel uncomfortable when you call me by my first name in school."

There are several benefits to using this approach. In contrast to typical "you-messages" (e.g., "You are being rude," "You ought to know better," "You're acting like a baby"), I-messages minimize negative evaluations of the student. They make it easier to avoid using extreme (and usually inaccurate) words like "always" and "never" (as in

"You *always* forget to do your homework" or "You're *never* prepared for class"). For these reasons, they foster and preserve a positive relationship between people. Since I-messages leave decisions about changing behavior up to students, this approach is also likely to promote a sense of responsibility and autonomy. In addition, I-messages show students that their behavior has consequences and that teachers are people with genuine feelings. Unlike you-messages, I-messages don't make students defensive and stubborn; thus, they may be more willing to change their behavior.

Most of us are not used to speaking this way, so I-messages can seem awkward and artificial. With practice, however, using I-messages can become natural. I once heard a four-year-old girl (whose parents had consistently used I-messages at home) tell her nursery school peer: "When you poke me with that pencil, it really hurts, and I feel bad 'cause I think you don't want to be my friend."

In addition to these nondirective approaches, there are also *more directive strategies* that you can try. Indeed, these may be particularly appropriate for African American students from low socioeconomic backgrounds. Lisa Delpit, African American author of *Other People's Children: Cultural Conflict in the Classroom* (1995), observes that framing directives as questions (e.g., "Would you like to sit down now?") is a "polite form of speech that is a mainstream, particularly female, structure" (Valentine, 1998, p. 17). According to Delpit,

> *Many kids will not respond to that structure because commands are not couched as questions in their home culture. Rather than asking questions, some teachers need to learn to say, "Put the scissors away" and "Sit down now" or "Please sit down now." (Valentine, 1998, p. 17)*

As Delpit suggests, the most straightforward approach is to *direct students to the task at hand* ("Get to work on that math problem"; "Your group should be discussing the first three pages"). You can also *remind the student about the rule* or behavioral expectation that is being violated (e.g., "When someone is talking, everyone else is supposed to be listening"). Sometimes, if inappropriate behavior is fairly widespread, it's useful to review rules with the entire group. This is often true after a holiday, a weekend, or a vacation.

Another strategy is to *give students a choice between behaving appropriately or receiving a penalty* for continued inappropriate behavior (e.g., "If you can't handle working in your group, you'll have to return to your seats"; "You either choose to raise your hand instead of calling out, or you will be choosing not to participate in our discussion"). Statements like these not only warn students that a penalty will be invoked if the inappropriate behavior continues, they also emphasize that students have real choices about how to behave and that penalties are not imposed without reason.

> *Donnie's class is having difficulty settling down and paying attention. She looks at her watch and then comments quietly, "We can either do this now, or we can do this at 2:00 [after school]. I know that I'm in no rush to go home."*

> *One of Sandy's male students comes in wearing a T-shirt (over another shirt) that promotes the use of marijuana. She quickly moves over to him and calmly tells him the shirt is inappropriate for school. She gives him a choice: "If you really feel you must wear it, go to the office. Your other option is to turn it inside out or to take it off." He takes it off.*

And in the following example, we see how Fred embellishes this strategy with a little humor:

> *The bell rings; Fred moves to a podium in the front of the room and tries to get his students' attention. They continue talking. "Ladies and gentlemen, if you want a zero for life, talk now. If you don't, listen." Students laugh and settle down.*

Deliberately Ignoring the Misbehavior

If misbehavior is extremely brief and unobtrusive, the best course of action may be *inaction.* For example, during a discussion a student may be so eager to comment that she forgets to raise her hand; or someone becomes momentarily distracted and inattentive; or two boys quietly exchange a comment while you're giving directions. In cases like these, an intervention can be more disruptive than the students' behavior.

One risk of ignoring minor misbehavior is that students may conclude you're unaware of what's going on. Suspecting that you're not "with-it," they may decide to see how much they can get away with, and then problems are sure to escalate. You need to monitor your class carefully to make sure this doesn't happen.

Another problem is that occasional ignoring can turn into full-fledged "blindness." This was vividly demonstrated in a study of a student teacher named Heleen (Créton, Wubbels, & Hooymayers, 1989). When Heleen was lecturing, her students frequently became noisy and inattentive. In response, Heleen talked more loudly and looked more at the chalkboard, turning her back on her students. She did not allow herself to see or hear the disorder—perhaps because it was too threatening and she didn't know how to handle it. Unfortunately, Heleen's students seemed to interpret her "blindness" as an indication that noise was allowed, and they became even more disorderly. Heleen eventually recognized the importance of "seeing" and responding to slight disturbances, in order to prevent them from escalating.

Dealing with More Serious Misbehavior: Using Penalties

Sometimes, nonverbal cues or verbal reminders are not enough to convince students that you're serious about the behavioral expectations that you've established. And sometimes misbehavior is just too serious to use these kinds of low-level responses. In cases like these, it may be necessary to impose a penalty in order to enforce your expectations for appropriate behavior.

In some cases, teachers discuss penalties when they teach rules and procedures, so students understand the consequences of violating a rule from the very beginning. We saw Sandy do this with her students in Chapter 4, when she laid out the penalties for coming late to class. This practice prevents unpleasant "surprises," and hopefully minimizes protests of blissful ignorance—"But you didn't *tell* me that would happen!"

Selecting Penalties

It's often difficult for beginning teachers to decide on appropriate penalties. One student teacher in social studies recently vented his frustration in this way:

> *These two kids come to class every day and sit and do absolutely nothing. They don't create a big disturbance, and they're not really nasty or belligerent; they just won't do any work. They prefer to sit there and talk, and draw cartoons, and goof off. I keep telling them they're getting a zero for each day they just sit, and that they're going to fail for the marking period, but they just don't care. I've told them I'm going to call their parents, but they just laugh. I don't want to send them to the disciplinarian's office, because my cooperating teacher says I could get a reputation as a teacher who can't control the class, and I'd really like to get a job in this district. So I'm really at a loss. These kids are really smart, and I hate to see them fail. But what can I do?*

During one meeting, I posed this question to all four teachers and learned about the types of penalties that they typically use. The question brought a variety of responses, but one theme emerged clearly. In Fred's words:

> *It's important to remember that the goal of a penalty is not to hurt kids, but to help them change their behavior. It's not to put kids down; it's to bring them up. If kids see that, then they'll accept the penalty. But if the behavior doesn't change, it's not a good penalty, no matter what it is.*

With this idea in mind, let's consider the seven categories into which these teachers' penalties generally fall.

Mandatory Private Conferences

When students do not respond to nonverbal cues or verbal reminders, our teachers generally call a private conference, often after school or during a free period. During these conferences, they express their disappointment in the student's behavior. We normally don't think of this as a penalty, but since students in these classes really like their teachers, they feel bad when their teachers are upset. In serious, almost sorrowful tones, our teachers express their disappointment and surprise at the inappropriate behavior and direct students to think about the consequences of their actions. Sometimes, they will negotiate a plan for change, trying to get the students to take responsibility for their behavior. For example, when a student in Sandy's class failed a test, she held a private conference with him after school. Sandy shares this account of their meeting: "We talked about how he had been doing in class, and what had happened in this particular exam. It turned out that he had gone clubbing until 11:30 the night before the test. I told him, 'Well, that was your choice, and this was the outcome. What do you think? Do you like this outcome?' Obviously he didn't. We agreed that the next time there was a test, he wouldn't stay out late the night before and see if it makes a difference. I really think it's important to approach teenagers this way—to put the responsibility back on them whenever possible."

Loss of Privileges

Sometimes, students lose the right to sit wherever they like, particularly if their behavior is having a negative impact on other students. Other privileges that can be taken away include working with a friend, free time, chewing gum, freely moving around the room, and joining in a class popcorn party.

Isolation from the Group

All four teachers will move students to an isolated or secluded area of the room if they are unable to work productively, but they try to be positive rather than negative about the move. Fred will signal a student to move to a place that's "less distracting." When Sandy covered a seventh-grade class, she sometimes had to tell a student, "Come with me. Let's go to the back of the class and see what you can do back here where you can concentrate better. This will be your own private office." This strategy can be particularly effective with students who suffer from attention deficit/hyperactivity disorder (ADHD). These students have trouble dealing with the distraction and stimulation of the typical classroom environment; moving temporarily to a secluded area of the room can provide a much needed opportunity to refocus.

Exclusion from Class

All four teachers believe that "kicking kids out" is a strategy that should be reserved for major disruption. As Donnie points out, "Some students *want* to get out; they'll provoke a teacher just so they can leave the room. I know teachers who throw kids out all the time, but what's the point? Kids can't learn if they're in the office."

Despite their preference for handling problems within the room, the teachers recognize that there are times when this is just not possible. Sandy remembers how she sent a student to the "time-out" room when his behavior was so infuriating that she couldn't discuss it calmly: "I was so mad, I knew I was losing it. I was yelling, and the kid was yelling. So it was better for him to be out of the room. But 10 minutes later, I called and told him to come back. By then we had both cooled down and we were able to talk." Sandy has also worked out a system with another teacher so that she can send a student to his classroom if necessary. In the other room, the student must sit quietly and do chemistry work, ignored by both teacher and students.

Fred also sends students to the office if their behavior is really out of control. He recalls one student who was severely disturbed: "I had it worked out with the office, so they knew what to do with him when he showed up. In the beginning, I had to kick him out three times a week, but slowly he got better about controlling his behavior, and we got it down to once every two weeks. But this only worked because class was a good place to be. He had friends there, we laughed every day, he got to do good stuff. If he hadn't liked it—and me—getting to leave would have been a reward."

Detention

For routine violations of rules (e.g., coming late to class), Donnie, Sandy, and Fred use regular school detention as a penalty. However, they are cautious about using this for "big" problems. As Sandy puts it, "If students are disrespectful, or really having problems controlling themselves, I prefer to talk privately with them. What's going to be learned from 45 minutes of detention?"

Written Reflections on the Problem

Sometimes, a situation is so complex that it warrants serious reflection in writing. Fred recalls this incident: "My senior honors class was supposed to do a short research paper on China. When I began to grade the papers, it seemed to me that a lot of the citations were suspicious. I did some checking at the library, and found that some students had simply taken material from an encyclopedia and made up the references. I went into class and told them how serious this was, and how they would all get zeros for their papers if they couldn't validate their references. But I gave them a way out: they could write a letter to me explaining what they had done and why, and they had to make 'reparation' by doing two additional research papers with valid citations. The letters were really revealing. A lot of these kids were absolutely clueless about why it's important to reference accurately. One kid came in and thanked me for making a big deal about this. He said he really didn't know that what he was doing was dishonest."

Contacting Parents

Donnie, Sandy, Christina, and Fred all contact parents or guardians if a student shows a pattern of consistent misbehavior. For example, when a student in Sandy's class repeatedly "forgot" to do his homework, Sandy told him she would be calling his parents to discuss the problem. She tried to make it clear that she was calling not in anger but out of serious concern. She also wanted to convey the idea that "between all of us, maybe we can help you get it together."

These penalties illustrate the ways Christina, Donnie, Fred, and Sandy choose to deal with problems when they have a degree of flexibility. In addition, there are times when they are required to follow school policies mandating particular responses to specific misbehaviors. Consider the example of cutting class. In Christina's school, two instances of cutting a class result in no credit earned for that course. In Sandy's school, one class cut requires teacher detention, parent notification, and a loss of open campus privileges for two weeks; two class cuts result in office detention for three hours, and a loss of open campus privileges for four weeks; three cuts result in exclusion until a parent conference is held. In Fred's school, one cut requires parental notification and a warning letter; two cuts result in "student/counselor contact" and "administrator/parent contact," a possible conference, and a warning letter. The third cut requires removal from class with a grade of AW (administrative withdrawal) and placement in study hall.

It's also important to note that about 90 percent of schools now have *"zero tolerance" policies* with predetermined consequences for the possession of firearms or other weapons, and about 80 percent have such policies for incidents of violence and use of tobacco (Johnston, 1999). Such policies usually result in automatic suspension or expulsion, although there is wide variation in severity.

If you have special education students in your classes, it's essential that you consult with their caseworkers about appropriate disciplinary strategies. Serious behavior problems require a team effort, and parents, special education teachers, psychologists, and administrators can all provide valuable insights and suggestions. Also be aware that the Individuals with Disabilities Education Act (IDEA) Amendments of 1997 include several stipulations about the rights of students with disabilities with respect to discipline. For example, if the problematic behavior is a manifestation of a student's disability, suspension and expulsion may not be allowed (Janney & Snell, 2000). A recent case provides a good example of this policy. In June 2000, a federal magistrate ruled that a district near Madison, Wisconsin, was wrong to expel a disabled student involved in a vandalism spree that resulted in $40,000 damage to two elementary schools. A psychiatrist argued that the offense was a manifestation of the student's attention deficit hyperactivity disorder (ADHD). The magistrate agreed (Sack, 2000).

Selecting Penalties That Are Logical Consequences

Whenever possible, penalties should be *logically related to the misbehavior* (e.g., Curwin & Mendler, 1988; Dreikurs, Grunwald, & Pepper, 1982). For example, when a student in Christina's class failed to work constructively in his small group, he had to work by himself until he indicated a readiness to cooperate. Similarly, if students make a mess in the home economics kitchen, a logical penalty would be to make them clean it up. If an individual forgets her book and can't do the assignment, she must borrow someone's book and do the assignment during free period. A student who hands in a carelessly done paper has to rewrite it.

Dreikurs, Grunwald, and Pepper (1982) distinguish logical consequences like these from traditional punishments, which bear no relationship to the misbehavior involved. An example of such a traditional punishment would be to have students write "I will not come late to class" 50 times. Here are some other examples of punishments that are unrelated to the offense:

> A student continually whispers to her neighbor. Instead of isolating the student (a logical consequence), the teacher makes her do an additional homework assignment.

> A student forgets to get his parent's permission to go on a field trip. Instead of having the student write a letter home to parents about the need to sign the permission slip (a logical consequence), the teacher gives him detention.

A student continually calls out during a whole-class discussion. Instead of having him make a cue-card to post on his desk ("I won't call out") or not allowing him to participate in the discussion, the teacher gives him an F for the day.

According to Dreikurs and his colleagues, punishment is likely to be seen as an arbitrary exercise of power by a dictatorial teacher. Sometimes, youngsters do not even associate the punishment with the misbehavior, but rather with the punisher. Instead of teaching students about the unpleasant results of their inappropriate behavior, unrelated punishments teach students only to make certain they don't get caught the next time around!

Imposing Penalties

It's frustrating when students misbehave, and sometimes we let our frustration color the way we impose penalties. I've seen teachers scream at students from across the room, lecture students on their history of misbehavior, insinuate that they come from terrible homes, and attack their personalities. Clearly, behavior like this destroys children's dignity and ruins the possibility of a good relationship with students. How can you avoid creating a situation like this?

First, if you're feeling really angry at a student, *delay the discussion.* You can simply say to the individual, "Sit there and think about what happened. I'll talk to you in a few minutes." During one observation in Fred's room, it was clear that he was becoming really annoyed at two students who were talking while he was introducing a film the class was about to watch. Twice during his comments he turned and told them to stop talking, but their conversation would begin again. I watched with curiosity to see if he would do anything further, but he continued the lesson. At the end of the period, however, he promptly went over and quietly spoke with the two offending students. Later, he reflected on their conversation:

> *I told them I couldn't talk while they were talking, that it distracted me and made me really mad—especially since I was talking about Gandhi, who's one of my favorite guys. They apologized; they said they had been talking about some of the ideas that had come up in class. I told them I was really glad they were so excited, but they had to share their thoughts with the whole class, or wait until after class to talk. I think they got the message. Talking with them after class had three advantages: It allowed me to continue with my lesson, it gave me a chance to calm down, and it made it possible to talk to them privately.*

As Fred's comments point out, by delaying discussion, you have a chance to calm down and to think about what you want to say. You'll also be more able to separate the student's character from the student's behavior. Your message must be: *"You're* okay, but your *behavior* is unacceptable."

Second, it's a good idea to *impose penalties privately, calmly, and quietly.* Despite the temptation to yell and scream, the softer your voice and the closer you stand, the more effective you tend to be (Curwin & Mendler, 1988). Remember, students are very concerned about saving face in front of their peers. Public sanction may have the advantage of "making an example" out of one student's misbehavior, but it has the disadvantage of creating resentment and embarrassment. In fact, a study by Turco and Elliott (1986) found that fifth-, seventh-, and ninth-graders viewed public reprimand as the *least acceptable method* of dealing with problems. Our four teachers agree. Sandy observes:

> *Let's say you've just given back some paper you graded. A student looks at his or her paper, crumples it up, and throws it on the floor. If you yell, "Pick that paper up," you've created a confrontational situation. It's a lot better to go over and talk privately and calmly. If you say something like, "If you have a problem with your grade, we can talk about it," then the kid doesn't lose face. It's really important not to back students into a corner; if you do, they'll come out fighting and create an even bigger problem than before."*

Finally, after imposing a penalty, it's a good idea to get back to the student and *reestablish a positive relationship.* At the beginning of this chapter, we saw how Sandy made a point of helping William with his lab experiment after giving him detention. Similarly, complimenting a student's work or patting a back communicates that there are no hard feelings.

The Issue of Consistency

As Emmer, Evertson, and Worsham (2000) note, "The dictum 'be consistent' has been repeated more frequently than the pledge of allegiance" (p. 134). Beginning teachers are taught that if they do not consistently enforce the rules, students will become confused, will begin to test the limits, and misbehavior will escalate.

There is research evidence to support this emphasis on consistency. Recall Evertson and Emmer's (1982) study of effective classroom management on the junior high level (discussed in Chapter 4). This study showed that more successful managers responded in a consistent, predictable fashion, often invoking the rules or procedures in order to stop the disruptive behavior. In contrast, the ineffective managers were more likely to act inconsistently: Sometimes they ignored the behavior; sometimes they invoked a prestated consequence (e.g., detention); sometimes they warned students of penalties, but then didn't act on their warnings. Inevitably, behavior problems increased in frequency and severity.

Although the importance of being consistent is obvious, teachers sometimes feel trapped by the need for consistency. (See the discussion in Chapter 5 about being fair.) When a normally conscientious student forgets a homework assignment, it seems unreasonable to send the same note home to parents that you would send if a student repeatedly missed assignments. Furthermore, what is an effective consequence for one person may not be effective for another (Dreikers, Grunwald, & Pepper, 1982). Having detention might be a negative experience for an individual who is eager to get to soccer practice; for an individual who has nothing special waiting at home, detention (particularly if it's in the classroom with the teacher) could actually be a positive, rewarding experience.

In order to get out of this bind, it's desirable to develop a *hierarchy of consequences* that can be invoked if rules are violated. Some teachers develop a graduated list of generic consequences that can be applied to all misbehaviors. Consider the following hierarchy as an example:

First violation:	Verbal warning
Second violation:	Name is written down
Third time:	Conference with teacher
Fourth time:	Call parents
Fifth time:	Send to principal

Another approach is to develop a graduated list of consequences for individual classroom rules. Curwin and Mendler (1988) suggest the following consequences for not bringing in homework:

1. Reminder.
2. Warning.
3. Student required to hand homework in before close of school that day.
4. Student required to stay after school to finish homework.
5. Conference between teacher, student, and parent to develop an action plan for completing homework on time.

Sandy used this approach when she developed her graduated list of consequences for coming late (see Chapter 4), and she makes sure to enforce the consequences no matter who is involved. She tells us:

Kids have got to see that you're fair. If my best student walks through that door late, I have to give the same detention that I'd give to my worst student. If I don't give detention, the kids will see that and think to themselves, "She's playing favorites. She's letting him get away with coming late." That's the end of my relationship with them.

Although all four teachers are absolutely consistent when dealing with straightforward behaviors like coming late, they consider these the "little problems." With the "big things," they prefer to talk privately with students and to develop a plan of action that is tailored to the individual student. By holding "mandatory private conferences," the four teachers can show students they are consistent in terms of enforcing class rules and dealing with problem behavior, but they can remain flexible with respect to the solution.

Penalizing the Group for Individual Misbehavior

Sometimes teachers impose a consequence on the whole class even if only one or two individuals have been misbehaving. The hope is that other students will be angry at receiving a penalty when they weren't misbehaving and will exert pressure on their peers to behave. Our four teachers are unanimous in their negative response to this practice.

Donnie observes, "If you even attempt to do this, students will be furious. You'll alienate the whole class." And Fred puts it this way: "I do this when I'm teaching about the causes of revolutions. It's a great way to foment a rebellion!"

Dealing with Chronic Misbehavior

Some students with persistent behavior problems fail to respond to the routine strategies we have described so far: nonverbal cues, verbal reminders, and penalties. What additional strategies are available? In this section, we consider three different approaches. First, we examine a problem-solving strategy, which views inappropriate behavior as a conflict to be resolved through discussion and negotiation. Next, we take a look at four self-management approaches based on principles of behavior modification—namely, self-monitoring, self-evaluation, self-instruction, and contingency contracting. Finally, we discuss an unconventional strategy called "reframing," in which teachers formulate a positive interpretation of problem behavior and then act in ways that are consistent with that interpretation (Molnar & Lindquist, 1989).

Resolving Conflicts through Problem-Solving

Most teachers think in terms of winning or losing when they think about classroom conflicts. According to Thomas Gordon, author of *T.E.T.—Teacher Effectiveness Training,*

> *This win–lose orientation seems to be at the core of the knotty issue of discipline in schools. Teachers feel that they have only two approaches to choose from: They can be strict or lenient, tough or soft, authoritarian or permissive. They see the teacher–student relationship as a power struggle, a contest, a fight. . . . When conflicts arise, as they always do, most teachers try to resolve them so that they win, or at least don't lose. This obviously means that students end up losing, or at least not winning. (1974, p. 183)*

A third alternative is a "no-lose" problem-solving method of conflict resolution (Gordon, 1974) consisting of six steps. In Step 1, the teacher and the student (or students) *define the problem.* In Step 2, everyone *brainstorms possible solutions.* As in all brainstorming activities, suggestions are not evaluated at this stage. In Step 3, the *solutions are evaluated:* "Now let's take a look at all the solutions that have been proposed and decide which we like and which we don't like. Do you have some preferences?" It is important that you state your own opinions and preferences. Do not permit a solution to stand if it is not really acceptable to you. In Step 4, you and the students involved *decide on the solution that you will try.* If more than one student is involved, it is tempting to vote on the solution, but that's probably not a good idea. Voting always produces winners and losers unless the vote is unanimous, so some people leave the discussion feeling dissatisfied. Instead, try to work for consensus.

Once you have decided which solution to try, you move to Step 5 and *determine how to implement the decision:* who will do what by when. Finally, in Step 6, *the solution is evaluated.* You may want to call everybody together again and ask, "Are you still satisfied with our solution?" It is important that everyone realize that decisions are not chiseled in granite and that they can be discarded in search of a better solution to the problem.

During one meeting, Donnie explained how she used problem solving when some of her students were not sitting in their assigned places during assemblies:

> *Whenever there's an assembly program, we're supposed to walk together to the auditorium and sit together. But it's crowded in the halls on the way to the auditorium, and everyone "loses" kids; someone has darted here or there, joined another class, faded into the crowd. By the time we get to the auditorium, the kids are scattered all over. They sit with other classes, and they act up. The teachers don't really know who they are, and sometimes the kids even give wrong names when the teachers ask. The behavior in assembly programs can be really bad. I decided this was a problem that we had to deal with before another assembly program was held.*
>
> *I told the class that I felt this was a problem, and they agreed. Then I explained that we were going to brainstorm solutions. Boy, these kids can really be hard on each other! They came up with about eight different solutions:*
>
> *Kick the offenders out of the assemblies.*
>
> *Don't let past offenders go to assemblies at all.*
>
> *Suspension.*
>
> *Kids have to get permission to sit with another class.*
>
> *Bring your friend to sit with you and your class (your friend would have to have special permission from his/her teacher).*
>
> *Invite parents to assemblies (kids would act better).*
>
> *Take attendance once you get to the assembly.*
>
> *Have a buddy system.*
>
> *The next day, we talked about each of these possible solutions, focusing on how they would affect everyone. I told them I didn't like the one about kicking people out of the assemblies because assembly programs were part of their education. I also explained that teachers don't have the right to suspend students, and if we chose that one, we'd have to get the disciplinarian involved. The kids said they could live with getting permission, and they also liked the buddy system. They said buddies should also have the responsibility of telling the person next to them to stop if he or she was disruptive. So we agreed to try those two. We also*

agreed that I would use the "teacher look" technique if I saw kids acting up and then write up a referral to the disciplinarian if they didn't stop.

We haven't had an assembly program yet, so I don't know how this is going to work, but I think it was good to get the kids involved in trying to solve the problem. Maybe they'll be more interested in trying to improve the situation.

Approaches Based on Principles of Behavior Modification

Behavior modification programs involve the systematic use of reinforcement to strengthen desired behavior. Probably more research has focused on the effectiveness of behavior modification than any other classroom management approach, and dozens of books on behavior modification techniques are available for teachers (e.g., Epanchim, Townsend, & Stoddard, 1994).

More recently, however, educators have come to view full-blown behavior modification approaches as ill suited for most regular classroom teachers. First of all, a single teacher working with a class of 30 students cannot possibly keep track of—let alone systematically reinforce—all the desirable behaviors each student exhibits (Brophy, 1983). Secondly, in order to extinguish inappropriate behavior that is maintained by teacher attention, behavior modification calls for teachers to ignore the behavior. Although this is effective in one-to-one situations, ignoring misbehavior in the crowded, public environment of the classroom can cause problems to escalate (an issue that was discussed earlier). This is even more likely to occur if teachers forget that ignoring is not a behavior management strategy by itself, but must be paired with attention for positive and appropriate behaviors. Finally, traditional behavior modification techniques emphasize external control by the teacher, rather than trying to foster internal control by the student.

For all of these reasons, educators have begun to recommend behavioral approaches that involve the student in *self-management:* self-monitoring, self-evaluation, self-instruction, and contingency contracting. The goal of these self-management strategies is to help students learn to regulate their own behavior. The perception of control is crucial in this process: When we feel in control, we are much more likely to accept responsibility for our actions.

The object of *self-monitoring* is to help individuals gain an accurate picture of their own behavior. Some students may not realize how often they're out of their seats or how frequently they sit daydreaming instead of focusing on their work. Others may be unaware of how often they call out during class discussions or how many times they make nasty comments to other members of their small group. Youngsters like this may benefit from a self-monitoring program, in which they learn to observe and record a targeted behavior during a designated period of time. Interestingly, self-monitoring can have positive effects even when youngsters are *inaccurate* (Graziano & Mooney, 1984).

Recording can be done in two ways. The first approach has individuals tally each time they engage in the targeted behavior. For example, students can learn to chart the number of math problems they complete during an in-class assignment, the number of times they blurt out irrelevant comments during a discussion, or the number of times they raise their hand to speak. In the second approach, individuals observe and record the targeted behavior at regular intervals. At the designated time, the student marks the recording sheet with a "+" or a "−," depending on whether she is engaged in appropriate or inappropriate behavior.

These two approaches are well illustrated in an early study conducted by Broden, Hall, and Mitts (1971). In the first part of the study, Liza, an eighth-grade girl who had difficulty paying attention in history class, was directed to record her "study" or "on-task" behavior on the sheet shown in Figure 12-1. Before Liza began recording her behavior, she was on task only about 30 percent of the time. During the self-recording phases, Liza averaged on-task rates of 76 percent to 89 percent.

The second part of the study involved Stu, an eighth-grade boy whose math teacher wanted to find a way "to shut Stu up" (p. 195). According to the teacher, Stu continually talked out in class, disturbing both the teacher and the other students. Having Stu record his talking-out behavior on the simple form shown in Figure 12-2 led to a decrease in his calling out, although the self-monitoring seemed to lose its effectiveness after a while (possibly because the teacher never acknowledged Stu's improved behavior).

Self-evaluation, a second self-management approach, goes beyond simple self-monitoring by requiring individuals to judge the quality or acceptability of their behavior (Hughes, Ruhl, & Misra, 1989). Sometimes self-evaluation is linked with reinforcement, so that an improvement in behavior brings points or rewards.

A study by Smith, Young, West, Morgan, and Rhode (1988) provides a good example of how these strategies can be used to reduce off-task, disruptive behavior. The study involved four students (ages 13 to 15) who spent half of each day in a special education

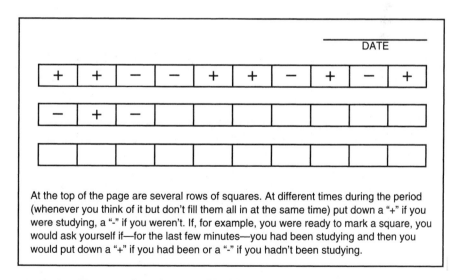

At the top of the page are several rows of squares. At different times during the period (whenever you think of it but don't fill them all in at the same time) put down a "+" if you were studying, a "-" if you weren't. If, for example, you were ready to mark a square, you would ask yourself if—for the last few minutes—you had been studying and then you would put down a "+" if you had been or a "-" if you hadn't been studying.

FIGURE 12-1. The recording sheet used by Liza

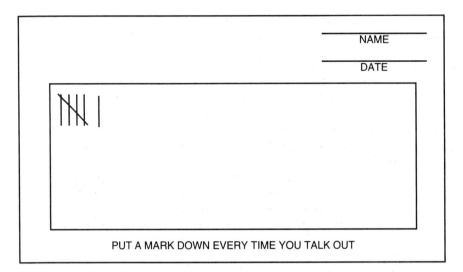

FIGURE 12-2. The recording sheet used by Stu

resource room; three students were classified as behaviorally disordered, and one was classified as learning disabled. All four students were taught to rate how well they followed the resource room rules using a simple scale that went from zero ("unacceptable") to five ("excellent"). Ratings were converted to points that could be exchanged for snacks, school supplies, or magazines at the end of each class period. Since bonus points were earned when students' ratings closely matched their teacher's ratings, the students were rewarded not only for behaving well but also for rating themselves accurately.

By tracking students' behavior over time, the investigators were able to show that the self-evaluation procedures were extremely effective in decreasing students' inappropriate behavior in the resource room. Darren, for example, went from an average of 71 percent off-task, disruptive behavior to 17 percent. Sadly, the results weren't as impressive when self-evaluation was tried in the regular education classes, where the teachers were less consistent in doing the ratings.

Recently, Fred decided to try a self-evaluation procedure with a boy in his Contemporary World Issues class. Daniel was in serious danger of failing the course; although he was not disruptive, Daniel was consistently inattentive and rarely completed assignments. Fred and Daniel discussed self-evaluation, and Daniel was enthusiastic about trying it. Together, they designed a simple sheet, which they agreed that Fred would keep and give to Daniel to fill out at the end of each class period. As you can see from Figure 12-3, the form requires Daniel to describe and evaluate his behavior.

During one meeting with all the teachers, Fred described how the self-evaluation procedure worked out:

We did it faithfully for three weeks, and it really worked. Sometimes I forgot to give Daniel the self-evaluation sheet at the end of the period, and he

```
┌─────────────────────────────────────────────────────────┐
│              WHAT DID YOU DO IN CLASS?                   │
│                                                         │
│  1. How well did you behave?                            │
│          Were you attentive?                            │
│          Did you complete assignments?                  │
│          Did you contribute to class discussion?        │
│          Did you think?                                 │
│          Did you learn something?                       │
│                                                         │
│  2. What score would be accurate?     1    2    3    4  │
│                                  (Excellent)    (Poor)  │
│                                                         │
│  Monday:                                                │
│                                                         │
│  Tuesday:                                               │
│                                                         │
│  Wednesday:                                             │
│                                                         │
│  Thursday:                                              │
│                                                         │
│  Friday:                                                │
│                                                         │
└─────────────────────────────────────────────────────────┘
```

FIGURE 12-3. Darren's self-evaluation form

actually reminded me. I took that as a sign of his commitment. His behavior really improved; he started paying attention and completing assignments for the first time all year. At the end of three weeks, Daniel was out for several days. When he got back, we didn't pick it up again, and I didn't push it. He was doing what he was supposed to be doing, without any monitoring.

The third self-management approach is *self-instruction,* in which youngsters learn to give themselves silent directions about how to behave. Most self-instruction strategies are based on Meichenbaum's (1977) five-step process of cognitive behavior modification: (1) an adult performs a task while talking aloud about it, carefully describing each part; (2) the youngster performs the task while the adult talks aloud (overt, external guidance); (3) the youngster performs the task while talking aloud to self (overt self-guidance); (4) the youngster performs the task while whispering (faded, overt self-guidance); (5) the youngster performs the task while thinking the directions (covert, self-instruction). This approach has been used to teach impulsive students to approach tasks more deliberately, to help social isolates initiate peer activity, to teach aggressive students to control their anger, and to teach defeated students to try problem solving instead of giving up (Brophy, 1983).

There is evidence that even seriously emotionally disturbed adolescents can learn to engage in self-instruction. In a study conducted in a self-contained special education class (Ninness, Fuerst, Rutherford, & Glenn, 1991), three teenage males who displayed high rates of off-task and inappropriate behaviors (running, fighting, fondling, spitting, throwing objects, jumping, or inappropriate language) were given formal instruction in social skills and self-management for one hour a day. Students were taught to raise their hands to ask questions, to avoid distractions of other students, and to talk politely to teachers and students. While others played the role of distractors, students rehearsed overt statements such as "I'm not going to let him or her bother me. I'm going to keep doing my work," and they practiced avoiding eye contact with those who annoyed them. In addition, students were taught to evaluate their own on-task and socially appropriate behavior, using a scale ranging from one to four. A bonus point was awarded on any occasion in which a student's self-assessment was within one point of the teacher's assessment.

After five weeks, the training in social skills and self-management was discontinued, and a series of experimental conditions was begun. In one condition ("instructed"), students were left alone for 20 minutes in the classroom with instructions to assess and record their behavior. In a similar condition ("instructed under provocation"), students were told to self-manage while others deliberately tried to provoke and distract them. Two other conditions investigated students' behavior when the teacher left the room without giving explicit instructions to self-manage ("uninstructed" and "uninstructed under provocation").

The results of the study demonstrated that training in self-management can dramatically improve students' behavior. Prior to the training, off-task and socially inappropriate behavior in the classroom averaged 92 percent, 95 percent, and 76 percent for Subjects 1, 2, and 3, respectively. All three subjects improved substantially during the course of the five-week self-management training—and all three demonstrated *near-zero off-task or socially inappropriate behavior during the experimental situations.*

Before we leave the discussion of self-monitoring, self-evaluation, and self-instruction, it is important to note that self-management strategies hold particular promise for students with disabilities in general education settings. Only a handful of studies have been conducted in inclusive secondary classrooms, but they indicate that students with disabilities can be taught to use self-management to improve both their social and academic performance (McDougall, 1998). On the other hand, this training requires time and expertise that general education teachers may not have (McDougall, 1998). If you decide to try one of these self-management strategies, you should consult with your school's psychologist, a counselor, or a special education teacher.

Contingency Contracting

A contingency or behavior contract is an agreement between a teacher and an individual student that specifies what the student must do to earn a particular reward. Contingency contracts are negotiated with students; both parties must agree on the behaviors students must exhibit, the period of time involved, and the rewards that will result. To be most effective, contracts should be written and signed. And, of course, there should be an opportunity for review and renegotiation if the contract is not working.

In South Brunswick High School, the guidance counselors, the Vice-Principal for Student Affairs (the school's disciplinarian), and the attendance officers regularly use contracts to deal with students who exhibit serious problems (e.g., extremely disruptive behavior, poor attendance, failing grades). An example of a typical contract appears in Figure 12-4.

SOUTH BRUNSWICK HIGH SCHOOL
STUDENT PERSONNEL SERVICES

CONTRACT

TO: WHOM IT MAY CONCERN

DATE:

RE: AGREEMENTS FOR XXX XXXXXX TO REMAIN IN/SUCCEED IN
        QQ QQQQQ'S CLASS

AFTER A FRUITFUL DISCUSSION BETWEEN XXXX, YYYYY, AND ZZZZZ,
THE FOLLOWING DECISIONS WERE REACHED:

1.   XXX WILL BE IN CLASS ON TIME WITH BOOK, NOTEBOOK, AND
      WRITING UTENSIL.

2.   ALL HOMEWORK ASSIGNMENTS WILL BE TURNED IN ON TIME
      AND COMPLETE.

3.   QQ QQQQQ WILL MEET WITH XXX AFTER SCHOOL ON
      THURSDAYS TO ASSIST XXX WITH THE QUARTERLY PROJECT.

4.   XXX WILL CHANGE HIS SEAT AWAY FROM RRRRR, AND PAY
      ATTENTION DURING CLASS.

5.   OTHER:

UPON SUCCESSFUL COMPLETION OF THIS CONTRACT, XXX WILL PASS
THIS CLASS WITH A "C" OR BETTER FOR THIS QUARTER.

STUDENT_____   TEACHER_____
PARENT_____   COUNSELOR_____

FIGURE 12-4. An example of a contract

Using an Ecosystemic Approach:
Changing Problem Behavior by Reframing

We often explain problem behavior by focusing on the characteristics of individual students (e.g., "He's insolent and sarcastic because he comes from a broken home"; "She never participates in class because she's so shy"). These explanations may have some validity, but they are unlikely to help us bring about positive change. Since we cannot alter a student's home environment or basic personality, we may conclude there is nothing we can do and fail to consider ways in which the social context of the classroom is contributing to the problem.

On the other hand, if we take an *ecosystemic perspective,* we recognize that problem behaviors are part of a stable pattern of interpersonal interactions. In other words, the classroom constitutes an *ecosystem,* in which every individual's behavior influences and is influenced by everyone else's behavior. According to Alex Molnar and Barbara Lindquist (1989), this is a more optimistic way of approaching problems, because it means that we can influence problem behaviors by making changes to the ecosystem. As they put it, "when you want something to change, you must change something" (p. 10).

Given the fact that behaviors can have multiple interpretations, Molnar and Lindquist suggest that a powerful way to change the ecosystem is to formulate an *alternative, positive interpretation of the problem behavior and to act in ways that are consistent with the new interpretation.* This technique is called *reframing.* Let's look at a few examples adapted from Molnar and Linquist's book, *Changing Problem Behavior in Schools* (1989).

Problem behavior:	Brian continually blurts out answers during discussions.
Standard interpretation:	Brian is trying to get attention.
Standard response:	Teacher ignores Brian as long as possible, but eventually chastises him.
Alternative interpretation:	Brian is so intensely engaged in the discussion he forgets to raise his hand.
Problem behavior:	Shandra never participates in class discussions. She also takes a long time to get started on written classroom assignments, so she makes little progress by the end of class.
Standard interpretation:	Since Shandra is capable of doing the work, she is simply being resistant and lazy.
Standard response:	Teacher talks with Shandra about the importance of participating and doing classwork. When that doesn't work, teacher has conference with parents. Teacher also tries giving Shandra special attention for participation.
Alternative interpretation:	Shandra needs to think carefully before participating in discussions or doing written work. She wants to get all her thoughts together before speaking or writing. (Shandra is not resistant or lazy; she is careful and deliberate.)

Not all teachers will find these alternative interpretations plausible, but that doesn't matter. What *does* matter is that you generate an interpretation that is plausible to *you.* Then the *alternative frame can suggest alternative responses.* Reframing helps you to get "unstuck" from routine, unproductive ways of dealing with problem behavior and to consider fresh approaches that change the social context or ecosystem of the classroom.

The following account was written by a student teacher who tried reframing:

Ruben is a sophomore in my English 2 class. He loves to be the center of attention. He is constantly disrupting the class by talking over me during a lesson. He also shouts across the room to his friend Oscar. . . . In addition, Ruben does not do any class work or homework on his own. . . .

My initial reaction to Ruben's behavior was that of frustration. I thought he wanted to irritate me and the only way he knew how was to disrupt the entire class. . . . I tried several techniques to change his behavior. I started by separating Ruben from his friends, specifically Oscar, and putting his desk in the middle of a group of [other] students . . . but it only made matters worse. He started talking . . . to the students around him and now the yelling across the room got louder. Ruben would also copy the other students' work and hand it in. The second thing I did was to try to talk to him. I explained that I thought he was an intelligent boy, and that he should use his energy toward his success and stop disrupting me as well as the other students. I also told Ruben that I thought it was rude and he promised he would change. But within a few days, he went back to his old behavior. The third approach I took was reprimanding him. I gave Ruben detention and this made him behave for about 40 minutes of the class, but then his behavior reverted. I finally called in his mother, but once again his [good] behavior did not last. In the end I found myself frustrated and angry with him. I began to yell at him whenever he was out of control.

Ruben was taking too much of my class time and attention, and I was exhausted by the end of third period. . . . I decided to view this problem from a different perspective. I [reframed it this way]: Ruben performs better in class when he voices his opinion and demonstrates his understanding. . . . Since he likes and is good at using his speaking skills, I assigned him [the job of] classroom manager. As classroom manager, Ruben was able to walk around class checking homework assignments [and] taking attendance. . . . He was [also] allowed to open the journal topic discussion and have students share their journal entries for the first 10 minutes of class. He conducted the class in an organized fashion and he was able to interact with his fellow classmates. . . .

Allowing Ruben to walk around the room and take responsibility for certain tasks gave him the chance to speak to his friend Oscar on the other side of the room as well as others. It also gave him a chance to voice his own opinion and thoughts, so the yelling mostly ceased to exist. . . . [I also think] that he wants to set a good example to his classmates and he does not want to be rude to me because he sees me as a companion who has given him the opportunity to utilize his skills. . . . His class work and homework have improved drastically. Ruben now wants to resign as classroom manager and he would like to choose the next one for the new marking period.

Wow! It really worked! I won't deny the fact that I thought the entire method . . . was impossible. I was in need of a change for all of my students' sake and I was desperate. I am glad that I did try it because . . . it made me realize that a problem behavior can change and [a student] can become an asset to my classroom setting. The change has not only improved my relationship with Ruben, but with the entire class.

In accordance with an ecosystemic perspective, this student teacher first recognizes her interpretation of Ruben's problem behavior: *He is trying to irritate her and disrupt the class, and he does not want to learn literature.* She also recognizes that this interpretation has led to unproductive responses. She and Ruben are in a rut, and a different approach is obviously needed. Although she is skeptical, she tries to reframe the situation. She formulates an alternative, positive interpretation of the behavior that she finds plausible: *Ruben needs to voice his opinion and demonstrate his understanding.* She then acts in ways that are consistent with the new interpretation: *She gives him a job that allows him to express his views, interact with peers, and use his understanding to conduct the class.* This leads to a decrease in both yelling and interruption. In short, by changing her own behavior to reflect the new interpretation, this student teacher has changed the ecosystem of the classroom, bringing about a positive change in Ruben's behavior.

Dealing with Thorny Problems

Every year, student teachers from extremely different placements return to their seminars with similar tales of behavior that they find especially vexing or troublesome. It's impossible to generate recipes for dealing with these problems, since every instance is unique in terms of key players, circumstances, and history. Nonetheless, it is helpful to reflect on ways to deal with them *before* they occur and to hear some of the thinking that guides the actions of our four teachers. In this section of the chapter, we will consider three behaviors that keep teachers awake at night wondering what to do.

Defiance

Some years ago, Claire came to seminar looking shaken and upset. When I inquired what was wrong, she shared this story:

My ninth-graders were really rowdy today. I'm not sure what was going on, but they just wouldn't stop talking and laughing and calling out. One boy in particular, Jamal, was really annoying me. He wouldn't stay in his seat; he kept going to the back corner of the room where his buddies sit. I kept telling him to sit down, and he'd slowly saunter over to his desk. But then a few minutes later, I'd see he was up again. Finally, I got so mad, I just yelled across the room, "Jamal, I've had it with you. Get out! Go the office!" And he looked at me and in this real slow, mocking voice he said, "Make me." I just froze. This kid is more than six feet tall and really strong. He towers over me. I had no idea what to do. Finally, I said something stupid like, "I'm not going to make you, but you just better sit down." Then I just ignored him for the rest of the period. I felt like a complete jerk, and he knew it.

Claire's interaction with Jamal was traumatic for her and unfortunate for him, but it gave our seminar group an opportunity to examine ways of dealing with defiance. As we pondered alternative strategies, it became obvious that *the best course of action would have been to avoid the situation in the first place.* For example, after she had repeatedly told him to sit down without success, she might have approached him and quietly, but firmly, let him know that he had the choice of getting to work or facing one of the consequences for inappropriate behavior (e.g., "Jamal, here are your choices. You can sit down and begin working or you can go to Ms. Rosen's classroom for time out"; "Jamal, you can sit down and begin working now or you can work on it after school"). Unfortunately, by shouting across the room, Claire created a public power struggle. She backed Jamal into a corner with no "graceful exit," and Jamal was forced to challenge her if he wanted to save face with his peers.

Having said that, we still need to consider Claire's options once Jamal defied her order to get out. When I recounted this episode to our four teachers, they gave these suggestions for dealing with defiance:

Don't lose your cool: Stay in control of yourself. Even though your first inclination may be to shout back, don't. (It may help to take a few deep breaths and to use self-talk: "I can handle this calmly. I'm going to speak quietly.")

Direct the rest of the class to work on something (e.g., "Everyone do the next three problems," or "Start reading the next section.").

Move the student away from peers: Talk to the student in an area where you can have more privacy. This eliminates the need for the student to worry about saving face.

Stand a few feet away from the student (i.e., don't get "in his face"): A student who is feeling angry and defiant may interpret closing in on him as an aggressive act (Wolfgang, 1999).

Acknowledge the student's feelings: "I can see that you're really angry . . ."

Offer a choice: In Jamal's case, the confrontation was no longer about doing the work, but about going to the office. So the choices should focus on this issue: "Jamal, I can see that you're really upset, and we'll have to talk later. But meanwhile, here are the choices. You can go to the office, or I'll have to send for someone to come and get you."

Interestingly, as the teachers and I discussed ways of responding to defiance, I began to understand that this was not a major problem for any of them. When Sandy commented that she could "count on one hand the cases of insubordination" she had encountered in a lifetime of teaching, the others nodded in agreement. So I asked why they thought that students in their classes were rarely defiant. The teachers were unanimous in their response: They don't allow minor problems to escalate into major ones. Donnie put it this way:

> I sometimes see students in the office, and I ask them, "Why are you down here?" They'll tell me, "I was thrown out for chewing gum." But you know that couldn't be the whole story. It probably started out with gum chewing, but escalated into a real power struggle. And for what? We need to make sure that we don't blow up situations way out of proportion.

And Fred had one last suggestion for new teachers: "If defiance is *not* a rare thing in your classroom, then it's time to think seriously about what you're doing with those kids. Some examination of your own practice is clearly in order." (See Chapter 14 for a related discussion of defusing potentially explosive situations.)

Failure to Do Homework

When students consistently fail to do homework assignments, you need to consider just how valuable those assignments are and if you have communicated that value to students. Fred comments:

> I am convinced that if teachers were evaluated on the basis of the amount and quality of their homework assignments, students would have much less homework and would do more of it! I never give homework assignments unless I can explain the reason to my students. Having students understand the importance of doing a particular task at home cuts down dramatically on the number of missing assignments.

In a similar vein, Sandy tells her students "there's a reason for every assignment I give":

> I tell them, "I will not insult your intelligence by giving you garbage assignments that waste your time. Every assignment is necessary for what we're currently working on; you have to do it to meet with success.

It's also important to reflect on how much homework you're assigning, if it's too difficult for students to complete independently, and whether the time allotted is sufficient. Recall that in Chapter 5, Christina talked about an instance when students had been disgruntled by the amount and difficulty of the homework she had assigned: "They kept saying it was like college work and . . . they were only 15!" Together, Christina and her students forged an agreement that was mutually satisfactory. Some due dates were postponed, in-class time was provided so that students could work in groups on some of the work, and Christina made sure she was available for help after school.

Here are some additional strategies that can help increase the likelihood of students completing homework:

Review, collect, or grade assignments. If you assign homework and then fail to check that students have done it, you're conveying the message that the homework just wasn't that important. Not all homework has to be graded, or even collected, but it's wise to check that students have done it and to record that fact in your grade book.

Give "homework quizzes." Since Donnie finds that getting some students to do homework is a "constant struggle," she gives students a daily quiz with one or two problems that are just like those assigned the night before for homework. In addition, she gives a "homework quiz" every week or two. She selects five problems that were previously given for homework and allows students to refer to their homework papers, but not their books.

Require a "product" in addition to reading. When Christina assigned 17 pages of *The Martian Chronicles* for homework, she discovered that fully one-half of the class had not done the reading—despite the fact that she had warned them about having a quiz. According to Christina, "students just don't count reading as homework." She has learned that they are far more likely to do the reading if she also has them do something *with* it (e.g., use Post-it notes to mark your three favorite passages; list 10 words or phrases the author uses to give clues about the protagonist's character; generate three questions about the reading to ask your classmates).

Accept no excuses. Sandy warns new teachers: "There are valid reasons for not doing homework. But if you start judging what's valid and what's not, that leads to a host of problems. My students know that I don't accept late homework. Period. If they don't have it, they come in and do it after school, because it's necessary for going on. But they get no credit for it."

Provide in-school support. Sometimes, students' home circumstances may interfere with doing homework. They may be in the midst of a family crisis. They may be living in an abusive situation. They may have after-school jobs or other responsibilities that leave little time for schoolwork. Donnie shares this incident: "Just last week I was visiting a friend in the hospital and ran into one of my students—a girl who often dozed off in class and frequently didn't have her homework. It turned out that she worked at the hospital every day from 3:00 to 11:00! This explained a lot! She's got a full-time job in addition to going to high school."

In situations like this, you might work with the student to develop a plan for getting homework done in school. Perhaps the student can do her homework during lunch or during a study hall. (If lunch is 40 minutes, a student can eat in 20 minutes and still have time to get started on homework.) Perhaps she can stop by your room before or after school for 15 minutes.

Despite your best efforts, some students will still not turn in homework. In this case, you need to meet individually to discuss the problem, generate possible solutions, and decide on an action plan. This might include contacting parents and asking for their cooperation and assistance, writing a contingency contract, or assigning a "homework buddy" to help the student remember and complete homework. Listen to Fred:

> *Many teachers have hard and fast rules about homework, with serious consequences if homework is not turned in on time. But I've come to believe that this kind of rigidity often does more harm than good. I try to work individually with kids who seem to be "irresponsible" with regard to homework. Together, we develop a plan for improving in this area.*

Cheating

A number of studies suggest that cheating is more prevalent than we like to think. According to Evans and Craig (1990), 61 percent of middle school students and 71 percent of secondary students perceive cheating to be a serious problem in their schools, while Schab (1991) found that more than two-thirds of high school students admit to having cheated on tests. And cheating isn't confined to those who are afraid of failing: In the 1998 Survey of High Achievers conducted by *Who's Who Among American High School Students,* four out of five high-achieving teenagers admitted having cheated in some way (Ditman, 2000).

In particular, the advent of the Internet has made the problems of plagiarism and purchasing papers more problematic than they used to be. Websites offer research papers for sale or give them away; often the papers are not well written and contain spelling and grammatical errors—a fact that can actually help students avoid suspicion (Ditman, 2000).

Once again, it's better to prevent the problem than to deal with it after the fact. This means finding ways to *diminish the temptation to cheat.* A recent study by Anderman, Griesinger, and Westerfield (1998) indicates that students are more likely to report cheating when they perceive the teacher as emphasizing performance over mastery (i.e., when it's more important to get an A on a test than to really learn the material). Similarly, students report more cheating when the teacher relies on extrinsic incentives to stimulate motivation (e.g., giving homework passes to students who get A's on a test) rather than trying to foster genuine interest in academic tasks. In light of this research, you need to make sure that the work you assign and the tests you give are fair and worthwhile and that you use the information they provide to help students master the material (Savage, 1999). You can also help students avoid the temptation to cheat by not basing students' grades on one or two "high-stakes" tasks (Savage, 1999). Although students may complain about frequent testing or assignments, they are less likely to cheat if they know that no one task will determine success or failure in the course.

At the beginning of the year, our four teachers also take the time to define cheating and to discuss how they feel about it. For example, Christina gives a "plagiarism speech," in which she carefully explains what constitutes plagiarism. Sandy elaborates on the distinction between helping one another with homework and cheating. She emphasizes the fact that cheating will lead to a loss of respect and trust. Similarly, Fred gives what he calls his "cheating sermonette": "Listen, you can lie and cheat and you may not be caught. . . . But if you don't cheat, you will be admirable."

In addition to reducing temptation, you can also take a number of simple precautions to *minimize opportunity.* When giving tests, for example, it's helpful to circulate throughout the room, use new tests each year, and create different forms of the same test for students seated in different rows. (With the help of a computer program, Donnie actually makes up four different forms for each test she administers.) I recently heard about a teacher who let four students take a make-up test out in the hallway. Not only was the test the same as the one the rest of the class had taken two days before (and which these students had heard about), the four students were allowed to sit together—unsupervised—to complete the test. Even the most ethical of students would find it hard to resist an opportunity like this! If you are assigning papers, make sure that you give realistic deadlines, provide enough preparation so that students feel comfortable, and require links with classwork and textbooks (Ditman, 2000). Christina has students turn in bits and pieces of their research papers all along the way (e.g. note cards, an outline, the first paragraph, a first draft), making it far more difficult for students to use a research paper obtained from a website.

Obviously, despite all your precautions, incidents of cheating will occur. It then becomes necessary to confront the students involved. Here are some suggestions for handling those encounters:

Talk privately. Once again, avoid creating a situation where the student may be publicly humiliated. This is likely to lead to a series of accusations and denials that gets more and more heated.

Present your reasons for suspecting cheating. Lay out your evidence calmly and firmly, even sorrowfully. (One "electronic" hint: If you suspect plagiarism, you might get help from www.plagiarism.org.)

Express concern. Make it clear that you do not expect this kind of behavior from this student. Try to find out why the student cheated (e.g., Was he simply unprepared? Is she under a lot of pressure to excel?)

Explain consequences. Some schools have predetermined consequences for cheating, such as giving a zero on the assignment, detention, and parental notification. If so, you need to follow your school's policy.

If allowed, provide an alternative method for earning credit (on the first offense). If your school policy allows, offer the student another way to demonstrate mastery of the material (e.g., taking a make-up test after school, writing a different report).

Discuss the consequences for subsequent cheating. Alert the student to the consequences for additional cheating incidents. Emphasize that you are available for assistance if cheating was the result of academic difficulties (i.e., there is no need to cheat because of problems with the material). If the student is under pressure at home to succeed, you may want to talk with parents. If students have no appropriate place to study at home, you might explore alternatives (e.g., studying at school or the public library).

Concluding Comments

In a study of the ways that teachers cope with problem students, Brophy and Rohrkemper (1981) found that a basic distinction between more effective and less effective teachers was their *willingness to take responsibility*. More effective teachers used a wide variety of strategies: Some used behavioral approaches—negotiating contracts, providing rewards, praising desirable behavior—while others tried to build positive relationships, provide encouragement, and foster self-esteem. Regardless, effective teachers were willing to assume the responsibility for managing youngsters' behavior. In sharp contrast, *less effective teachers tended to disclaim responsibility and to refer problems to other school personnel* (e.g., the principal, guidance counselor, etc.).

Clearly, our four teachers are willing to take responsibility for the behavior of their students. They recognize that they are accountable for what happens in their classrooms. Furthermore, they are willing to admit when they have contributed to problems that occur. Listen to Christina:

> When I first started to use groupwork, it wasn't clear to me that students needed a lot of structure, and I didn't provide enough detailed instruction. So students wouldn't really understand what the task entailed. I'd tell them, "You have 20 minutes," but I wouldn't tell them how much time they should spend on each part of the assignment. Or I wouldn't explain what each person in the group was supposed to do. . . . When I would realize the groupwork was falling apart, I'd say, "This is what you should be doing now." I'd add the instructions I should have given at the beginning!

I agree with Christina, Sandy, Donnie, and Fred that teachers need to assume responsibility for students' behavior problems, and I hope that this chapter will help you to feel more competent in this area. Nonetheless, there are times when you have to acknowledge that an individual's problem is so deeply rooted that interventions like the ones discussed in this chapter just don't work. As Donnie observes: "Teachers have to recognize that there are kids you can't help by yourself. Then it's important to go to guidance and try to get assistance." We turn to this topic in Chapter 13.

✦ Summary

Inappropriate behavior threatens order by interrupting the flow of classroom activity. This chapter discussed ways of responding to a variety of problems—from minor, nondisruptive infractions to chronic, more serious misbehaviors.

Guidelines for dealing with misbehavior

- Use disciplinary strategies that preserve the dignity of the student.
    Separate the student's character from the specific misbehavior.
    Encourage students to take responsibility for regulating their own behavior.
- Try to keep the instructional program going with a minimum of disruption.
- Consider the context of students' actions. Behavior that is acceptable in one context may be unacceptable in another.
- Match your disciplinary strategy to the misbehavior.

Strategies for dealing with minor misbehavior

- Nonverbal interventions.
- Verbal interventions:
    Direct student to the task at hand.
    State student's name.
    Remind student of rule.
    Call on student.
    Use gentle humor.
    Use an I-message.
- Ignoring misbehavior that is fleeting.

Strategies for dealing with more serious misbehavior

- Plan penalties ahead of time.
- Choose penalties that are logically related to misbehavior.
- Impose penalties calmly and quietly.
- Reestablish a positive relationship with the student as quickly as possible.
- Develop a range of alternative consequences.

Strategies for dealing with chronic misbehavior

- Problem-solving process:
    Step 1: Define the problem.
    Step 2: Brainstorm possible solutions.
    Step 3: Evaluate solutions.
    Step 4: Decide on a solution to try.
    Step 5: Determine how to implement the decision.
    Step 6: Evaluate the solution.
- Behavior modification approaches:
    Self-monitoring
    Self-evaluation
    Self-instruction
    Contingency contracting

- An ecosystemic approach:
  Recognize your current interpretation of the problem.
  Formulate an alternative, positive interpretation (reframe the situation).
  Act in ways that are consistent with the new interpretation.

Dealing with thorny problems

Defiance
Failure to do homework
Cheating

Effective teachers are willing to take responsibility for managing students' behavior. Work on developing a system for dealing with misbehavior that suits your personality and your teaching style. You may have a student whose problems are too severe for you to deal with. If so, it is your responsibility to get this student outside help.

Activities

1. Beginning teachers sometimes overreact to misbehavior or take no action at all because they simply don't know what to do or say. Read each of the following situations and devise a nonverbal intervention, a verbal cue, and an I-message.

Example	Nonverbal	Verbal	I-Message
A student writes on the desk.	Hand the student an eraser.	"We use paper to write on."	"When you write on the desk, the custodian complains to me, and I get embarrassed."
A student makes a big show of looking through her book bag for her homework, distracting other students and delaying the start of the lesson.	Give the "look."	"We're ready to begin."	"When you take so long to get your things out, I can't begin the lesson, and I get very frustrated by the lost time."

a. A student is copying from another student's paper.

b. A student takes another student's notebook.

c. A student sharpens his pencil during your presentation.

d. A student calls out instead of raising her hand.

2. When a misbehavior occurs, there usually isn't much time for careful consideration of logical consequences. I've listed a few typical misbehaviors for your practice. What are two logical consequences for each example?

   a. As part of a small group, Lou monopolizes the discussion and tells everyone what to do in an authoritarian manner.

   b. At the end of the year, Arianna returns her book with ripped pages and the cover missing.

   c. Shemeika yells out answers throughout your class discussion, even though you have instructed students to raise their hands.

   d. Whenever you're not looking, Tom practices juggling with three small bean bags he has brought to school.

   e. Instead of working on the class activity, Tanya examines the contents of her cosmetic kit.

3. Develop a behavior modification plan (such as self-monitoring or a contingency contract) to deal with the following problems:

   a. Arthur is a seventh-grader who exhibits aggressive behavior. Hardly a day goes by that another student hasn't come to you complaining of Arthur's pushing, teasing, or name-calling. You've talked to his parents, but they are at a loss about what to do.

   b. Cynthia, an eleventh-grader, rarely completes her work. She daydreams, socializes with others, misunderstands directions, and gets upset when you speak to her about her incomplete work. The problem seems to be getting worse.

4. Try reframing a problem behavior according to an ecosystemic approach. First, think of a problem you are currently having. What is your current interpretation of the behavior? How do you typically respond to the behavior? Next, consider some positive alternative interpretations of the behavior. Based on one of the explanations, how might you respond differently?

5. What would you do in the following situation? You are reviewing homework from the night before. You call on James to do number 5. He slumps in his seat and fidgets with the chain around his neck. You tell him the class is waiting for his answer to number 5. Finally he mutters, "I didn't do the f___ homework."

✦ For Further Reading

Curwin, R. L., & Mendler, A. N. (1988). *Discipline with dignity.* Alexandria, VA: Association for Supervision and Curriculum Development.

Curwin, R. L., & Mendler, A. N. (1999). *Discipline with dignity for challenging youth.* Bloomington, IN: National Educational Service.

Gordon, T. (1974). *T.E.T.—Teacher Effectiveness Training.* New York: Peter H. Wyden.

Janney, R., & Snell, M. E. (2000). *Behavioral support.* Baltimore: Paul Brookes. (In the series *Teachers' guides to inclusive practices.*)

Molnar, A., & Lindquist, B. (1989). *Changing problem behavior in schools.* San Francisco: Jossey-Bass.

✸ References

Anderman, E. M., Griesinger, T., & Westerfield, G. (1998). Motivation and cheating during early adolescence. *Journal of Educational Psychology, 90*(1), 84–93.

Broden, M., Hall, R. V., & Mitts, B. (1971). The effect of self-recording on the classroom behavior of two eighth-grade students. *Journal of Applied Behavior Analysis, 4,* 191–199.

Brophy, J. E. (1983). Classroom organization and management. *The Elementary School Journal, 83*(4), 265–285.

Brophy, J., & Rohrkemper, M. (1981). The influence of problem ownership on teachers' perceptions of and strategies for coping with problem students. *Journal of Educational Psychology, 73,* 295–311.

Cairns, L. G. (1987). Behaviour problems. In M. J. Dunkin (Ed.), *The International Encyclopedia of Teaching and Teacher Education.* New York: Pergamon Press, pp. 446–452.

Créton, H. A., Wubbels, T., & Hooymayers, H. P. (1989). Escalated disorderly situations in the classroom and the improvement of these situations. *Teaching & Teacher Education, 5*(3), 205–215.

Curwin, R. L., & Mendler, A. N. (1988). *Discipline with dignity.* Alexandria VA: Association for Supervision and Curriculum Development.

Delpit, L. (1995). *Other people's children: Cultural conflict in the classroom.* New York: The New Press.

Ditman, O. (July/August 2000). Online term-paper mills produce a new crop of cheaters. *Harvard Education Letter, 16*(4), 6–7.

Doyle, W. (1986). Classroom organization and management. In M. C. Wittrock (Ed.), *Handbook of research on teaching.* New York: Macmillan, pp. 392–431.

Doyle, W. (1990). Classroom management techniques. In O. C. Moles (Ed.), *Student discipline strategies: Research and practice.* Albany, NY: SUNY Press.

Dreikurs, R., Grunwald, B. B., & Pepper, F. C. (1982). *Maintaining sanity in the classroom: Classroom management techniques* (2nd ed.). New York: Harper & Row.

Emmer, E. T., & Aussiker, A. (1990). School and classroom discipline programs: How well do they work? In O. C. Moles (Ed.), *Student discipline strategies.* New York: SUNY Press, pp. 129–165.

Emmer, E. T., Evertson, C., & Worsham, M. E., (2000). Classroom management for secondary teachers. (5th ed.). Boston: Allyn and Bacon.

Epanchin, B. C., Townsend, B., & Stoddard, K. (1994). *Constructive classroom management: Strategies for creating positive learning environments.* Pacific Grove, CA: Brooks/Cole.

Evans, E. D., & Craig, D. (1990). Teacher and student perceptions of academic cheating in middle and senior high schools. *Journal of Educational Research, 84,* 44–52.

Evertson, C. M. (1989). Classroom organization and management. In M. C. Reynolds (Ed.), *Knowledge base for the beginning teacher.* New York: Pergamon Press, pp. 59–70.

Evertson, C. M., & Emmer, E. T. (1982). Effective management at the beginning of the school year in junior high classes. *Journal of Educational Psychology, 74*(4), 485–498.

Good, J. E., & Brophy, T. L. (1994). *Looking in classrooms*. (6th ed.). New York: HarperCollins.

Gordon, T. (1974). *T.E.T.—Teacher Effectiveness Training*. New York: Peter H. Wyden.

Graziano, A. M., & Mooney, K. C. (1984). *Children and behavior therapy*. New York: Aldine.

Hughes, C. A., Ruhl, K. L. & Misra, A. (1989). Disordered students in school settings: A promise unfulfilled? *Behavioral Disorders, 14,* 250–262.

Janney, R., & Snell, M. E. (2000). *Behavioral support*. Baltimore: Paul Brookes.

Johnston, R. C. (November 24, 1999) Decatur furor sparks wider policy debate. *Education Week, 19*(13), pp. 1, 12.

Kounin, J. S. (1970). *Discipline and group management in classrooms*. New York: Holt, Rinehart and Winston.

Lasley, T. J., Lasley, J. O., & Ward, S. H. (1989). Activities and desists used by more and less effective classroom managers. Paper presented at the annual meeting of the American Educational Research Association, San Francisco.

McDougall, D. (1998). Research on self-management techniques used by students with disabilities in general education settings: A descriptive review. *Remedial and Special Education, 19*(5), 310–320.

Meichenbaum, D. (1977). *Cognitive behavior modification*. New York: Plenum.

Molnar, A., & Lindquist, B. (1989). *Changing problem behavior in schools*. San Francisco: Jossey-Bass.

National Center for Educational Statistics. (1998). *Violence and discipline problems in U. S. public schools: 1996–97, NCES 98-030*. Washington, DC: U. S. Department of Education, Office of Educational Research and Improvement.

Ninness, H. A. C., Fuerst, J., Rutherford, R. D., & Glenn, S. S. (1991). Effects of self-management training and reinforcement on the transfer of improved conduct in the absence of supervision. *Journal of Applied Behavior Analysis, 24*(3), 499–508.

Pittman, S. I. (1985). A cognitive ethnography and quantification of a first-grade teacher's selection routines for classroom management. *The Elementary School Journal, 85*(4), 541–558.

Richard, A. (September 8, 1999). As students return, focus is on security. *Education Week, 19*(1), 1, 14–15.

Sack, J. L. (June 7, 2000). ADHD student's expulsion voided. *Education Week,* p. 4.

Savage, T. V. (1999). *Teaching self-control through management and discipline* (2nd ed.). Boston: Allyn and Bacon.

Schab, F. (1991). Schooling without learning: Thirty years of cheating in high school. *Adolescence, 26,* 839–847.

Smith, D. J., Young, K. R., West, R. P., Morgan, D. P., & Rhode, G. (1988). Reducing the disruptive behavior of junior high school students: A classroom self-management procedure. *Behavioral Disorders, 18,* 231–239.

Turco, T. L., & Elliott, S. N. (1986). Assessment of students' acceptability ratings of teacher-initiated interventions for classroom misbehavior. *Journal of School Psychology, 24,* 277–283.

Valentine, G. (Fall 1998). Lessons from home (an interview with Lisa Delpit). *Teaching Tolerance, 7*(2), 15–19.

Wolfgang, C. H. (1999). *Solving discipline problems: Methods and models for today's teachers*. (4th ed.). Boston: Allyn and Bacon.

Helping Students Who Are Troubled

Chapter 6 described recent changes in the American family—the increase in the number of single parents, the vanishing "stay-at-home" mother, and the growing population of ethnic groups that do not speak English. I pointed out that these changes make it more difficult to achieve close family–teacher communication than in earlier years. But other societal trends will also affect you as a teacher. Consider these statistics from the Annie E. Casey Foundation (1999) and the Children's Defense Fund (1999):

Despite the economic boom of the 1990s, the proportion of children living in poverty—14.7 million or nearly 21 percent—changed little from the previous decade. During the 1990s, there was a significant increase in the number of children living in "working-poor" families, from 4.3 million in 1989 to 5.6 million in 1997. The U.S. child poverty rate is among the highest (if not *the* highest) in the developed world.

More than 10.7 million children, or 15 percent, do not have health insurance. These children are more likely to suffer from health problems because they have fewer physician visits each year and are less likely to receive adequate preventive services and immunizations.

Nineteen percent of American children, or nearly 13.3 million, are growing up in homes where the head of the household is not a high school graduate. Children born to a mother without a high school diploma are twice as likely to drop out of school as the children of a mother who is a high school graduate.

The United States ranks first among industrialized nations in rates of teenage pregnancy. The teen birth rate is twice as high as the next highest country (United Kingdom). Children born to teenage mothers are more likely to drop out of school, give birth out of wedlock, divorce or separate, and be dependent on welfare.

The number of abused and neglected children doubled between 1986 and 1993. Child abuse, neglect, and family violence are all closely linked with alcohol and other drug use. Three-quarters of the 12 million Americans who say they regularly use illegal drugs have children under the age of 12 at home. Illicit drugs are involved in half the reported incidents of family violence, while alcohol is involved in three-quarters of the cases.

Nationally, there are 9.2 million children, or 13 percent, growing up with four or more risk factors (e.g., poverty, absence of health insurance, low parental educational level). Nearly 30 percent of all black children and nearly 25 percent of all Hispanic children are in this high-risk category, compared to only 6 percent of all white children.

The message in these alarming statistics is clear: Large numbers of America's youth are at risk—for school failure, substance abuse, physical problems, psychological and emotional disorders, abuse and neglect, teenage pregnancy, and violence. (For a chilling picture of the plight of America's children, see Figure 13-1.) Moreover, *when these young people come to school, their problems come with them.* This means that teachers have to deal with issues that were unimaginable in an earlier era—issues that require knowledge and skills far beyond those needed to be an effective instructor.

How can you provide extra support for the at-risk students who may be in your classroom? *First, you need to be alert to the indicators of potential problems.* As an adult immersed in adolescent culture, you will probably develop a good idea of what typical teenage behavior is like. This allows you to detect deviations or changes in a student's behavior that might signal the presence of a problem. In *Teacher as Counselor: Developing the Helping Skills You Need* (1993), Jeffrey and Ellen Kottler suggest that you learn to ask yourself a series of questions when you notice atypical behavior:

> *What is unusual about this student's behavior?*
>
> *Is there a pattern to what I have observed?*
>
> *What additional information do I need to make an informed judgment?*
>
> *Who might I contact to collect this background information?*
>
> *What are the risks of waiting longer to figure out what is going on?*

Every 1 second	a public high school student is suspended.*
Every 9 seconds	a high school student drops out.*
Every 10 seconds	a public school student is corporally punished.*
Every 20 seconds	a child is arrested.
Every 24 seconds	a baby is born to an unmarried mother.
Every 37 seconds	a baby is born to a mother who is not a high school graduate.
Every 44 seconds	a baby is born into poverty.
Every 1 minute	a baby is born to a teen mother.
Every 2 minutes	a baby is born at low birthweight (less than 5 lbs., 8 oz.).
Every 4 minutes	a baby is born to a mother who had late or no prenatal care.
Every 4 minutes	a child is arrested for drug abuse.
Every 8 minutes	a child is arrested for a violent crime.
Every 9 minutes	a baby is born at very low birthweight (less than 3lbs., 4 oz.)
Every 19 minutes	a baby dies.
Every 42 minutes	a child or youth under 20 dies from an accident.
Every 2 hours 20 minutes	a child or youth under 20 is killed by a firearem.
Every 3 hours	a child or youth under 20 is a homicide victim.
Every 4 hours	a child or youth under 20 commits suicide.
Every day	a young person under 25 dies from HIV infection.

*Based on calculations per school day (180 days of seven hours each)

FIGURE 13-1. Moments in America for All Children
Reprinted by permission. Children's Defense Fund, The State of America's Children Yearbook 2001. *Washington, D.C.: Children's Defense Fund, 2001.*

Does this student seem to be in any imminent danger?

Who can I consult about this case?

During one meeting, the teachers talked about how they try to be alert to problems their students might be experiencing. Sandy told us how she tries to distinguish between problems that warrant immediate action and those that do not, and how she collects additional information:

I watch for changes in students' behavior. If I see anything that looks like drug abuse, I report it immediately. If it doesn't seem like a drug problem, I generally approach the student and ask what's going on. If the kid seems depressed, I'll say something like, "Hey, you seem a little down today. Are you having a problem? Do you want to talk?" We all have bad days, and adolescents have wide swings of mood; it's the nature of the beast. A day or two of strange behavior doesn't necessarily mean there's a big problem. Adolescents aren't very good at masking their emotions, and most of the time they're upset because they had a fight with their mother, or the dog had to be put to sleep, or their boyfriend or girlfriend broke up with them. But if a kid is acting weird or seems depressed for longer than a few days, I check with other teachers to find out if they're seeing anything unusual too. If they've also noticed problems, I go to the principal or the vice-principal; often they know if something is going on at home. If there appears to be a real problem, I'll report it.

As Sandy's comment suggests, *a second way you can help students with serious problems is to be informed about the various special services that are available and to know how to obtain access to those services.* Keep in mind these words of Maynard Reynolds, a leading special educator:

It is too much to ask that a beginning teacher know about all of the problems he or she will encounter in teaching; but it is not too much to ask that the beginning teacher recognize needs for support and assistance when challenging problems arise, and to understand that it is a sign of professionalism to seek help when needed rather than a sign of weakness. (Reynolds, 1989, p. 138)

Since specific resources and reporting procedures vary from district to district, it is essential that you learn about the special services in your own school and find out if there are special referral forms. Depending on the situation, you may want to consult with the principal or vice-principal, student assistance counselor, school social worker, substance awareness coordinator, nurse, guidance counselor, or the "CORE" team (a group consisting of all these individuals, working together to identify, refer, and support at-risk students experiencing problems). Some schools, like New Brunswick High School, where Donnie teaches, and South Brunswick High School, where Fred teaches, even have "School Based Youth Services Programs" (SBYSP), centers in the school where outside agencies provide a wide variety of support services to students and their families. Gail Reynolds is the director of the SBYSP at New Brunswick High School. She explains about "School Base":

We have five main programs in New Brunswick: counseling services— which include substance abuse programs; a teen parenting program; health screening and services; employment training; and recreation. Our largest service is the counseling program. We've got trained social workers and psychologists who work with the students who have the most difficult problems and who need longer-term interventions than the guidance office could provide. We also run groups for kids who are acting out, who don't have any impulse control, who come from really chaotic families, who are really depressed.

In addition to the counseling, we provide health screening and services. We have a coordinator who's a social worker and a nurse right here in the school. They make assessments, refer kids to the Eric B. Chandler Health Center [a nearby health clinic] or to Planned Parenthood as needed, set up the appointments for them, and actually get the kids there and back.

In our teen parenting program, we run two groups—one on life skills preparation (getting ready for the world of work) and one on child development and parenting skills. We also have a child care center right here in the school that can accommodate up to 19 infants and toddlers; we have a van, and every morning we pick up the mothers and their babies and bring them here, and we bring them home every night.

Having all these programs right here in the school is the best way for us in New Brunswick. We found that if we have the programs off-site, the kids just don't follow through. We used to make referrals to a counseling center nearby and set up the appointment, but then the kid wouldn't go, so what good does it do? This way, the programs are immediately available to them. The kids are comfortable in school; they know you; they trust you. Of course, the down side is that a lot of kids are super sensitive about their friends seeing them come to School-Base. It's hard to maintain strict confidentiality in a school setting. But that's one reason why we have recreation and employment programs. We're trying to send the message that you don't have to have a problem to come here.

This chapter examines some of the serious problems that teachers may encounter in today's high schools—substance abuse, abuse and neglect, eating disorders, and depression/suicide. As you will see, this chapter not only describes the experiences of our four teachers, it also draws upon the wisdom of counselors who work directly with troubled students in each of the four districts, New Brunswick, Highland Park, Woodbridge, and South Brunswick.

What Are the Problems? And What Can You Do?

Substance Abuse

In order to deal with problems rooted in drugs and alcohol, many schools have established student assistance programs (SAPs) and have hired full-time student assistance counselors (SACs). Note that the initials "SA" do *not* stand for substance abuse. The wording is deliberate. Although SAPs focus on identifying and helping students at risk for alcohol and other drug problems, they generally adopt a broad-based approach. There are two good reasons for this strategy. First, drug problems usually occur in conjunction with other problems—depression, abuse, academic difficulties, family problems, pregnancy (Gonet, 1994). Second, it's less stigmatizing to go to a student assistance counselor than a substance abuse counselor. Shirley Sexton, the SAC in Christina's school, emphasizes this point: "It's really important not to be known as the 'drug lady.' I try to make it clear that I'm available to talk about all kinds of problems that kids may be experiencing—from bereavement to divorce to communication problems with parents."

With respect to alcohol and drugs, SACs can provide help to students who are the *children of alcoholics/addicts (COAs) and students who are themselves substance abusers.* Let's turn first to the problems of COAs and consider the cases of Amanda and Eric (adapted from Powell, Zehm, & Kottler, 1995).

Amanda's father is an alcoholic who becomes aggressive and abusive when he drinks. At age 13, Amanda is her mother's primary source of support and works hard to make her family appear normal. She has assumed many adult responsibilities that would normally be carried out by the father of a household. At school, she is a very successful student; her teachers describe her as superdependable and motivated. They don't realize that she is filled with feelings of inadequacy and confusion, that her behavior is prompted by a compulsive need to be perfect. Nor do they notice that in between classes and at lunch time Amanda spends most of her time alone. Amanda avoids forming friendships because she is afraid of revealing the family secret.

Eric is a ninth grader whose teacher describes him as sullen, disrespectful, and obstructive. He frequently fights with other students and has been suspended several times for antisocial behavior. His mother claims not to understand his behavior; she reports that Eric never acts this way at home and implies that his teachers are the cause of his perpetual negative attitude. Yet he often has violent outbursts at home. At the core of Eric's behavior is anger: He is enraged by the rejection he feels from his alcoholic father and feels resentful that his mother spends so much time wallowing in self-pity. He soothes his pain by planning ways to leave home when he's old enough to drop out of school. He is on the verge of jumping into his own life of addiction.

Substance abuse touches secondary classrooms every time youngsters like Amanda and Eric enter the room—and their presence is not a rare occurrence. It is estimated that one in every four students sitting in a classroom comes from a family in which one or both parents are addicted to drugs or alcohol (Powell, Zehm, & Kottler, 1995). When these youngsters are angry and disruptive like Eric, it is relatively easy to recognize that a problem exists; it is far more difficult when students are compliant perfectionists like Amanda.

Leslie Lillian, a student assistance counselor in Fred's district, stresses that COAs can exhibit a wide variety of behaviors (see Table 13-1):

Some children become perfectionists and peacemakers. They want to prevent situations that might evoke their parents' anger because their

TABLE 13-1. Characteristics of Children of Alcoholics/Addicts

Difficulty in creating and maintaining trusting relationships, often leading to isolation.

Low self-esteem.

Self-doubt.

Difficulty in being spontaneous and open, caused by a need to be in control and to minimize the risk of being surprised.

Denial and repression because of the need to collaborate with other family members in keeping "the secret."

General feelings of guilt about areas for which the child had no responsibility.

Uncertainty about his/her own feelings and desires caused by shifting parental roles.

Seeing things in an "all or nothing" context, which sometimes manifests itself in a perfectionist fear of failure.

Poor impulse control, which may result in acting-out behavior, probably caused by lack of parental guidance, love, and discipline.

Potential for depression, phobias, panic reactions, and hyperactivity.

Preoccupation with the family.

Abuse of alcohol and/or drugs.

Source: Towers, 1989.

> *parents' responses are so unpredictable. It's as if they think to themselves, "I'm not going to disturb anything; I'm not going to do anything wrong; I'll try and keep the peace, so that no one will be angry."*
>
> *Some children become class clowns; maybe they've found that making people laugh breaks the tension, or maybe they're seeking attention. Others become very angry; they may begin to lie, or steal, or cheat. Some become sad and melancholy; everything about them says, "Nurture me." We see a whole spectrum of reactions—and it's the same spectrum of behaviors that we see in kids from violent homes.*

It's important to understand that for COAs, family life revolves around the addiction. Rules are arbitrary and irrational; boundaries between parents and children are blurred; and life is marked by unpredictability and inconsistency. Leslie comments:

> *These kids never know what they're going home to. One day, they may bring a paper home from school that's gotten a low grade, and the parent might say, "That's OK, just do it over." Another day, they might get beaten up for bringing home a paper like that.*

Sadly, it's often difficult for COAs to reach out for help. In a chemically dependent family, everyone works to maintain the family secret. Tonia Moore, Highland Park's student assistance counselor, finds that COAs move back and forth between "wanting to report the lies and wanting to believe the lies":

A while back I worked with a sister and brother; the girl was in elementary school and the boy was in high school. Their mother was an alcoholic, and she would tell them if they did well on their report cards, she would stop drinking. They'd go to church and pray for that; they'd even dream about it. I would tell them, "Don't count on it. It's not that easy for your mom to stop drinking, even though she wants to." But they wanted to believe it would happen. They really tried to improve their grades, and they did, and she still didn't stop. They were heartbroken.

Sometimes, she'd come to back-to-school night, and you could tell she'd been drinking. The boy would put his arm around her and try to keep her from making a scene. And then the next day, he'd come in to see me, all embarrassed, and apologize for her behavior. He'd say she wasn't feeling well, that she had the flu, even though he knew that I knew she was an alcoholic. He'd participate in the secret, he'd try to cover up, even as he confided in me. Children of substance abusers have such a tremendous need to have things be normal.

One of the most frustrating aspects of working with COAs is the realization that you do not have the power to change the child's home life. Instead, you must concentrate on what you *are* able to do during the time the student is in your classroom. Many of the strategies are not different from those I have espoused for all students. (See Table 13-2). For example, it is essential that you establish clear, consistent rules and work to create a climate of trust and caring.

TABLE 13-2. Ways of Helping Children of Alcoholics/Addicts

1. **Be observant.** Watch your students not just for academic or behavior problems, but also for the more subtle signs of addiction and emotional distress. Remember that COAs can be overachieving, cooperative, and quiet, as well as disruptive and angry.
2. **Set boundaries that are enforced consistently.** When chaos exists at home, some sense of order is crucial at school.
3. **Be flexible.** Although it is necessary to set boundaries, classroom rules that are too rigid and unyielding may invite students to act out.
4. **Make addiction a focus of discussion.** Find a way to deal with this subject. Incorporate addiction into literacy instruction (e.g., through children's literature, writing), science, social studies, etc.
5. **Make it clear you are available.** Communicate that you are eager and open to talk to children. Reach out to the troubled student in a gentle, caring way. "I notice you are having some difficulty. I just want you to know that I care about you. Call me any time you are ready to talk. And if you would rather speak to someone else, let me find you someone you can trust."
6. **Develop a referral network.** Find out what services are available to help and refer the student for appropriate professional care.
7. **Accept what you can do little about.** You can't make people stop drinking or taking drugs.

Source: Adapted from Powell, Zehm, & Kottler, 1995.

In addition to using these strategies, you should find out if your school has student assistance counselors or other special services personnel who can provide help. Find out if support groups for COAs are available. For example, Tonia runs groups at school, sometimes alone and sometimes with the guidance counselor. Tonia speaks about the benefits that joining such a group can bring:

There's such a sense of relief. The comments are always the same: "I thought I was the only one." "I didn't know anyone else was going through this stuff." The shame is so great, even at a very young age, and the need to keep it all a secret is so hard. There's instant camaraderie.

We'll often start off by asking, "On a scale from 1 to 10, how are you feeling today?" That allows us to get a sense of the group and to learn quickly who's in the middle of a crisis. Then we'll ask them to share something positive that happened this week and something negative that happened. We'll ask who needs group time. We do activities that help to ⋅ build self-esteem. We do role playing to get at feelings—being disappointed, being unsafe, being embarrassed, being angry that you can never make plans, that you can never say, "My mother will be there," or even "I'll be there."

Unfortunately, COAs may be reluctant to join such groups. Shirley Sexton has recently started three groups for students at JFK, one on bereavement, one on divorce and separation, and one for COAs. Although students immediately signed up for the first two groups, thus far she's gotten little response to the third. Shirley is not surprised. "It'll take some time," she explains. "Talking about your parents' alcoholism or addiction is a touchy issue."

If there are no groups for COAs in your school, find out if your community has any support groups like *Alateen,* for children from 8 to 19. This group is part of the Al-Anon Family Groups and abides by the same "12 steps" as Alcoholics Anonymous. (See Figure 13-2.)

A second way that substance abuse can affect high school classrooms is when students themselves abuse drugs and alcohol. The extent of this problem is not entirely clear. In the late 1990s, substance abuse among teenagers appeared to show a decline. One survey, for example, found that the percentage of 12- to 17-year-olds who reported using illicit drugs at least once in the past 30 days had dropped from 11.4 percent in 1997 to 10 percent in 1998 (Coles, 1999). Similarly, another study found that "risky behavior" (e.g., drug use, sexual activity) among teenagers dropped significantly from 1991 to 1997 (Coles, 2000). On the other hand, the same study found that Hispanic teenagers' use of alcohol, marijuana, or other illegal drugs rose by nearly 50 percent during this period, and the Centers for Disease Control and Prevention found an increase in cocaine and marijuana use from 1991 to 1999 (Coles, 2000).

Alateen, part of the Al-Anon Family Groups, is a fellowship of young people whose lives have been affected by alcoholism in a family member or close friend. We help each other by sharing our experience, strength and hope.

We believe alcoholism is a family disease, because it affects all the members emotionally and sometimes physically. Although we cannot change or control our parents, we can detach from their problems while continuing to love them.

We do not discuss religion or become involved with any outside organizations. Our sole topic is the solution of our problems. We are always careful to protect each other's anonymity as well as that of all Al-Anon and AA members.

By applying the Twelve Steps to ourselves, we begin to grow mentally, emotionally and spiritually. We will always be grateful to Alateen for giving us a wonderful, healthy program to live by and enjoy.

FIGURE 13-2. Suggested preamble to the Twelve Steps
Source: From Alateen: Hope for Children of Alcoholics, 1989.

Regardless of the actual numbers, it is clear that substance abuse and addiction remain serious problems. Carol Lowinger, the student assistance counselor in Fred's school, comments on teenage drug use:

> *There's been an influx of heroin that's incredibly potent. The kids are snorting it—they don't use needles, so they think it's safer. There's still some cocaine and, of course, there's always marijuana. But we're also seeing more designer drugs, hallucinogens, and amphetamines. And drinking is consistently high. I don't really see it going up or down.*

As Carol's comment indicates, marijuana and alcohol are still the drugs of choice, although an increasing number of teenagers are experimenting with "designer drugs" such as "Ecstasy," methamphetamines or crank (Sandham, 2000), heroin, and even Ritalin, which is often prescribed for attention-deficit/hyperactivity disorder (Portner & Galley, 2000). Rohypnol, a depressant known on the streets as "rufies," "ropies," or "roofies," is also becoming popular. Known as the "date rape drug," rohypnol has no taste or color, and when dissolved in alcohol, it produces disinhibition and amnesia.

To a large extent, SACs rely on teachers to refer students who might be having problems with alcohol and other drugs or who might be at risk for such problems. But teachers may be particularly reluctant to make referrals about suspected drug use. Five different reasons for this reluctance emerged during my conversations with teachers and counselors. First, some teachers think drug use is just not all that serious. According to Carol:

> *Some teachers have a tendency to minimize the situation—especially if it involves alcohol or pot. They just don't consider pot to be a "real" drug. They think, "Oh, all kids do this; it's not that big a deal."*

In addition, Carol speculates that some teachers feel it's not their role to get involved, while others want to play the role of confidante:

Sometimes, teachers are overwhelmed by all the responsibilities of teaching. They feel like they have more than enough to do without getting involved in students' personal problems. They tell themselves, "It's not my role to report this; I'm here to teach." But other times, teachers don't refer because they want to try to help the kid themselves. You know, a lot of teachers really like the role of mediator, caretaker, trusted confidante. They like the fact that a student is confiding in them about a problem, and sometimes they make a pact of confidentiality with the student: "You can tell me your secret. I won't tell anybody." But if the kid is in serious trouble, that can be a problem. First of all, they don't really have the training to help the way a counselor could. Second, they might be sending a message to the kid that it's not okay to go to a counselor or a mental health professional— and that's not a message we want to send. We want kids to see that we all need a variety of people in our lives, people who can help us in many different ways. We don't want kids to think that one person is all they need, and if they have the teacher they don't need to go to anybody else. Third, they could actually be serving as a "professional enabler"—they're allowing the kid to continue behavior that could be self-destructive. That's not helpful to the kid. What you've got to do is say to the kid, "I care too much about you to allow this to continue. We've got to get help for you."

A fourth reason for teachers' reluctance to refer is the belief that they are "turning kids in" when they would rather "give the kid a break" (Newsam, 1992). Sandy herself comments on this attitude:

Some teachers are afraid to report suspected drug use because they don't want to create a hassle for the kid. They don't want to get the kid in trouble. They may also be afraid that reporting kids will ruin their relationship with students. But I haven't found that to be the case. Sometimes, the kid will come back and say, "Why did you do that?" But I say, "This is too big for us. We need more help." Sometimes, I'll even have kids come to tell me about a problem with a friend. They know I'll find help. That's what they want.

Finally, teachers may be reluctant to report suspected drug use because they are unsure about the indicators. Tonia is very sensitive to this problem:

Teachers tell me, "I have no idea what substance abuse looks like. It wasn't a part of my training. I wouldn't know when to refer a student." I tell them, that's okay. You can't tell substance abuse just by looking. There has to be a chemical screening. But you can see changes in behavior. You know

enough about kids to know when somebody's behavior has changed, or if
their behavior is different from all the other kids. You don't need to know
the student is using; you just need to suspect that there may be drug use
or a problem related to drug use.

What are the behaviors that might lead you to suspect drug use and to make a referral? Figure 13-3 shows the behavior checklist used at South Brunswick High School.
Many schools use forms that are very similar to this one. Keeping your school's behavior checklist handy can help you stay alert to the possibility that students are using drugs
or living with addiction in their families.

It's important to distinguish between situations in which a pattern of behavior problems suggests possible *drug use outside of school* and situations in which a student appears to be *under the influence of drugs during school, at school functions,* or *on school
property.* When you see students who might be "under the influence," you cannot wait
to fill out a behavior checklist; you need to alert the appropriate personnel as soon as you
possibly can. Fred shares this experience:

A few years ago, I had this really bright kid in my first-period class. He was
a star football player; he could have gone to college anywhere. But then he
got into drugs. I remember one day in particular when he came into class
high. I didn't realize it at first, because he just sat down quietly and every-
thing seemed okay. But then he got up to sharpen his pencil, and I could
see that he was walking funny. He was actually leaning to one side. It
looked like he was going to fall over. I never saw anyone walk like that. I
gave the rest of the class an assignment and asked him to come with me
out into the hall. I tried to be really discreet; I didn't want everyone
watching and talking about him. I planned to call the assistant principal, but
the principal happened to be walking by just at that minute, so he took him
to the nurse.

In New Jersey, teachers are legally required to report "as soon as possible" a student
who appears to be under the influence of drugs. Tonia explains one of the reasons for
mandating an immediate response:

It used to be that teachers would come to me at the end of the day and
say, "I was really worried about X today. I think he was really on something."
That's no good. I need to know at the time. After all, that student could fall
down the stairs, or the student could leave the building during lunch time
and get killed crossing the street. We have to deal with the problem imme-
diately. It can really be a matter of life and death.

Make sure you know to whom you're supposed to refer students who appear to be
under the influence of drugs. In Fred and Christina's schools, teachers call an administrator, who comes to the classroom and accompanies the student to the nurse. In Sandy's

---

STUDENT ASSISTANCE PROGRAM
BEHAVIOR CHECKLIST

The goal of the Student Assistance Program is to help students who may be experiencing problems in their lives. These problems can be manifested in school through any combination of behaviors. The following is a list of typical behaviors students having problems may exhibit. While most students engage in many of the behaviors at one time or another, the student who may be having trouble will show a combination or pattern of these behaviors.

Student: _____   Grade: _____

Staff
Member: _____   Date: _____

Academic Performance
____Drop in grades
____Decrease in participation
____Inconsistent work
____Works below potential
____Compulsive overachievement
      (preoccupied w/school success)

School Attendance
____Change in attendance
____Absenteeism
____Tardiness
____Class cutting
____Frequent visits to nurse
____Frequent visits to counselor
____Frequent restroom visits
____Frequent request for hall passes

Social Problems
____Family problems
____Run away
____Job problems
____Peer problems
____Constantly borrowing money
____Relationships problems

Physical Symptoms
____Staggering/stumbling
____Incoherent
____Smelling of alcohol/marijuana
____Vomiting/nausea

____Glassy, bloodshot eyes/dark
____Poor coordination
____Slurred speech
____Deteriorating physical
      appearance
____Sleeping in class
____Physical injuries
____Frequent physical complaints
____Dramatic change in musculature

Extracurricular Activities
____Lack of participation
____Possession of drugs/alcohol
____Involvement in thefts and
      assaults
____Vandalism
____Talking about involvement in
      illegal activities
____Possession of paraphernalia
____Increasing noninvolvement
____Decrease in motivation
____Dropping out missing practice(s)
____Not fulfilling responsibilities
____Performance changes

Disruptive Behavior
____Defiance of rules
____Irresponsibility, blaming, lying,
      fighting
____Cheating

FIGURE 13-3. The referral form used in South Brunswick

<table>
</table>

____Sudden outburst, verbal abuse	____Defensive
____Obscene language, gesture	____Withdrawn/difficulty relating
____Attention-getting behavior	____Unrealistic goals
____Frequently in wrong area	____Sexual behavior in public
____Extreme negativism	____Seeking adult advice without a
____Hyperactivity, nervousness	specific problem
____Lack of motivation, apathy	____Rigid obedience
____Problem with authority figures	____Constantly seeks approval

Atypical Behavior

____Difficulty in accepting mistakes

____Boasts about alcohol or drug use, "partying bravado"

____Erratic behavior

____Change of friends

____Overly sensitive

____Disoriented

____Inappropriate responses

____Depression

Other

____Students talking about alcohol or other drugs

____Having beeper

____Bragging about sexual exploits

____Mentions concerns about significant other's alcohol or other drug use, gambling

____Staff knowledge of addiction in family

Additional Comments:

_____

FIGURE 13-3. *(cont.)*

school, teachers send students to the nurse, who then contacts the student assistance counselor. In Donnie's school, teachers call a security guard who takes the student to the nurse.

Since you cannot be sure that a student is using drugs just by looking, it's important not to be accusatory when you talk with the student. Sandy describes how she usually handles this situation:

If I see a kid with his head down on the desk, I'll go over and ask real quietly, "Do you need to see the nurse?" Usually they'll say, "No, I'm just tired," or "No, I'm bored." I'll tell them, "But this is chemistry! This is supposed to be fun." Usually, the head stays up after that. But if the head goes back down, I'll say, "I think you need to see the nurse. You don't seem to be feeling well." I'm not confrontational, and I try to show the kid that I'm acting out of concern. Sometimes I'm wrong, and it turns out that the kid just stayed up until 4:00 AM doing a term paper. That's fine. It's better to err on the side of caution.

Making a referral can be difficult, but you need to remember that turning away and remaining silent can send the message that you condone the behavior—or that you don't care enough to do anything. You also need to remember that referral is not the end of your responsibility. Listen to Fred:

The referral is not the end of your job. You still have to stay involved. I try to let the kid know that he can come and talk to me. But I also let him know that I care enough not to tolerate drugs in my class, that I won't cut him any slack, and that I won't make excuses for him.

One final note: If you suspect that a student is in possession of drugs or alcohol in school (e.g., in a purse or backpack), it's best to bring that person to the appropriate school official rather than undertake a search by yourself. In a landmark case (*New Jersey v. T.L.O.,* 1985), the United States Supreme Court ruled that a school official may properly conduct a search of a student "when there are reasonable grounds for suspecting that the search will turn up evidence that the student has violated or is violating either the law or the rules of the school" (Fischer, Schimmel, & Kelly, 1999). In other words, students in school have fewer protections than are normally afforded to citizens under the stricter "probable cause" standard (Stefkovich & Miller, 1998). Nonetheless, searching a student's belongings is best left to an administrator who is aware of the subtleties of the law.

Abuse and Neglect

During one conversation with Donnie, she emphasized the difficulty of detecting abuse and neglect among older students:

At the high school level, abuse and neglect are not as obvious as they are at the elementary level. Kids cover up more. But it's clear that a lot of them live in situations that are really awful. Teachers have to watch really carefully and listen to all the conversations that you're not supposed to hear. That way you can learn about what's going on in kids' lives and in the community.

As Donnie points out, abuse of adolescents is often well hidden. Furthermore, adolescents just don't seem as vulnerable as younger children: They may have as much strength or weight as adults; they seem able to run away from abusive situations; and they appear to have more access to potential help outside the family. For these reasons, it's easy to think that abuse and neglect are not problems at the high school level. But adolescents still need protection. During one meeting, Christina recalled a girl who had worn a short-sleeved shirt in December when temperatures were in the 20s:

It was as if she was saying, "Please look at my arm." I did—and saw she had bruises all over it. As a new teacher, I was a little nervous about handling this the right way, so I went to consult with a more experienced teacher. We spoke with one of the school counselors, who took the student to the nurse.

It's also important to realize that girls are not the only victims of abuse. Consider this tale, shared by Donnie:

A number of years ago, I had a 16-year-old football player in my class. I noticed that he seemed really quiet, which was unusual for him. I asked him to come see me after school. When he came in, I said, "You don't seem yourself. Is everything OK?" To my amazement, he started to cry. It turned out he had been seduced by a 35-year-old woman living next door. Obviously, she didn't tie him down, but having sex with a minor constitutes sexual abuse. It was the last thing I expected. I figured he had broken up with his girlfriend, or he was having a problem on the football team. I was really hit between the eyes, and I was furious. I kept thinking, "How could she do that? He's just a kid." I had difficulty thinking straight. I thought, "Now what do I do?" I was the first person he had told. It was after school, and the psychologist was gone, the counselor was gone. But I convinced him to go with me to the principal. The office took over from there.

It has been estimated that almost 2 million school-age youngsters are victims of child abuse and neglect each year (Parkay & Stanford, 1992). In order to protect these youth, most states have laws requiring educators to report suspected abuse to the state's "child protective service." Although definitions of abuse vary, states generally include nonaccidental injury, neglect, sexual abuse, and emotional maltreatment. It is essential that you become familiar with the physical and behavioral indicators of these problems. (See Table 13-3.)

Teachers are often reluctant to file a report unless they have absolute proof of abuse. They worry about invading the family's privacy and causing unnecessary embarrassment to everyone involved. Nonetheless, it's important to keep in mind that *no state requires the reporter to have absolute proof before reporting.* What most states do require is "reason to believe" or "reasonable cause to believe or suspect" that abuse has occurred (Fischer, Schimmel, & Kelly, 1999). If you are uncertain whether abuse is occurring, but have reasonable cause, you should err in favor of the youngster and file a report. Waiting for proof can be dangerous; it may also be illegal. If a child is later harmed, and it becomes clear that you failed to report suspected abuse, both you and your school district may be subject to both civil and criminal liability (Michaelis, 1993).

It's essential that you learn about the reporting procedures in your state *before* you are faced with a situation of suspected child abuse. Some states explicitly name the school personnel who are required to file the report. (In New Jersey, for example, teachers are required to file a report directly to the child protective service in order to avoid unnecessary delays.) Other states have more general provisions that require reporting by "any person" who works with children; this would clearly include teachers, nurses, therapists, and counselors (Fischer, Schimmel, & Kelly, 1999). Often, a teacher who suspects child abuse notifies the principal, who then reports to the appropriate state agency. If, however, the administrator fails to make the report, the teacher should do so. Studies suggest that two-thirds of reports from teachers stop at the principal's desk (Bancroft, 1997). Also keep in mind that every state provides immunity from any civil suit or

TABLE 13-3. Physical and Behavioral Indicators of Child Abuse and Neglect

Type of Child Abuse or Neglect	Physical Indicators	Behavioral Indicators
Physical abuse	Unexplained bruises and welts: —on face, lips, mouth —on torso, back, buttocks, thighs —in various stages of healing —clustered, forming regular patterns —reflecting shape of article used to inflict (electric cord, belt buckle) —on several different surface areas —regularly appearing after absence, weekend or vacation Unexplained burns: —cigar, cigarette burns, especially on soles, palms, back, or buttocks —immersion burns (socklike, glovelike, doughnut shaped on buttocks or genitalia) —patterned like electric burner, iron, etc. —rope burns on arms, legs, neck, or torso Unexplained fractures: —to skull, nose, facial structure —in various stages of healing —multiple or spiral fractures Unexplained lacerations or abrasions: —to mouth, lips, gums, eyes —to external genitalia	Wary of adult contacts Apprehensive when other children cry Behavioral extremes: —aggressiveness —withdrawal Frightened of parents Afraid to go home Reports injury by parents
Physical neglect	Consistent hunger, poor hygiene, inappropriate dress Consistent lack of supervision, especially in dangerous activities or long periods Constant fatigue or listlessness Unattended physical problems or medical needs Abandonment	Begging, stealing food Extended stays at school (early arrival and late departure) Constantly falling asleep in class Alcohol or drug abuse Delinquency (e.g., thefts) States there is no caretaker

TABLE 13-3. *(cont.)*

Type of Child Abuse or Neglect	Physical Indicators	Behavioral Indicators

Sexual abuse	Difficulty in walking or sitting
	Torn, stained or bloody
	  underclothing
	Pain or itching in genital area
	Bruises or bleeding in external
	  genitalia, vaginal, or anal areas
	Venereal disease, especially in
	  preteens
	Pregnancy
		Unwilling to change for gym or
		  participate in PE
		Withdrawal, fantasy,
		  or infantile behavior
		Bizarre, sophisticated, or
		  unusual sexual behavior or
		  knowledge
		Poor peer relationships
		Delinquent or run away
		Reports sexual assault by
		  caretaker

Emotional maltreatment	Habit disorders (sucking, biting,
	  rocking, etc.)
	Conduct disorders (antisocial,
	  destructive, etc.)
	Neurotic traits (sleep disorders,
	  speech disorders, inhibition
	  of play)
	Psychoneurotic reactions
	  (hysteria, obsession,
	  compulsion, phobias,
	  hypochondria)
		Behavior extremes:
		—compliant, passive
		—aggressive, demanding
		Overly adaptive behavior:
		—inappropriately adult
		—inappropriately infantile
		Developmental lags (physical,
		  mental, emotional)
		Attempted suicide

Source: Child Abuse and Neglect: A Professional's Guide to Identification, Reporting, Investigation, and Treatment. Trenton, NJ: Governor's Task Force on Child Abuse and Neglect, October 1988.

criminal prosecution that might result from the reporting of suspected child abuse or neglect—as long as you have acted "in good faith" (Fischer, Schimmel, & Kelly, 1999).

States also vary with respect to the form and content of reports required. Most states require an oral report, followed by a more detailed written report, and some states also have a 24-hour, toll-free hot line. Generally, you should be prepared to provide the student's name and address; the nature and extent of injury or condition observed; and your own name and address (Fischer, Schimmel, & Kelly, 1999).

The variation among states underscores the importance of becoming familiar with the procedures and resources in your own school. The best way to do this is to speak with people who can provide guidance and direction—experienced teachers, the principal, the school nurse, members of the CORE team, and the student assistance counselor.

Eating Disorders

During a visit to one of Fred's honors classes in late April, I was shocked by the emaciated appearance of one of his female students, Sara. Her eyes and cheeks were sunken in, and her arms looked like twigs. I couldn't take my eyes off her. After class, Fred shared the story:

This kid is a straight A student—she'll probably be valedictorian or salutatorian of her class. Everything she does is perfect. I don't think she's ever gotten less than 100 on any test or assignment I've given. And she's a fantastic soccer player. As a matter of fact, she's being recruited by a number of schools that want her to play soccer. To me, it looks like she couldn't even kick the ball. But I know that she practices every day, and she runs too.

A couple of Sara's friends have come to talk with me after school— they're worried about her too. They say that she insists she's fat and that she hardly eats. She seems to be particularly obsessed about not eating anything with fat in it—no pizza, no cheese, no cakes or cookies, and of course no meat of any kind. Apparently, all they ever see her eat is bagels and lettuce!

I've talked with Sara—I've told her that I'm really worried about her, but she insists that she's fine and that everyone's overreacting. I've also reported the situation to the school psychologist and the SAC [student assistance counselor], and I know that they've called Sara's parents. I even called her parents myself. But her parents don't acknowledge that there's a problem. It's just so sad, but what else can we do?

Given our society's obsession about thinness, it's not surprising that teenage girls often become concerned about body image. But Sara's intense preoccupation with losing weight goes way beyond ordinary concern. Sara seems to suffer from anorexia nervosa, an eating disorder that generally begins during adolescence and primarily afflicts white females, although it's increasing among black females and does occur among males (Gonet, 1994). Anorexic adolescents literally starve themselves; even so, they continue to feel fat and may actually perceive that they are becoming heavier. Sara's involvement in running and soccer is also typical; in an attempt to lose weight more quickly, anorexics may combine excessive physical exercise with dieting.

Another eating disorder is bulimia nervosa, in which individuals starve themselves, then binge (often on high-calorie or high-sugar foods), and finally purge themselves (by inducing vomiting). Individuals with bulimia may be underweight, overweight, or average, but they share an intense fear of gaining weight. They may also feel that they have lost control over their lives; thus, they seek to control their eating and their weight (Gonet, 1994).

Of the two eating disorders, bulimia is more common, while anorexia is more severe and can actually be fatal. But both are long-term illnesses that require treatment; they will not go away by themselves. This means that you need to be alert to the signs of eating disorders and report your concern to the appropriate person in your school. Too often, teachers overlook eating disorders since concern about weight is a "normal pathology" in our society. Furthermore, the young women who most frequently suffer from eating disorders are often high-achieving, compliant, perfectionist students who cause no problems in class. Naomi Wolf, author of *The Beauty Myth* (1991), recalls how no one in her school tried to intervene when she was an anorexic teenager:

> *There were many starving girls in my junior high school, and every one was a teacher's paragon. We were allowed to come and go, racking up gold stars, as our hair fell out in fistfuls and the pads flattened behind the sockets of our eyes. . . An alien voice took mine over. I have never been so soft-spoken. It lost expression and timbre and sank to a monotone, a dull murmur the opposite of strident. My teachers approved of me. They saw nothing wrong with what I was doing, and I could swear they looked straight at me. My school had stopped dissecting alleycats, since it was considered inhumane. [But] there was no interference in my self-directed science experiment: to find out just how little food could keep a human body alive. (p. 202)*

Suicide

Suicide among adolescents is an increasingly serious problem. In 1960, the suicide rate among 15- to 19-year-olds was 3.6 per 100,000. By 1990, the figure was 11.1. Today, suicide is second only to automobile accidents as the leading cause of death among young people in this age group (National School Safety Center, 1990). More teenagers die each year from suicide than from cancer, heart disease, AIDS, pneumonia, lung disease, and birth defects *combined* (Portner, 2000a). Gays and lesbians are three times more likely than their peers to commit suicide (Remafedi, 1994). And for every teenager who actually "succeeds" at suicide, 100 more attempt it (Portner, 2000a).

Adolescent suicides are often triggered by some kind of stress such as breaking up with a friend, arguments with parents, or school problems (Portner, 2000a), but suicide is *not* the result of a single event. Most suicide victims have had a long history of problems, all of which contributed to the final event (Underwood & Dunne-Maxim, 1993). Risk factors include biological factors, substance abuse, depression, a sense of alienation and isolation, a lack of family stability, and child abuse—but it is normal for many individuals to experience one or more of these risk factors and not be suicidal.

Some of the warning signs that indicate the potential for suicide are listed in Table 13-4. As you look over this table, keep in mind that suicidal intent is often well hidden; conversely, it is normal for individuals to exhibit one or more of these indicators and *not* be suicidal. Nonetheless, if you see signs of suicide potential, if the youngster communicates an intent to commit suicide (in writing or verbally), or if you receive a report of such signs from another student, you should immediately communicate the information to the principal or the student assistance counselor. Many schools have a crisis management team that will be responsible for meeting with the student to determine the extent of the problem. Don't take it upon yourself to counsel the student or to give assurances

TABLE 13-4. Signs of Suicide Potential

Use of drugs or alcohol.

Extensive preoccupation with death fantasies.

Absence of a support system.

A specific plan for committing suicide.

Available means to carry out the plan (e.g, loaded gun; bottle of sleeping pills at home).

A history of self-destructive acts.

A gesture that may be interpreted as a cry for help.

History of relative having committed suicide.

Significant mood changes from depression to elation.

Noticeable, negative changes in appearance or academic performance.

Source: Adapted from Kottler and Kottler, 1993.

that "life will get better." Nor should you be afraid of violating a student's privacy rights (Portner, 2000b).

The crisis management team also coordinates the school's responses when a suicide occurs. The school's task is to deal with the grief of the members of the school community. Students need to accept the reality of the loss and to begin to work through the pain of grief (Underwood & Dunne-Maxim, 1993). It's essential that the school not ignore the suicide, but make sure it is talked about in a structured, controlled manner.

Talking with Students Who Have Problems

As I've stressed earlier, it is not your job to be a school counselor, therapist, or confidante for all your students. You have neither the time nor the training to serve in those roles. Nonetheless, there will be instances in which students will reach out to you for understanding. A student might confide her fears about being pregnant; another might tell you about his alcoholic parents; still another might want to talk about her feelings of inadequacy and isolation. What will you do? As I've already indicated, in many cases, the appropriate response is to put the student in touch with a special service provider who has the expertise needed to intervene. Listen to Sandy:

> Sometimes students will try to trap you into inappropriate confidentiality. They'll say, "I need to tell you something, but you have to promise not to tell anyone else." Right away, I tell them, "I can't promise that, because if this is too big for us to handle, I need to tell people who can help. We have a school psychologist, a student assistance counselor, a principal, a guidance counselor, a nurse. All these resources are here to help you. If you tell me what's bothering you, I can get you to the right person." Sometimes, the kid will say, "I don't want to tell that person; I don't know them." Then I say, "OK, you can tell me, and I'll tell them."

In addition to getting professional help for a student with a serious problem, you can also be helpful by developing the communication skills discussed in Chapter 5—attending and acknowledging, active listening, open-ended questioning, and problem solving. Remember, listening attentively to students and showing you care can be powerful ways of helping students who are hurting.

Concluding Comments

The problems that students bring to school can seem overwhelming, especially for beginning teachers who are still learning the basics. And in fact, there may be students whose problems are so great, you really cannot help. As Fred reminds us, "There's failure in this business. These problems transcend the classroom, and there's only so much an individual teacher or the school can do." Sandy echoes this thought:

> *When the school has done everything it can, and you know the child is still hurting, you feel so helpless. It's infuriating when you can't do anything. But when this happens, you just have to say, "I tried. Now I need to let go."*

"Letting go" means recognizing that you may not be able to change a student's life; it *doesn't* mean abandoning your responsibility for making that student's time in school as productive and meaningful as possible. Carol Lowinger, the SAC at Fred's school, believes that, to some extent, teachers need to treat troubled students "like everyone else":

> *Sometimes teachers think, "These kids are going through a hard time; I'll give them a break." But out of this sense of caring, they give kids breaks they shouldn't get. Kids need to be held accountable. They have to learn to live in the real world where you can't hide behind your problems. You have to learn to cope, and you* mustn't *learn "I don't have to cope." I'm not saying that we shouldn't give them some leeway if their problems are really great; obviously, we need to be flexible and supportive. But they still need to be responsible for their current behavior. If we always bail kids out, we're enabling. That's not helpful—and it's even dangerous.*

When students have serious problems, it's more important than ever to create a classroom that is safe, orderly, and humane. You may not be able to change youngsters' relationships with their families, but you can still work to establish positive teacher-student relationships. You may not be able to provide students with control over unstable, chaotic home lives, but you can allow them opportunities to make decisions and to have some control over their time in school. You may not be able to do anything about the violence that permeates the neighborhoods in which they live, but you can structure classroom situations to foster cooperation and group cohesiveness. In Fred's words, "You can show them you care enough about them not to let them slough off. You can still keep teaching."

✵ Summary

Because large numbers of America's youth are at risk for school failure, substance abuse, physical problems, psychological and emotional disorders, abuse and neglect, teenage pregnancy, and violence, today's teachers have to deal with issues that require knowledge and skills beyond those needed to be an effective instructor. There are two primary ways that teachers can help students with serious problems:

- Teachers need to be alert to the indicators of potential problems.
- Teachers need to be informed about the various special services that are available and to know how to obtain access to those services.

The chapter briefly discussed four serious problems that teachers may encounter:

- Substance abuse:
  Students may be children of alcoholics/addicts (COAs) and/or may be abusing drugs and alcohol themselves.
  COAs can benefit from support groups.
  Teachers must be watchful for students who may be abusing drugs and alcohol and refer students to the SAC or other appropriate persons.
  Teachers must distinguish between situations in which drugs are being used outside of school and situations in which students are under the influence during school.
- Abuse and neglect:
  Educators are required to report suspected abuse and neglect to the state's child protective service.
  No state requires the reporter to have absolute proof before reporting.
  Most states require "reason to believe" or "reasonable cause to believe or suspect."
- Eating disorders:
  Students who suffer from eating disorders are often high-achieving, compliant, and perfectionist students who cause no problems in class.
- Suicide:
  Most suicide victims have a long history of problems.
  Teachers should immediately report suspicions or reports of intended suicide to the principal or student assistance counselor.

Sometimes the problems that students bring to school can be overwhelming, especially for beginning teachers who are coping with the basics. And in fact, there may be students whose problems are so great, you just cannot help. Nonetheless, you can still try to create a classroom environment that is safe, orderly, and humane. You can show students you care by holding them accountable for their behavior and by continuing to teach.

Activities

1. In the school where you are observing or teaching, interview the student assistance counselor, a guidance counselor, or the director of special services to determine the policies for reporting drug abuse. Get copies of the referral forms that are used and compare them with the form shown in this chapter.

2. Reporting suspected abuse and neglect varies from state to state. Find out the policies used in your state. Also find out if your school has particular policies and procedures you are to follow. In particular, get answers to the following questions:

   Who is required to report abuse and neglect?
   When should you report child abuse? (When you have reasonable cause to suspect? Reasonable cause to believe?)
   To what state agency do you report?
   What information must be included in the report?
   Do you have to give your name when reporting?

For Further Reading

Drug Strategies (1999). *Making the grade: A guide to school drug prevention programs.* Washington, D.C.: Drug Strategies.

Fischer, L., Schimmel, D., & Kelly, C. (1999). *Teachers and the law.* New York: Longman.

Kottler, J. A., & Kottler, E. (1993). *Teacher as counselor: Developing the helping skills you need.* Newbury Park, CA: Corwin Press.

Powell, R. R., Zehm, S. J., & Kottler, J. A. (1995). *Classrooms under the influence: Addicted families/addicted students.* Thousand Oaks, CA: Corwin Press.

References

Annie E. Casey Foundation (1999). *Kids count data book: State profiles of child well-being (1999).* Baltimore, MD: Annie E. Casey Foundation.

Bancroft, S. (1997). Becoming heroes: Teachers can help abused children. *Educational Leadership, 55*(2), 69–71.

Children's Defense Fund (2001). *The state of America's children yearbook 2001.* Washington, D.C.: Children's Defense Fund.

Coles, A. D. (September 8, 1999). Teenage drug use continues to slide. *Education Week,* 10.

Coles, A. D. (June 14, 2000). Lately, teens less likely to engage in risky behaviors. *Education Week,* 6.

Fischer, L., Schimmel, D., & Kelly, C. (1999). *Teachers and the law.* New York: Longman.

Gonet, M. M. (1994). *Counseling the adolescent substance abuser: School-based intervention and prevention.* Thousand Oaks, CA: Sage Publications.

Kottler, J. A., & Kottler, E. (1993). *Teacher as counselor: Developing the helping skills you need.* Newbury Park, CA: Corwin Press.

Michaelis, K. L. (1993). *Reporting child abuse: A guide to mandatory requirements for school personnel.* Newbury Park, CA: Corwin Press.

National School Safety Center (1990). *School safety check book.* Malibu, CA: Pepperdine University Press.

Newsam, B. S. (1992). *Complete Student Assistance Program Handbook.* West Nyack, NY: The Center for Applied Research in Education.

Parkay, F. W., & Stanford, B. H. (1992). *Becoming a teacher* (2nd ed.). Boston: Allyn and Bacon.

Portner, J., & Galley, M. (May 31, 2000). More students are abusing Ritalin, DEA official testifies. *Education Week,* 8.

Portner, J. (April 12, 2000a). Complex set of ills spurs rising teen suicide rate. *Education Week,* 1, 22–31.

Portner, J. (April 12, 2000b). Suicide: Many schools fall short on prevention. *Education Week,* 1, 20–22.

Powell, R. R., Zehm, S. J., & Kottler, J. A. (1995). *Classrooms under the influence: Addicted families/addicted students.* Thousand Oaks, CA: Corwin Press.

Remafedi, G. (1994). *Death by denial.* Boston: Alyson Publications.

Reynolds, M. C. (1989). Students with special needs. In M. C. Reynolds (Ed.), *Knowledge base for the beginning teacher.* Oxford, England: Pergamon Press.

Sandham, J. L. (May 24, 2000). Cranked up. *Education Week,* 36–41.

Stefkovich, J. A., & Miller, J. A. (April 13, 1998). *Law enforcement officers in public schools: Student citizens in safe havens?* Paper presented at the conference of the American Educational Research Association, San Diego, California.

Towers, R. L. (1989). *Children of alcoholics/addicts.* Washington D.C.: National Education Association.

Underwood, M. M., & Dunne-Maxim, K. (1993). *Managing sudden violent loss in the schools.* Piscataway, NJ: Governor's Advisory Council on Youth Suicide Prevention.

Wolf, N. (1991). *The beauty myth: How images of beauty are used against women.* New York: Anchor Books, Doubleday.

Chapter Fourteen

Preventing and Responding to Violence

*By the year 2000 all schools in America will be free of drugs and violence and the unauthorized presence of firearms and alcohol, and offer a disciplined environment that is conducive to learning. (*Goals 2000: Educate America Act, *1994)*

In the late 1990s, a series of school shootings in Mississippi, Kentucky, Arkansas, Pennsylvania, Tennessee, and Oregon made it clear that this laudable national goal, adopted by Congress and signed by President Clinton, was certainly out of reach. But nothing prepared the country for the events of April 20, 1999. On that day, two seniors at Columbine High School in Littleton, Colorado, shot and killed 12 students and a teacher before turning their guns on themselves. Overnight, the topic of school violence catapulted to the front page. Copycat shootings, bomb scares, and threats of violence created unprecedented terror and upheaval during the final weeks of the school year. Parents agonized about sending their children to school. Politicians, policy makers, and pundits talked about youth violence as a "national epidemic" and speculated on the causes. School officials across the country worried that "their schools could become the next Columbine High" and increased security measures (Drummond & Portner, 1999).

But just how widespread is school violence? Was Columbine symptomatic of a growing epidemic, or a horrible but isolated incident? Let's look at some facts and figures.

How Much Violence Is There?

Data on the frequency and severity of school violence come from a study conducted by researchers from the Centers for Disease Control (Brener, Simon, Krug, & Lowry, 1999). *Surprisingly, the study found that violence at high schools had actually decreased in the 1990s.* From 1993 to 1997, for example, the number of high school students who said they had carried a weapon "such as a gun, knife, or club" on school property decreased 28 percent, from 11.8 percent to 8.5 percent. The number of students who carried a gun decreased 25 percent, from 7.9 percent to 5.9 percent. And the percentage of students in a physical fight on school property decreased 9 percent, from 16.2 percent to 14.8 percent.

Other research supports these findings. The Justice Department has reported that the number of violent crimes committed by children and teenagers has declined substantially since 1993 and is at the lowest rate since 1986 (Glassner, 1999). The Washington-based Justice Policy Institute found that the number of school-associated violent deaths has decreased 40 percent, from 43 in 1998 to 26 in 1999 (Portner, 2000). The U. S. Departments of Education and Justice have confirmed that schools remain among the safest places for children and youth. During the 1999-2000 school year, for example, 90 percent of the nation's schools reported no serious crime, while 43 percent said they experienced no crime at all (U.S. Department of Education, 2001).

It is hard to believe numbers like these when we read headlines about murderous rampages and see television news clips of students fleeing from schools under siege. Indeed, surveys indicate that students do not *feel* safer, even though they report fewer fights and weapons. On the contrary, the number of public school students who said they always feel safe in school fell from 44 percent in 1998 to 37 percent in 1999 (Glassner, 1999). And in a telephone poll conducted by *The Wall Street Journal* and NBC News in 1998, 71 percent of the respondents said they thought it was likely a school shooting could happen in their community (Portner, 2000). Clearly, teachers and administrators must work to decrease students' fears and anxiety, as well as actual incidents of school violence. But what can actually be done?

Improving Security Systems

In the wake of Columbine, school officials all across the country reexamined their safety and security measures. Schools installed metal detectors and surveillance cameras, stationed police officers in high schools, introduced photo identification cards, practiced "lock-downs" and safety drills, and required clear plastic backpacks or banned them completely. Although enhanced security is a logical reaction to the threat of violent crime, studies suggest that measures like these may actually make students feel *less* safe and may not reduce incidents of violent crime (Barton, Coley, & Wenglinsky, 1998; Portner, 2000). Furthermore, some educators worry that security measures create a negative environment, turning schools into prisonlike, oppressive institutions (Astor, Meyer, & Behre, 1999; Berreth & Berman, 1997; Noguera, 1995).

It is clear that enhanced security systems alone will not solve the problem of school violence, nor will they allay students' fears and anxieties. Creating safer schools—and schools that *feel* safer—requires a collaborative effort to reach out to students (especially those on the margins), build a climate of tolerance, and recognize the early warning signs of potential violence. This chapter examines some of the ways that individual teachers can contribute to this effort.

Strategies for Preventing Violence

Building Supportive School Communities

Although we focused on creating safer, more caring classrooms in Chapter 5, it's important to revisit this topic in relationship to violence prevention. Numerous educators argue that violence prevention has to focus on the creation of more humane environments in which students are known and feel supported (Astor, Meyer, & Behre, 1999; Noguera, 1995). Indeed, Richard Riley, President Clinton's Secretary of Education, has suggested that schools look beyond traditional security issues to find better solutions for students who need help: "We need to make sure that in every community, in school, every child is connected to at least one responsible, caring adult" (Richard, 1999). Marylu Simon, the superintendent of Sandy's district, echoes this sentiment:

> *A safe school is one that is responsive to students, where the staff knows the kids, where you can get help for troubled kids right away. . . . We don't talk much about metal detectors or security measures here. Our approach to violence prevention emphasizes connecting to kids and addressing their social–emotional needs. We try hard to make sure that one group isn't elevated over another. . . . and to respect differences among kids.*

Creating a supportive school community is not easy, especially in large high schools, where feelings of anonymity, alienation, and apathy are leading causes of problems. Following the suggestions in Chapter 5 should help to build a sense of community in the classes you teach. In addition, a number of useful suggestions come from *Responding to Hate at School* (1999) published by Teaching Tolerance, a project of the Southern Poverty Law Center.

Be Alert to Signs of Hate

Take note if book reports, essays, or journal entries convey messages of hate or violence, and report your concerns to the principal or a school counselor. Be aware of online hate sites and recruitment by hate groups. (The Southern Poverty Law Center's Intelligence Project can help you stay informed about this.) Help students recognize hate literature containing swastikas, derogatory references to race or ethnicity, and caricatures of racial/ethnic groups, and discuss what students can do if they find or someone gives them a hate flier. At Halloween time, discourage costumes that involve negative stereotyping (e.g., "Gypsy" costumes or "homeless person" outfits) or organizations that promote hate (e.g., Ku Klux Klan robes).

Examine the Ways Your School Recognizes Student Achievement

Traditions that contribute to a sense of superiority among some students may lead to feelings of frustration or inadequacy in others. Are athletes disciplined less severely for offenses? Are their achievements highlighted more than the achievements of other students? Do honors students and student leaders enjoy special privileges? Take action to avoid institutionalized favoritism. Find ways to recognize and celebrate different kinds of achievement.

Curb Peer Harassment

We already touched on peer harassment in Chapter 5, but this problem clearly warrants further discussion. Every day, students suffer teasing, name calling, ridicule, humiliation, ostracism, and even physical injury at the hands of their peers. The problem is substantial: In a large-scale, national study of 15,686 students in grades 6 through 10 (Nansel, Overpeck, Pilla, Ruan, Simons-Morton, & Scheidt, 2001), about 30 percent of the sample reported moderate or frequent involvement in bullying—as a bully (13 percent), one who was bullied (10.6 percent), or both (6.3 percent). Also frightening is the fact that peer harassment is quasi-acceptable (Hoover & Oliver, 1996). Bullies can be popular, and their behavior is often dismissed as normal. When the bullies are males, for example, it is not uncommon to hear adults dismiss their behavior by reminding us that "boys will be boys."

Teasing is the most frequent bullying behavior at all ages, but it can be difficult for students to draw the line between playful exchanges and hurtful harassment. Hoover and Oliver (1996) suggest that whether an exchange represents teasing or friendly banter may have to do with the social level or popularity of the individuals involved. If a higher-status student mocks a lower-status student, the exchange is likely to be seen as an attack. Teasing someone of the same status is more likely to be interpreted as playful. Figure 14-1 contains some "Teasing Dos and Don'ts" that may help your students understand when teasing is acceptable and when it is not.

During one discussion with Christina, she related a story that illustrated the pain that "friendly" teasing can cause.

This year I've got a freshman named Anita in one of my classes. Last year, I had her boyfriend, who's a junior. He's been in a lot of trouble. For example, last year he was arrested the day before the HSPT. But he's been doing a really good job of turning his life around. Anyway, one day I heard kids teasing Anita about him. They'd ask if he was on house arrest, or if he was in jail again. She looked unhappy about it, but she didn't say anything to me. After class, I told her that I had heard what the kids were saying, and I asked how she felt about it. She indicated that she didn't like it, but she didn't

---

DO:

1. Be careful of others' feelings.
2. Use humor gently and carefully.
3. Ask whether teasing about a certain topic hurts someone's feelings.
4. Accept teasing from others if you tease.
5. Tell other if teasing about a certain topic hurts your feelings.
6. Know the difference between friendly gentle teasing and hurtful ridicule or harassment.
7. Try to read others' "body language" to see if their feelings are hurt—even when they don't tell you.
8. Help a weaker student when he or she is being ridiculed.

DON'T:

1. Tease someone you don't know well.
2. [If you are a boy] tease girls about sex.
3. Tease about a person's body.
4. Tease about a person's family members.
5. Tease about a topic when a student has asked you not to.
6. Tease someone who seems agitated or who you know is having a bad day.
7. Be thin-skinned about teasing that is meant in a friendly way.
8. Swallow your feelings about teasing—tell someone in a direct and clear way what is bothering you.

FIGURE 14-1. Teasing do's and don'ts
Reprinted, with permission, from The Bullying Prevention Handbook: A Guide for Principals, Teachers, and Counselors *by John H. Hoover and Ronald Oliver. Copyright 1996 by the National Educational Service, 304 W. Kirkwood Ave., Suite 2, Bloomington, IN 47404, 800-733-6786, www.nesonline.com*

want to make a "big deal." She said she didn't want to get them in trouble. I offered to talk to the other kids—without indicating that I had spoken with her. I told her I'd make it clear that she hadn't asked me to intervene. The next day, I took the kids aside—there were two boys specifically—and said I had overheard them saying these things to Anita, and that I didn't think it was appropriate. They said they were "only teasing." I told them, "But teasing can hurt." I said that from the expression on Anita's face, it was clear that she didn't think it was funny. They looked surprised—as if they just hadn't given it any thought before. They promised to stop it, and they did.

In an effort to curb peer harassment, you need to be alert to hurtful comments about race and ethnicity, body size, disabilities, sexual orientation, unfashionable or eccentric dress, use of languages other than English, and socioeconomic status. Barone (1997) reports that counselors, teachers, and administrators tend to underestimate the amount of bullying that exists in their schools. In a survey administered to eighth-graders and school staff, Barone found that almost 60 percent of students reported having "been bothered by a bully or bullies" in middle school. In contrast, staff members believed that only 16 percent of the students had been victims of bullies.

Teachers also need to make it clear that disrespectful speech and slurs—even when used in a joking manner—are absolutely unacceptable. This means intervening if you hear a student use a hateful epithet (e.g., "That word hurts people, so you may not use it in this classroom" or "Disrespectful words are never acceptable in this school" or even "Watch your language, please!"). According to Stephen Wessler (2000/2001), a former prosecutor of school hate crimes, intervention "breaks the pattern of escalation from language to more focused harassment to threats and, finally to violence" (p. 31). If you stay silent, students are likely to think you condone the degrading language. You're also serving as a poor role model for students, modeling passivity instead of the courage, skills, and empathy to speak up.

Teaching Conflict Resolution

Concerns about safety and order have led to a raft of violence prevention programs such as conflict resolution training, peer mediation, and social problem solving. These programs emphasize anger management and impulse control; effective communication skills; social perspective taking (i.e., understanding that others can have a different and equally valid perspective on the same situation); resisting peer pressure; and prejudice, sexism, and racism (Dusenbury, Falco, Lake, Brannigan, & Bosworth, 1997). All programs also teach students a series of steps for dealing constructively with conflicts. These generally consist of strategies for cooling down, expressing feelings (in the form of I-messages), generating solutions, evaluating consequences, selecting the best action, and implementing the plan.

There is great diversity in approaches, but generally the programs fall into two categories: those that train the entire student body in social problem-solving and conflict resolution strategies and those that train a particular cadre of students to mediate disputes among their peers (Johnson & Johnson, 1996). An example of a program that targets the entire student body is Johnson and Johnson's *Teaching Students to be Peacemakers* (1995). The program spans Grades 1 through 12; each year all students learn increasingly sophisticated negotiation and mediation procedures. Research conducted by Johnson and Johnson indicates that students trained in the peacemaker program are able to apply the negotiation and mediation procedures to a variety of conflicts—both in and out of the classroom. In addition, training results in fewer discipline problems that have to be managed by the teacher and the principal (Bodine & Crawford, 1998).

In a peer mediation program, selected students guide disputants through the problem-solving process. The advantage of using peers as mediators rather than adults is that students can frame disputes in a way that is age appropriate. Generally working in pairs, mediators explain the ground rules for mediation, provide an opportunity for disputants to identify the problem from their differing perspectives, explain how they feel, brainstorm solutions, evaluate the advantages and disadvantages of each proposed solution, and select a course of action. These steps can be seen in the example of a peer mediation that appears in Figure 14-2.

Peer mediation programs are becoming increasingly popular in schools across the country. Sandy's school has had a peer mediation program for the last six years, and Tonia Moore, the student assistance counselor, believes that it has definitely helped to reduce incidents of violence:

Before we had peer mediation, we had lots of kids getting suspended for fighting; now we rarely have fights. Kids will tell the peer mediators when something is brewing, and they can prevent the problem from erupting into a physical fight. Peer mediation gives kids a structure they may not have developed yet for dealing with emotional issues. Sometimes, kids will mock the structure—they tell me, "All we do in peer mediation is hear our own words repeated back to us." But they still go; they still use it. We have to recognize that settling problems this way is a very new approach for some kids; this may be the first time they've ever done anything like this. It's a real life change for them.

Thus far, anecdotal evidence supports Tonia's conviction that peer mediation programs can substantially reduce violent incidents. Some researchers contend that peer mediation actually has more impact on the *mediators* than on the disputants, since they acquire valuable conflict resolution skills and earn the respect of their peers (Bodine & Crawford, 1998; Miller, 1994). If this is so, it means that high-risk students—not just the "good kids"—must be trained and used as mediators.

In schools with ethnic and racial diversity, it's extremely important to sensitize peer mediators to cultural differences (Hyman, 1997). For example, African American, Italian, and Eastern European cultures encourage emotional expressiveness, and this frequently involves the dramatic use of hands and body language. On the other hand, English and Scandinavian cultures value the control of overt emotionality. Thus, an innocuous interaction can turn into an angry exchange if students from these different

Trouble in the Classroom

Situation: Jimmy has been sitting in front of Eduardo all year in math class. Eduardo has this habit of tapping his foot on Jimmy's chair. It's been driving Jimmy crazy.

Jimmy: You jerk! Why don't you stop bothering me?

Eduardo: Who are you calling a jerk? I don't know what you are talking about.

Jimmy: If you touch my chair one more time, I'm going to let you have it.

Eduardo: I'll touch your chair all I want. See if I care.

The boys start pushing and the teacher asks them if they would like to go to mediation.

The boys agree.

▶ **Step 1** **Introductions and Ground Rules**
Mediator 1:
Our names are _____ and _____ and we are student mediators. We are not here to punish you or tell you what to do. We are here to help you solve your conflict. What are your names? (Write them on the form.) Thank you for coming. Everything you say here is CONFIDENTIAL, except if it involves drugs, weapons, or abuse. Then, we'll have to report it to our advisor or stop the mediation.

Mediator 2:
There are five rules you must agree to before we begin. They are:
1. **Be willing to solve the problem.**   2. **Tell the truth.**
3. **Listen without interrupting.**   4. **Be respectful: no name calling or fighting.**
        5. **Take responsibility for carrying out your agreement.**
Do you agree to the rules? (Be sure the students agree.)

▶ **Step 2** **Telling the Story**
(Each person tells his/her side of the story. Mediator chooses the person who begins.)

Mediator 1:   Jimmy, tell us what happened.

Jimmy: I was minding my own business when this creep starts hitting my chair.

Mediator 1:   No name calling, please.

Jimmy: Okay. Like I said, I was sitting in my chair when he started hitting it, like he always does, just to bother me. I'm not going to take it anymore.

Mediator 1:   You said that you were sitting in your chair when Eduardo started hitting it. How do you feel about this situation?

FIGURE 14-2. Peer mediation script
Reprinted with permission from Grace Contrino Abrams Peace Education Foundation Inc., 1992

Jimmy:	I feel angry because he's doing this all the time. He does it just to get me mad.
Mediator 1:	You feel angry because he does it all the time just to get you mad.
Mediator 2:	Eduardo, tell us what happened.
Eduardo:	I always tap my foot. I do it to keep myself awake. It's just a nervous habit. You can ask anybody, I always tap my foot.
Mediator 2:	You said that you always tap your foot to keep yourself awake and it's a habit. How do you feel about what happened?
Eduardo:	I feel upset because I really didn't mean to start a fight. He's too picky.
Mediator 2:	You feel upset because you didn't mean to start a fight and you also think that Jimmy is too picky. Is there any other information that we need to know? (If yes, ask each one to speak following the same rules. If no, continue to Step 3.)

▶ Step 3   Searching For Solutions

One mediator asks questions, the other writes the suggested solutions on paper. This is not the time for choosing—only thinking.

Mediator 1:	You both listened to each other's side of the story. How do you think this conflict can be solved? What could you do to solve this conflict? We're going to write down all your ideas. Later, you'll pick the idea or ideas you like best.
Jimmy:	I could apologize for calling Eduardo a creep.
Eduardo:	I could tap my foot on my bookbag, instead of his chair so it won't make a noise.
Jimmy:	I could ask the teacher to move my seat to the front of the room.
Eduardo:	We could exchange seats with each other.
Mediator 1:	Any more ideas? (If none, go to Step 4.)

▶ Step 4   Choosing the Solution

Mediator 2:	Let's go over the suggestions you both made. Which ones do you think will solve this conflict?
Jimmy:	I'll apologize for calling you a creep. I got mad and the words just came out.
Eduardo:	I'll apologize for tapping on your chair. I didn't know that it was bothering you. I will tap on my bookbag from now on.
Jimmy:	It sounds good to me.
Mediator 2:	Is this conflict solved? (If they both say "yes" have them fill out their section of the Mediation Report Form. If not, go back to Step 3.)

FIGURE 14-2. *(cont.)*

▶ Step 5	**In The Future**
Mediator 1:	What do you think you could do differently to prevent this from happening again?
Jimmy:	I'm going to try to tell people what is bothering me before I explode.
Eduardo:	I'm going to try to be more aware of bothering other people.
▶ Step 6	**Choosing**
Mediator 2:	Jimmy and Eduardo, congratulations for solving your conflict. To keep rumors from spreading, please tell your friends that the conflict has been resolved: Thank you for coming to mediation.

FIGURE 14-2. (*cont.*)

backgrounds misread cues. Consider an argument between Salim, who comes from Lebanon, and Jim, whose family heritage is British and German:

SALIM: Jim, why did you laugh in class when I was reading that part from *Romeo and Juliet* out loud?

JIM: I don't know. Something was funny.

SALIM: What was funny? (Salim wonders if Jim was laughing at him. His voice becomes louder as he uses his hands to help express himself.)

JIM: Listen, I have to get to my next class. I'll talk to you later. (Jim begins to get uncomfortable about Salim's raised voice and hand waving.)

SALIM: Just tell me what was funny. (Salim now feels he is being ignored. He steps in front of Jim, who has turned to walk away.)

JIM: Why are you waving your fist at me? I told you I don't have time now. Now get out of my way. You better not try anything! (Salim's hand waving and attempt to get Jim's attention was misinterpreted.)

SALIM: I am not waving my fist. I just want to know why you laughed.

JIM: I wasn't laughing at you. I was laughing about what those words meant. This is ridiculous. I'm not going to stand here and argue about such a silly thing.

SALIM: What words were so funny? (Salim will forget the matter if he believes he wasn't insulted.)

JIM: I don't have time for this. (Jim turns to walk away. This action is a direct insult to Salim. It means he is being treated with contempt, when all he asked for were the words that were funny. He would actually like to know what he missed.) (Hyman, 1997, p. 255)

Hyman suggests that Jim's immediate response might have been adequate for someone he knew well or who was not part of a culture in which any possible insult is treated seriously:

Salim, who does not believe in violence, had no intention of becoming aggressive, but he was worried that he did not understand if there was something funny in the text he was reading. However, Jim's initial response made him wonder if Jim were laughing at him. Salim's hand waving and animated body language are typical in his culture, but to Jim, they suggest real danger. (p. 255)

Obviously, peer mediation is not an option when the conflict involves drugs, alcohol, theft, or violence, since these are criminal actions. But mediation *can* help to resolve disputes involving behavior such as gossiping, name calling, racial putdowns, and bullying, as well as conflicts over property (e.g., borrowing a book and losing it). Even then, mediation must be voluntary and confidential. In cases where school rules have been violated, mediation should not substitute for disciplinary action; rather, it can be offered as an opportunity to solve problems and "clear the air."

Knowing the Early Warning Signs of Potential for Violence

In 1998, at the request of President Clinton, the U. S. Department of Education and the Department of Justice published a guide to assist schools in developing comprehensive violence prevention plans (Dwyer, Osher, & Warger, 1998). The guide contains a list of "early warning signs" that can alert teachers and other school staff to students' potential for violence, as well as signs that violence is imminent. These appear in Tables 14-1 and 14-2.

It's important to remember that the early warning signs are not an infallible predictor that a child or youth will commit a violent act toward self or others (Dwyer, Osher, & Warger, 1998). Also keep in mind that potentially violent students typically exhibit multiple warning signs. Thus, be careful about overreacting to single signs, words, or actions, and don't be biased by a student's race, socioeconomic status, academic ability, or

TABLE 14-1. Early Warning Signs

Social withdrawal.
Excessive feelings of isolation and being alone.
Excessive feelings of rejection.
Being a victim of violence.
Feelings of being picked on and persecuted.
Low school interest and poor academic performance.
Expression of violence in writings and drawings.
Uncontrolled anger.
Patterns of impulsive and chronic hitting, intimidating, and bullying behaviors.
History of discipline problems.
Past history of violent and aggressive behavior.
Intolerance for differences and prejudicial attitudes.
Drug use and alcohol use.
Affiliation with gangs.
Inappropriate access to, possession of, and use of firearms.
Serious threats of violence.

TABLE 14-2. Imminent Signs of Violence

Serious physical fighting with peers or family members.
Severe destruction of property.
Severe rage for seemingly minor reasons.
Detailed threats of lethal violence.
Possession and/or use of firearms and other weapons.
Other self-injurious behaviors or threats of suicide.

physical appearance. Lindy Mandy, a counselor in Fred's school, acknowledges the tension between needing to identify students who may pose a risk for violence and *social profiling*:

> We have kids who wear the gothic look, and after Columbine, we wanted to reach out to them. But you have to be so careful about stereotyping, thinking that everyone who dresses in gothic must be potentially violent or alienated. It really made us think about our process. At what point does identifying kids who might be violent become social profiling?

The difficulty of distinguishing between a real threat to safety and harmless student expression is underscored by a 2000 federal court ruling in Washington State (Walsh, 2000). In this case, a high school junior submitted a poem to his English teacher about a lonely student who roamed his high school with a pounding heart. The poem contained this passage:

> As I approached the classroom door, I drew my gun and threw open the door. Bang, Bang, Bang-Bang. When it was all over, 28 were dead, and all I remember was not felling [sic] any remorce [sic], for I felt, I was, cleansing my soul.

The student's teacher alerted administrators, and the poem was reviewed by a psychologist, who determined that the student was unlikely to cause harm to himself or others. Nonetheless, the district decided to expel him on an emergency basis. After the student was examined by a psychiatrist, the district rescinded the expulsion, and the student completed his junior year. The boy's parents then sued the district, claiming that the school had violated his First Amendment right to free speech and asking that the expulsion be removed from their son's record. On February 24, 2000, a federal district judge ruled for the family, maintaining that the district had overreacted in expelling the student. She suggested that there were less restrictive ways the district could have ensured the safety of students and school personnel, such as imposing a temporary suspension pending psychiatric examination.

Stories like this can discourage teachers from reporting essays or artwork that contain threatening messages or behavior that suggests a potential for violence. But it's better to alert school officials about what you have learned than to ignore indicators and be sorry later. Find out what the reporting procedures are in your school: Do you report your concerns to the principal? The school nurse? A counselor? Do you notify parents? Remember that parental involvement and consent are required before personally identifiable information is shared with agencies outside the school (except in case of emergencies or suspicion of abuse). The Family Educational Rights and Privacy Act (FERPA), a federal law that addresses the privacy of educational records, must be observed in all referrals to community agencies (Dwyer, Osher, & Warger, 1998).

In addition to knowing the early warning signs, teachers can help prevent violence by being observant in hallways, cafeterias, stairwells, and locker rooms—"unowned" spaces where violence is most likely to erupt (Astor, Meyer, & Behre, 1999). Chester Quarles, a criminologist who specializes in crime prevention, suggests that teachers attempt to make eye contact whenever they pass students in the halls:

> *The subliminal message being exchanged is that "I know who is here and I know who you are. I can remember your features. I can identify you." The influence of careful observation is a strong criminal deterrent for everyone that you observe. . . . Observant teachers . . . can decrease the probability that any of the people they encounter will commit a delinquent act against another that day. (1989, pp. 12–13)*

Being Attentive to Whispers and Rumors

The high-profile school shootings that we have witnessed in the last decade are what the Secret Service calls *targeted violence*—incidents in which the attacker selects a particular target prior to the violent attack. As part of the Safe School Initiative (October 2000) of the U.S. Secret Service and the U.S. Department of Education, researchers studied 37 school shootings involving 41 attackers who were current or recent students at the school. Here are some of the preliminary findings:

Incidents of targeted violence at school are rarely impulsive. In well over three-quarters of the incidents, the attacker *planned* the attack. A few attackers developed the plan the same day as the attack, but more than half developed the plan at least two days before.

In more than three-quarters of the cases, the attacker told someone about his idea or plan. Some peers knew details of the attack, while others just knew that something "spectacular" was going to happen in school on a particular day.

In over two-thirds of the cases, the attackers felt persecuted, bullied, harassed, and injured.

More than three-quarters of the attackers were known to hold a grievance at the time of the attack. Half had revenge as a motive.

These findings contradict the common perception that students who commit targeted acts of violence have simply "snapped." Nor are they loners who keep their plans to themselves. This means that school staff must be attentive to whispers that something is afoot and impress upon students the need to report rumors of potential violence. As Tonia Moore puts it, "You have to have your radar out all the time."

De-escalating Potentially Explosive Situations

Explosive situations often begin benignly. You make a reasonable request ("Would you join the group over there?") or give an ordinary directive ("Get started on the questions at the end of this section"). But the student is feeling angry—maybe he has just been taunted and humiliated in the hallway; maybe her mother has just grounded her for a month; maybe the teacher in the previous class has ridiculed an answer. The anger may have nothing to do with you at all, but it finds its outlet in your class. In a hostile mood, the student fails to comply immediately and may even respond defiantly. Unfortunately, at this point, teachers often contribute to the escalation of a conflict by becoming angry and impatient. They issue an ultimatum: "Do what I say or else." And now teacher and student are combatants in a potentially explosive situation neither of them wanted.

Let's consider an example (adapted from Walker, Colvin, & Ramsey, 1995) of a teacher–student interaction that begins innocuously enough, but quickly escalates into an explosive situation:

> *Students are working on a set of math problems the teacher has assigned. Michael sits slouched in his seat staring at the floor, an angry expression on his face. The teacher sees that Michael is not doing his math and calls over to him from the back of the room where she is working with other students.*

TEACHER: Michael, why aren't you working on the assignment?

MICHAEL: I finished it.

TEACHER: Well, let me see it then. [She walks over to Michael's desk and sees that he has four problems completed.] Good. You've done 4 but you need to do 10.

MICHAEL: Nobody told me that!

TEACHER: Michael, I went over the assignment very clearly and asked if there were any questions about what to do!

MICHAEL: I don't remember that.

TEACHER: Look at the board. I wrote it there. See, page 163, numbers 11–20.

MICHAEL: I didn't see it. Anyway, I hate this boring stuff.

TEACHER: OK, that's enough. No more arguments. Page 163, 11 through 20. Now.

MICHAEL: It's dumb. I'm not going to do it.

TEACHER: Yes you are, mister.

MICHAEL: Yeah? Make me.

TEACHER: If you don't do it now, you're going to the office.

MICHAEL: F——— you!

TEACHER: That's enough!

MICHAEL: You want math? Here it is! [He throws the math book across the room.]

At first glance, it appears that the teacher is being remarkably patient and reasonable in the face of Michael's stubbornness, defiance, and abuse. On closer examination, however, we can detect a chain of successive escalating interactions, in which Michael's be-

TABLE 14-3. Managing Potentially Explosive Situations

- Move slowly and deliberately toward the problem situation.
- Speak privately, quietly, and calmly. Do not threaten. Be as matter-of-fact as possible.
- Be as still as possible. Avoid pointing or gesturing.
- Keep a reasonable distance. Do not crowd the student. Do not get "in the student's face."
- Speak respectfully. Use the student's name.
- Establish eye-level position.
- Be brief. Avoid long-winded statements or nagging.
- Stay with the agenda. Stay focused on the problem at hand. Do not get sidetracked. Deal with less severe problems later.
- Avoid power struggles. Do not get drawn into "I won't, you will" arguments.
- Inform the student of the expected behavior and the negative consequence as a choice or decision for the student to make. Then withdraw from the student and allow some time for the student to decide. ("Michael, you need to return to your desk, or I will have to send for the principal. You have a few seconds to decide." The teacher then moves away, perhaps attending to other students. If Michael does not choose the appropriate behavior, deliver the negative consequence. "You are choosing to have me call the principal.") Follow through with the consequence.

Source: Adapted from Walker, Colvin, & Ramsey, 1995.

havior moves from questioning and challenging the teacher to defiance and abuse, and for which the teacher is also responsible (Walker, Colvin, & Ramsey, 1995). Could the teacher have broken this chain earlier? The probable answer is yes.

First, the teacher should have been sensitive to Michael's angry facial expression and the fact that he was slouching down in his seat. Facial expression, flushing, squinty eyes, clenched fists, rigid body posture, pacing and stomping—these all suggest an impending eruption (Hyman, 1997). Second, teachers can usually avoid defiant situations if they do not corner a student, do not argue, do not engage in a power struggle ("I'm the boss in this classroom, and I'm telling you to . . .") and do not embarrass the student in front of peers. Table 14-3 summarizes specific recommendations.

With this background, let's go back to Michael and see how the teacher might have dealt with the situation to prevent it from escalating.

Students are working on a set of math problems the teacher has assigned. Michael sits slouched in his seat staring at the floor, an angry expression on his face. The teacher notices Michael's posture and realizes that he is feeling upset about something. She goes over, bends down so that she is on eye-level with Michael, and speaks very quietly.

TEACHER: Are you doing OK, Michael? You look upset. [Teacher demonstrates empathy.]

MICHAEL: I'm OK.

TEACHER: Well, good, but if you'd like to talk later, let me know. [Teacher invites further communication.] Meanwhile, you need to get going on this assignment.

MICHAEL: I already did it.

TEACHER: Oh, good. Let me see how you did. [She checks the paper.] OK, you've done the first four, and they're fine. Now do the next four problems and let me see them when you're done. [She walks away, giving the student space.]

Being Alert for the Presence of Gang Activity

Violence is sometimes related to the presence of gangs that use schools for drug activity and weapons trafficking, for extortion and intimidation, and for recruiting members (Verdugo, 1997). Although many schools and districts deny gang presence, educators who have studied gangs (Lal, Lal, & Achilles, 1993) report that gang activity has infiltrated schools throughout the country. Indeed, Kodluboy and Evenrud (1993) contend that "gang activity is present within the boundaries of virtually every major school district in America" (p. 257).

It's not easy to identify a gang, since teenagers frequently "run in packs" and try to look and act just like everyone else. But Kenneth Trump, coordinator of the Youth Gang Unit of the Cleveland Public Schools, reminds us that the key to gang activity is negative behavior:

Kids who sit together in the lunch room don't constitute a gang. But when groups start assaulting other students or creating an atmosphere of fear and intimidation, they become a gang. In short, groups of students reach gang status when their behavior, either individually or collectively, is disruptive, antisocial, or criminal. (1993, p. 40).

In order to determine the extent to which gangs are present in your school, you need to be familiar with the indicators summarized in Table 14-4. In addition, you may find it helpful to use a gang assessment tool developed by the National School Safety Center (1992; see Figure 14-3). Each "yes" response earns the indicated number of points. The total score is an assessment of the severity of the problem and can suggest the possible need for school security measures: 0–15 points indicate no significant gang problem; 20–40 points, emerging gang problem; 45–60 points, a significant gang problem that must be addressed; 65 points or higher, acute gang problem that requires urgent attention and intervention.

According to Donnie, gang activity in New Brunswick was intense about five years ago, when the city's adolescents were divided into "uptown" and "downtown" gangs:

What you saw was that the kids who lived in the projects stayed together and kept up a feud with the kids on the other side of Livingston Avenue. They'd fight about drugs, about somebody from one side of town going out with a girl from the other side of town, about somebody "ratting" on

TABLE 14-4. Signs of Gang Presence

Gathering or hanging out:	Gang members may establish territory (e.g., in the lunch room, on playing fields, and in bleachers). Once these areas are claimed, other students will stay away.
Nonverbal and verbal signs:	Gang members often have special ways of signaling one another and conveying messages: "Flashing"—the use of finger and hand signs. "Monikers"—nicknames emphasizing a member's particular attribute (e.g., "Shooter" uses a gun well; "Lil Man" is short).
Graffiti:	Signs, symbols, and nicknames on notebooks, papers, clothing, and walls; graffiti advertises the gang and its members and may contain challenging messages to other gangs; when graffiti is crossed out, that constitutes a direct challenge from a rival gang.
Stance and walk:	Unique ways of standing and walking that set them apart: "Standing duck-footed"—feet are pointed outward. "Holding up the wall"—leaning back with one hand in the pocket and one foot against a wall.
Symbols:	Tatoos, earrings, colors, scarves, bandannas, shoelaces, caps, belts (change over time).

Source: Adapted from Lal, Lal, & Achilles, 1993.

1. Do you have graffiti on or near your campus? (5)

2. Do you have crossed-out graffiti on or near your campus? (10)

3. Do your students wear colors, jewelry, clothing, flash hand signals or display other behavior that may be gang-related? (10)

4. Are drugs available near your school? (5)

5. Has there been a significant increase in the number of physical confrontations or stare-downs within the past 12 months in or around your school? (5)

6. Is there an increasing presence of weapons in your community? (10)

7. Are beepers, pagers, or cellular phones used by your students? (10)

8. Have you had a drive-by shooting at or around your school? (15)

9. Have you had a "show-by" display of weapons at or around your school? (10)

10. Is the truancy rate of your school increasing? (5)

11. Are there increasing numbers of racial incidents occurring in your community or school? (5)

12. Is there a history of gangs in your community? (10)

13. Is there an increasing presence of "informal social groups" with unusual names—for example, "Woodland Heights Posse," "Rip Off and Rule," "Females Simply Chillin'" or "Kappa Phi Nasty"? (15)

FIGURE 14-3. Gang assessment tool.
Reprinted with permission from School Safety Update, March 1992, p. 8.
Copyright 1992 by the National School Safety Center, Westlake Village, CA.

somebody else. Whenever there was a gang fight over the weekend or at night, the kids would all come in buzzing the next day. One year, a kid got killed in a gang fight, and there was a tremendous amount of tension that spilled over into the school. It would simmer down, and then every year, there'd be a big memorial to him that would rekindle all the trouble. But it seems as if the main kids who were involved have moved on. Things have been a lot quieter the last few years.

As Donnie's comment suggests, gangs consist of the "main kids" and those who are on the periphery. In fact, Lal, Lal, and Achilles (1993) suggest that there are at least four types of gang members. *Hard core* members, "in for life and ready to die," determine the character of the gang and are most likely to be involved in illegal behavior. *Affiliates* constitute the "homeboys" or the basic membership. *Peripheral* members exist in a "gray area," dressing like a member, flashing signs, and engaging in minor activities. *Wannabes* are sometimes viewed as "posers" or "pretenders" who are experimenting with gang behavior. In addition, *homegirls,* relatives and girl friends, are sometimes "appendages" to male gangs (Verdugo, 1997), although they have recently begun forming their own gangs. Knowing about the types of gang members can help you to identify the leadership of a gang, focus your efforts on the core individuals, and avoid exaggerating the extent of the problem (Verdugo, 1997).

Asking Students to Contribute to Violence Prevention Efforts

It is critical to learn what students' views are with respect to violence and violence prevention strategies—and to include not just the "good ones," but also "the toughies, the gangbangers, the disruptive, the withdrawn, and the unmotivated" (Curwin, 1995, p. 75). Encourage students to organize their own antiviolence events. Solicit their perceptions of the school's high-conflict areas (e.g., hallways, cafeterias, restrooms) and their ideas about how to make these safer. Invite students to develop an antibullying campaign.

A good example of the way students can become meaningfully involved is the Health Informed Teens' Own Program on Sexuality (HITOPS) that Tonia Moore helps to run at Highland Park High School. Together with the health teacher, Tonia runs sessions for juniors who have volunteered to become student experts on health and sexuality issues (e.g., pregnancy prevention, postponing sexual involvement, sexual harassment, homophobia). The students then conduct lessons for their peers. According to Tonia, the hardest issue for students to grasp was sexual harassment:

They kept dismissing it as teasing or flirting. They'd say, "But it's only in fun." It was really hard for them to understand that what counted was not how it was intended, but how it was received. It took time, but they finally got it, and they've done a really good job of communicating the message. Kids will listen a lot more closely to what their peers say than to what adults say.

Responding to Violence

Coping with Aggressive Behavior

Despite your best efforts at prevention, there are times when students erupt in hostile, aggressive behavior. A girl screams profanities and knocks a pile of dictionaries to the floor. A boy explodes in anger and throws a chair across the room. Someone yells, "I'll kill you," and hurls a notebook at another student. In situations like this—every teacher's nightmare—it's easy to lose self-control and lash out. As Fred puts it,

> The normal *reaction is to become angry and aggressive and to get in the kid's face. But* teachers can't react normally. *That will only make things worse, and your responsibility is* to make things better.

In order to "make things better," you need to think carefully about what you will do to defuse the aggression and protect yourself and your students. Let's consider an episode that occurred in Sandy's classroom.

> As usual, I was standing at the doorway as the kids were coming into the classroom. I noticed Robert come in without his backpack or any books. That didn't look right, and I watched him cross the room and go over to Daniel, who was sitting at his desk. Robert picked up the desk and the leg of Daniel's chair and overturned them, cursing and screaming the whole time. I ran over. The first thing I said was "Daniel, don't raise your hands." He was on the floor on his back, and Robert was standing over him screaming. I kept saying, "Robert, look at me, look at me, look at me." Finally, he made eye contact. Then I said, "You need to come with me." We began to walk toward the door, but he turned back and started cursing again. Very quietly and firmly I told him, "You need to come with me now." He followed me to the door, and as I reached the door I picked up the phone and called the office and said there was a problem and to send someone up. Then we stepped out into the hallway. Robert was angry and was going to leave, and I asked him to please stop and talk to me about what was going on, what was bothering him. I didn't yell, I didn't say, "How could you do something so stupid?" (even though that's what I felt like saying). I said, "Obviously you're upset about something. Tell me about it." It turns out that these two were friends, but Robert found out that Daniel was sleeping with his [Robert's] girlfriend. I heard a lot I didn't really want to hear, but it kept him occupied until the vice-principal came up.
>
> Once the vice-principal took Robert, I got Daniel out into the hallway and asked him if he was OK, and if he needed to go to the nurse, or needed to be out of the classroom. He said no, he was OK. I told him, "You were very

smart for not raising your hands against Robert." He returned to his seat, and all the kids started saying, "Daniel, are you OK?" and crowding around him. I told them, "Robert's in the office. Daniel's OK. Let's get started on chemistry." At the end of the period, the office called for Daniel to go to the peer mediation room to have the dispute mediated.

In addition to going to peer mediation, Robert was suspended for three days. But the day he was suspended, he came back after school hours (something he wasn't supposed to do) to apologize for his language. I accepted his apology, but I said that there were other ways to handle the situation and to express anger. It was a very low key discussion. I didn't make light of what had happened, but I told him I was glad he realized the danger of the situation.

After the suspension, Daniel came to me before homeroom to say he was feeling frightened about coming to class that day. It was going to be his first meeting with Robert, and Robert sits right in front of him. I said that I had already changed both their seats. I told him, "Don't worry, I'll be watching." When they came in, I told them each "You have a new seat," and showed them where to sit. There was no problem from that point on.

Analysis of Sandy's response to Robert's outburst reveals some important guidelines for dealing with aggression in the classroom. Let's examine her behavior more closely and consider the lessons to be learned.

1. Although Sandy admits that she wanted to respond with anger ("What is wrong with you?!"), she remained outwardly calm and in control. By doing so, she was able to *prevent the situation from escalating.* She lowered the level of emotion in the class and decreased the chance of becoming a victim herself. She then directed Daniel not to raise his hands against Robert. This prevented Robert's aggressive actions from escalating into a full-scale physical fight. Next, she issued quiet, firm, repetitive instructions for Robert to look at her. This created a lull in the altercation, during which she was able to separate the two boys ("You need to come with me."). Since Daniel was lying on the floor under the desk, it was easier for her to have Robert move away. In other cases, however, it may be advisable to remove the targets of the aggression. You can direct them to go to a nearby teacher's classroom, preferably with a friend, since they are bound to be angry and upset ("Take Scott and go to Ms. Thomson's room so we can get this sorted out") or have them move to a far corner of the room, out of the aggressor's line of sight.
2. Sandy's next action was to report that there was a problem in her room and *to summon help.* Never send angry, aggressive students to the office alone: You cannot be certain they will actually get there, nor do you know what they will do on the way. If you do not have a telephone or intercom, quietly instruct a responsible student to go for assistance.

Who should be summoned will vary, so it's important for you to check on the procedures in your own school. Fred would call one of the two SROs—security resource officers—who patrol the hallways. Christina and Sandy would call the main office. Donnie would contact one of the security guards.

3. While Sandy waited for someone from the office to provide assistance, she spoke privately and quietly with Robert in an attempt to *defuse the aggression.* She did not rebuke or threaten punishment. Instead, she acknowledged his anger and showed her willingness to listen.

Again, it's critical that you resist the temptation to "react normally" and lash out at the student. You need to speak slowly and softly and to minimize threat by not invading the student's space and keeping your hands by your side. Allow the student to relate facts and feelings, even if it involves profanity, and use active listening ("So you were really furious when you found out what was happening . . ."). Do not disagree or argue.

If, despite your efforts to restore calm, the student's aggression escalates, it is best to move away unless you are trained in physical restraint techniques. Even then, don't use restraint unless you are strong enough and there are no other options. As Hyman (1997) emphasizes, "The last thing you ever want to do is to physically engage an enraged student who may be out of control" (p. 251).

4. When Robert came to see Sandy after school, he gave her the opportunity to discuss what had happened, to reinforce alternative ways to handle anger, and to accept his apology. He also gave her the chance to *reestablish a positive relationship.* Fred emphasizes how important this is:

Suspending a violent kid isn't the end of the situation. At some point, the kid is going to come back, and then it's your job to rebuild the relationship. You need to reassure them that they're still a member of the class. You need to tell them, "OK, you messed up. But I'm on your side. You can learn from this."

5. Once Robert was on his way to the office and Daniel was back in his seat, Sandy scanned the room in order to *determine how the other students were feeling* and what to do next. She decided that her best course of action was to provide them with the basic facts ("Robert is in the office. Daniel's OK.") and to begin the lesson ("Let's get started on chemistry."). She certainly did not want to explore with her class the reasons behind Robert's aggressive actions.

Sometimes, however, your students may be so upset and frightened that it's impossible to continue working. Tonia Moore suggests that it's important to allow them to express their feelings:

If the students are upset, you have to give them the opportunity to talk about what happened and to acknowledge their fear. You don't want to pretend nothing happened and then send them on to the next class all churned up inside.

Responding Effectively to Physical Fights

What do you do if you're on the scene when a fight erupts? I asked the teachers that question one evening, as we talked about the problem of violence in schools. They were unanimous in their response:

1. **Get help.** All four teachers stressed the importance of immediately calling for other teachers and for the principal or vice-principal. Once other people are there to help, it's easier—and safer—to get the situation under control.
2. **Tell students to stop.** Often, students don't want to continue the fight, and they'll respond to a short, clear, firm command. If you know the combatants' names, use them.
3. **Disperse other students.** There's no need for an audience, and you don't want onlookers to become part of the fray. If you're in the hallway, direct students to be on their way. If you're in the classroom, send your students to the library or to some other safe place.
4. **Do not intervene physically**—unless the age, size, and number of combatants indicates that it's safe to do so, there are three or four people to help, or you have learned physical restraint.

As we discussed the issue of fighting in school, the teachers repeatedly stressed the fact that *fights are fast.* They can erupt quickly—so you don't have a lot of time to think through a response—and they're usually over in less than 30 seconds (although that can seem like a lifetime). There was also amazing unanimity among the teachers on the issue of fights among girls versus boys. As Donnie put it: "Teachers shouldn't think that fighting is only going to happen among boys. Girls fight too—and girl fights are terrible. Girls kick, pull earrings, bite, scratch, and when you try to stop it, they turn on *you.*"

Finally, it's important to remember that you must report violent acts. Every school system needs to have a violent incident reporting system that requires you to report what happened, when and where it happened, who was involved, and what action was taken (Blauvelt, 1990). Remember that assault and battery, possession of a weapon on school property, and vandalism are *crimes*—not just violations of school rules—and that they must be reported to the police (Blauvelt, 1990).

Concluding Comments

Amid the reports of school shootings and murderous rampages, two stories provide inspiring examples of what can happen when a school makes a concerted effort to create a peaceful community. The first story takes place in Huntington Beach High School in California (Shore, 1995). With 2,000 students, the school was plagued by chaos, vandalism, and violence. In 1991, educators decided to implement deliberate programs to provide a more personalized education—one in which students are known by adult professionals in the school. Administrators, special services personnel, and teachers created a "hot list" of students viewed as not on track to graduate due to academic or behavior problems. The adults in the school then worked to know those students by name. They initiated an adopt-a-kid program that matched adult volunteers with one or two students of their choosing; formed weekly groups to discuss the progress of students on this list; presented "most improved student" awards; held student forums in the principal's conference room; instituted a green-ribbon campaign to promote antiviolence attitudes; and instituted block scheduling and tutorial periods. Together, these measures resulted in a much improved school climate. Expulsion and suspension rates dropped, students on the hot list improved their grades, test scores rose, and students' attitudes toward school improved dramatically. As Shore reports, it is now common to see administrators out in the halls between classes, talking to students, and calling them by name. One teacher reported that the reforms resulted in "the best year he could remember in 18 years at the school." Another commented that for the first time, she felt safe in a school assembly with the entire student population present.

The second story is set in Patterson High School, another school with 2,000 students, located in Baltimore, Maryland (McPartland, Jordan, Legters, & Balfanz, 1997). There, students roamed the halls instead of being in class; windows were smashed; fires were set in the school's trophy cases; and food fights disrupted lunch periods. In an effort to enforce discipline, students were regularly suspended and expelled. Poor student attendance led to course failures, grade retentions, and high drop-out rates.

Finally, with the help of consultants from the Johns Hopkins University Center for Research on the Education of Students Placed at Risk (CRESPAR), Patterson faculty created six small learning academies, each with a unique academic and career focus. Each academy now enrolls between 240 and 350 students and has its own faculty of 14 to 18 teachers. The smaller size allows students and teachers to know everyone's name. Students in grades 10 through 12 stay with the same homeroom teacher, a relationship that fosters a more personalized climate. The first 15 minutes of each day are set aside for advice and mentoring, and a four-period day cuts down on hallway traffic, thus decreasing opportunities for trouble. These innovations have created a climate conducive to learning: Students go to class instead of roaming the halls, the building is free of graffiti, and student attendance and promotion rates have surged.

The transformation of Huntington Beach and Patterson High has much to teach us. Installing metal detectors and state-of-the-art security systems can only go so far. To create a more peaceful school community, teachers and administrators must reach out to students and *build connections*. In the final analysis, it is the presence of caring administrators and teachers that holds the greatest promise for preventing violence.

❧ Summary

In the late 1990s, a series of horrific school shootings catapulted the topic of school violence to the front page. Politicians, policy makers, and pundits talked about youth violence as a national epidemic. Although data on the frequency and severity of school violence indicate a decrease, students, teachers, and parents are fearful, and the perception that violence is increasing is widespread.

School officials have tried to counter the problem of school violence by installing metal detectors and sophisticated security systems, but it is clear that these will not solve all the problems. This chapter presented a variety of strategies for preventing and responding to violence.

Prevention strategies

- Build supportive school communities:
    Be alert to signs of hate.
    Examine the ways your school recognizes student achievement.
    Curb peer harassment.
- Teach conflict resolution.
- Know the early warning signs of potential for violence.
- Be attentive to whispers and rumors.
- De-escalate potentially explosive situations.
- Be alert for the presence of gang activity.
- Ask students to contribute to violence prevention efforts.

Responding to violence

- Cope with aggressive behavior:
    Prevent escalation.
    Summon help.
    Defuse the aggression.
    Reestablish a positive relationship with the aggressor.
    Determine how the other students are feeling.
- Respond effectively to physical fights:
    Get help.
    Tell the students to stop.
    Disperse onlookers.
    Do not intervene physically unless it is safe.

Metal detectors and security systems can only go so far. It's essential to build connections with students. In the final analysis, it is the presence of caring administrators and teachers that holds the greatest promise for preventing violence.

Activities

1. Interview an experienced teacher, the student assistance counselor, the school nurse, or a guidance counselor about the school's efforts to prevent violence.

   If you think a student exhibits some of the early warning signs of potential for violence, to whom do you report?
   Is there an official form to file?

Do you contact parents?

Are school personnel aware of gang activity?

What are the indicators of gang membership and gang activity?

2. Consider the following situations. What would you do in each case?

   a. As students enter your classroom, you overhear a girl teasing Annamarie about the boy Annamarie's dating. They go to their seats, but the taunts continue. Suddenly, Annamarie stands up, turns to the girl, and shouts, "You shut up, bitch. Just shut up, or I'll get you!"

   b. Your students are taking a brief quiz on the homework. Those who have finished already are reading. As you circulate throughout the room, collecting the finished papers, you notice that James is looking at a catalog of weapons. He makes no attempt to conceal it.

   c. Jesse comes to your first period class wearing a T-shirt with a Celtic cross surrounded by the words "White Pride World Wide."

   d. You ask Taysha where her textbook is. She mutters something under her breath. When you tell her you didn't hear what she said, she shouts, "I left the f———— book in my locker!"

3. Find out if the school where you are observing or teaching has a peer mediation program.

   How are students selected to be peer mediators?

   Who schedules peer mediation sessions?

   What is the procedure for requesting peer mediation?

   Can a teacher insist/suggest that two students go to peer mediation?

✦ For Further Reading

Begun, R. W. (Ed.) (1996). *Ready-to-use social skills lessons and activities for grades 7–12.* West Nyack, NY: The Center for Applied Research in Education.

Bodine, R. J., & Crawford, D. K. (1998). *The handbook of conflict resolution education: A guide to building quality programs in schools.* San Francisco: Jossey-Bass.

Canter, L., with Garrison, R. (1994). *Scared or prepared: Preventing conflict and violence in your classroom.* Santa Monica, CA: Lee Canter & Associates.

Hoover, J., & Oliver, R. (1996). *The bullying prevention handbook: A guide for teachers, principals and counselors.* Bloomington, IN: National Educational Service.

Hyman, I. A. (1997). *School discipline and school violence: The teacher variance approach.* Boston: Allyn and Bacon.

Lieber, C. M. (1994). *Making choices about conflict, security, and peacemaking. Part I: Personal perspectives: A high school conflict resolution curriculum.* Cambridge, MA: Educators for Social Responsibility.

National School Safety Center (1990). *School Safety Checkbook.* Malibu, CA: Pepperdine University Press.

Perlstein, R., & Thrall G. (1996). *Ready-to-use conflict resolution activities for secondary students: Strategies for dealing with conflict in real-life situations plus guidelines for creating a peer mediation program.* West Nyack, NY: The Center for Applied Research in Education.

Schrumpf, F., Crawford, D. K., & Bodine, R. J. (1997). *Peer mediation: Conflict resolution in schools* (rev. ed.). Champaign, IL: Research Press.

Teaching Tolerance (1999). *Responding to hate at school: A guide for teachers, counselors and administrators.* Montgomery, AL: The Southern Poverty Law Center.

Walker, H. M., Colvin, G., Ramsey, E. (1995). *Antisocial behavior in school: Strategies and best practices.* Pacific Grove, CA: Brooks/Cole.

✱ Organizational Resources

The Anti-Defamation League (ADL), 823 United Nations Plaza, New York, NY 10017 (www.adl.org; 212-885-7800)—dedicated to combating hate crime and promoting intergroup cooperation and understanding.

National School Safety Center, 141 Duesenberg Dr., Suite 11, Westlake Village, CA 91362 (www.nssc1.org; 805-373-9977)—resource for school safety information, training, and violence prevention.

National Educational Service, 304 W. Kirkwood Ave., Suite 2, Bloomington, IN 47404 (www.nesonline.com; 1-800-733-6786)—provides a variety of resources and materials for understanding, preventing, and reducing violence in schools.

Drug Strategies, 1575 Eye Street, NW, Suite 210, Washington, DC 20005 (www.drugstrategies.org; 202-289-9070)—publishes a guide on conflict resolution and violence prevention curricula.

The Southern Poverty Law Center, 400 Washington Avenue, Montgomery, AL 36104 (www.teachingtolerance.org)—Provides teachers at all levels with ideas and free resources for building community, fighting bias, and celebrating diversity through the Teaching Tolerance project.

The Safe and Drug Free Schools website for the U.S. Department of Education (www.ed.gov/offices/OESE/SDFS/news.html) provides reports and articles on school safety and school violence.

✱ References

Astor, R. A., Meyer, H. A., & Behre, W. J. (1999). Unowned places and times: Maps and interviews about violence in high schools. *American Educational Research Journal, 36*(1), 3–42.

Barone, F. J. (1997). Bullying in school: It doesn't have to happen. *Phi Delta Kappan, 79,* 80–82.

Barton, P. E., Coley, R. J., & Wenglinsky, H. (1998). *Order in the classroom: Violence, discipline, and student achievement.* Princeton, NJ: Educational Testing Service.

Berreth, D., & Berman, S. (1997). The moral dimensions of schools. *Educational Leadership, 54*(8), 24–26.

Blauvelt, P. D. (1990). School security: "Who you gonna call?" *School Safety Newsjournal,* Fall, 4–8.

Bodine, R. J., & Crawford, D. K. (1998). *The handbook of conflict resolution education: A guide to building quality programs in schools.* San Francisco: Jossey-Bass.

Brener, N. D., Simon, T. R., Krug, E. G., & Lowry, R. (1999). Recent trends in violence-related behaviors among high school students in the United States. *Journal of the American Medical Association, 282,* 440–446.

Curwin, R. L. (1995). A humane approach to reducing violence in schools. *Educational Leadership, 52*(5), 72–75.

Drummond, S., & Portner, J. (May 26, 1999). Arrests top 350 in threats, bomb scares. *Education Week,* pp. 1, 12–13.

Dwyer, K., Osher, D., & Warger, C. (1998). *Early warning, timely response: A guide to safe schools.* Washington, D.C: U.S. Department of Education.

Dusenbury, L., Falco, M., Lake, A., Brannigan, R., & Bosworth, K. (1997). Nine critical elements of promising violence prevention programs. *Journal of School Health, 67*(10), 409–414.

Glassner, B. (August 13, 1999). School violence: The fears, the facts. *The New York Times,* p. A21.

Hoover, J., & Oliver, R. (1996). *The bullying prevention handbook: A guide for teachers, principals and counselors.* Bloomington, IN: National Educational Service.

Hyman, I. A. (1997). *School discipline and school violence: The teacher variance approach.* Boston: Allyn and Bacon.

Johnson, D. W., & Johnson, R. T. (1995). *Teaching students to be peacemakers* (3rd ed.). Edina, MN: Interaction Book Co.

Johnson, D. W., & Johnson, R. T. (1996). Reducing school violence through conflict resolution training. *NASSP Bulletin, 80*(579), 11–18.

Kodluboy, D. W., & Evenrud, L. A. (1993). School-based interventions: Best practices and critical issues. In A. P. Goldstein and C. R. Huff (Eds.), *The gang intervention handbook.* Champaign, IL: Research Press.

Lal, S. R., Lal, D., & Achilles, C. M. (1993). *Handbook on gangs in schools: Strategies to reduce gang-related activities.* Newbury Park, CA: Corwin Press.

McPartland, J., Jordan, W., Legters, N., & Balfanz, R. (1997). Finding safety in small numbers. *Educational Leadership, 55*(2), 14–17.

Miller, E. (1994). Peer mediation catches on, but some adults don't. *Harvard Education Letter, 10*(3), 8.

Nansel, T. R., Overpeck, M., Pilla, R. S., Ruan, W. J., Simons-Morton, B., & Scheidt, P. (2001). Bullying behaviors among US youth: Prevalence and association with psychosocial adjustment. *Journal of the American Medical Association, 285*(16), 2094–2100.

Noguera, P. A. (1995). Preventing and producing violence: A critical analysis of responses to school violence. *Harvard Educational Review, 65*(2), 189–212.

Portner, J. (April 12, 2000). School violence down, report says, but worry high. *Education Week,* 3.

Quarles, C. L. (1989). *School violence: A survival guide for school staff, with emphasis on robbery, rape, and hostage taking.* Washington D.C.: National Education Association.

Remboldt, C. (1998). Making violence unacceptable. *Educational Leadership, 56*(1), 32–38.

Richard, A. (September 8, 1999). As students return, focus is on security. *Education Week,* 1, 14–15.

Shore, R. (1995). How one high school improved school climate. *Educational Leadership, 52*(5), 76–78.

Stephens, R. D. (1994). Planning for safer and better schools: School violence prevention and intervention strategies. *School Psychology Review, 23*(2), 204–215.

Trump, K. (1993). Tell teen gangs: School's out. *American School Board Journal, 180*(7), 39–42.

U.S. Department of Education (February/March 2001). Studies report declining rate of school violence. *Community Update, 85,* 1–2.

U.S. Secret Service Safe School Initiative (October 2000). *An interim report on the prevention of targeted violence in schools.* Washington, D.C.: U.S. Secret Service National Threat Assessment Center in collaboration with the U.S. Department of Education.

Verdugo, R. (1997). *Youth gangs: Findings and solutions for schools, communities, and families.* Washington, D.C.: National Education Association.

Walker, H. M., Colvin, G., Ramsey, E. (1995). *Antisocial behavior in school: Strategies and best practices.* Pacific Grove, CA: Brooks/Cole.

Walsh, M. (March 8, 2000). Law update: A fine line between dangerous and harmless student expression. *Education Week,* 14.

Wessler, S. L. (2000/2001). Sticks and stones. *Educational Leadership, 58*(4), 28–33.

Index